Contemporary
Canadian
Marketing Cases

Contemporary Canadian Marketing Cases

THIRD EDITION

H. F. (Herb) MacKenzie

Brock University

PEARSON

Prentice
Hall

Toronto

Library and Archives Canada Cataloguing in Publication

Contemporary Canadian marketing cases / [compiled by] H.F. (Herb) MacKenzie. — 3rd ed.

ISBN 978-0-13-205973-2

1. Marketing—Canada—Case studies. I. MacKenzie, H. F.

HF5415.12.C3C65 2007   658.800971   C2007-901620-0

ISBN-13: 978-0-13-205973-2
ISBN-10: 0-13-205973-8

Editor in Chief, Business and Economics: Gary Bennett
Acquisitions Editor: Don Thompson
Marketing Manager: Eileen Lasswell
Developmental Editor: Rema Celio
Production Editor: Avivah Wargon, Patricia Jones
Copy Editor: Erica Fyvie
Proofreader: Susan McNish
Production Coordinator: Avinash Chandra
Composition: Laserwords
Art Director: Julia Hall
Cover Design: Miguel Acevedo
Cover Image: Digital Vision/Datafunk

Statistics Canada information is used with the permission of Statistics Canada. Users are forbidden to copy the data and redisseminate them, in an original or modified form, for commercial purposes, without permission from Statistics Canada. Information on the availability of the wide range of data from Statistics Canada can be obtained from Statistics Canada's Regional Offices, its World Wide Web site at http://www.statcan.ca, and its toll-free access number 1-800-263-1136.

1 2 3 4 5   11 10 09 08 07

Printed and bound in the United States.

Contents

H. F. (Herb) MacKenzie

Keith Thomas has just been hired as sales manager for Industritech's western Canadian office. He has conducted a sales analysis and now must decide what action, if any, he should take.

H. F. (Herb) MacKenzie

The Health Care Corporation of St. John's has called for tenders for a meal delivery system to service its six locations. The case provides some insight into the purchasing process for expensive products, as well as the opportunity for students to actually get involved in the negotiating process through a practical simulation.

H. F. (Herb) MacKenzie

A salesperson relates four ethical scenarios that he faced during 15 years in business-to-business sales and sales management. Each scenario calls for action.

Preface

Contemporary Canadian Marketing Cases, Third Edition, is a collection of 40 marketing cases by many of Canada's best case writers. I believe you will find an improved selection of cases in this edition, and that they will provide you with the flexibility to personalize a course that will offer enjoyment and learning for you and your students.

Two primary considerations helped focus my selection of cases. First, cases provide an excellent basis to build rapport among everyone involved in the case-learning environment; cases should be engaging for both students and instructors. I have included cases on current marketing issues, in the context of a variety of Canadian industries. There are cases that involve business and consumer markets, for-profit and not-for-profit businesses, services marketing (tourism, hospitality, and the arts), entrepreneurship and franchising, online marketing, co-op marketing, service failure and recovery, and international marketing.

Second, the best cases provide a rich environment for student learning. You will find lots of suggestions in the teaching notes to help you decide upon a teaching strategy for these cases. Many cases can be used for in-class exercises. You will also find a balance between narrowly-focused and comprehensive cases, and between cases that are best for classroom discussion and those that can serve well for written assignments or examinations.

Exhibit 1 lists the 40 cases in this edition. While many cases have breadth well beyond what is indicated in this table, I have organized them on the basis of why they were chosen for this edition of the casebook.

—H.F. (Herb) MacKenzie
Brock University, St. Catharines, Ontario

| EXHIBIT 1 | Primary (P) and Secondary (S) Focus of Cases | | | | | | | | | | | |

		Introduction to Marketing	Marketing Environment	Strategy Planning, Implementation	Customer Buying Behaviour	Marketing Research, Sales Forecasting	Segmentation, Targeting, Positioning	Product and Services Marketing	Channels and Channel Management	Marketing Communications	Pricing Strategy	Ethics, Not-for-Profit Marketing	International Marketing
1	Cott Corporation	P											S
2	Financial Analysis Exercises	P											
3	Marketing OxyContin		P							S		S	
4	SaskTel and Max Interactive		P									S	
5	Pantry Pride Stores			P	S					S		S	
6	Centre for the Arts			P						S	S		
7	Wing and a Prayer			P	S	S							
8	Lucas Foods			P									
9	Comfort in the Night			P	S	S							
10	Steinhouse Knitting Mills			P	S			S	S				
11	Casablanca Kids			P			S	S	S				
12	Rocky Mountain House Co-op			P	S			S	S	S	S		
13	Executive Training Inc.			P	S	S	S	S		S	S		
14	Dillon Controls Ltd.				P	S							S
15	Nickel Belt Paving				P					S			
16	Toronto Door & Trim				P				S				
17	Ontario Rutabaga Council				P	S	S	S		S			
18	Marketing-in-Focus Inc.					P		S					
19	African Market Square Inc.					P	S		S				
20	Agro Seeds						P						

EXHIBIT 1	**Primary and Secondary Focus of Cases** (continued)

		Introduction to Marketing	Marketing Environment	Strategy Planning, Implementation	Customer Buying Behaviour	Marketing Research, Sales Forecasting	Segmentation, Targeting, Positioning	Product and Services Marketing	Channels and Channel Management	Marketing Communications	Pricing Strategy	Ethics, Not-for-Profit Marketing	International Marketing
21	Milton Quality Inn						P	S					
22	"Greener Pastures"						P		S				
23	MN Design						P			S			
24	Therm-eze						P		S		S		
25	Protocase						P	S	S				
26	Wilderness Nfld. Adventures						P		S				S
27	ABS Global (Canada) Inc.						P	S	S	S			
28	EverLine							P					S
29	Hannas Seeds								P				
30	MediaSpark								P				
31	TFI Food Equipment Solutions								P	S			
32	Murray Industrial Limited								P			S	
33	Wee Piggies & Paws								P		S		
34	Literacy Partners of Manitoba									P		S	
35	"The Holey War"									P			
36	5-to-10-a-day Program									P		S	
37	Stavanger Safety Equipment									P			
38	Industritech Inc.									P			
39	Health Care Corporation									P	S		
40	Some Ethical Dilemmas											P	

Introduction for Students

LEARNING FROM CASES

One of the most valuable experiences for marketing students is the opportunity to participate in marketing case analyses and discussions. However, if you are to benefit most from this experience, it is important to be an active participant. Many students, particularly if their educational experiences have focused on readings and lectures, find it difficult to do case analyses and to express themselves in case discussions. This is unfortunate because case analyses and discussions can add a whole new dimension to your marketing education and to your personal growth.

While lectures may be the most efficient method of transmitting knowledge, case analyses and discussions foster learning through the development of independent thought and creativity, interpersonal communication, and decision-making skills. The focus changes from simply content to both content and process. This means that students must share responsibility for their learning, while instructors must be confident about sharing power in the classroom, encouraging student views and participation. This provides a positive learning environment for everyone.

INDIVIDUAL CASE PREPARATION

Cases vary in scope. Some are comprehensive cases that require a complete analysis, including consideration of the marketing environment, buyer behaviour, segmentation, targeting, and positioning strategies, as well as product, price, promotion, and distribution strategies. Other cases are more narrowly focused. When reading through a case, pay particular attention to the opening and closing sections to gain some idea of what the case involves and what decisions you are required to make.

Then, you should read the case more carefully. This is when you should underline important facts and make notes in the margins concerning your thoughts as you learn more about the case. Some careful thought after this reading will help you decide how to proceed: what decisions you must make, what numerical analysis is important, what alternatives may be appropriate, and what qualitative facts you must consider before making action-related recommendations. A word of caution here is to avoid focusing on one alternative too early as that will constrain your analysis. In most situations, there are several good alternatives, and effective managers recognize that different courses of action may enable an organization to meet its objectives.

Once you have completed your analysis, it is time to think about action—what you will do. It is sometimes easy to argue that more information is needed before you should act, but the reality is that many times managers are required to make decisions with incomplete or imperfect information. You may need to make some assumptions, and you should test the robustness of those assumptions. For example, your success may depend upon competitive reaction to your market strategy. You may need to assume that a competitor response will be to reduce its price by 10%. What effect will this have on the success of your strategy? What if the competitor reduces its price by 15%, or even 20%? How would this affect your performance? Would these competitor price reductions require additional changes in your marketing strategy?

A final recommendation when doing individual case preparation is to stay within the context of the case. While you may have information relating to events subsequent to the writing of the case, you should try to ignore this information when doing your analysis and deciding your recommendations. Cases are written concerning problems and issues at a particular point in time and the situations that the decision maker faced at that time. You should analyze the case with the information that the decision maker had because that is the information that would have determined his or her actions. After the case discussion, or if the instructor requests, you may wish to contribute additional knowledge.

While you can do too little analysis on a case, you can also do too much. You need to consider what you are expected to do with your case analysis. If you are to make a formal class presentation or to hand in a written analysis and action plan, more time and effort will be required than if you are preparing for a large group discussion. For most cases, you should spend two to four hours doing your individual analysis. Beyond some point, however, there is a diminishing return from working alone on a case. You need to consider participating in a small group discussion.

SMALL GROUP DISCUSSIONS

In some classes, you may be assigned to a small discussion group or you may wish to consider forming your own group. Discussing your analysis and recommendations among a small group of peers allows you to refine and test your thinking. It provides additional learning opportunities for all participants. Many students feel more comfortable presenting and defending their recommendations, and the assumptions they have used, in this environment. To be effective, groups should consist of approximately four to six members committed to doing individual case analyses before the meetings and contributing during the meetings. The duration of these small group discussions may vary depending on the case, but you should expect to spend 20 to 30 minutes for each meeting.

LARGE GROUP DISCUSSIONS

In an effective case course, the most significant learning takes place in large group discussions. Even if your instructor has organized the course around formal group presentations, there is usually time for questions and discussions after each presentation.

To get the most from large group discussions, you should be committed to active participation. You must be able to listen to what others are saying and follow where the discussion is going. That means you should limit or eliminate note-taking. It is difficult to listen to what others are saying if you are focused on taking notes. That is a strategy you use when someone is transferring knowledge to you, such as during a lecture. During large group discussions, you should be learning from the process, not focusing simply on the content. It is important to listen to understand what is happening if you wish to make an appropriate contribution. At the end of an effective case discussion, you should be able to review what has happened and summarize what you have learned from the experience.

Participation is essential when working with case analyses. Some students find this process exciting and challenging, while others are intimidated and fear speaking in a large group of their peers. Small group discussions prior to class often help. Another consideration is your seating position in class. Some students gravitate to the back of the class as they find this seating position less threatening. You may wish to consider moving forward. Many students find it easier to participate from the front row. From that seating position, the size of the classroom seems smaller, and the interaction with the instructor seems more personal.

Also, participation becomes easier with practice. Like most worthwhile skills, if you do not practise, you will not improve. By partaking early on in the dialogue, it is often easier to continue making contributions as the case continues. For students less confident during discussions, another good opportunity for participation is when the direction of the discussion changes. As your confidence increases, you can increase your involvement in large group discussions.

MARKETING STRATEGY

When developing marketing strategies, managers must consider both internal and external factors that may affect marketing decisions. A marketing strategy is a plan of action focused on developing, pricing, promoting, and distributing need-satisfying goods and services to target customers. The development of a marketing strategy requires the consideration of many aspects. It often helps to have an outline to guide your thinking. Organized around internal and external analysis and action, Exhibit 1 provides a framework of factors to consider during this development.

EXHIBIT 1	A Framework for Case Analysis and Action

Internal Analysis:

Objectives	Strengths/Weaknesses
Sales growth	Marketing and sales (people and knowledge)
Market share	
Increased profit	Other personnel
Product development	Financial condition
Innovation	Costs and revenues
Quality (products and service)	Marketing information systems
Reputation and image	Production capacity
Employee satisfaction	Distribution channels
	Reputation and image
	Quality (products and service)

External Analysis:

Customers	Competitors
Size and growth	Relative size or market share
Segments (sizeable, measurable, accessible, responsive)	Market leaders or followers

EXHIBIT 1	A Framework for Case Analysis and Action (continued)

Purchase criteria (quality, price, service, etc.)	Strengths and weaknesses
Roles (initiator, user, influencer, decider, buyer, gatekeeper)	Reaction profile (aggressive or passive)
Relationship needs (transactional, or long-term orientation)	
Buying conditions (limited or extended problem solving, new task buy, straight rebuy, or modified rebuy)	
Search (extent and type)	

Opportunities / Threats	Distribution Channels / Suppliers
Competition	Relationships (power, dependence, interdependence, cooperation)
Buyer needs (unmet, changing)	Availability, development, capacity
Channels (availability, development capacity)	Technological capabilities
Resources (human, financial, material)	Financial condition
Technology	Cost
Market (size, growth, share)	
Economic conditions	
Political and legal changes	

Action:

Product	Price
Quality (higher, competitive, lower)	Level (premium, competitive, low)
Service (superior, competitive, inferior)	Discounts (cumulative, noncumulative, warranty or guarantee, level trade, cash, seasonal)
Branding (generic, family vs. independent, manufacturer vs. distributor)	
Line (depth and breadth)	
Packaging	

Promotion	Distribution
Objectives (inform, persuade, remind)	Intensity (intensive, selective, exclusive)
Budget	Motivation (margin, support)
Mix (advertising, personal selling, sales promotion, publicity)	
Push vs. pull (or both)	

As you can see from this exhibit, there are many things to consider at the analysis stage, and many more to consider before deciding upon a course of action. A framework helps reduce confusion by providing a basis for beginning your analysis and deciding action. Hopefully, you will find it useful and the case process enjoyable and rewarding.

Cott Corporation

H. F. (Herb) MacKenzie

Cott Corporation is the world's largest supplier of retailer-branded, carbonated soft drinks, producing and distributing products to mass-merchandise, grocery, drugstore, and convenience store chains from its 15 beverage manufacturing facilities in Canada, the United States, and the United Kingdom. For example, Cott produces private-label brands for Wal-Mart in the United States, and President's Choice drinks for Loblaw Cos. Ltd. in Canada.

Cott began operations in Quebec in 1952, importing carbonated beverages from the United States. Eventually, the company started producing its own product in Canada. Expansion followed to Ontario, western Canada, and the Atlantic provinces, and to both the United States and Europe. Cott has differentiated itself through innovation, and by producing quality products, providing superior service, and achieving cost efficiency. Cott's growth can be largely attributed to these factors and to its strategic retail branding and category management expertise, which it customizes to meet the specific needs of each retail customer.

Because Cott manufactures branded products for its customers, its products compete with manufacturer, or national, brands for shelf space and for sales in retail stores where they are sold. Its largest competitor is the U.S.-based Coca-Cola Company, the global soft-drink industry leader. Coca-Cola has approximately 21% market share of the nonalcoholic, ready-to-drink beverage market in both Canada and the United States; however, the company and its subsidiaries sell products in nearly 200 countries around the world. Approximately 70% of volume and 80% of profit come from global markets. When Cott-produced products compete with Coca-Cola products outside Canada and the United States, special issues may arise due to changes in the market environment.

In Britain, for example, the largest supermarket chain, J. Sainsbury PLC, contracted with Cott Corporation for the supply of a retailer-branded cola. At the time, Coca-Cola had a 60% share of the £670-million cola market in Britain. The Sainsbury cola was packaged in red-and-white cans, as was Coca-Cola. Where "Coca-Cola" was written vertically down the can, Sainsbury had "Cola" written in a similar but slightly more silvery red script. The Sainsbury brand also had the word "Classic" on the can, along with "Original American Taste." Sainsbury stocked the competing products side by side, but priced its private-label brand 25% less than the "real thing." While Coca-Cola might have sued, it is questionable whether it could have won. The cola giant would have had an easier time almost anywhere else in Europe where many countries have a general concept of unfair competition, a concept missing from British law, which focuses on a narrow definition of trademark.

Japan has one of the world's most competitive soft-drink markets. Approximately 500 manufacturers offer more than 7000 different soft drinks, and introduce about 1000 new ones annually. Cott Corporation does not yet operate there; however, Coca-Cola Japan manages more than 25 brands and 60 flavours. The company and its Japanese partners maintain 930 000 vending machines, as this method of distribution accounts for more than 50% of all soft-drink sales there. Some years, Japan has provided as much as 20% of the company's global profit. However, the company's most popular product in Japan is not its flagship brand, but a milky sweet drink called Georgia coffee.

In the future, if Cott wishes to continue its strong growth trend, it may wish to consider entry into Japan or some other Asian market.

Financial Analysis Exercises

H. F. (Herb) MacKenzie

Fundamental to any marketing analysis is an analysis of the financial and economic data relevant to each situation. You must understand what the numbers are telling you: where you are. This, along with more qualitative considerations, will suggest various courses of action. You must then be able to assess the effect of implementing these actions on financial performance: where you will be.

The following exercises provide the opportunity to practise sales, markup, and breakeven analyses, and analyses related to each element of the marketing mix.

A. SALES ANALYSIS

Canada Controllers, Inc. manufactured electric motor starters and motor control centres, used in all types of industrial plants, including mines, pulp mills, and manufacturing plants. Motor starters were installed on or near individual pieces of equipment and usually operated only a single motor. They ranged in price from $50 to several thousand dollars. Motor control centres consisted of dozens or even hundreds of motor starters that were combined in a customized enclosure and were capable of starting motors in various locations of the plant from a centralized location. They ranged in price from less than $50 000 to several hundred thousand dollars.

Analyze the following sales data for Canada Controllers, Inc.:

Year	Company Sales	Industry Sales
1998	$ 10 250 970	$ 74 600 000
1999	11 844 888	92 300 000
2000	13 384 152	111 700 000
2001	14 722 155	133 500 000
2002	16 040 063	158 900 000

Analyze the following sales data for 2002:

Product Line	Company Forecast	Company Sales	Industry Sales
Control centres	$ 2 500 000	$ 3 233 727	$ 20 250 000
Motor starters	11 500 000	10 406 040	122 400 000
Repair parts	2 000 000	2 400 296	16 250 000
Total	$16 000 000	$16 040 063	$158 900 000

Analyze changes in the following sales data from 2001 to 2002:

Product Line	2001		2002	
	Sales (units)	Sales ($)	Sales (units)	Sales ($)
Control centres	28	$ 1 766 740	38	$ 3 233 727
Motor starters	16 775	11 041 600	18 305	10 406 040
Repair parts	*	1 913 815	*	2 400 296
Total		$14 722 155		$16 040 063

*Unit volume of repair parts not monitored.

B. MARKUP ANALYSIS

1. Northgate Convenience store wishes to sell two cans of either Coke or Pepsi for $1. If the store does not sell anything at a markup lower than 25%, what is the maximum price that it can pay for a can of either brand?

2. Tom Thompson owns an apple orchard in Alberta. He was hoping to sell his apples at roadside for $0.59 per pound, and he wanted to make a 50% markup based on his total growing cost. What is the highest cost Tom can have to produce his apples and achieve his goals?

3. Harvey Hornswaggle has just left Newfoundland for a job in Cambridge, Ontario. He has decided to bring along a truck full of partridgeberry jam, and he has been busy buying it from all the people he knows who make it. He has been paying $2 per jar for 500 millilitre jars, and he hopes to sell them through grocery wholesalers around the Toronto area. According to his friend, Fred Nitney, wholesalers generally expect to make 20% markup on their cost, and retailers generally will not sell items like this unless they make 30% markup on their selling price. Harvey thinks he should make $1 per jar. What is Harvey's markup on his cost? What is Harvey's markup on his selling price? What price will Mrs. Consumer have to pay in order for all channel members to achieve their desired margins?

C. BREAKEVEN ANALYSIS

1. Geeta, Khawla, and Ann Marie were three final-year university students who decided to operate an on-campus business producing and selling novelty t-shirts that also promoted their university name. At first the university was somewhat uncooperative, but eventually it decided to allow the students to have an unused room in the student union building for a nominal charge of $800 total for the eight months during the regular school year. Although they were allowed to use the university name, they were prevented from using the official university logo. The young women decided that they each wanted $2000 income for the year for operating the business. Advertising and promotion costs were estimated at $400 for the year. They decided that the selling price for their t-shirts would be $12, and their best estimate of required sales to break even was 1800 shirts.

   a. What was the variable cost?

   b. What was the contribution margin?

   c. What was the margin as a percentage of sales?

   d. What was the margin as a percentage of cost?

2. Moose Elbow Archery manufactures a high-quality crossbow for hunting. The company has been in business for three years, and its anticipated fixed costs for 2007 are estimated at $200 000. It sells the crossbow for $250 to retailers throughout North America. The company's variable cost to produce each crossbow is $200. Sales for 2004 are expected to be $1 250 000.

   a. What is the breakeven point in units?

   b. What is the breakeven point in dollars?

   c. What is the company's expected profit for 2007?

   The owner's daughter, a business student at a Western Canadian college, thought that the 2007 sales forecast was too optimistic. She forecasted sales of only $875 000.

   d. What would the company's expected profit be if her estimate is accurate?

   e. If the owner of the company believes that his daughter's forecast was correct, should he shut the company down?

3. Peter Rushton operated a small bakery and deli that sold most items at wholesale as well as retail. Many of his bakery items were sold to retailers around the city, who then resold his items to their customers. Peter reviewed his sales for 2006:

	Bakery	Deli	Wholesale
Sales	$372 201	$217 544	$443 265
Cost of goods	77 413	84 566	117 022
Contribution	294 788	132 978	326 243

Peter's major problem is that he has limited space. He has only six tables in his deli, each with two seats. The backroom operations where he prepares many deli items for his catering business is also limited. Peter now has an opportunity to rent the retail space next door to his business as the current owner has left. This would increase his rent by $48 000 per year. He estimates that it would also cost approximately $30 000 for renovations to make the new area acceptable.

How much additional business does Peter need to make to cover his increased costs?

D. EVALUATING ADVERTISING EFFECTIVENESS

You are the advertising manager for a firm that manufactures piping products for the pulp and paper, and petrochemical industries. You have been working with a national advertising firm to develop an advertisement. You have decided to place it in trade magazines targeted at purchasing agents in these industries, and to also develop it for a more targeted direct mailing to a list of 1000 purchasing professionals that work in these industries. To control advertising expenses, you will use exactly the same ads for both advertising campaigns. The results of the two campaigns follow:

- *Campaign A.* You have placed the ad in two trade magazines: *Pulp & Paper Canada* and *Canadian Oil & Chemical.* The cost to advertise in the first magazine was $4745, and to advertise in the second magazine was $4350. It was expected the ad would be read by 700 purchasing agents in the target industries. The ad generated 206 inquiries, and 105 were later qualified by telemarketers (an average of four calls per hour, and they were paid $16.50 per hour) as worthy of followup by a sales representative. The ad was believed responsible for 28 sales, averaging $63 344 with a 21.4% gross margin.

- *Campaign B.* A copy of the ad was mailed to 1000 purchasing professionals on a mailing list that had been purchased for $1100 from a mailing list supplier. Other costs included printing, $1285; cover letters and envelopes, $115; and postage, $990. The ad resulted in 310 inquiries, and 164 were later qualified by telemarketers (an average of four calls per hour, and they were paid $16.50 per hour) as worthy of followup by a sales representative. The ad was believed responsible for 44 sales, averaging $41 445 with a 22.2% gross margin.

E. EVALUATING SALESPERSON EFFECTIVENESS

You are the sales manager for a large Canadian consumer goods company, and you are evaluating three salespeople that were hired last year. Salespeople work 230 days per year, and the average across your entire sales force was eight sales calls per day. Which salesperson is the most effective, and why?

Salesperson	Karen King	Bob Bishop	Anne Hand
Territory	Calgary	Toronto	New Brunswick
Calls per day	10	8	6
Direct selling costs	$72 000	$74 000	$82 000
Conversion rate (orders/calls)	22%	26.1%	29%
Average sales/call	$3666	$4123	$3255
Average gross margin	21.1%	22.7%	23.3%
Average time per sales call	32 minutes	42 minutes	36 minutes

F. EVALUATING DISTRIBUTION CHANNELS

Upper Canada Clothing Company has been selling its industrial clothing across Canada for over 20 years. It has a four-member sales force, with three in Ontario and one in Quebec. Total sales by this sales force in 2006 were $3.9 million. Total industry sales for competing products in Ontario and Quebec were $15.8 million. The company also has nine manufacturer's agents, who are paid an 8% commission on sales. Their 2006 performance follows:

Territory	No. of Agents	Sales	Market Share
British Columbia	2	$ 886 458	17. 5%
Alberta	2	742 458	13. 4%
Saskatchewan and Manitoba	2	1 244 553	19.5%
Atlantic provinces	3	937 887	26.3%
Total		$ 3 811 356	

The agents that sell your clothing sell between three and eight other non-competing product lines. One of the agents in British Columbia has recently complained about the commission she is being paid, and has informed you that your major competitor is paying its agents a 10% commission. You have decided that it is time to reassess your channel strategy. You are wondering whether you should continue with your current strategy, or replace all manufacturer's agents with company salespeople. The direct selling costs (salaries and selling-related expenses) for each salesperson you hire would be $90 000. You would need one salesperson for each territory. After an analysis of the situation, what would you recommend?

G. EVALUATING PRODUCT LINES

As the product manager responsible for the artificial tree line of a manufacturer of Christmas-related products, with plants in three provinces, you have been instructed to review the four items manufactured at your plant to see if one or more items could be eliminated. The company has added so many items to its product mix over the past decade that the president has decided to reduce the number of items by 20 to 40%. Each product manager has been asked to do a similar analysis. What would you recommend to the president based on the following information?

Product	Suggested Retail Price*	Projected 2006 Unit Sales Volume	Estimated Average Growth Rate 2007–2011
Spruce	$ 90	31 000	10%
Blue spruce	$100	46 000	12%
Fir	$140	62 000	6%
Pine	$180	10 200	4%

Production overhead costs	$ 800 400
Plant administrative expenses	$ 140 510
Allocation of corporate overhead	$ 110 500
Inventory turnover	2.2 times per year
Inventory carrying costs	5.25%

Direct variable cost as a percentage of manufacturer's selling price:

Spruce	75%
Blue spruce	73%
Fir	75%
Pine	80%

*All sales were through retailers who insisted on a markup of 50% on sales, and who expected shipments F.O.B. destination. The average cost of shipping a tree was $ 2.50.

The company did not have a sales force, but sold through manufacturer's agents who received a 5% commission on sales.

Marketing OxyContin in Canada

Anne M. Lavack and Chris Brischuk

INTRODUCTION

In January 2004, the marketing director for Purdue Pharma's Canadian division sat in his Pickering, Ontario, office, pondering some thorny issues regarding marketing the company's best-selling product, OxyContin, to Canadian doctors and pharmacists. Purdue Pharma had been severely criticized in the United States regarding the aggressive marketing of OxyContin, a prescription drug that can become extremely addictive when abused. Purdue Pharma had been publicly accused of questionable marketing practices, including not giving appropriate warnings to U.S. doctors about when and to whom the drug should be prescribed. As he reviewed the company's strategy for marketing OxyContin in the United States to date, the marketing director wondered what steps should be taken for marketing the product in Canada in the future, to avoid similar types of criticism.

BENEFITS OF OXYCONTIN

OxyContin is a semi-synthetic opioid-class analgesic, intended for relief of moderate to severe pain. The active narcotic ingredient in OxyContin tablets is oxycodone, a compound

This case was written by Anne M. Lavack and Chris Brischuk, University of Regina, Regina, Saskatchewan. It is based on publicly available information from news sources and websites. The case is intended to provide a basis for classroom discussion and learning, and is not intended to portray methods or decisions that are right or wrong. Copyright © Anne M. Lavack. Reprinted with permission.

that is similar to morphine, and is found in pain-relief drugs such as Percocet and Percodan. OxyContin is available in strengths of 10 mg, 20 mg, 40 mg, and 80 mg tablets.

Research and development costs for OxyContin exceeded $40 million, and Purdue Pharma obtained formal approval for the drug from the U.S. Food and Drug Administration (FDA) in December of 1995. OxyContin was developed by taking an existing morphine-like product, oxycodone, and applying a time-release coating technology. As a result, OxyContin contains more oxycodone than other drugs, and the time-release formulation allows patients to take it just twice a day, rather than several times a day.

OxyContin hit the U.S. drug market in 1996 and had first-year sales of $55 million, which ballooned to over $1 billion in annual sales by 2000 (with nearly six million prescriptions written for it that year). The drug was also approved for sale in the Canadian market in 1996. Only 600 Canadian prescriptions were written for OxyContin in 1996, but this rapidly rose to 126 000 prescriptions in the year 2000. The estimated U.S. sales of OxyContin by year are shown in Exhibit 1. To put the numbers into perspective, overall sales of narcotic painkillers (including OxyContin) totalled $4.67 billion in 2000, up 136% from 1998—so OxyContin's share of the market was fairly substantial.

EXHIBIT 1	Annual U.S. Sales of OxyContin						
Year	1996	1997	1998	1999	2000	2001	2002
Sales Figures	$55M	$100M	$308M	$600M	$957M	$1.176B	$1.27B

OxyContin's initial popularity wasn't a huge surprise to its manufacturer, Purdue Pharma, who hailed the drug as superior to other intense painkillers. OxyContin "contains no other active ingredients which can cause side effects" and "the drug's special time-release mechanism means a patient needs to take only one pill every 12 hours, a vast improvement for seriously ill patients who formerly had to take other pain medicines as often as 6 times a day." Purdue Pharma felt that OxyContin would be safer and less appealing to abusers than other pain-relieving drugs because of the time-control system that allowed the active drug, oxycodone, to slowly enter the body over an entire day. The label on the package clearly warned patients to only swallow the tablets (i.e., not to crush them) in order to avoid rapid release of a potentially toxic amount of oxycodone.

The benefits of OxyContin were reported immediately by physicians and grateful patients. "There are people in severe pain whose lives have been totally transformed by this drug," according to J. David Haddox, Purdue Pharma's senior medical director for health policy.

Patients who suffer chronic and terminal pain claimed that the strong, long-lasting dosage available in OxyContin had made their lives and day-to-day tasks bearable once again. "All I know is it worked better than anything else," said 31-year-old patient Jeanette Murray, who took OxyContin after suffering irreparable nerve damage in her neck. Jeanette started taking 40 mg OxyContin pills twice a day and found she could finally bathe and dress herself again. "I felt hope for the first time," she said.

PROBLEMS OF OXYCONTIN ABUSE IN THE UNITED STATES

Soon after the drug became a popular prescription painkiller, it became additionally popular for an alternative reason. Illicit drug users quickly learned that if the OxyContin tablet was crushed and snorted, or dissolved and injected, the pill's time-release properties were destroyed, allowing the user to experience a large rapid dose of narcotic. This led to an enormous abuse of the drug, especially in some small communities with large populations of unemployed people and those suffering from disabilities.

A U.S. General Accounting Office report pointed out that "the original label's safety warning advising patients not to crush the tablets because of the possible rapid release of a potentially toxic amount of oxycodone may have inadvertently alerted abusers to methods for abuse." Once addicts figured out how to abuse OxyContin, the drug immediately increased in popularity. Some abusers of the drug claimed the high they got from OxyContin was comparable to that of heroin, but at a much cheaper price, and easier to get on the street. The addiction was like that of heroin as well, with users needing more and more OxyContin just to feed their addiction in order to make it through the day without feeling the symptoms of withdrawal. This caused many users to ultimately take such large amounts of the drug that they would overdose, causing respiratory failure and, in many cases, death. In Exhibit 2, the dramatic increase in the number of U.S. deaths and emergency room visits involving oxycodone (the chief ingredient in OxyContin) is shown for the years 1996 through 2000.

EXHIBIT 2	Deaths and Emergency Room Visits Involving Oxycodone				
	1996	1997	1998	1999	2000
Emergency Room Visits	3 190	4 857	5 211	6 429	10 825
Deaths	51	99	181	268	n/a

The majority of OxyContin that was abused was obtained at pharmacies through prescriptions written by physicians. Some OxyContin abusers obtained their own prescriptions by faking or exaggerating pain, and obtaining prescriptions from more than one doctor (also known as "double-doctoring"), or tampering with handwritten prescription forms by changing the number of pills prescribed. Some patients who suffered legitimate pain received prescriptions for OxyContin, and then sold their stock on the black market in order to benefit financially. Some of these were also involved in "double-doctoring" or tampering with prescriptions, in order to increase the amount of OxyContin they could sell. Several senior citizens were charged with drug trafficking after they were caught selling their own OxyContin pills in order to supplement their modest old-age pension income and pay for other prescriptions.

OxyContin addiction could also lead to violence. Cravings for OxyContin could become so intense that some addicts would do almost anything in order to get their hands on the pills for just one more fix. OxyContin addicts have been involved in holding up and breaking into pharmacies, breaking into doctors' cabinets, and even breaking into the homes of people who are legitimate users of the drug. Some addicts have gone as far as physically threatening doctors and their families in order to have a prescription written, prompting some doctors to give up their licence to write prescriptions for narcotics.

A few doctors have been involved in illegally writing prescriptions for OxyContin. One doctor in Ohio set up a phony clinic and was writing OxyContin prescriptions to "patients" at a premium, knowing the drug would be used for illegal consumption. "Drug abuse goes through fads and epidemics, and OxyContin is on the upturn," according to Don Nelson, a pharmacologist with Ohio Drugs and Poison Control. "When people become aware of a script doctor, they come in droves."

Widespread abuse of OxyContin was first reported in economically poor areas of rural Kentucky, New England, and other eastern U.S. states. Many drug abusers turned to OxyContin as a way to deal with their mundane and sometimes depressing day-to-day lives. For example, eastern Kentucky has one of the nation's highest cancer rates, and many residents suffer from chronic mining and timber injuries. OxyContin seemed like the most potent antidote yet to local despair. "If there's ever a drug that will knock depression out for the short term, it's OxyContin," according to therapist Mike Spare. "The euphoria sucks you in." It was this escape that made OxyContin such a popular choice among users. Social problems were deeply ingrained in these rural communities, and the drug of choice, even among teens, became "Oxy." Use among teenage high school students represented a very disturbing pattern of abuse.

OXYCONTIN IN CANADA

The abuse of OxyContin was originally isolated within poorer areas of the eastern United States, but it gradually moved up the coast and across the border into Atlantic Canada. The border towns of Calais, Maine, and St. Stephen, New Brunswick, were prime examples of how the abuse had crossed the border. Because of cheaper prescription drug prices in Canada, users from Calais would visit St. Stephen, NB, to buy OxyContin on the black market. The abuse of OxyContin spread up the coast from New Brunswick, through Nova Scotia, Prince Edward Island, and into Newfoundland and Labrador. Reports out of Yellowknife also suggested that a market for the drug was developing, after seizures of black market OxyContin occurred there in January 2004.

The popularity of OxyContin use in the Atlantic provinces has resulted in the same types of social problems that were experienced in the United States. "Homes of people with cancer are getting broken into," according to Constable Greg Gouthro of the Cape Breton Regional Municipality street crime unit. "People are even stealing it from their own relatives who have the disease. In the past few months we've had an increase in armed robberies directly related to the drug."

Most of the media attention on the OxyContin problem in Canada centred on Newfoundland and Labrador, where six deaths in 2003 were blamed on OxyContin overdoses. Health officials in that province quickly recognized the problem, and set up a task force in December 2003 to see how the abuse could be stopped in the province.

PURDUE PHARMA: LAWSUITS AND BAD PUBLICITY

Many groups have accused Purdue Pharma of over-aggressively marketing OxyContin, not educating doctors and patients about the possible risks, and of being more concerned about profits than about public safety and well-being. In the United States, many recent lawsuits have been lodged against Purdue Pharma, claiming that OxyContin has ruined lives, and demanding compensation from the company. Although over 30 of these lawsuits against OxyContin have been dismissed, in July 2003 an Ohio court ruled that a class-action lawsuit against Purdue Pharma could proceed on the grounds that the company had been overly aggressive in promoting OxyContin to physicians and pharmacists. An Ohio Court of Appeal agreed to hear Purdue Pharma's challenge to this class-action suit in 2004. Ohio plaintiffs' counsel Stanley Chelsey of Cincinnati's Waite, Schneider, Bayless, and Chelsey predicts that if the certification is upheld, it could bankrupt the company.

Even though it isn't the only prescription drug that is abused, OxyContin is the brand name that is most widely discussed in the media and best known by the general public, thanks to famous abusers such as U.S. radio talk show personality Rush Limbaugh and musician Courtney Love. Therefore, of all the prescription drug manufacturers, Purdue Pharma has the most to lose as long as the controversy lingers. The blame that Purdue Pharma takes for overdose deaths may not be fully substantiated either. Many addicts abuse multiple drugs, so OxyContin is often only one of several drugs involved in a particular overdose death.

Even with all of the pressure that Purdue Pharma has been under in the United States over OxyContin, this prescription drug still has many supporters. Richard Weiner, executive director of the American Academy of Pain Management, contends that when taken as directed, OxyContin is a safe, effective pain medication with few side effects, and that reports of related deaths almost always involve other substances. The roughly one million patients using the drug aren't the ones getting hooked, agrees J.S. Hochman, a Houston-based pain specialist. He cites myriad studies showing that patients properly treated with opiates have about a 1% chance of becoming addicted. Hochman says, "They don't get goofy, high, or giddy, and there's no euphoria—the pain is simply gone."

In the United States, Purdue Pharma has tried to overcome the bad publicity by undertaking many different initiatives all over the country. Under pressure from the U.S. federal government, the company has already devoted significant resources and money to curbing illegal drug use, including rewriting product safety warnings and distributing tamper-resistant prescription-writing pads to doctors that include safety features to make forgery impossible. Purdue Pharma has also agreed to put money into the development and implementation of prescription monitoring software in Florida. The company is running a campaign across the United States, entitled "Painfully Obvious," aimed at teaching adolescents about the perils of prescription drug abuse.

Even with all of these efforts, Purdue Pharma still faces much scrutiny from anti-drug advocates in the United States, and has been desperately trying to find a way to break the negative stigma associated with OxyContin. The company fears that given the recent problems of OxyContin abuse in Newfoundland and Labrador, the same issues could arise in Canada.

CONCLUSION

In marketing OxyContin to Canadian physicians and pharmacists, Purdue Pharma had a significant dilemma on its hands. The product was by far the most successful in the history of their company, representing more than 80% of the company's net sales. However, there was a concern that a large part of these sales may be based on drug abuse, rather than on appropriate use of the drug.

As the Canadian marketing director reviewed the information on his company's successes and failures with OxyContin in the U.S. market, he wondered what sort of marketing strategy should be utilized in Canada. Every year since 1996, when OxyContin was introduced in Canada, Canadian physicians had been writing more and more OxyContin prescriptions for patients. Prescriptions dispensed by pharmacies Canada-wide had soared 400% since 2000. But how much of this represented legitimate use of the drug, and how much of it represented illicit or black-market abuse? Because OxyContin was Purdue Pharma's flagship brand and represented such a large proportion of corporate sales, any significant decline in OxyContin sales could have an enormous effect on the company. Yet, there were significant issues regarding corporate social responsibility.

There was a key issue regarding whose responsibility it was to prevent prescription drugs from being abused. It seemed possible that the Canadian government might regulate the issue, allowing only doctors who were pain and cancer specialists to write prescriptions for painkillers like OxyContin—but would this unnecessarily limit access for patients in need of the drug? Or should Purdue Pharma be held responsible for warning physicians, pharmacists, and patients about the possible perils of OxyContin and what could be done to prevent abuse—and how far should these warnings go? Should the company put money into educational programs in schools, similar to what the U.S. arm of the company had done? Should it aid in the funding of detoxification programs for those addicted to OxyContin? These questions had to be weighed carefully in developing Purdue Pharma's Canadian marketing campaign, since they would influence how aggressively OxyContin could be marketed, and the degree to which Purdue Pharma would need to undertake additional measures to improve their public profile.

SaskTel and Max Interactive Services

Natalie Turnley-Johnston,
Anne M. Lavack, and Gina Clark

SaskTel is a provincial Crown corporation that serves as a monopoly provider of local telephone service throughout Saskatchewan, as well as a competitive provider for a variety of other telecommunications services (e.g., long-distance, mobile phone, Internet, home security). As a Crown corporation, the SaskTel mandate is to provide reliable, high-quality telecommunications service to the people of Saskatchewan at a reasonable cost.

A key question for SaskTel is the degree to which it should offer services that compete with the private sector. For example, in 2002 SaskTel introduced Max Interactive Services, which allows customers to enjoy unlimited high-speed Internet service on their televisions and computers as well as a full lineup of digital-quality television channels, including local radio and television programming.

The new Max service was criticized in the Saskatchewan legislature, where the opposition Saskatchewan Party expressed concerns about the appropriateness of spending millions of dollars of public money to compete with services offered by the private sector. This leads to a key question: under what conditions is it appropriate for a Crown

This case was prepared by Natalie Turnley-Johnston with assistance from Gina Clark, under the supervision of Anne M. Lavack, Ph.D., in the Faculty of Business Administration at the University of Regina. The case is intended to provide a basis for classroom discussion and learning, and is not intended to portray methods or decisions that are right or wrong. Quotes shown in the text are from publicly available web sources. Copyright © Anne M. Lavack. Reprinted with permission.

corporation to compete with the private sector? Based on this concern, what should SaskTel do in the future?

ABOUT SASKTEL

SaskTel has a long history in the province of Saskatchewan (see Exhibit 1). The Department of Railways, Telegraphs, and Telephones was first established by the Government of Saskatchewan in 1908 to service rural and remote communities. The early 1900s saw a series of acquisitions of small telephone companies in Saskatchewan, so that the province became united under one telephone company. In 1947, the telephone system became a provincial Crown corporation and was renamed Saskatchewan Government Telephones. An act of legislature was passed in 1969 which renamed the telephone system corporation as Saskatchewan Telecommunications (SaskTel).

EXHIBIT 1	History of SaskTel

YEAR	HIGHLIGHTS
1908	• SaskTel begins under the Department of Railways, Telegraphs, and Telephones.
1909	• SaskTel acquires the Bell Telephone Company, Wapella-Harris Telephone Company, and the Saskatchewan Telephone Company.
1911	• SaskTel purchases Saltcoats District Telephone Company as well as the North-Western Telephone Company and the Swift Current system.
1923	• Lines are provided that allow for the very first church broadcast in all of Canada.
	• Long-distance lines that allow for radio broadcasting are developed.
1947	• The telephone system becomes known as Saskatchewan Government Telephones and becomes a provincial Crown corporation.
1957	• The first radio relay system is created, which allows for live network television programs to be broadcast coast to coast.
1960s	• Long-distance centres are built in Regina and Saskatoon, leading to the introduction of Direct Distance Calling.
	• Touch-tone phones are introduced.
	• Renamed Saskatchewan Telecommunications (SaskTel).
1970s	• Saskatchewan becomes the first province to bury all its toll lines.
	• Private-line service is established.
	• SaskTel begins a province-wide relay service for the hearing impaired.
1980	• Directory assistance becomes computerized.
1989	• Cellular service is introduced in Saskatchewan.
1995	• Custom calling services including call display, call trace, and call return are introduced to Saskatchewan.
	• Internet services are introduced.
2000	• High-speed Internet is available to over 50% of Saskatchewan and cellular service to over 90%.

EXHIBIT 1	History of SaskTel (continued)
2002	• Max Interactive Services are developed.
2003	• Max Front Row is added to Max.
2004	• SaskTel International has projects and contracts in Africa (Tanzania) and Ukraine.
	• SaskTel develops a partnership with SaskEnergy, TransGas, Sask Pipelines, and other pipelines to establish "Sask 1st Call."

SaskTel is the monopoly provider for local telephone service in Saskatchewan. It is guided by a vision of innovation, competitive communication solutions, and the delivery of sound financial returns and public policy benefits for the people of Saskatchewan. SaskTel currently employs over 4000 Saskatchewan residents from 50 different communities. A 12-member Board of Directors is responsible for supervising the management and affairs of SaskTel.

SaskTel's corporate values include honesty, integrity, mutual respect, open communication, teamwork, and excellence. This means providing customers with value through service, quality, and choice, as well as providing modern products, services, and processes. SaskTel's policy is to remain on the leading edge of technology, while maintaining superior customer service and minimal service fees.

SaskTel is committed to innovation within its organizations, which has led to the introduction of numerous technological advancements within Saskatchewan including the introduction of cellular services in Saskatchewan in 1989; the introduction of Internet services in 1995; and the introduction of Max Interactive Services in 2002. SaskTel has a variety of subsidiaries, divisions, and affiliates (outlined in Exhibit 2), which allows the organization to provide a comprehensive portfolio of telecommunications services.

EXHIBIT 2	SaskTel Subsidiaries & Related Companies

DirectWest Publishing Partnership. DirectWest is fully owned by SaskTel and has been publishing Saskatchewan telephone directories for over 45 years. Recent additions to DirectWest's activities include online advertising, email marketing, and website development.

Hospitality Network Canada Partnership. This venture was established in 1994 based on private Saskatchewan business interests offering entertainment services to Saskatchewan's hospitality industry. This partnership has helped the Hospitality Network to become Canada's main provider of telephone and television services to those in long-term care homes and hospitals. SaskTel currently owns 94.0% of the Hospitality Network.

SecurTek Monitoring Solutions Inc. (SecurTek). SecurTek provides commercial and residential security monitoring services to people in Alberta, Saskatchewan, British Columbia, and Manitoba, and selectively in Ontario. SaskTel partners with small local businesses with established security sales and services to provide comprehensive security services. Security monitoring services are provided through the SaskTel call centre.

Streamlogics Inc. (Streamlogics). Streamlogics Inc. is the main supplier of web presentation and collaboration solutions for over 500 businesses, associations, and government organizations worldwide. Streamlogics Inc. provides services such as webcasting, web conferencing, and media hosting. SaskTel combined existing data hosting and video streaming competencies with their extensive sales and marketing experience in creating Streamlogics.

EXHIBIT 2	SaskTel Subsidiaries & Related Companies (continued)

Business Watch International. This subsidiary makes it possible for pawnshops and other second-hand property dealers to inform law enforcement of their transaction data over the Internet. SaskTel created an equity ownership in Business Watch International in order to blend private sector ideas with the corporation's hosting, Internet, and ebusiness expertise and security protocols.

Interactive Tracking Systems Inc. (Itracks). Itracks is a data collection company that specializes in online data solutions. SaskTel provides its call centre expertise to Itracks.

SaskTel Wireline. The company provides traditional voice services as well as evolving data, data storage, web hosting, text messaging, enhanced call features, dial-up and high-speed Internet, as well as message manager and the increasingly popular Max television service.

SaskTel Wireless (SaskTel Mobility). SaskTel Mobility provides high-quality wireless communication and information services to Saskatchewan and various North American markets.

SaskTel International. This fully owned subsidiary provides engineering consulting, project management, and software solutions around the world. SaskTel International has sold computer software and hardware throughout North America and the United Kingdom, offered engineering consulting and managed products in Tanzania and the Philippines, and has provided products and services to Argentina, the Bahamas, People's Republic of China, Jamaica, Malaysia, Mexico, Poland, and Puerto Rico.

SaskTel has repeatedly been recognized as a top employer in Canada, and as a significant contributor to the Saskatchewan community. Some of SaskTel's recent awards and accomplishments are listed in Exhibit 3.

EXHIBIT 3	SaskTel—Recent Awards and Accomplishments (2000-2004)

Year	Awards/Accomplishments
2000	• Recognized as one of Canada's Top 100 Employers
	• Named one of the Best Companies to Work for in Canada by *Report on Business Magazine*
	• Received the Top Employers of Youth Award and the Royal Bank Partners in Education National Award from the Conference Board of Canada
2001	• Recognized as one of Canada's Top 100 Employers
	• Received the Top Employers of Youth Award
	• Received the 2001 Saskatchewan Labour Force Development Board Training for Excellence Award for Aboriginal Participation
	• SaskTel International received an award from the Canadian International Development Agency and the Canadian Manufacturers and Exporters for its work in bringing telephone service to Northwest Tanzania
2002	• Recognized as one of Canada's Top 100 Employers
	• National Award for Learning Technologies in the Workplace
	• Training for Excellence Award from the Sask. Labour Force Development Board

EXHIBIT 3	SaskTel—Recent Awards and Accomplishments (2000-2004) (continued)
	• SaskTel Pioneers given three awards at the Canadian Pioneers Annual Conference: two People Who Care Awards and one Education Excellence Award
2003	• Recognized as one of Canada's Top 100 Employers
	• Included on *Globe & Mail* 2004 list, "The Fifty Best Employers in Canada"
2004	• Recognized as one of Canada's Top 100 Employers for the fifth consecutive year
	• Labelled "telecom provisioning king" by industry expert, Telecom Research Institute
	• Became Canada's first hosting provider to achieve Signature Certified Status through the HP Service Provider Certification Program
	• Aboriginal Government Employees Network Industry Award

As well, SaskTel is an active promoter of events, major organizations, and tourist attractions that enrich the quality of life for Saskatchewan's people. Some of the sponsored events and organizations include the Kinsmen Telemiracle Telethon, the SaskTel Saskatchewan Jazz Festival, the Saskatchewan Roughriders Football Club, and the Saskatchewan Curling Association. SaskTel is also involved in numerous initiatives to support Saskatchewan youth. (See Exhibit 4.)

EXHIBIT 4	Community Involvement with Youth

SaskTel Youth Initiative Programs and Activities

- Organizes the SaskTel Aboriginal Youth Awards of Excellence
- Annually awards eleven SaskTel scholarships worth $3000 each to students studying in a telecommunication-related subject
- Annually awards six $1500 scholarships to encourage Aboriginal students to study telecommunication-related fields at post-secondary institutions, in conjunction with the Saskatchewan Institute of Indian Technologies
- Annually awards a four-year bursary of $10 000 a year for post secondary studies, in honour of former board member A.E. Blakeney
- Sponsors the Kids Help Phone in Saskatchewan
- Organizes the Student Venture Management Competition to promote entrepreneurship and encourage students in Saskatchewan to consider jobs in areas related to telecommunications

TelCare is another example of SaskTel's commitment to the community. Through this program, 1600 SaskTel employees provide a voluntary deduction from their payroll to contribute approximately $200 000 annually to the TelCare fund, which supports a variety of charitable organizations. The SaskTel Pioneers, comprising 4350 current and former SaskTel employees and family members, volunteer about 60 000 hours of their time to over

100 ongoing community projects every year, and also raise approximately $300 000 annually for community projects.

MARKETING PRODUCTS AND SERVICES

SaskTel offers telephone, Internet, and other technological products and services that suit the needs of businesses and consumers. (See Exhibit 5 for a list of SaskTel's products and services.)

EXHIBIT 5	Products and Services	
Subsidiary/Affiliate	**Product or Service**	**Description**
SaskTel Wireline	Calling Features	• Includes features such as call and name display, call waiting, call return, call forward, and three-way calling
	Message Manager	• Provides users with the ability to send, receive, and reply to phone messages
	Web Conferencing	• Combines data and video, and SaskTel Teleconferencing allows for online meetings
	High-speed Internet	• Fast Internet access that doesn't require a second phone line, is always on, and offers email and personal web space
	Wireless Internet	• Fast Internet that does not tie up the phone line; perfect for those in rural areas that don't have high-speed Internet access
	Dial-up Internet	• Ties up the phone line; includes all the software needed to use the Internet
	Dedicated Internet	• Always connected, doesn't tie up phone lines, unlimited usage, and allows people within an organization to share access
	Max Interactive Services	• Provides users with high-speed Internet use from their television
		• Add-ons include Max Caller ID, which displays the name and number of incoming calls on your television screen, as well as Max Front Row, which is a video-on-demand service
SaskTel Wireless	Wireless Products and Services	• Includes wireless phones, plans, accessories, data phones, data plans, and prepaid phone cards
SecurTek	SecurTek	• 24-hour monitored home safety system protects homes from intrusion, fire, flood, and abnormal temperatures

Although SaskTel has a monopoly on basic telephone service in Saskatchewan, customers have a choice of suppliers when it comes to long-distance service, mobile phone service, Internet service, and television service. Therefore, SaskTel has worked hard to bundle and cross-sell its products. A customer who has basic phone service can be offered long-distance service, mobile phone service, Internet service, and Max expanded television service, and each of these products has a variety of configurations to meet the needs of specific customer segments. Furthermore, customers can bundle these products together in order to earn discounts. The ability to earn reduced rates for using multiple services increases customer loyalty to SaskTel.

In order to effectively sell bundled services to consumers, SaskTel makes use of modern database marketing techniques which involve collecting and storing detailed information on current and prospective customers. With the information in this database, SaskTel is able to identify the most profitable customer segments and create marketing campaigns that directly target the intended consumer. This can involve identifying customers who currently use only one or two of SaskTel's services and persuading them to sign on for additional services. The objective is to help increase customer loyalty and expand into previously non-serviced markets. This helps to build SaskTel's revenues.

SaskTel has considerable marketing savvy at its disposal, with over 100 people employed in marketing and communications within the organization. SaskTel also works with outside advertising agencies to ensure that its advertising is highly creative and effective.

THE CASE OF "MAX"

On September 12, 2002, SaskTel introduced Max Interactive Services—a service that offers customers high-speed Internet connectivity on their television and computer as well as digital music and television, all over the customers' current phone lines. With this service, customers are able to go online, talk on the phone, watch television, and even run their SaskTel SecureTec security system simultaneously.

However, the introduction of Max has not been without its critics. Much of the criticism SaskTel has experienced has come from the Saskatchewan legislature, where the opposition Saskatchewan Party expressed concerns. Eight months after Max was launched, SaskTel had invested $21 million in Max on costs such as advertising and promotion, but only 5000 customers were subscribing to the service. In response to this, Saskatchewan Party Leader Brad Wall complained, "After all of that cost and after all of that advertising that we've seen on the television, they've got 5000 customers, $21 million spent. Has cabinet even put a ceiling, a cap, on how much SaskTel will spend on this initiative?"

Twelve months after the introduction of Max Interactive Services, the number of subscribers had reached 10 000. According to Don Ching, SaskTel President and Chief Executive Officer, "We are extremely pleased with the success of Max and the fact that our customers have found it to be such a great service. SaskTel continues to be a leader in our industry, as other telephone companies also realize that it is essential in the convergent marketplace to offer services such as Max." Mr. Ching also thanked current Max customers for their patience, as he noted that, "With the popularity of Max, our installation team has been extremely busy keeping up with the demand."

However, Saskatchewan Party Leader Brad Wall criticized the organization again, reiterating the fact that with advertising, promotion, and other costs totalling over $21 million, SaskTel had spent over $2000 per customer to attract 10 000 customers. Brad Wall suggested that SaskTel should stay out of risky ventures like Max and instead focus its efforts on its core services.

Some users of Max also had mixed feelings about the effectiveness of the new Max technology. Murray Hill, technology writer at the *Regina Sun,* expressed a concern about the quality of the Internet experience. He explained, "The problem is video cards—TVs don't have them, so you're browsing the Net with the resolution your TV allows you, which is usually pretty low." Hill added, "Because of that, webpages are slow to load and you'll have to scroll around to see what you'd normally see on a computer screen." Overall, however, Murray Hill gave the service a positive review and recommendation.

Although Max had a slow start, by 2005 there were over 25 000 households subscribing to Max, representing a 15.19% penetration in the Saskatchewan market.

There are four Max packages for customers to choose from: Basic Max ($49.95), More Max ($69.90), Mega Max ($89.95), and Ultimate Max ($109.80). All of the packages include unlimited high-speed Internet, digital television channels, Max Pages, Max Mail, Max Front Row service, 45 Galaxie digital music channels, and 33 Saskatchewan radio stations. Exhibit 6 provides details about the specific components within each of the four Max packages.

EXHIBIT 6	Max Packages	
Type of Package	**What It Includes**	**Price**
Basic Max	Standard features include: • Over 30 digital television channels • Unlimited high-speed Internet • Max Pages • Max Mail • Max Front Row service • 45 Galaxie digital music channels • 33 Saskatchewan radio stations	$49.95/month (before possible savings)
More Max (option #1)	• All the standard features of Basic Max • Access to Movie Mania, which provides customers with a selection of exclusive television series and movies that can be watched repeatedly and on demand	$69.90/month (before possible savings)
More Max (option #2)	• All the standard features of Basic Max • Choice of five Theme Packs, which are groupings of channels from a similar category	$69.90/month (before possible savings)
Mega Max (option #1)	• All the standard features of Basic Max • Choice of ten Theme Packs	$89.95/month (before possible savings)
Mega Max (option #2)	• All the standard features of Basic Max • Five Theme Packs and Movie Mania	$89.95/month (before possible savings)
Ultimate Max	• All the standard features of Basic Max • 12 Theme Packs and Movie Mania	$109.80/month (before possible savings)

Customers receive $10.00 off the price of the Max package if they are also SaskTel mobility customers, and an additional $5.00 off if they are on a SaskTel long-distance plan. All of the Max packages also have optional add-ons of Max Caller ID, Max Games, and additional channels. Max Caller ID displays the number and name of incoming calls on the television screen and is available for $2.00 a month. Max Games provides subscribers with twelve different games that can be played on the television screen, and is available for $4.95/month. Customers wanting additional channels can choose from a number of Theme Packs for $4.95 per package (each package contains between four and nine channels).

By offering television programming, SaskTel Max Interactive Services is competing against cable providers such as Access Communications Inc. and Shaw Communications Inc., as well against satellite TV providers such as Bell ExpressVu and Star Choice. In addition, although SaskTel is the only one of its kind to offer a combined Internet and television service such as Max in Saskatchewan, there are other companies offering similar services all across Canada. For example, Manitoba Telecom Services Inc. offers customers digital television service, while Telus Corp. offers digital television, pay-per-view, and video-on-demand service to British Columbia and Alberta residents.

In 2003, SaskTel introduced Max Front Row, a video-on-demand service. The service offered customers a number of ever-changing videos to choose from. Although the movies are purchased through the television, they have similar features to a regular rental. Customers can fast-forward, play, rewind, pause, and stop the movie being viewed. In addition, there are no late charges; customers can choose their own start time and receive unlimited access to the video for 24 hours. Parental controls allow parents to monitor what is being watched and a purchase password prevents accidental charges. New-release movies can be rented for $4.95, second-run movies for $3.95, adult movies for $8.95, kids' packs for $3.95, and kids' movies for $0.95.

FINANCIAL

Over the past five years, SaskTel has seen a steady increase in its total revenue. Its net income has remained fairly flat over this time period, totalling approximately $94 million in 2004–05. As a Crown corporation, the organization's mandate is to break even. It is also acceptable to return a small net profit to the provincial government, which the provincial government can use to offset the cost of other services to taxpayers. A five-year synopsis of financial data for SaskTel is presented in Exhibit 7.

EXHIBIT 7	Five-Year Financial Data & Service Statistics				
Finance	2000	2001	2002	2003	2004
(Thousands of Dollars)					
Operating Revenue	$785 609	$863 426	$893 485	$897 150	**$932 358**
Operating Expenses	675 194	710 579	753 999	783 850	819 071
Other	24 447	(9 360)	(40 625)	(21 009)	8 135
Interest and Related Costs	41 525	41 990	33 715	9 265	26 952
Net Income	93 337	101 497	65 146	83 026	**94 470**
Dividends	87 280	91 347	58 631	76 564	**88 009**

EXHIBIT 7	Five-Year Financial Data & Service Statistics (continued)				
Gross Construction Expenditure	$ 116 227	$ 128 271	$ 166 979	$ 137 208	$ 126 141
Property, Plant, & Equipment	2 309 505	2 411 795	2 512 258	2 510 199	2 568 011
Long-term Debt (gross)	390 203	478 934	473 907	442 614	407 241
Financial Ratios					
Return on Equity	14.9%	16.0%	10.1%	13.0%	14.4%
Debt Ratio	40.1%	38.9%	38.5%	32.7%	25.7%
Employees and Payroll					
Number of Permanent Employees (excluding part-time):					
Diversified Operations *	507	747	802	763	782
SaskTel Wireline	3 370	3 354	3 370	3 390	3 321
Total	3 877	4 101	4 172	4 153	4 103
Salaries Earned (thousands)	$ 228 374	$ 225 767	$ 255 166	$ 270 332	$278 050
Operational Highlights					
Network Access Services	621 766	616 292	613 695	610 720	606 959
Internet Access Services	88 427	106 204	128 501	148 853	162 646
Cellular Access Services	218 856	240 492	259 071	286 250	321 673
Originated Long-distance Minutes (thousands)	1 406 739	1 442 165	1 437 747	1 433 936	1 426 493

*Includes SaskTel International, SaskTel Wireless, DirectWest SecurTek, and others.

CONCLUSION

SaskTel is involved in offering a variety of telecommunications services that go beyond its core identity as a monopoly provider of basic local telephone service. Most would agree that it is entirely appropriate to have a Crown corporation that is a monopoly provider of a basic utility service, like local telephone service. This can be an effective method for keeping basic local telephone rates at the lowest possible level, thereby ensuring that basic phone service is available to citizens at every income level.

However, some have suggested that it may not be appropriate for a Crown corporation to compete against the private sector in areas such as expanded television offerings, Internet services, and mobile phone services. There is sometimes a concern that the organization may be subsidizing its areas of competition by charging more than is necessary for the basic telephone service. On the other hand, if the organization is competing successfully and profitably in these other areas, these competitive efforts may allow the organization to subsidize the cost of basic telephone service accordingly, enabling lower local telephone service rates than would otherwise be possible.

Pantry Pride Stores

H. F. (Herb) MacKenzie

Brenda Howley was a marketing consultant in Somewhere, Ontario. She and her husband, Cameron Porter, a prominent corporate tax lawyer, earned a combined income over $250 000 (before taxes). They had two small children, both under five years of age.

Brenda enjoyed grocery shopping as it gave her a break from her professional and family obligations. She referred to it as "mindless" work, but she prided herself on being good at it. Brenda usually alternated between two major grocery chains in her town, Pantry Pride Stores and Freshway.

Following a series of dissatisfying experiences at one of her regular grocery stores, she decided to write to the company president. Her letter follows.

EXHIBIT 1	Letter to President of Pantry Pride Stores

March 19, 2007
16 Eden Loch Road
Somewhere, ON
E9E 3Z8

President
Pantry Pride Stores
555 Garden Place
Mississauga, ON
L9Q 8Y8

Dear Sir or Madam:

I write you today because I have been a customer of Pantry Pride Stores for over 30 years, but I am increasingly disturbed by a series of experiences I have had at the Victoria Street location in our town.

Over the past year, I have been charged incorrect prices at the checkouts seven times—three times at your competitor, Freshway, and four times at Pantry Pride. I must say, I admire the response I received each time at Freshway, but I have left your store dissatisfied each time. Let me recount some of my experiences for you so that you might appreciate the difference between what I have experienced at both stores.

My first experience was at Freshway. I had purchased a 2-litre container of ice cream. When I went through the checkout, I was overcharged $0.50. The ice cream was supposed to be on sale for $2.59, but the scanner read the regular price of $3.09. I complained to the woman at the service desk, and she insisted that I accept a full refund of $3.09. I told her I would be happy to simply get my $0.50, but she insisted that it was store policy that when customers get charged the wrong price at the checkout, they get a full refund and get the item free of charge. She refunded my money, apologized for the mistake, and asked me to please return to the store for my future grocery needs. Since then, I have had two similar experiences at Freshway.

Now, I will recount four experiences at your store. My first experience was about a year ago. I was overcharged $1 on a bottle of olive oil. I took it to the service desk and advised the woman there that I had been overcharged for the item. At that point, I did not know that you had a similar policy to Freshway, and I did not care as I was perfectly willing to settle for a $1 refund. However, the woman on the service desk asked another employee standing nearby to check the price. The second woman seemed visibly displeased that someone should ask her to do a price check, and that may explain her subsequent behaviour. I watched her stop to talk to one of the cashiers on her way to the grocery aisle, and when she finally disappeared down the aisle and failed to return after about ten minutes, I went to see if she was still there. She was having a personal conversation with another shopper, so I returned to wait at the service desk to see how long the whole process would take. During this period, I read your sign that explained store policy with respect to overcharged prices. Eventually, when the woman returned from doing her price check, she did not address me at all, but simply said to the woman at the service desk, "She's right. Give missus a buck." As you might expect, I was quite upset with the process at this point, and I took further exception to being called "missus." I immediately informed her that I recognized her as a long-time employee of Pantry Pride Stores, and that I would have expected her to know her store policy better than me. I told her I would be pleased to explain it to her if she had not had the opportunity to read it. I grudgingly got a refund on the item.

With respect to my second experience, I admit the error was partly mine. I saw a sign that advertised white onions on special, and I decided to buy one. When I got to the checkout, I was charged a higher price than the advertised special. I asked that the price be checked, and the cashier held it in the air and asked one of the male employees who was nearby to check the price. His comment was, "One onion! &$*%\#!" I mentioned to the cashier that he appeared to be having a bad day and her comment was, "Oh. That's just Ken. He's always having a bad day." The result after the price check was that the price charged was correct. Apparently, I just took a

EXHIBIT 1	Letter to President of Pantry Pride Stores (continued)

large white onion from under the sign that advertised white onions, but I really had a Spanish onion (as were all of the others under the sign). I simply paid the price and left.

On the third occasion, which occurred less than two months ago, I noticed the service desk was very busy and, to save time, I remarked to the cashier that I should get an item free as it was scanned at the checkout at a price higher than advertised. She tried to tell me that as I had not paid for the item, she could simply adjust the price. When I insisted that was unacceptable as she did not catch the error, she called over a supervisor who asked the same question, "Did she pay for it yet?" When told no, she instructed the cashier to adjust the price. I objected again, and the store manager was called for a third opinion. He agreed with me that the store policy stated that the customer would receive any item free if it scanned at a price higher than advertised at the checkout, and he instructed the cashier to deduct the item from the sale. He remarked to the two women, "Remember, we talked about this last week." I left the store thinking that customer service improvements were about to be made.

Unfortunately, late one evening last week, I had my most dissatisfying experience. When overcharged by a young man at the cash register, he asked another cashier (which happened to be the same one I had my previous experience with) what he should do. She told him to give me $0.50 and to put a note in the cash register and someone would fix it in the morning. I informed her that I was more knowledgeable with respect to store policy than she was, and that she should get some additional training as we had already been through this about a month previously. Her remark, in front of a dozen customers, was "We were told by the manager not to mention this policy unless the customer mentions it first."

That was very unsettling. First, it indicates that this store grudgingly implements store policy, and only for those customers who know what it is and who insist on it. It further implies that employees at this store are willing to take advantage of less knowledgeable customers, or those customers who are less likely or unwilling to complain. In my view, this is very unethical marketing behaviour. It is also disturbing that someone in a management position in your company supports that employees will, unknowingly or, worse, knowingly, act in an unethical manner with respect to your customers. Those employees who realize that they are being asked to behave unethically may be uncomfortable doing so and, in a better economic climate, may seek employment elsewhere.

I apologize for the length of my discourse, but I want you to be aware that the problem you have at this location is one I take seriously. When I talked last year to the president of one of Canada's largest hotel chains, he explained his philosophy of customer guarantees to me. I recall he commented that for them to be effective, customers must know what the guarantees are, they must receive compensation when the company fails with respect to its promises, and employees must see that the company pays when they fail. I would suggest that you either scrap this similar store policy, or that you train your managers as to why it is important and why it should be implemented properly.

Sincerely,

Brenda L. Howley

Brenda L. Howley

c.c.   Manager, Pantry Pride Stores
Somewhere, ON

When she finished writing her letter, Brenda mailed a copy to the president. She then decided to visit Pantry Pride for one of her regular shopping trips, and she took another copy of the letter, intending to personally deliver it to the store manager.

Centre for the Arts

H. F. (Herb) MacKenzie

Debbie Slade, managing director for the Centre for the Arts (www.arts.brocku.ca), was preparing for a meeting with Erin White, the marketing coordinator. Debbie had called the meeting to discuss what to do concerning the centre's theatrical programming. It was Monday, October 27, 2003, two days before the centre was scheduled to present *Halo*. This would be the first theatrical performance for the 2003/2004 professional entertainment season, and ticket sales were disappointingly low. Early indications were that sales for the other two theatrical performances were likely to be similar. Debbie was concerned in the short term with what to do to increase sales for this performance, but also for the other two theatrical performances that were scheduled for the current season. More important, she had to decide the longer-term issue of what role live theatre should have within the centre's programming; that is, what she should do for the 2004/2005 season and beyond.

THE VENUE

The Centre for the Arts is an integral part of Brock University. The Departments of Dramatic Arts and Music are given scheduling priority as the centre's facilities are needed for the practical components of their studies. The centre is mandated to stimulate cultural interest in the arts within the Niagara Region. See Exhibit 1 for a statement of the centre's vision, mission, and values and beliefs. It provides hands-on experience for Brock students, as well as for high school students and community users. Through its live performances and educational programs, the centre has been successful in attracting thousands of visitors annually to Brock University.

The Centre for the Arts is intended primarily as an educational and cultural resource for Brock University. Therefore, there are clear priorities when it comes to determining usage for its facilities:

1. Department of Dramatic Arts—for rehearsals, performances, and exhibitions (required 700 hours over 18 weeks during the 2003/2004 season; expected to increase needs by 30% beginning the following year)

2. Department of Music—for performance classes and concerts (required 300 hours during the 2003/2004 season for lunch-hour concerts, the Encore Concert Series, and pedagogical examinations)

3. Niagara Symphony Orchestra

4. Faculty of Education

5. University departments/groups for performances, lectures, speakers, etc.

6. Community groups

7. Centre for the Arts professional entertainment events

EXHIBIT 1	Vision, Mission, and Values and Beliefs of the Centre for the Arts

VISION

To be Niagara's *best* cultural centre, to foster excellence in the performing arts, and to be a leader in the arts community by providing access to all citizens to the live performing arts.

MISSION

To stimulate cultural interest in the performing arts within the university and the Niagara community.

VALUES and BELIEFS

1. To provide leadership for the arts and live entertainment in the community.

2. To program local, national, and international artists to reflect community needs by offering a balanced performing arts program that is shared by educational, community, and professional use on an equitable and flexible basis.

3. To provide a facility that is accessible to all citizens through a variety of programming and culturally diverse programs based on availability, market demand, and fair pricing.

4. To maintain and enhance the centre's facilities and operations at the highest possible standard in order for the Centre for the Arts to continue to be a valuable community and national asset.

The Centre for the Arts employs ten full-time staff members. The managing director, Debbie Slade, is responsible for directly managing the other nine employees, and for indirectly managing 60 part-time student workers and 25 volunteers. The marketing coordinator, Erin White, is responsible for managing the advertising and promotion budget; media releases; magazine, radio, and newspaper advertising; and hospitality for guest artists. She is also responsible for selling advertising space in promotional programmes distributed by the centre, as well as media and other kinds of sponsorship and in-kind gifts. A production manager is responsible for all of the technical operations of the centre; directly managing three technicians responsible for sound equipment, lighting, and computers; enforcing fire regulations; and acting as assistant managing director when Debbie Slade is absent. An audience services supervisor is responsible for selecting, training, and supervising part-time staff, and managing concession inventory and bar supplies. There is also an administrative assistant, a box office manager, and a box office assistant. The number of staff has not increased since 1987, although the scope of operations has more than doubled. See Table 1 for a list of scheduled performance for the 2003/2004 professional entertainment season.

Table 1	Season Schedule 2003/2004
Tower of Power	October 4
Remy Shand	October 9
Zucchero	October 22
Two Planks and a Passion Theatre: *Halo*	October 29
Chantal Kreviazuk	October 30
Harlem Gospel Choir	October 31
The Royal Winnipeg Ballet: *The Magic Flute*	November 15
The Second City National Touring Company:	
The Puck Stops Here!	November 26
Brass Rings: *A Time for Christmas*	December 4
Natalie MacMaster	December 5
Cantabile	December 10
Ron Sexsmith *with Mad Violet*	December 16
Holly McNarland *with Shaye*	January 15
The Heillig Manoeuvre	January 17
The Flaming Idiots	January 18
Motus O: *A Midsummer Night's Dream*	January 24
The Musical Box:	
Genesis: Selling England by the Pound	January 28
Dave Coulier	January 29
Smythe and Saucier	February 8
Kiran Ahluwalia	February 19
Nearly Neil and the Solitary Band	February 21

Table 1	Season Schedule 2003-2004 (continued)
Sampradaya Dance: *Revealed by Fire*	February 28
Gregg Lawless and the Acoustic Orchestra	March 3
Jory Nash and Aengus Finnan	March 6
One Acre Productions: *Fingers and Toes*	March 11
John McDermott	March 12 & 13
Roger Whittaker	March 14
The Cottars	March 19
Jane Bunnett and the Spirits of Havana	March 25
Sinha Danse: *Loha / Thok*	March 27
Cleo Laine & the John Dankworth Group	April 1
Catalyst Theatre: *The Blue Orphan*	April 7
Nnenna Freelon	April 16
David Usher	April 17
Shona Reppe Puppets: Cinderella	April 18
Rik Emmett	April 21
Buddy Wasisname and the Other Fellers	April 28
The Big Band Broadcast	April 30

THE ACT

Halo, a compassionate and funny play written by actor and playwright Josh MacDonald, tells the story of the sighting of an image of Jesus that appeared in small-town Nova Scotia. The play is based on a true story, the Christ-like apparition having appeared under the floodlights on the outside wall of a Tim Hortons in Bras D'Or, Cape Breton, and first noticed by staff at the Lick-A-Chick restaurant across the road. The apparition appeared for several days, resulting in nightly traffic jams around the donut shop when as many as 4000 people came to view it.

The main character in the play is Casey Quinn, a high school dropout who has taken a full-time job at the local Tim Hortons. Casey, who resents the rigidity of her local community, has become an outcast. She ridicules the faith of her boyfriend and boss, while she befriends the new priest in the community. Following the appearance of the apparition, the community becomes a "faith circus" where everyone, including Casey, has something to learn. While this is happening, a local Christmas tree farmer and devout Catholic, Donald McMullen, has been sitting at the bedside of his daughter who has been in a coma for the past two years. Donald's faith is tested and his motivations examined when his older daughter, Lizzie, joins him at the bedside. The two stories come together to provide a powerful and hilarious look at modern faith and community.

The play was being performed by a cast of seven members of theatre company Two Planks and a Passion Theatre (www.twoplanks.ca), founded in 1992 in rural Kings County, Nova Scotia. The company's mission is "to commission, develop, and produce challenging Canadian drama with strong roles for women that is reflective of the lives of the audiences for whom they perform, and to disseminate this work to communities large and small nationwide." Other works that the company created and produced include *Westray: The Long Way Home* and *Hockey Mom Hockey Dad.*

The touring performers had booked numerous performances across eastern Canada, beginning with the Confederation Centre, in Charlottetown, PEI, on October 16 and ending on November 8 at the Markham Theatre in Markham, Ontario. The St. Catharines performance was booked for October 29, 2003 at the 538-seat Sean O'Sullivan Theatre, Centre for the Arts, Brock University. One of the main advantages that the centre had was its membership in the CCI Group. As a result, it could procure the services of a number of performing artists through a network of block booking with other members, thereby getting reduced artistic fees because of "volume" booking. The artistic fees charged to the centre for *Halo* amounted to $4000.00. Artistic fees varied depending on the venue, and the centre simply adjusted box office prices to reflect the fees it paid.

COSTING *HALO*

When Debbie reviewed the other costs associated with *Halo*, she noted that she would have to spend $600.00 for hotel accommodations for the performers. The promotional costs that were either spent or committed at that time included $950.00 for flyers, brochures, and posters; $475.00 for print advertising (newspapers), and $450.00 for radio advertising. Projected costs also included three local crew members to unload and set up stage props and equipment for two hours each ($27.00 per hour); four local crew members to take down the stage props and equipment and load them for shipment for one hour each ($27.00 per hour); one spot operator for two-and-a-half hours ($27.00 per hour); one house manager for four hours ($15.00 per hour); two catering staff for five hours each ($8.50 per hour), and eight ushers for three-and-a-half hours each ($9.85 per hour). The only other actual cost involved would be to service the credit card administration as credit card companies charge a small percentage for a handling fee. Debbie's best guess was that it would be somewhere between $150.00 and $200.00. Debbie included a cost of $915.00 for theatre rental, although this was not actually paid to the university as a rental fee. The reason it was included was because it was an opportunity cost since that is what would be received if the theatre were actually rented for another purpose. When all costs are finally known, including this opportunity cost for theatre rental, the centre could make up to 10% profit. Any revenue above this amount would then be split 80% / 20% between the artist or artists and the promoter. This arrangement had become increasingly popular over the past few years and was now being demanded by almost all performers.

SALES TO OCTOBER 27, 2003

Prior to the meeting, Debbie Slade asked for an up-to-date summary of sales. With two days remaining before the performance was scheduled, there were only 225 paid seats. Table 2 shows a breakdown of sales. Historically, there were very few, if any, seats sold the last few days before a theatrical performance.

Seat prices varied depending on the particular performance. Prices for musical performances varied from $55.00 per single seat for John McDermott or Natalie MacMaster, to $49.50 for Chantal Kreviazuk or Remy Shand, to $32.00 for the Cottars or Buddy Wasisname and the Other Fellers, to $28.50 for Ron Sexsmith or Holly McNarland.

Table 2	Sales to October 27, 2003			
Buyer Type	Seats	Revenue	GST	CRF
Advance (Ticket Office)	57	$ 1624.50	$ 106.02	$ 57.00
Advance (Internet)	16	456.00	29.76	16.00
Group Tickets	36	923.40	60.48	36.00
Brock Staff/Faculty	2	51.30	3.36	2.00
Gold Members	45	1057.50	69.30	45.00
Platinum Members	69	1414.50	92.46	69.00
Total	225	5527.20	361.38	225.00

Theatrical performances were priced at the lower end of the range. All three performances scheduled for the 2003/2004 season were priced $28.50 for single seats, with a 10% discount for groups of ten or more, or for Brock University staff and faculty; $23.50 for Gold members; and $20.50 for Platinum members. Brock University had 490 faculty members and 16 librarians in its Faculty Association, and 654 staff. The centre sold approximately 600 memberships annually, mostly outside the university. Memberships were almost equally divided between Gold memberships and Platinum memberships. Gold members paid $50.00 annually. For this, they got advance notice of upcoming performances and special events, plus an opportunity to purchase tickets prior to their being offered to the general public. They also got reduced prices of up to 20% and could buy as many as six discounted tickets per show. Membership also entitled them to three complimentary parking vouchers valued at $3.00 each, an invitation to a special "Member's Night" sneak preview, and complimentary tickets to selected shows. Platinum members paid $100.00 annually and received all the benefits of Gold members, but got discounts of up to 25% and five complimentary parking vouchers, and they could buy up to ten discounted tickets per show. Platinum members also got advance purchase privileges prior to Member's Night.

From total revenue, the Centre for the Arts had to pay GST to Revenue Canada, and a $1.00 per seat charge that was to contribute to a capital reserve fund that was used to repair and renovate the facilities when needed. One of the main marketing objectives for the 2003/2004 season was to have an average 80% capacity paid attendance, with 50% of all tickets sold through membership. While the centre was not specifically focused on generating a profit, Debbie was certainly aware that generating some positive financial contribution would position the centre better within the university hierarchy, and this would make it easier to negotiate for things that it might need in the future.

MARKETING

Erin White is the marketing coordinator for the Centre for the Arts. Erin received a B.A. in Media Communications from Brock University in 1998 before being hired by a small theatre company in Fort Erie, not far from St. Catharines. The job was very much "trial by fire." The position was supported by a grant from Human Resources Development Canada. Otherwise, the company had limited resources and no understanding of business. Taking an opportunity for a more stable position, Erin joined Conference Services at Brock University, where she worked for two years and gained some marketing and promotion experience. Then, she moved to the Centre for the Arts, responsible for marketing and promotion.

The major promotional item for the centre was a full-colour, 12.0 × 16.5 cm. glossy brochure with a page dedicated to each of the scheduled performances. The brochure was distributed at the start of the season to all Gold and Platinum members and to 17 000 people registered in the centre's database. It was also distributed throughout Brock University via its internal mail system, to local hotels and libraries, and then it continued to be distributed at the box office throughout the performing season. Direct mail was commonly used to promote a specific item or series. For example, to promote the three theatrical performances scheduled for the 2003/2004 season, the centre made a series of mailings in late September: 404 letters were sent to people in the database who had bought theatre tickets within the previous two years, 284 letters were sent to church and seniors groups, and 24 letters were sent to "theatre educators" at local high schools. For the latter group, the centre made a special offer for secondary school students of $11.75 per ticket for a group of ten or more, plus one free ticket for every ten tickets purchased.

The centre received some free radio publicity on local radio stations that aired "A Brock Minute" each day, a short description for the local community of what was happening throughout Brock University. Aside from this, radio was a regular medium for promoting the centre. For *Halo*, for example, four radio ads per day were booked on each of three local radio stations—105.7 Easy Rock FM, 97.7 Hits FM, and 610 CKTB AM Talk Radio—for the six days before the scheduled performance.

Print advertisements were placed locally each week during the programme season from early September through late April. These quarter-page print ads usually featured a particular performance, and sometimes more than one if there were several performances scheduled within a particular week. The *St. Catharines Standard* gave the centre a 25% discount based on its seasonal volume. *Pulse Niagara*, a regional paper that was distributed throughout the Niagara Region promoting upcoming events, gave a one-for-one promotional deal—"buy one and get one free." *Halo* was advertised in both papers each of the two weeks prior to its scheduled performance.

Other promotional media included email newsletters to select patrons who had agreed to receive them, occasional letters to Brock University staff and faculty, and large, 28.0 × 43.25 cm. posters. Exhibit 2 shows the promotional poster for *Halo*. Volunteers distributed several hundred of them to businesses around town and throughout Brock University. Students at Brock University were encouraged to buy "walk-up" tickets on the night of performances. The price to students was just $6.00 per seat. For popular performances, of course, there were never walk-up seats available. For some comedy or musical performances, a dozen or so students might decide to see if seats were available at the last minute. For theatrical performances, it was highly unlikely that there would be any additional seats sold the last few days before a performance, including student walk-up purchases.

THE MEETING

Debbie Slade had asked to meet with Erin to discuss the upcoming performance of *Halo* when it became apparent that the performance would likely not generate enough boxoffice revenue to cover its costs. Together they reviewed the promotion for the show and what could possibly be done.

EXHIBIT 2	*Halo* Promotional Poster

The two women agreed that cancelling the performance was not an option, and spending any additional money at this time would most likely be ineffective. Several alternatives were discussed, however. One alternative was to contact the 300 Gold and 300 Platinum members who had not purchased tickets for the performance and make them a special "buy one and get one free" offer. If this were successful, it might create some interest and gain additional sales for the later theatre performances as well. Unfortunately, given the sales that had already been made, there was also the possibility that it would create dissatisfaction among those who had booked and paid for their seats early. A similar option was to make the same offer to Brock University staff and faculty as they could be reached on short notice through the Brock University email system. There were only two tickets sold so far to staff and faculty, and that was most likely a single sale for two tickets. If the staff or faculty member became aware of this and was disappointed, it would be easy to provide him or her with two additional tickets to the performance, or to another performance.

Another option that was discussed was to provide free tickets for local radio stations to give away to listeners. One issue was whether single tickets should be given away, or whether pairs of tickets should be given away. Another issue was what paying patrons might feel if they found that too many people in the audience were attending without having paid for their admission. This type of promotion would not generate much revenue immediately, but would help build awareness around the local community and might encourage potential new patrons to attend and they might possibly then purchase tickets for other performances, or even purchase a membership. Some additional revenue might be received through concession sales. The average patron spent approximately $4.00 for food and beverage items. Promotional tickets might generate a few immediate sales if ticket winners decided to buy additional tickets for friends or family, but Debbie and Erin agreed that this was really not likely to produce many additional sales.

As they discussed this option, Debbie also suggested they could give some free tickets to other people who recently made some contribution to the Brock University community. One example would be volunteers who had helped with the university's United Way campaign. Giving them free tickets would help recognize their volunteer work, might also encourage some of them to attend other theatrical performances, and, at the very least, would help fill the theatre. If paying patrons viewed the theatrical performances as popular, it would encourage them to purchase tickets to other shows in advance to ensure that they were available. Either alternative providing free tickets would at least fill seats and this was important for the performers, for other patrons, and for reviewers, who often tended to write poor reviews of poorly attended performances.

As the meeting neared its end, Debbie turned to Erin:

> I guess, for your part, I would appreciate if you could look over the revenue and cost projections and see if there is anything we can do immediately or for the other two scheduled theatrical performances. While we do not have to generate a profit on every performance we book, there will be increasing pressure on us to increase revenue, particularly as demand increases within the university for the facilities. We may have to book fewer performances in future years and we may have to become more concerned about which ones help us generate sales. Once I have your ideas, I will be better able to decide what to do about the larger programming issue. It could be that theatre is better left to other venues around the community.

Wing and a Prayer

Marvin Ryder

Stefan Bakarich had found just the right name for his mobile bungee jumping operation—"Wing and a Prayer." It was March 1994, and he had eight weeks to the May Victoria Day Weekend—the first long weekend of the summer. If he had it figured correctly, Stefan would rent a construction crane, assemble a group of friends, and tour southwestern Ontario offering bungee jumps at tourist attractions. He and his friends could earn enough money to return to university in the fall while being paid to have fun and work on their tans over the summer.

SOME HISTORY

Bungee jumping started as a ritual practised by "land divers" on Pentecost Island in the New Hebrides of the South Pacific. To cleanse themselves of wrongdoing or as acts of courage, native men constructed 30-metre towers from thin trees. Climbing to the top, they dove off with vines tied around their ankles. Their heads would just touch the ground as the vine became taut. In the 1960s, a group of Oxford University students (who called themselves the Oxford Dangerous Sports Club) brought bungee jumping to the modern world. As a commercial curiosity, the sport was born in New Zealand in 1988 where ancient vines were replaced with modern manufactured fibre cords tested to withstand more than 1361 kilograms, and where bamboo pole towers were replaced with bridges spanning deep river gorges.

The sport became popular on the west coast of the United States in the late 1980s and swept across the country in the early 1990s showing phenomenal growth. In 1991, only 20 companies in the United States offered bungee jumps. In 1992, that number had grown to 200 and by 1993, more than 400 companies in the United States were in the bungee jump business. Participation in the sport had also grown. In 1992, 1.5 million Americans experienced a bungee jump, spending more than $100 million for the thrill. In 1993, 2.5 million Americans participated, spending more than $125 million.

In Canada, the first commercial bungee operation (Bungy Zone) opened south of Nanaimo on Vancouver Island on August 4, 1990. By 1993, 30 000 people had jumped at this one site. Some Bungy Zone statistics: oldest jumper was 73, youngest was 14, and heaviest was 150 kilograms. The most paid bungee jumps by one person was 30. The typical jumper was a thrill-seeking male aged 18 to 25. Ninety-nine percent of people who paid the fee completed the jump. Ten percent of jumpers took a second jump on the same day. Participation statistics were not available for Canada but, in 1993, there were about 35 companies that arranged bungee jumps off bridges, towers, cranes, and hot air balloons. The West Edmonton Mall had introduced indoor bungee jumping. Nanaimo had even hosted bungee jumping in the nude.

Stefan had taken his first bungee jump in May 1993. He tried to describe his experience to a friend.

> I dove straight out, in my best imitation of Superman. At first, the free-fall was exhilarating. But it was also disorienting, and after a moment I panicked. I wished there was something to grab hold of. The sound of the wind was almost deafening. The ground below rushed toward me, until everything became a blur. It was hard to believe that I was feeling 3Gs—just like airforce pilots.
>
> Suddenly, the world seemed upside-down. The ground was receding, and now I was completely confused. I was up in the air again when I realized that the cord had held.
>
> I started to descend once more. This time, there was no fear, just enjoyment. I rebounded up and down four more times, with each rise becoming smaller. Finally, the bungee cord had no more bounce, and I was lowered onto the pad where my feet were untied. Friends told me I had The Look—a certain glow common to those who had just found God or had escaped the electric chair.

During the summer of 1993, Stefan took a bungee jump training course, worked for two-and-a-half months at an amusement park in the United States, and jumped 150 more times.

OPERATIONS

Stefan's experience with a crane-based company inspired him. He had taken careful notes about its operation so that he could replicate its success in Canada. For a typical jump, a patron would be taken, in a specially designed metal cage, 40 metres to the top of a crane—a ride of 60 seconds. These jump platforms were available for $500 to $1000, though Stefan thought he could design and build one over the next eight weeks. At the top, the patron would be placed in one of two harnesses and given special instructions about jumping. One harness went around a person's ankles so that he or she would fall head first. The feet were tightly bound together with a towel and tethered to the bungee cord by a nylon strap and carabiner, a common piece of mountaineering equipment. The other harness could be strapped around a person's waist so that he or she would fall feet first. Each harness was commercially available at a cost of $150 to $300. While the patron took some time to build courage, the length of the bungee cord was adjusted to that person's weight. These "top of crane" activities could take between two and four minutes. Jumping out from the cage and away from the crane, the patron would take three seconds to fall until the bungee cord became taut and caused them to bounce. Waiting for the bouncing to stop, lowering the basket, retrieving the jumper, and removing the harness from her/him would take another two minutes.

Stefan had researched potential suppliers and had a firm estimate of costs. He would have to pay $100 per operating hour for construction crane rental which included $1 million of liability insurance, fuel to run the generator, and a driver. Given the lack of office-building construction, many companies had cranes parked in their compounds. These construction companies had been quite interested in Stefan's lease proposal. A crane operator would cost an additional $40 per operating hour. He felt the cost was justified as a skilled employee operating the crane would minimize the chances of something going wrong.

He and a jump assistant would be on the jump platform helping with instructions, adjusting the bungee cord, strapping on the harness, and communicating via walkie-talkie to the crane operator. On the ground, one person would use a microphone and sound system to speak to any crowd that had gathered and encourage them to participate. Two other people would assist on the ground by getting potential patrons to sign a liability waiver form, weighing jumpers to determine the proper bungee cord, collecting the jump fee, and talking personally with patrons in the crowd. While people under 18 could jump, a parent's or guardian's signature would be required on the waiver form. Excepting the crane operator and himself, all staff would each be paid $8 per operating hour.

Of course, a bare crane is not very attractive, so Stefan would have to invest $700 in some cloth banners which, when hung on the crane, would also be used for promotion. Some portable tables, folding chairs, walkie-talkies, and a sound system would have to be purchased for $1700. This cost also included portable "snow" fencing which would be used to limit public access to the crane, jump platform, and retrieval area. During less busy times, the sound system would play hip hop, dance, house, and rap music to help attract and build a crowd. His major cost was an inflatable target pad that would be used to catch a jumper only if the bungee cord broke. Though pads came in many sizes, he felt it was a wise precaution to choose the largest size available at a cost of $12 000. As he estimated the business would have a three-to-five-year life, the pad and other equipment could be used year after year.

He had modelled his fee schedule on the American amusement park: $65 for the first jump and $55 for a second jump on the same day. If the patron used the waist harness rather than the ankle harness, both prices were reduced by $10.

Realistically, the company would operate for the 110-day period from the Victoria Day weekend in late May to the Labour Day weekend in early September. As Stefan did not want to be bothered with portable lighting, he would start operations no earlier than a half-hour after sunrise and cease operations no later than a half-hour before sunset. The company would never operate during a thunderstorm or in high winds and Stefan thought that the start of a week and overcast/rainy days would see less demand for the service.

SAFETY

Bungee jumping was not without its risks. In August 1992, a man was killed in Peterborough, Ontario, when he jumped from a crane. That same year, two people died in the United States and one in New Zealand from accidents. The Canadian Standards Association, a nonprofit agency, had not determined any rules for bungee jumping so regulations varied by province. Some provinces had no regulations, but Ontario, working with the Canadian Bungee Association, had amended the Amusement Devices Act to regulate bungee jump operations starting in the spring of 1994.

In the legislature, Ontario Consumer and Commercial Affairs Minister Marilyn Churley said, "Operators can't just take a construction crane and set it up and have people jump off. We don't think that's safe. The government is committed to establishing and enforcing safety standards to minimize the risks to Ontarians who take part in this activity. Maintaining high standards of safety may also limit bungee operators' exposure to lawsuits and reduce the high cost of liability insurance."

Bungee jump operators were required to obtain a licence and permit ($310 fee) from the ministry prior to any jumps taking place. Before a licence could be issued, the operators' equipment designs first had to be approved by ministry engineers ($400 fee) after which a thorough on-site physical inspection of the bungee operation would be completed ($200 fee). The technical dossier of designs was to include: the jump height; a description of bungee cords including manufacturer, type of cord, and weight range of jumpers; an indication if the jump was static or portable; a description of the hoisting device including name of manufacturer, year, serial number, and safe working load; depth of water or air bag; type of harnesses to be used and types of jumps offered; wind speed restrictions; and number and function of jump personnel.

A 40-page code of safe conduct for bungee jumping operations was also in place. The code had been recommended by the Task Force on Bungee Jumping, a working partnership between government and the Canadian Bungee Association. The code required a number of safety features that must be in place on bungee equipment and technical specifications for the structure, platform, bungee cords, harness, and all other equipment used in the activity. It also outlined the qualifications for bungee jump employees, including certificates in first aid and cardio-pulmonary resuscitation (CPR), and training specific to bungee jumping. Another requirement was a good first aid kit with a spinal board and speed splints which would cost an operator an additional $500.

These changes were introduced to regulate careless operators and were aimed primarily at mobile bungee operations as they had less-experienced staff and more failure-prone equipment due to being repeatedly set up and dismantled. Prior to the legislation, some operators had voluntarily introduced dual carabiners for ankle harnesses so there was a backup if one failed.

Stefan planned his own set of rules. No pregnant women. No people with heart conditions. No people with high blood pressure. No people who suffered from epilepsy. No people with neurological disorders. No people under the influence of alcohol and/or drugs. He would allow no reverse jumping (anchoring and loading the bungee cord from the ground to propel the jumper upward), no sandbagging (loading excess weight with the jumper to be released at the bottom to gain more momentum) and no tandem jumping (two or more jumpers harnessed together).

A bungee cord was made from several bound strands of latex rubber, doubled back on itself thousands of times, sheathed in cotton and nylon. The cost of these cords varied from $300 to $1000. The cord could stretch to five times its original length. For safety, most operators retired a bungee cord after 150 jumps. Prior to the popularity of jumping, these cords were used by the U.S. Air Force on aircraft carriers, and so were constructed to military specifications.

SOME DECISIONS

To start his business, Stefan needed capital to acquire bungee cords, harnesses, the landing pad, and his operating equipment. He was aware of two Ministry of Economic Development and Trade loan programs. As a returning Canadian university student, he could apply for a $3000 interest-free loan. To qualify for this loan, he had to be over 15, returning to school, and operating a business in Ontario between April 1, 1994 and September 30, 1994. Whatever loan amount he received would be payable on October 1, 1994.

He had also heard of the Youth Venture Capital Program. It provided loans of up to $7500 to help unemployed Canadian youth aged 18 to 29 start a business in Ontario. The interest rate on the loan would be prime plus 1% and he would be expected to make principal and interest payments each month. He would also be expected to contribute a minimum of one-quarter of the loan amount to the operating capital of the firm. This program was not intended to fund a summer job experience.

Neither program would provide him with all the capital he required. He approached his parents. While not completely sold on the venture, his parents thought it would be a good learning experience so they agreed to loan him $3000 interest-free, though they expected to be repaid at the end of the summer.

Needing more money, Stefan shared his plan with Zach Thompson, a friend on the university water polo team and a recent bungee jumping enthusiast. Zach had also worked part-time with a bungee jump operator but he had only jumped 40 times in the last year. He would act as a jump assistant. Zach proposed a partnership and a joint application for any government loan. Profits would be split 50-50. Like Stefan, he would replace a "paid" worker on the jump crew but would not draw any hourly wages. Of all people Stefan contacted, Zach asked the most questions.

Where would they operate the business? Stefan thought they could create a base of operations in Grand Bend. When special events occurred, like the Western Fair in London, Ontario, or the Zurich Bean Festival, they could pull up stakes and move to that location for a few days.

Would they offer only bungee jumps? Zach thought they could sell some complementary products. A colourful logo could be designed for Wing and a Prayer and applied to t-shirts and baseball caps. Selling for $20 and $10 respectively, these items would have a 100% markup on cost and could add extra revenue. Zach had also thought about selling a personalized video. That would mean purchasing a camcorder ($1800), developing some stock footage for opening and closing credits, and somehow editing/processing the video footage on-site so the patron could quickly get her/his tape. Zach thought they could sell the videos for $25. Building on these ideas, Stefan thought about offering a colourful poster that might be especially popular among children. To produce 1000 posters would cost $800 but they could be sold for $4 to $6, generating a very healthy profit margin.

Would they make any money? That required some financial analysis, including a breakeven analysis. Zach felt they needed to assess a second scenario: the likelihood that they would make enough money to return to university in the fall. These analyses would be needed along with their marketing plan when any loans were sought.

If this was going to be their summer occupation, they needed to get started right away.

Lucas Foods

John Fallows and Walter S. Good

Bib Martin was marketing manager of Lucas Foods, a diversified food manufacturing and wholesaling company based in Edmonton. The company has recently had some success with a new product, Gold Medal Crumpettes. Jerry Lucas, the president of Lucas Foods, asked his marketing manager to recommend an appropriate strategy for the new product that would best capture the available opportunity and support the mission of the company.

THE INDUSTRY

Lucas Foods was in the food manufacturing and wholesaling business, marketing a broad product line that included frozen egg products, shortening, flour, baking mixes, spices, and bulk ingredients. Its primary customers were the five major national food wholesalers, with smaller regional wholesalers and independent grocery stores accounting for a smaller portion of its sales.

Prepared by John Fallows under the direction of Walter S. Good of the University of Manitoba as a basis for classroom discussion rather than to illustrate either effective or ineffective handling of an administrative situation. Copyright © by the Case Development Program, Faculty of Management, University of Manitoba. Support for the development of this case was provided by the Canadian Studies Program, Secretary of State, Government of Canada. Reprinted with permission.

Gold Medal Crumpettes was a recent entry in Lucas Foods' bakery products group. The product fell into the product class commonly known as biscuits. Competitive products in this class included crumpets, scones, English muffins, and tea biscuits. Competition also came from a variety of substitute products such as toast, donuts, and muffins. Biscuit producers included such prominent names as Weston Bakeries and McGavin Foods Ltd., domestically, as well as the American firm of S. B. Thomas, which concentrated on English muffins and dominated the market for that product.

Lucas Foods estimated that the product life cycle for specialty bakery goods was from five to seven years. Generally, if a new product was going to be successful, it enjoyed quick acceptance in the marketplace. Introduced in 1984, Gold Medal Crumpettes had limited distribution. They had been sold in Alberta and Saskatchewan and were recently introduced in Manitoba, Montana, and Minnesota. Safeway was the only major chain to carry the product in Canada, but sales growth had been steady to date.

HISTORY OF LUCAS FOODS

The company was originally formed under another name over 50 years ago. It specialized in frozen egg products and later diversified into cabbage rolls and frozen meat products. The company was purchased by a major brewery in 1972, but the frozen egg portion of the business was sold back to the original owners six years later. They sold the business to Jerry Lucas in 1979. Since then, sales have doubled to their present annual level of $12 million.

The company followed a "portfolio approach" to its product line, regularly adding or deleting items according to established criteria with respect to the marketing cycle. With the single exception of frozen egg products, no specific product or product family dominated its overall product offering. (An exception was made for frozen egg products because of their unique life cycle and recession-proof qualities.)

In its statement of business mission, Lucas Foods indicated a desire to grow to an annual sales level of $50 million and to become a major national food manufacturer and wholesaler, as well as an exporter. Its major competitive weapons were believed to be its excellent reputation, product knowledge, marketing expertise, and level of customer service.

MARKETING GOLD MEDAL CRUMPETTES

Lucas Foods believed that the consumption of biscuit items was uniform across age groups, seasons, and geographic locations. It is a mature market. The merchandise itself was targeted toward the "upscale buyer." Package design, pricing policy, and product ingredients positioned Gold Medal as high-priced and high-quality relative to the competition. Therefore, the primary variables for segmenting the market were socioeconomic: Gold Medal Crumpettes were a luxury item.

The Crumpettes were designed to incorporate the taste and texture of scones, English muffins, and biscuits. They could be eaten with or without butter, either toasted or untoasted. They were available in four flavours: plain, raisin, cheese, and onion, and the company had plans to add three more flavours, including pizza. The product could be stored frozen. The name, Gold Medal Crumpettes, was specifically selected to imply quality.

Since wholesale food distribution in Canada was dominated by relatively few firms, management felt that it had little choice in the distribution of its products. Lucas Foods did not own a large warehouse to store its finished baked goods, but manufactured Gold Medal Crumpettes to order. The merchandise was then transported by common carrier to various customers under net-30-days credit terms.

The goal of the company's promotional efforts was to stimulate and encourage consumer trial of the product. There was some radio advertising when the product was first introduced. Although Lucas suggested the retail price, the distributor, especially in the case of Safeway, did most of the promotion. Typical promotions have been:

- Hostesses distributing free samples in supermarkets
- Crossover coupon promotions with jam companies
- Mail-out coupons to consumers
- Free products to stores
- Temporary price reductions for distributors

So far, $50 000 had been spent on the promotion of Gold Medal Crumpettes. To complement these promotional efforts, Lucas Foods had three salespeople who, along with the marketing manager, regularly called on all major accounts.

Gold Medal's high price was consistent with its positioning and was arrived at after evaluating consumer surveys and the company's production costs. The expected price-sensitivity of the market was also considered. A package of eight biscuits retailed for $1.89. The product was sold to supermarket chains in cases of 12 packages, with a factory price of $12 per case. Manufacturing costs, including allocated overhead, were $8.40 per case. This provided a contribution margin of $3.60 per case, or 30%. Production capacity was available for up to 16 000 cases per month.

CAPTURING THE OPPORTUNITY

The estimated total potential market for Gold Medal Crumpettes is shown in Exhibit 1. Bib Martin guessed that Lucas Foods held a 16% share of the Alberta market.

The Alberta consumer had been very receptive to the product, but outside Alberta, the company had only a limited reputation and was not well known as a wholesale food supplier. This lack of awareness made it more difficult for the product to obtain the acceptance of retailers. Also, the company faced an almost total lack of consumer awareness outside the province.

If Gold Medal succeeded in obtaining quick acceptance in new markets, competitors might view the development of a similar product as an attractive proposition. This could be particularly distressing if the competitor taking such an action was a major producer with

EXHIBIT 1	Total Potential Market for Gold Medal Crumpettes (yearly sales)	
	Cases	Volume
Alberta	43 000	$ 520 000
Canada	960 000	$ 11 500 000
United States	9 660 000	$ 115 000 000

an existing broad distribution system. Therefore, the speed with which Gold Medal Crumpettes could be introduced and developed into a dominant market position was very important to the long-term survival and profitability of the product. There was also the question of whether the degree of consumer acceptance the product had achieved in Alberta could be repeated in other areas.

Pricing research conducted by the company indicated that consumers were not prepared to cross the $2 price level at retail. If production costs were to rise and force an increase in selling price, sales might decline. Also, while the current exchange rate allowed Lucas to be quite competitive in the U.S. market, a strengthening of the Canadian dollar could damage the company's export position.

SELECTING A STRATEGY

Bib Martin had to propose a marketing strategy to Jerry Lucas that he felt would best take advantage of the opportunity available to Gold Medal Crumpettes. He was considering three alternatives:

1. Maintain the product's existing market coverage and strategy. This implied limiting distribution of the product and focusing the company's efforts on the Prairie provinces and the states of Montana and Minnesota.

2. Phased expansion. This would involve expanding across Canada, region by region, to become a major force in the Canadian biscuit market and begin selective entry into the U.S. market.

3. Rapid expansion. This approach would involve an attempt to expand rapidly in both countries, to precede and preferably preempt competitive products in all markets, and to seek a dominant position in the North American biscuit market.

During their early discussions, Jerry pointed out that the company had the financial capacity to undertake any of these options. It was a question of how best to focus the available resources.

Before evaluating his alternatives, Bib prepared a list of criteria to guide Jerry in coming to an appropriate decision:

- The alternative should be feasible.
- The alternative should be profitable.
- The market opportunity should be exploited as far as possible while still meeting the first two criteria.
- The alternative should fit into the activities of the company.
- The alternative should be consistent with the mission of the company.
- The alternative should be consistent with Lucas Foods' portfolio management approach concerning return, risk, and diversity.
- There should be early evidence to support the alternative.

Comfort in the Night

Edward Bruning and Charles Mossman

Janet Meredith had just finished talking to another 1-800 caller from a cancer clinic that placed an order for five samples of *Comfort in the Night: A Cancer Companion*. The clinic administrator had heard of *Comfort in the Night* from a family member of one of the patients, and was interested in reviewing the product for the clinic's outreach support program. Just like the previous 12 months, this day in early February 1999 was going to be long and stressful, taking orders, speaking with suppliers, and contacting potential distributors. At ten o'clock, Janet was going to have a meeting with Donna Holsan, the second principal of their firm, Comfort and Counsel. They were going to discuss how to market their high-quality product. An essential element of their discussion would be defining Comfort and Counsel's competitive position and strategy.

Janet and Donna believed that a critical element for the continuation of their venture would be to secure financing for Comfort and Counsel's entry into the large North American market. Janet's brother, a business professor at the local university, had mentioned in a recent conversation over dinner that potential investors would demand a solid financial forecast for their proposed expansion. In order to explain the profit

This case was written by Edward Bruning and Charles Mossman of the Faculty of Management, University of Manitoba, as a basis for classroom discussion, rather than to illustrate effective or ineffective management actions. Names and other identifying information have been disguised to protect confidentiality. The authors appreciate the assistance of Ryan Kalmakoff in accumulating information for this case, and financial support from the Centre for International Business Studies at the University of Manitoba. Copyright © 2007. Reprinted with permission.

potential of their venture, Janet and Donna would need to construct a thorough marketing plan. The conversation with Donna at ten o'clock would focus on developing their marketing plan, specifically the market definition and development component.

HISTORY

It was during the summer of 1990 when Janet and Donna first felt that there was an unfulfilled need among people with cancer, their families, and friends. They required something that could help them cope with the emotional and physical consequences of this deadly disease. Janet had experience as a public relations practitioner, and Donna as an editor and audio recorder. Through their professional and personal experiences, they realized that many people were looking for some cushion of comfort that could provide information and support for dealing with the ravages of cancer. Something must be done to give patients and their families a basis for hope and healing. The idea eventually came to life as *Comfort in the Night: A Cancer Companion*.

The first prototype of *Comfort in the Night* appeared long before the idea materialized into the two women's business venture. When asked what prompted development of *Comfort in the Night*, Janet recalled:

> . . . years ago, my aunt, who had cancer, was very unhappy with the emotional support she was getting. I remember her saying to me, 'I'm in pain. I can't do the things I'm used to doing. Some days I can't even get out of bed, and I don't want to bother my family. What can I do, Janet?' We mulled it over and finally I went to the local library, our church, and other sources and created this very amateurish cassette tape, full of little sayings, church music, and information on coping. This cassette brought a little part of the world to my aunt every day. It was her companion throughout the lonely evening hours, and helped her get through the night.

This relatively simple audio device was the forerunner of *Comfort in the Night*. The two entrepreneurs formed their company, Comfort and Counsel, and began distributing copies of cassette tapes to local help groups, friends, churches, and health care clinics. Everyone who reviewed the product was impressed and offered to pass the word about the therapeutic benefits it offered people in need of psychological support.

The principals of Comfort and Counsel had made an extensive investment of time and financial resources over the last few years. They had taken the concept from the needs study stage through all phases of data collection and development, culminating in a finished product. The creative process itself involved over 300 interviews, 500 hours of taped conversations, and two months of transcribing every word to paper. But in early 1999, with the product at the market launch stage, the question of how to finance and develop the market further had to be addressed. Comfort and Counsel lacked the capital to spend large amounts on an advertising campaign or other promotional programs. Neither partner possessed sufficient personal resources to support the venture through an equity investment. With no well-to-do relatives or friends on whom the partners could call for financial support, it was necessary to seek financing from an outside lender or investor.

Before a bank or venture capitalist would consider their request for financial backing, it was necessary for the Comfort and Counsel principals to thoroughly define their market and devise an action plan for developing it. Neither Janet nor Donna had experience in designing marketing plans, and they were at a loss as to how to go about the task. They felt strongly that there was a large demand for their product in Canada and the United States. The cancer incidence rates among men and women in North America were quite high, particularly for older people. The partners believed that large urban markets in Canada offered the greatest likelihood for success during the initial start-up period. When their product had become well-established in Canada, the next step would be to focus on large, urban markets in the United States.

PRODUCT

Comfort in the Night: A Cancer Companion was a series of audiotapes providing emotional and practical support for cancer patients and their families. The greatest strength of the product was its high quality and level of integrity. It was unique in that the creators of the product had recorded nearly 500 conversations with cancer patients, their partners and family members, as well as front-line cancer care providers. Thus, the patient received many supportive comments and empathy from people who had already experienced the pain of cancer, along with health care information to assist in managing the disease.

Diagnosis and *Questions & Choices* were the first two programs in the *Comfort in the Night* series. They focused on clients with an early diagnosis of cancer. The back cover of each program carried endorsements by prominent professionals. The leading cancer clinic in Toronto wrote positively about *Comfort in the Night* in its weekly newsletter to patients. In addition, the Mayo Cancer Clinic in Rochester, Minnesota, and the MD Anderson Center in Houston, Texas, both formally approved *Comfort in the Night* after a three-tier review process, and were now using these programs as outpatient resources.

Diagnosis was designed to reduce the stress and anxiety of a cancer diagnosis, and to provide comfort and companionship to people recently diagnosed with cancer and their families. *Questions & Choices* discussed issues that might arise after diagnosis and during the time of treatment. Both programs comprised two 60-minute cassette tapes. Purchasers of the product received a personal diary with daily "words of comfort" along with each program set of cassette tapes. The product concept was to establish an intimate connection with the cancer patient through the cassette tapes and to assist him or her through the initial periods of fear, anger, and depression. Taken together, the two programs formed part of a collection specifically directed at early diagnosis and treatment. Donna managed production of the tapes and worked with a local recording studio. Janet designed the packaging and promotional material, and was responsible for developing the distribution network for selling the programs. Production costs had been around $125 000 per program, and were expected to continue at about this level.

In the future, Comfort and Counsel was considering the possibility of developing products that were more focused and tailored to the needs of patients living with different types of cancer. Videocassette tapes would focus on: 1) patients diagnosed in advanced disease stages or with recurrence; 2) effective partner and family communication patterns; and 3) grief. In addition to these themes, several more specialized series had been identified, two of which were currently in progress: 1) a breast cancer program; and 2) a sexuality program that focused on issues related to male and female reproductive diseases. Another product under consideration was a companion tape for partners of afflicted persons.

Comfort in the Night's success was based on establishing an honest, open relationship with people who had suffered greatly and needed sympathy and understanding. Based on comments from many of the people, Janet and Donna believed competitors' products were poor-quality substitutes for *Comfort in the Night*. However, no systematic market analysis had been conducted.

MARKET

Janet and Donna had decided that the primary market for their product comprised those patients diagnosed as having cancer in Canada and the United States. Cancer strikes a disproportionately large number of the senior population (55 and older). However, younger people might also be part of the target market, since it was often the children of the diagnosed who made purchases. Cancer diagnosis was increasing at a rate of 3% per year. One and one-half million new cases were recorded in the United States alone during 1997. Ten percent of the North American population suffered from some form of cancer. Table 1 presents cancer incidence rates for Canadian men and women by age.

Table 1	Cancer Incidence Rates per 100 000 persons, Women and Men, Canada, by age category, 1998						
Gender	Below 30	30 to 40	41 to 50	51 to 60	61 to 70	71 to 80	Over 80
Women	63.76	223.04	622.91	1263.18	2136.65	3045.76	3579.43
Men	55.90	124.43	341.30	1109.01	2882.08	5291.33	6951.88
Total	119.66	347.47	964.21	2372.19	5018.73	8337.09	10531.31

Source: Cancer Bureau, Health Canada, 1998.

According to the National Alliance of Breast Cancer Organizations, breast cancer had become the most common form of cancer for women in the United States and Canada. There were more than 1.6 million American breast cancer survivors. In 1997, 202 000 new cases of breast cancer were diagnosed, and about 54 000 women died from the disease. Breast cancer mainly affects women between the ages of 35 and 54. In fact, between these ages, American women were 40 to 50% more likely to develop cancer than were men. Beyond age 54, however, incidence rates for males exceeded rates for females by a magnitude of 40 to 50%.

Prostate cancer was the most common form of cancer affecting men. In 1997, over two million men were diagnosed with prostate cancer in the United States. While survival rates were reasonable, the affliction was considered quite severe. In addition, cases of lung and stomach cancer were relatively high for middle- and older-aged men. Canadian statistics reported in Table 1 indicate that the likelihood for a cancer diagnosis increased substantially for men beyond age 60.

The increase in incidence of cancer placed considerable pressure on the medical system to provide not only treatment, but also emotional and psychological support. Unfortunately, the costs of entering a psycho-oncological program were still very high for many patients. Constant increases in the number of cancer patients limited the time available for medical and support staff to properly address patients' emotional needs.

For the past several years, the evolution of cancer treatment centres had become very regionalized. The intensive training of medical personnel and the growing sophistication of medical equipment required to treat cancer had resulted in the concentration of treatment centres primarily in large regional cities, in both Canada and the United States. They served as central information sources for thousands of cancer patients. At the same time, resources to address the emotional needs of patients in small communities and in rural locations were very limited.

Health care funding in Canada declined substantially during the 1990s, particularly for programs dealing with the emotional and psychological needs of patients suffering from long-term, chronic illnesses. In the United States, a large and growing segment of the population lacked adequate support for addressing the physical, much less the psychological needs associated with cancer. Patients and families received very limited assistance from local public social service providers. Increasingly, cancer patients had become dependent upon family members, friends, churches, and charitable organizations for emotional support.

COMPETITION

Janet knew that as the number of people diagnosed with cancer during the past several decades had grown, the portfolio of products and services available to cancer patients had increased significantly. Numerous books, brochures, self-help seminars, educational classes, and prescription medicines had become available to patients and their families during the past decade. Moreover, non-governmentally sponsored support groups arose throughout communities in North America, offering an alternative to professional psycho-oncological care. More recently, afflicted persons were able to participate online with help groups through the Internet. Local television stations offered daytime viewing of the lives of people going through everyday life with cancer. Telephone call-in centres in numerous locations responded to the needs of cancer victims.

Support groups still could not cover everyone, since a number of patients, particularly those in rural areas, did not have regular access to a support group. Most elderly men and women were unfamiliar with the electronic intricacies of the Internet. Consequently, they were not always able to participate with online support groups. In addition, many might not feel comfortable discussing personal issues in a group setting.

TECHNOLOGY

Janet felt that new technology would have a significant impact on the type of media needed for program delivery. Technological improvements in media-related products had introduced many new market opportunities for communication and education specialists. Whereas audiocassettes dominated the adult education, self-help, and support group markets in the late 1980s and early 1990s, videotapes, web-based streaming videos, and digitized, readable-only and readable/rewriteable CDs were becoming common means of communicating information and entertainment. Local video stores were converting from tape to DVD-based products for viewing movies and action games. Many corporate training videos were CD-based. Furthermore, prices on videocassette players, DVD players, and CD drives had plummeted since 1997, while product quality skyrocketed.

The modern family now had access to relatively inexpensive entertainment, information, and group support worldwide at any time of day. Near-term demand projections reported in recent media publications indicated that anyone with a television in their home would soon have immediate Internet access at the push of a button. The PC revolution was at a point where, with minimal cabling and technical support, the TV could serve as the home interface for information, telecommuting, and entertainment.

Recently, hand-held devices were evolving to a point where electronic transfer of voice messaging, video streaming, and computing was possible, although not necessarily economical for the next several years. In the near future, consumers would be able to connect online to syndicated programming, specialized programming, DVD movies, and interactive voice messaging and conversations. These features would be available from a digital hand-held device for a reasonably priced, fixed monthly fee.

Developers of the technology argued that, for the typical consumer, loneliness would become an antiquated notion. Yet, Janet and Donna felt that the loneliness caused by a lack of true personal connections could create an even greater demand for support programs such as *Comfort in the Night*. They were available when people were in real need of emotional support.

DISTRIBUTION

Janet and Donna believed that their distribution strategy involved a number of critical decisions. Ultimately, the correct strategy could be determined by answering the following question: "Which marketing channels will use our meagre resources most effectively, and allow us to maintain maximum control of the marketing effort?" The partners wanted to control pricing and product integrity in order to benefit the maximum number of people in the market. Channel selection would be a critical issue for the future of Comfort and Counsel products. Janet and Donna had identified several options:

- Direct distribution to cancer patients and significant others by means of a 1-800 telephone number
- Direct distribution via the Internet
- Distribution through family physicians, oncologists, and psycho-oncologists
- Retail distribution through pharmacies, hospital gift shops, bookstores, and mass merchandisers
- Distribution through support groups and community health organizations
- Distribution through pharmaceutical/health maintenance organizations, or health insurance providers

The option, or options, chosen should allow Comfort and Counsel the ability to retain control of the components of product, price, and distribution, while allowing for large market exposure to meet profit and volume goals. Costs of promotion, inventory, and agent commissions would have to be carefully monitored and controlled. Janet and Donna felt that there was no slack for inefficiencies in market distribution.

PROMOTION

The message, and the selection of the medium used to communicate that message, was critical to a successful market entry program. Although Comfort and Counsel's products keyed into the lonely and solemn feelings of cancer patients, the message should appeal to the positive emotions from experiencing the products. Potential communication mix elements were:

- Internet
- Infomercials

- Direct mail
- Trade shows/Conferences
- Focused print advertising
- Public relations-based promotions

PRICE

Current pricing was at the traditional "book on tape" pricing, as opposed to other high-quality tape series offering a "portable support group." Table 2 provides a list of competitive products and market prices. Comfort and Counsel promoted *Comfort in the Night* as a high-quality niche product. Pricing was $49.99 for each program of two cassette tapes. Direct costs per program were $22.00, which covered production, marketing, distribution, shipping, and storage costs. Variable allocated overhead costs were $5.00 per unit. At current prices, therefore, Comfort and Counsel had to sell 5438 units to cover the fixed costs of $125 000. However, sales to date were only 1487 units. To have achieved a "break-even" with the level of cumulative sales and investment costs experienced would have required pricing each program at $111.06. Such a retail price was clearly far beyond what would be acceptable to potential customers.

Table 2	Selected Examples of Self-Help/Healing Audio Cassettes, Amazon.com, January, 1999 (prices quoted in U.S. dollars)	
Cassette Title	Price	Number of Cassettes
Women's Bodies, Women's Wisdom	16.95	1
Love and Survival: The Breakthrough Medical Program That Improves Your Mind and Memory	18.00	1
Personal Reflections and Meditations: A Journey Through Four Guided Meditations for Physical and Spiritual Healing	10.00	1
The Higher Self	17.00	1
Gathering Medicine: Stories, Songs and Methods for Soul-Retrieval	19.95	2
The New Physics of Healing	9.95	1
Cancer: Discovering Your Healing Power	10.00	1
Breast Health: A Holistic Approach to Breast Wellness Based on New Research, Nutrition, and Self-Knowing	11.95	1
Living with Depression and Manic Depression: Self-Help Strategies	11.95	1
How to Be an Exceptional Patient: Living with Love and Hope	18.00	2
Self Healing Affirmations	11.95	1
Healing Images	10.00	1

Note: For purposes of comparison, the partners assumed that CDN$1.00 equalled US$0.67.

THE MEETING

With some frustration at trying to find a solution to the difficult marketing strategy problems, Janet shuffled her papers, slid them into her briefcase, and left for the meeting scheduled with her partner, Donna. She knew that if they were going to turn their venture into a profit generating operation, they had to find a way to reach many more people. But, could they generate profits while maintaining product quality and integrity? After all, they had been pursuing this venture for some time now, and all they had to show for their efforts was depleted financial resources. Janet knew that for their operation to succeed, more effective market definition and planning must occur. The partners had to make key decisions on a marketing plan soon.

Steinhouse Knitting Mills (Canada) Ltd.

Mark Haber and Christopher A. Ross

In the fall of 1999, Abraham (Abe) Steinhouse and his son Mark were wondering what action they should take regarding their knitting business. Steinhouse Knitting specialized in the manufacture and sale of men's sweaters. In 1998, annual sales were $2.7 million. In 1999, with overheads at about $100 000 per month, excluding management salaries, estimated annual sales were approximately $2.4 million (U.S. sales excluded). This latter figure was approximately 30% of their 1988 peak sales of $7.5 million. Since 1988, sales had been declining steadily. In 1993, for example, annual sales were $3.5 million. Both Abe and Mark felt that changes had to be made to the operations of the business in order to reverse this downward trend and ensure the survival of the business.

HISTORY OF THE COMPANY

Abe's father founded Steinhouse Knitting in 1929. He had been trained as a knitter. He began operations making babies' wear—romper sets—in the back of a store, with 12 square metres of space. He had a great sense of quality, though, according to Abe, he did not have a great sense of fashion. He manufactured babies' wear because he liked it.

He also felt that the babies' wear industry was not as competitive as the ladies' or menswear industries. While he made the outfits at the back, his wife sold at the front.

Abe was still in high school when he started the business in 1952. He took care of invoicing, the payroll, and some of the bookkeeping. As he became familiar with the business he realized that there was a low upper limit to price in the children's sweater business. For example, while price points for children's sweaters were $3.95 to $4.95 at retail, the price points for men's sweaters were $10.95 to $12.95. As a result, he started making more and more men's sweaters.

By the time Abe was 17, the company had a staff of 20 employees working in 279 square metres of space. At this time too, Abe began working as a salesperson selling to independent stores. In 1957, Abe graduated from university. By 1958, the physical space for the business had grown to 1115 square metres and it was located on St. Lawrence Street, Montreal. In 1960, annual sales were $500 000. By 1967, Abe had started visiting Europe looking for new styles and had also started to buy sophisticated computerized knitting machines.

By 1986, the business was well established, profitable, and successful. There was enough money for the family to live comfortably. In August of that year, Mark Steinhouse, Abe's son, joined the business. Mark had graduated in industrial psychology from McGill University in Montreal. He entered the business immediately after graduating and has never worked in any other business. His cousin was in charge of production and Mark worked in shipping, cutting, and sewing. After gaining experience and knowledge of the inner workings of the business, Mark went out to sell. He sold to independent menswear stores for three years, a total of six selling seasons in all. Mark is 36 years old and Abe is 64.

In 1988, with sales at $7.5 million, including imports, and approximately 50 employees, the owners made the decision to move from St. Lawrence Street to an owned location. The company had been on St. Lawrence Street for 30 years. They built their own plant and moved, in May 1989, to Chabanel Street, in Montreal. In that same year, the company made a brief and unsuccessful foray into the U.S. market. The company hired two sales representatives, one in New York and the other in New Jersey. These two salespeople were successful in bringing in new business but one of them was caught in fraudulent activities. Steinhouse Knitting lost about US$65 000. After this event, the company exited the U.S. market in 1991.

In 1990 Abe bought his sister's share of the business. She and her son left the company. Steinhouse Knitting continued as usual with Abe's father, Abe, and Mark as the management team. Steinhouse Knitting re-entered the U.S. market in 1996, and by 1998 sales in that market were US$250 000.

In December 1997, the management of Steinhouse Knitting invited a family friend, Jacob Lieberman, to use part of their facilities as the head office of his sport-shirt manufacturing business, Styles JMD. The motivation behind this move was symbiotic: Styles JMD would benefit from economies of scale and Steinhouse Knitting would have a modern brand name, which also generated financial benefits. Steinhouse's executives owned 50% of JMD and financed the complete operation. The two businesses operated separately, although the owners shared ideas and overheads such as secretarial help, salespeople, and computing facilities. Styles JMD paid Steinhouse 5% of sales in lieu of rent and overhead. All manufacturing for the shirt business, however, was subcontracted. In 1998, the year that Abe's father passed away, annual Canadian sales for

Steinhouse Knitting were $2.7 million. By 1999, the sales of JMD shirts were about equal to the sales of Steinhouse's sweaters. Styles JMD also imported a small quantity of sweaters from Asia. Like Steinhouse Knitting, the customers of Styles JMD were also independent men's clothing stores in Canada and in the United States.

PRODUCT

Steinhouse Knitting manufactures and sells high-quality men's sweaters. The company produces three different brands: Steinhouse, Etcetera, and España. Customers perceive España as having the highest quality and price. However, for the three brands, the company does not differentiate on the basis of style, price, or fabrication.

Currently 80% of the yarn used in making the sweaters is sourced from one supplier in Toronto. All the yarn is NAFTA-approved. Consequently, Steinhouse Knitting does not pay any duties on sweaters shipped to the United States. When the yarn arrives at the factory door, it is knitted, washed, and finished. Fabric softener is then added. It is also pressed flat, even, and smooth. Employees cut the sweaters one at a time. They are then sewn, cleaned, and tagged prior to shipping. In total there are 27 operations involved in making a sweater. Mark commented on the process,

> [Our sweaters are] cut piece by piece as opposed to cutting in piles. That is one of the differences between a quality sweater and a so-so sweater. There are lots of differences among brands apart from the yarn. For example, an inexpensive manufacturer will not finish the sweater properly, and then when you buy the sweater it will shrink 10 to 15%. We take out the shrinkage; we tumble it with softener, so it is treated. We cut them one by one, so that each line will fall where it is supposed to fall. An inexpensive manufacturer will pile the material to cut and then when the sweaters are cut, the top one and the bottom one are off-centre.

Steinhouse Knitting has not changed its raw material inputs for the sweaters in the last ten years. All sweaters for the fall line are 70% acrylic and 30% wool. The fall line contributes 85% to annual sales. In the spring, the sweaters are 50% cotton and 50% acrylic. Management believed that their product quality was very good. There was a problem, however, in people's perception of acrylic. Most people cannot tell the difference between acrylic and wool, but when they read the manufacturer's label on a sweater and see "acrylic," they perceive a cheaper garment. However, the sweaters of Steinhouse Knitting are in the upper price ranges. There appears, therefore, to be an inconsistency between what customers perceive and the price points at which the sweaters are sold. Adding more wool is a possible solution to this problem. Even 5% angora, alpaca, or linen may make a difference, according to Mark. Abe pointed out, however, that European manufacturers used the same type of yarn as Steinhouse Knitting and that in the United States the image of acrylic was improving.

Steinhouse Knitting produces most of its sweaters to order. During the selling season, the salespeople visit the customers and book orders. All the orders are then entered into a computer, yarn is bought, and the orders are produced. Sometimes the company may have yarn in inventory ahead of time because, from experience, they may know what is popular. For example, there may be black sweaters in 20 different styles, so they may order 10 000 pounds (4536 kilograms) of black yarn. However, when the salesperson deposits the order with the company, Steinhouse begins production with inventoried raw material and does not wait until the yarn arrives. Thus, the company may purchase yarns ahead of time when they believe that the risk is minimal. It takes six to eight weeks to receive the yarn once the company places the order.

Steinhouse Knitting normally finishes the fall line at the beginning of January. From January to March, the factory is practically at a standstill. Only the principal employees are retained. The company may knit a few styles that they are confident will sell in the next period. Consequently, they will have some styles in stock, ahead of time. In past years, 10 to 15% of sweaters were knitted in advance.

The company makes about 30 different styles per season. Each style might be made in a polo, a cardigan, a crewneck, and a V-neck, and each might have four different colours, in four sizes. If the style is sized in "bigs and talls," these add eight more sizes. As a consequence, the company has many stock-keeping units (SKUs). The large number of SKUs sometimes results in inefficiencies, especially if the demand is only for a small quantity. About 10% of the SKUs are responsible for 50% of annual sales. In a few cases, only 100 sweaters may be made of a style. The company makes to order, but the order is rounded up to the nearest dozen. Thus, if an order is for 7.5 dozen, the company will make 8 dozen. If, subsequently, a retailer calls and requests additional sweaters and they are in stock, Steinhouse will ship them, but they will not make only one or two sweaters for a retailer. Retailers are therefore taking a chance that their order might not be able to be filled if they call for just one or two sweaters.

Like many other manufacturers in this industry, Steinhouse Knitting does not have an in-house designer. Prior to 1967, the company borrowed ideas for different styles of sweaters from competitors, from store displays, or from magazines. After a while, Steinhouse management began making annual trips to Europe to look at fashions and to examine different styles of sweaters. All the fashion in sweaters originates in Europe, according to Abe and Mark. Abe and Mark usually visit different European countries, shop at different stores, meet at some agreed point, and compare purchases. For the fall season of 1999, for example, they purchased upwards of 50 sweaters in Europe. Upon returning to Canada, they incorporated the best fashion ideas and colours into their own products while keeping their customers in mind. Because the equipment and machinery in Steinhouse Knitting is different from what is available in Europe, the products they make do not look exactly like the samples purchased.

Abe believes that the fashion business is like no other and that many factors determine the different trends. Men's sweaters are not as fashionable as they were even five years ago. The fact that yarn is still the same price it was 15 years ago indicates the market. The weather also determines the level of sweater sales. For the last three years in western Canada, for example, the winters were unseasonably warm. On the upside, in Europe, men's sweaters are becoming popular. It also seems that the name-brand concept may be weakening. This may benefit Steinhouse.

CUSTOMERS

Steinhouse customers are largely independent clothing stores. Steinhouse also sells to some stores with four or five outlets, and to Ernest with 34 stores and Bovet with 22 stores. Ernest and Bovet are private-brand sales and account for 20% of Steinhouse's annual sales. Quebec and Ontario account for 30% of sales each, 5% of sales goes to the Maritimes, 10% goes to Alberta, and the rest goes to Manitoba, Saskatchewan, and British Columbia. The typical order size is $1500. A few larger customers may buy

$10 000, and a few smaller customers may buy only $800. Retailers will sometimes call for one or two sweaters if a client is asking for a special size or colour and they are out of stock.

Management believes that the independent stores are quickly disappearing (Exhibit 1). In Mark's experience there is almost a constant stream of bankruptcies among these stores. Mark believes that their customers are disappearing because of competition from category killers such as Wal-Mart and Price-Costco, and strong, established brand names such as Hilfiger, Polo, Nautica, and Point Zero. Very little effort has been made to sell to other types of customers. Steinhouse Knitting did try to win Simon's as a customer, but was not successful. Simon's imports most of its sweaters from low-wage countries. "We cannot compete against Chinese and Bangladeshi prices, and these and similar countries are the major source for stores such as Simon's. We are the supplier of last resort," Abe said.

EXHIBIT 1	Men's Clothing Store Sales
Year	**Sales ($000 000)**
1999	1536.4
1998	1581.7
1997	1569.5
1996	1516.0
1995	1623.0
1994	1848.1
1993	1756.3
1992	1622.5
1991	1703.2
1990	2202.0

Note: In 1999, department stores generated 27.1% of men's clothing store sales, discount stores generated 16.5%, apparel specialty chain stores generated 31%, independent apparel stores generated 14.1%, and all other outlets generated 11.3%.

Source: Statistics Canada CANSIM database, Matrix 2400, 1999.

Steinhouse Knitting does not do any market studies. Customers, for example, are not consulted before Steinhouse management makes their annual trip to Europe. From experience, the company believes that a major influence on the purchasing behaviour of their retail customers is the previous year's sales. Retailers examine what was popular last year and tend to buy similar styles. Another influence on purchasing behaviour is the business climate at the time the sales representative makes a sales call. The company believes that, in general, the sales representative who calls on the retailer first gets most of the business. The company has some sense of the kind of consumers who purchase sweaters from the independent retailers. Again, because of long experience in the industry and good communication with their retailers, the management of Steinhouse Knitting believes that women purchase most of the men's sweaters, for their husbands or boyfriends. Women probably purchase 75% of all men's sweaters. "We believe that most of the women are over 40 years old because at our retail prices, they must have income levels that are moderate to better," Abe said.

A recent trend among customers is the growing popularity of the "big and tall" sizes. About 20% of Steinhouse sales in 1999 were "big and tall" sizes. The cause of this popularity is not known for sure—customers may be getting bigger. Another problem is the trend to "dressing down" or what is sometimes called "casual days." Because of increasing informality at work, customers are buying fewer suits, and suits are what brought many customers into the store. Because men buy fewer suits, they visit menswear stores less frequently and therefore they also buy fewer accessories such as sweaters. For many stores, suits accounted for 40 or 50% of sales. Accessories like sweaters, shirts, ties, handkerchiefs, and socks accounted for the other 50%. The weather over the last few years has also hurt business.

Both Abe and Mark also observed that customers were increasingly demanding higher-gauge, lighter sweaters made of natural fibres such as wool and cotton. Sweaters can be made in different gauges such as eight-, ten-, or twelve-gauge, for example. The higher the gauge, the finer the knitting and the lighter the sweater. This move to higher-gauge sweaters by customers is believed to be suitable for today. Fashion dictates change and thus other-gauge sweaters eventually appear. While their current machinery can knit natural fibres, the machines cannot produce higher gauges of knit. Thus, substantial retooling would be necessary and new machinery would be required if Steinhouse Knitting were to take advantage of this new demand. To convert all their machinery is a major investment. One of the biggest changes taking place in the industry is in the area of technology. Steinhouse's machinery can be programmed in a matter of hours, not a week as in the past, for example. New machines can be programmed to make the whole garment. They can also put the V-neck and buttonholes in sweaters. These machines are, however, very slow and costly. The yarn has to be perfect. The price of this kind of yarn is high and it is not always available in North America. Abe believes that at the present time none of these machines are running in North America. The last time the company put money into machinery was about six years ago when they bought two new knitting machines. The capital cost for modern knitting machines is about $250 000 to $300 000 each. Steinhouse needs about 20 machines but is hesitant to purchase these in this market. Compounding the problem is Steinhouse's large inventory of acrylic/wool fibres that cannot just be disposed of, although they expect to reduce it to a reasonable level.

PROMOTION

Steinhouse Knitting depends largely on commission salespeople to promote its products. Salespeople in Montreal are provided with an office, and paid a straight commission. In Canada, the company has salespeople all across the country: one in the Maritime provinces, three in Quebec, three in Ontario, one in the Prairie provinces, one in Alberta, and one in British Columbia. They pay their own expenses and the company pays them commissions upon delivery of goods to the customer. The average commission rate is 7.5%, which is standard in the menswear industry. If the salespeople discount prices to a customer, their commission is reduced. The company uses a sliding scale. For example, a discount of 10% reduces a salesperson's commission to 3%.

The salespeople visit customers twice a year—once for the fall line and once for the spring line. They do not do any servicing of customers between those two selling seasons. In the opinion of the salespeople it does not pay to visit customers at any other time. A sales booking season lasts from about four to six weeks, so the salespeople work for about three months of the year. For the rest of the year they are free to do whatever they wish.

Mark concluded, "I don't believe that our declining sales are because of our sales force. I believe that we have very good salespeople. In general, I am happy with our sales reps. I can't really blame it on them. They are pretty much stuck with the stores they have. Our reps sell to independent stores. Each one of those guys is losing market share—whether it is in British Columbia, northern Ontario, Toronto, Alberta, the Prairie provinces, or wherever. It is no secret that they are getting hurt by the same people we are getting hurt by."

The principal salesperson in Montreal recruited the salespeople in the United States. He called the U.S. accounts where Steinhouse Knitting was doing business and he obtained references about possible candidates for the job. As in Canada, commission salespeople are standard in the United States, except that a national sales manager might be hired. According to Mark, the hardest part about selling in the United States is finding good sales representatives. Current sales for the company in the U.S. are $250 000 and one person is responsible for about 85% of that. This sales representative covers the New Jersey / New York area. Because Steinhouse's customers in the United States are also independent menswear stores, the company entered the U.S. market with more or less the same marketing mix—aiming at the higher end of the market with products exported from the Montreal plant. In the U.S., while the compensation system is the same as in Canada, straight commission at 7.5% of sales, the salespeople may also receive "draws" of approximately $1000 to $2000 per month.

The company has never spent money on advertising, except in 1998 when it created a colour catalogue, at a cost of $25 000, and mailed it to its existing customers. The company participates in a number of trade shows. Steinhouse supported its re-entry into the United States in 1996, for example, by participating in trade shows. At the trade shows, it often succeeded in winning some accounts. They participated for five years, two seasons per year. Each year cost about $60 000, which is expensive in Mark's opinion, but the government subsidized each year by about $20 000.

PRICING

Retailers pay anywhere from $22 to $70 for Steinhouse sweaters. However the average price is approximately $40. Steinhouse's average gross margin is approximately 40% of sales and its receivable-days are about 95. Customers of the retail stores pay an average of $80 to $100 for a Steinhouse sweater. In contrast, the average retail price for an imported sweater is $40 or lower. In 1998, 67% of all sweaters sold in Canada were imported. These were mostly women's and children's. The major source of imports in 1996 was Hong Kong (transhipped from China), the United States, China, Italy, and Taiwan. Today in Canada, retailers have difficulty if they merely sell the sweater at double the price they paid for it. A typical retail store must have a gross profit of 50% after markdowns.

COMPETITION

In Canada, the major sweater manufacturers are located in Ontario, Quebec, and Manitoba. In 1996, the total sales of sweaters in Canada—domestic production and imports—equalled $0.5 billion dollars. According to Steinhouse Knitting management, a number of plants that specialized in men's sweaters have closed in recent years (Exhibit 2). Current competition includes Cooper Knitting and San Remo Knitting in Montreal. Cooper Knitting has approximately 50 employees and San Remo Knitting has over 100 employees. In Toronto, Straton Knitting has over 100 employees and Standard Knitting, in Winnipeg, Manitoba, has over 100 employees. Competitive profiles are shown in Exhibit 2.

In the view of Steinhouse management, competition is surviving because they are concentrating on the U.S. market. Others survive by reorienting their production to suit the demands of Wal-Mart and Zellers. Consequently, they operate more downmarket than

EXHIBIT 2	Competitive Profiles					
Name	Location	Age in Years	Employees	Sales ($000 000)	Exporting	Main Product
Boutique Knitting Mills[a]	Montreal	24	175	<$25	Yes–U.S., Europe, Aus. <$500 000	Ladies' sweaters
Grace Knitting[b]	Montreal	15	39	>$25	Yes–U.S. <$100 000	Ladies' sweaters
Niagara Knitting[c]	St. Catharine's	8	45	<$5	No	Uniforms and school sweaters
Standard Knitting Ltd.[d]	Winnipeg	23	100	<$25	Yes–U.S., Europe, Latin Amer	Men's sweaters
Straton Knitting Mills Ltd.[e]	Toronto	57	175	<$25	Yes–U.S., Japan, Asia <$1 000 000	Men's sweaters
San Remo[f]	Montreal	–	100	<$10	–	Men's sweaters
Cooper Knitting[g]	Montreal	70	50	<$10	Yes–U.S.	Men's sweaters

a. This company produces sweaters for men, boys, women, and girls in acrylic, wool, nylon, polyester and cotton.
b. This company produces sweaters for men and women, boys and girls, in wool, acrylic, and cotton.
c. This company produces primarily sweaters. Occupational clothing is secondary. They use standard materials and produce for the RCMP, Canada Customs, Correctional Services, and different police forces. It specializes in wind proof, lined sweaters.
d. This company produces primarily sweaters but also operates in the sporting goods industry. It uses cotton, wool, cashmere, silk, linen, and various blends. Its brand is Tundra.
e. This company mostly manufactures sweaters; it also produces some shirts. It uses the standard materials.
f. This company was owned by Dylex. Over 86% of its sales was to Tip Top, also owned by Dylex. Dylex sold Tip Top to Graft & Fraser, and San Remo is now for sale.
g. This company manufactures sweaters, with some private branding. It uses standard materials.

Steinhouse Knitting does. They sell 100% acrylic or 100% cotton sweaters to these discount stores at $12 to $13 per sweater. While the material and the machinery might be the same, the sewing and cutting of lower-quality sweaters is inferior to Steinhouse sweaters. Furthermore, these downmarket competitors do not finish their sweaters the same way Steinhouse does.

In fact, there has been a polarization in the marketplace. Steinhouse products are too expensive for Price-Costco, Wal-Mart, and Zellers. These stores buy directly from Asian manufacturers, who require letters of credit. Steinhouse is at a big disadvantage in terms of financing as well as labour. Steinhouse sells in the fall for delivery in March and is paid an average of 95 days after that. The high end of the market, on the other hand, sells the Italian brands—sweaters that sell for $200 or more. The large department stores focus on the name brands such as Nautica, Polo, Tommy Hilfiger, and Point Zero at slightly lower prices. So with their customers, the independent boutiques and small chains disappearing, Steinhouse Knitting is in a precarious position.

THE COMPANY: CURRENT PERSPECTIVES

Management believes that they have a company that is financially sound. The firm has no long-term debt. Finance is therefore not a constraint on decision-making. If they had to, they could buy new technology or different kinds of raw materials. They also believe that they have tremendous experience in manufacturing and selling men's sweaters.

THE FUTURE

Both Abe and Mark feel that producing ladies' sweaters is not a viable option. The ladies business is very competitive and they would have to compete against extremely competent businesses. In any event, it is a very different business—in management's view, as different from their current business as marketing is to finance.

Abe and Mark also feel that getting into department stores is not feasible. Department stores in Canada have, in fact, almost disappeared. Only The Bay and Sears remain, and they sell mostly imported sweaters or name brands. The discounters such as Wal-Mart and Price-Costco buy in such large quantities that they do not need wholesalers and purchase directly from manufacturers in low-wage countries. Both Abe and Mark believe that Steinhouse cannot match the prices of the imported sweaters.

One possibility is changing the mix of yarn in the sweaters. Some customers, particularly in the United States, have made such demands. By adding a bit of cashmere to the sweaters, for example, it is possible that the established brands of Steinhouse may be perceived differently. But they cannot compete with the Chinese who produce cashmere. Cashmere yarn costs $50 per pound and it takes 1.5 pounds to make a sweater.

Another possible route for survival and prosperity is to make a bigger push into the U.S. market, since Steinhouse can export to the United States virtually duty-free. The independents are also disappearing in the United States, but it is such a big market that it is still possible to get 100 or 150 stores as customers—enough to be profitable. In addition, the low value of the Canadian dollar relative to the U.S. dollar is a big advantage. But the

United States is a difficult market. Abe and Mark believe that to succeed they will have to modify their product, but in a way that it is different from American styles. Continuing to focus on the European styles is the answer, they believe. Right now they are crawling along but the goal is to double U.S. sales in the next two years. That target will depend on producing a lot more "big and tall" sizes.

A final alternative is to continue supplying customers who would like to have traditional Steinhouse products in their stores. At the same time, they could also import the type of sweaters that Steinhouse does not produce, from low-wage countries, and sell these to a different market segment. Sweaters imported from Asia, Italy, or Turkey would also yield a 35 to 40% gross margin. One obvious consequence is that the plant will continue to operate below capacity.

Both Abe and Mark were wondering what they should do. They are very comfortable and can afford to close the business. They want to stay in business, however. They also know that cycles change. Sweaters will be in fashion again and Abe is committed to be more demanding on his customers when it becomes a seller's market. The biggest fear is that as the market changes, there will be nobody to sell to. Exhibit 3 provides some salient characteristics of the clothing industry in general, of which the sweater industry is a part.

EXHIBIT 3	Some Salient Characteristics of the Clothing Industry

The clothing industry is labour intensive and can function with a limited number of special skills; clothing is therefore manufactured in almost every country of the world. Low-wage developing countries with an abundant supply of labour provide tough competition to countries such as Canada.

Statistics Canada classifies Clothing (SIC 24) into four sub-groups: Men's and Boy's Clothing (SIC 243), Women's Clothing (SIC 244), Children's Clothing (245), and Other Clothing (SIC 249) which includes sweaters, hosiery, fur, and occupational clothing.

In 1997, men's and women's clothing accounted for 68.1% of manufacturing output of this industry. Other clothing accounted for 25.8%, and children's clothing for 6.1%.

Clothing is manufactured in all regions of Canada except the territories. Fully 62% of establishments were located in Quebec in 1997, accounting for an equal % of the industry's shipments and 57.1% of employment. Ontario was home to 22.5% of establishments and produced 25.2% of the shipments.

Shipments originating in Quebec rose by 5.4% over the past decade, despite a decline of 42.5% in the number of establishments, indicating that there has been some consolidation of apparel production and efficiency gains.

The industry as a whole has been slow to adopt advanced manufacturing technology, although some sub-sectors such as knitting (which is more capital intensive than other sub-sectors) and menswear (which is less susceptible to style changes) have been quicker to embrace technological advancement.

The clothing industry consists of many small establishments. Of the 1665 establishments in 1997, 74.5% employed less than 50 people and contributed only 28.1% to the value of total shipments.

Canadian households in 1988 spent 6% of their personal disposable income on clothing and footwear. That was reduced to 4.7% in 1998. The demand for apparel has been affected by other competing priorities, such as the purchase of computers and electronics, by a trend towards shopping in discount stores, and by consumers' increased insistence on good value for the price paid.

Since 1989, domestic shipments of clothing have decreased persistently, except for 1995. Manufacturers have only been able to maintain the present level of production as a result of phenomenal growth in exports. While imports doubled, exports in 1998 were five times the value of 1988.

Source: Yasmin Sheikh, "Has the Clothing Industry Adapted to the Changing Economic Environment?" Statistics Canada site, December 1999 <www.statcan.ca/english/freepub/34-252-XIE/1999/34-252.htm>, accessed November 9, 2002. Yasmin Sheikh is a Statistics Canada economist in the Manufacturing, Construction and Energy Division of Statistics Canada.

Casablanca Kids

Lisa Giguere and David Rose

In October 2005, Ricki Glinert assumed the new position of Artist & Repertoire and Marketing Manager for Casablanca Kids, a private Canadian-based children's music label. The owners of Casablanca Kids believed that children's music required more attention and gave Ricki the task of increasing artist signings, overseeing product development, and increasing brand recognition and marketing of the product line to increase sales. As Ricki began gathering information to develop a plan for increasing sales and profitability in the next year, she realized that her new position was going to be very challenging.

THE COMPANY

Ed Glinert and Jennifer Mitchell founded Casablanca Kids in 2001, as a division of Casablanca Media Acquisitions Inc. ("Casablanca"). (Exhibit 1 provides biographies for Ricki Glinert, Jennifer Mitchell, and Ed Glinert.) Casablanca Kids produced children's music, while Casablanca's other divisions were involved in the production and distribution of a variety of music genres as well as music publishing and television production services. Casablanca Kids' products were well-produced quality entertainment of various musical styles (i.e., blues, jazz, reggae, etc.), designed for children, without being patronizing. The founders strongly believed that their company had one of the most impressive children's music catalogues in all of North America. They had titles from well-established artists, most of whom had over 20 years of experience in the industry. Notable signed artists included Sharon, Lois, and Bram, Fred Penner, Jack Grunsky, Al Simmons, Norman Foote, and Bob King. Casablanca Kids' releases included original CDs by established artists, compilation CDs by lesser-known artists, DVDs, and interactive games. According to Jennifer Mitchell, the company's products were "competitively priced at a mid-range level of approximately $9.99 to $12.99 per CD, midway between the high-end products and the discount products." As a testament to the quality of the product, Casablanca Kids had won numerous consumer choice awards including Parents' Choice Awards, National Parenting Publications Awards, iParenting Awards, and Juno Awards. However, Mitchell acknowledged that although

---

EXHIBIT 1	Biographies

Ricki Glinert, Artist & Repertoire and Marketing Manager
Ricki has over 25 years of experience in television production and has most recently focused on Kids' TV because she can look them directly in the eye. Ricki was the creator and producer of Treehouse TV's *Crazy Quilt*, as well as the creator and producer of *100% True* for Discovery Kids. She has also written numerous television series for kids and spent five years at TVO producing, directing, and writing in the children's department. Her credits include *Join In, Way Up There, World of Nature, and Mathica's Mathshop*. She has also worked on children's shows for OWL Communications and CTV. At Casablanca Television she has served as Executive in Charge of Production on the 13-part space series *Rocket Science* and produced, directed, and wrote the two-hour special on the science of wrestling, *Slam Bam*. Both of these series aired on the Discovery Channel.

Jennifer Mitchell, Vice-President
Jennifer has specialized in the areas of entertainment, media, and corporate law for the past 10 years, working with Edmund L. Glinert in private practice and co-founding Casablanca Media Acquisitions Inc. She has been involved in the acquisition and sale of numerous entertainment-related transactions as well as film and television tax shelters. Ms. Mitchell is the Senior Vice President of Casablanca Media Acquisitions Inc. and is involved in the buying, selling, administration, and development of music publishing and recording catalogues. She has been overseeing the day-to-day operations of all areas of Casablanca since its inception.

Ed Glinert, President
Ed has specialized in the areas of entertainment, media, and communications law for the past 25 years. Prior to becoming a lawyer, he founded, owned, and operated Frederick

EXHIBIT 1	Biographies (continued)

Lewis Artist Placement Bureau, one of Canada's largest theatrical agencies, from 1967 through 1971. From 1977 through 1982, he was also a co-owner of National Variety Promotions ("NVP"), one of Canada's largest adult contemporary concert promoters, which presented such acts as Liza Minnelli, Frank Sinatra, Don Rickles, and Steve Lawrence as well as producing the stage play, *Pirates of Penzance*, starring Barry Bostwick and Andy Gibb at the Royal Alexandra Theatre. In 1990, he co-founded The Children's Group, owner of the hit series *Classical Kids* which has been one of the most successful series of children's records in history. In 2000, he founded Casablanca Media Acquisitions Inc., along with Jennifer Mitchell.

these awards were meaningful to consumers, they had little impact on the retailers that Casablanca Kids relied on to distribute their products.

Typical of a company with less than $1 million in sales, Casablanca Kids faced some challenges. Its net income continued to decrease from declining sales and a lower profit margin as Wal-Mart continued to force retail prices down and CD manufacturing costs remained the same. (Exhibit 2 provides a breakdown of variable costs for CDs.) In 2005, over 50% of total sales volume was attributed to budget compilations (or discount CDs).

EXHIBIT 2	Variable Costs Per CD[1]		
	Dollar Store CD	Budget CD	Mid-Range CD
Retail Price	$1.00	$5.99	$9.99
Wholesale Price	$0.50	$2.99	$4.99
Distribution Costs 25%	$0.12	$0.75	$1.25
Manufacturing	$0.25	$1.00	$1.30
Mechanical Licences	$0.05	$0.32	$0.50
Master Licences	$0.05	$0.32	$0.50
Casablanca Income	$0.03–$0.04	$0.60	$1.44

[1]Figures represent estimates of average costs for music companies with less than $1 million in sales. Some figures may have been disguised.

Although margins on mid-range CDs were much higher, the discount CDs had a much higher potential sales volume.

Casablanca was considering whether to enter the dollar store market where margins would be even lower but volumes could be much higher, perhaps several hundred thousand units per sale.

Casablanca Kids had limited financial resources for any marketing initiatives. Compounding this challenge was the need to "front-end" the marketing of children's music products (i.e., upfront marketing costs that cannot be recouped until two years after the expenses are incurred). "Front-end" marketing costs totalled approximately 10% of

Casablanca Kids' mid-range CD sales. Marketing expenses were a requirement in order to promote mid-range CDs, whereas discount CDs were sold on the basis of low price with little marketing support. Dollar store CDs would receive no marketing support and would not even carry the Casablanca Kids name.

Casablanca Kids had no current television presence to assist in promoting the product line, as none of the company's signed artists currently had a regular television program. Further, Casablanca Kids was very reliant on a single act as over 50% of total Canadian sales volume was attributed to Sharon, Lois, and Bram.

THE CHILDREN'S MUSIC MARKET

While the total world market for children's music was unknown, Ricki thought there had been little sales growth during the past few years. Recently, the preschool market (children under the age of six) had been declining due to a decrease in the number of families having children. However, this market was expected to experience moderate growth within five years as the Echo generation (the children of the Baby Boom generation) started having children. Casablanca Kids estimated that Canada represented about 10% of the total world market for children's music, while the U.S. market was estimated to be as much as 45% of the total world market.

More detailed information was available about the overall music industry, compared to the limited data about the children's music market. According to figures available to Casablanca, in 2005:

- Tracking firm Nielsen SoundScan, which measured point-of-sale purchases across the United States, indicated that total album sales, including current and catalogue titles, fell 7.2% from 2004 to 618.9 million units, the lowest since 1996, when they were 616.6 million. After enjoying an "up" year in 2004, prompting predictions that the worst was over, sales flagged during 2005, hurt by competition from illegal downloads, rival forms of entertainment such as video games, and a lack of breakout musical acts.
- Overall music sales, which included albums, singles, music videos, and digital tracks, jumped 22.7% to just over a billion units in 2005. The rise was fuelled by a 194% increase in digital downloads.
- Sales of physical albums bought via the Internet were up 11.3%.
- Breaking down sales by genre, every type of music took a hit in 2005 with the exception of Latin, which saw a 12.6% increase.

DISTRIBUTION

The primary channel of distribution for Casablanca Kids' products in Canada was through two large music distributors, EMI and Universal. These two distributors accounted for approximately 75% of the total sales volume for the company. EMI and Universal sold the product directly to mass merchants including Wal-Mart, Zellers, and Best Buy; major book chains including Indigo and Chapters; major record chains such as HMV; and non-traditional outlets such as major grocery and drug chains. In terms of an overall promotion mix strategy, EMI and Universal used a push strategy, directing all marketing activities (mainly personal selling and trade promotion) toward wholesalers and retailers to encourage them to stock the product and promote it to the end-consumer.

Ricki recognized that sales in the children's music industry were dominated by mass merchant accounts including Wal-Mart, Zellers, and Best Buy. She thought that in 2005 Wal-
Mart accounted for 50% to 60% of total retail sales of children's music in Canada. She
described non-traditional outlets such as grocery and drug chains as "problematic since these
stores are not used to selling music. There is often low compliance from staff to ensure that
the product is properly merchandised." Compounding this issue was the fact that Casablanca
Kids did not have dedicated staff to call on retailers and maintain merchandising displays.

EMI and Universal also sold the product to wholesalers who would stock the titles for
smaller retail accounts including small chain stores and privately owned independent stores
who would be likely to purchase less than ten copies of a single title in the span of a year.

Direct sales accounted for the remaining 25% of total company sales volume. This
included sales to small retailers who might, for example, purchase products from the
Casablanca Kids website as well as direct sales to consumers who could purchase the product directly "off-stage" during the artists' concerts and from the online store at the
Casablanca Kids website (www.casablancakids.com). According to Ricki, "There are no
plans to expand the direct sales channel as this would require a huge financial investment."
Exhibit 3 provides an illustration of the various distribution channels.

EXHIBIT 3	Distribution Channels

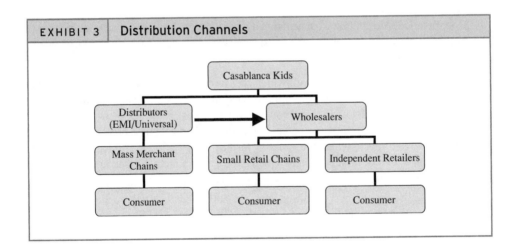

BUYING BEHAVIOUR OF RETAILERS

In the children's music industry, product was 100% returnable for a full refund. This
meant that retailers could return the product to Casablanca Kids for a full refund if the
product did not sell. In addition, the two primary distributors, EMI and Universal,
charged a refurbishing cost to Casablanca Kids for all returned product. Ricki felt that
mass merchants such as Wal-Mart were most concerned with profit per square foot and
would rather carry CDs from well-known adult artists that would be guaranteed to move
quickly. According to Ricki,

> If the CDs are not sold within a couple of weeks, mass merchants and non-traditional retail out-
> lets will return the product to Casablanca Kids for a full refund. They tend to buy low priced chil-
> dren's music products or brands advertised nationally on television. Mass merchant buyers are
> not particularly knowledgeable about children's music.

Ricki believed that children's music occupied the least amount of shelf space, relative to other categories of music, in all retail stores. Further, she recognized that with the maturation of the CD format, retailers were beginning to carry far less CD inventory in general.

BUYING BEHAVIOUR OF CONSUMERS

The primary purchasers of children's music were parents who tended to purchase the same music that was purchased for them as children, prompting Ricki to describe the industry as being "evergreen." In addition, grandparents, other relatives, and friends also purchased children's music as gifts. However, children's music was a low-priority purchase for the vast majority of buyers. According to Ricki,

> A fundamental problem is that the majority of parents don't believe that children need to be exposed to music. With the introduction of DVD players in automobiles, parents can now choose to let children watch a DVD in the car instead of listening to music.

Buyers of children's music could be divided into four main categories. The "keep them quiet" buyer group purchased children's music to keep children occupied and quiet, particularly during long car trips. These buyers were not well informed about the quality of children's music or the developmental benefits of exposing children to music at an early age. The second group of buyers, the "developmental buffs," believed that regular exposure to music from birth was fundamental to a child's brain development. This group purchased children's music because they firmly believed that exposing children to music at an early age made them smarter. These buyers were searching for a quality music product and were willing to pay a premium to ensure that children had the proper exposure to music. The third group, "music enthusiasts," were music lovers themselves and wanted to share their love of music with children. This group was very knowledgeable about a variety of music and was willing to pay more for a quality recording. A fourth group, "gift givers" included a wide range of behaviours, depending on a number of factors such as the occasion and the relationship of the giver to the child.

Most buyers who shopped at big box stores such as Wal-Mart and Zellers tended to be looking to purchase low-end product for $2.00 to $5.00 per CD. Although big box stores did stock some mid-range product, i.e., approximately $9.99 to $12.99 per CD, the focus was on offering a wide range of low-end product to meet the needs of the target customers. Conversely, buyers who shopped at specialty children's stores such as Mastermind were prepared to spend more money. As such, children's music sold in these specialty stores tended to be high-end product in the $16.00 to $19.99 per CD range.

Children's music was generally not purchased by the person who would listen to the music, i.e., the child, so the product had to be appealing to both the buyer (parents, relatives, friends) and the user (the child). Both parents and children chose children's music based on familiarity with the performing artist. According to Ricki,

> Most parents grew up listening to Sharon, Lois, and Bram. That's what is driving our high sales for this act. Parents are choosing Sharon, Lois, and Bram because they know that the music is great.

Ricki felt that the target demographic for Casablanca Kids' product was getting younger, as children were growing up at a younger age, a phenomenon often called "age compression." According to Ricki,

> With artists like Sharon, Lois, and Bram, we need to focus on younger children, as kids today are growing up faster at an earlier age. Our target demographic has become children under the age of

five. The industry is in a cycle of animation, meaning that the majority of children's music performers are animated characters. Children are being exposed to and love animated characters. This
presents a challenge as our signed artists are not animated, but are real people. However, this trend
is slowly beginning to change in our favour with the movement toward live performances.

PROMOTIONS

In terms of marketing to retail accounts, Casablanca Kids provided catalogues and "sell
sheets" that contained information about a CD that would be released in the near future.
The release information contained in both the sell sheets and catalogues served as marketing tools to convince the distributors, wholesalers, and retailers to carry the product. In
addition, Casablanca Kids advertised in trade magazines including *Canadian Music
Network, Canadian Entertainment Network,* and *Billboard Magazine.*

Marketing efforts by Casablanca Kids toward end-consumers were more limited.
Whenever possible, public relations was used as a tool to promote new releases in the
various media including print, television, radio, and the website. The main exception
was the budget compilation CDs, where the primary factor driving the consumer purchase decision was price. However, it was generally very difficult to interest the media
in the company's news. According to Ricki,

> The media is just not that interested in children's music. Ideally, we like to get positive product
> reviews in the media, but this is a challenge given the media's overall lack of interest in the
> industry.

Giveaways had proven to be a more successful form of promotion. For example,
Casablanca Kids often provided prizes for draws held at "Movies for Mommies," movie
viewings for mothers who brought their babies with them. Some advertising was placed in
parenting magazines and on children's television and radio shows, but only a very limited
amount due to the relatively high cost.

OPPORTUNITIES FOR GROWTH

In 2005, Casablanca Kids introduced *Jazz Baby,* a CD with traditional children's songs
recorded by celebrities and famous musicians including Jim Belushi, Cybill Shepherd,
Megan Mullally, and Taj Mahal. Short-term promotional plans for *Jazz Baby* included the
creation of t-shirts with the *Jazz Baby* logo and the possibility of a live concert on television, which would result in a DVD for sale.

Casablanca Kids was attempting to increase its music DVD product line. Given the
maturation of the CD format, more retail shelf space was available for music DVDs than
CDs. The company was also beginning to introduce interactive music games.

Casablanca Kids planned to aggressively enter the U.S. market in 2006. In the longer
term, the company planned to expand internationally into the U.K. market, given the cultural similarities between the Canadian and U.K. markets. However, each country had its
own group of notable children's music artists and it was very difficult for a children's
music artist to gain international exposure. Such exposure was only obtained through the
television media. The Wiggles, an Australian act, had gained international recognition
with children through their own television program, which aired in many countries. The
Casablanca Kids' artists were not well known in the United States, making it difficult for

the company to effectively penetrate the market. Recently, the company had been trying to sign more U.S. artists in an effort to overcome this lack of awareness.

Casablanca Kids had been exploring the potential of digital music stores as another distribution channel for the product. Use of this channel would require a relationship with a digital aggregator who would then distribute the Casablanca Kids recordings to the digital music stores. According to Ricki, the digital music market was growing significantly.

Another opportunity existed in the educational market, selling music to schools, but it was not a market that Ricki found attractive:

> The educational segment is difficult to penetrate and restricted by funding guidelines. In addition, it's very hard to reach the buyers, i.e., the teachers, and building relationships with these individual buyers would take a long period of time. If we were to go after this market, the best way for us to reach the buyers directly would be to have a strong presence at relevant industry trade shows. But this presents a challenge given our limited resources.

COMPETITORS

Casablanca Kids' largest direct competitor was Disney, who produced the best-known products in the industry. In 2005, Ricki estimated that Disney's share of the worldwide children's music market was approximately 30%. Other significant competitors included:

- Branded television characters, such as the Wiggles and Sesame Street
- "Tween" entertainers, such as Hilary Duff, who targeted children aged 9 to 12
- Budget compilation CDs consisting of collections of songs by unknown artists, selling for $1 to $2
- Video/early learning games, such as Baby Einstein (a Disney product)

In addition to direct competitors, indirect competition existed in the form of other children's entertainment products such as DVDs, toys, games, and books. The total market in Canada for children's entertainment products was estimated to be at least $2 billion. Most of the sales were through large retailers such as Wal-Mart and Zellers, with a much smaller amount through specialty retailers. Typically, products were not carried by the large discount retailers and the specialty retailers at the same time, with specialty retailers tending to carry newer, higher-end products. Once products ended up at the large discount retailers, where they were often heavily discounted, it was difficult for specialty retailers to continue selling them.

THE DECISION

Ricki wondered how she could increase the brand recognition and, therefore, sales of Casablanca Kids' products. The company had an established relationship with both EMI and Universal, but was that the best method of distribution? Were there other channels that might provide more support? The mass merchant retailers currently accounted for the vast majority of the company's sales, but would that continue, given their limited interest in children's music? Which consumer groups represented Casablanca's most attractive target market? She wondered how she could increase sales when it seemed like the distribution channels were not interested in carrying the products and consumers were not aware they existed. Ed and Jennifer were anxious to hear what Ricki had planned for the business, so she soon needed to make some important decisions.

Rocky Mountain House Co-op

Tom Funk

Frank Gallagher, general manager of Rocky Mountain House Co-op (RMHC) was sitting in his office reviewing the performance of his organization when Milt Zirk, petroleum manager of the company, hurried into the room. "Frank, I'm afraid I've got some bad news," exclaimed Milt. "The word is out that United Farmers of Alberta is planning to open a new petroleum outlet in Rocky Mountain House. The petroleum end of our business has been going fairly well for us over the past couple of years. This could really mess things up! You know they are very aggressive marketers, and because they are a co-op like us, they could really eat into our market share. Frank, I'm worried! We're going to have to make sure we're ready for them. We've got to develop a plan to minimize their impact on our sales and profits."

ROCKY MOUNTAIN HOUSE CO-OP

Rocky Mountain House Co-op is a retail outlet located in Rocky Mountain House, Alberta, approximately 80 kilometres west of Red Deer, on Highway 11. Rocky Mountain House is a community of approximately 6000 people with both an agricultural and commercial economic base. The area is characterized by mixed farming with most farms being relatively small and having at least some livestock. Industry in the area includes general business, trucking, construction, oil exploration, and logging.

The trading area served by RMHC is much larger than Rocky Mountain House itself and contains the following communities: Alder Flats, Alhambra, Caroline, Condor, Leslieville, Nordegg, Rocky Mountain House, and Stauffer. The trading area has an approximate population of 16 000 people and a radius of 50 kilometres although the trading area on the west extends nearly 100 kilometres to the Rocky Mountains. Exhibit 1 shows the Rocky Mountain House trading area.

RMHC is a co-operative type business. Co-operatives are like regular businesses except they are owned by their users who purchase shares in the business. Instead of earning "profits" co-operatives earn "savings" which can be returned to members through "patronage dividends." RMHC is owned by 7332 active members. For the most part, these "owners" are people in the trading area who have become members by purchasing shares in the organization. Each share is valued at $1 and a minimum of five shares must be purchased to become a member. The main reason for being a member is to share in the savings of the business through patronage dividends. Patronage dividends are based on the amount of business a member does each year and have amounted to about 5% of purchases at RMHC over the past several years. In addition, members have a voice in the affairs of the co-op through their right to elect a board of directors to represent their views.

RMHC is involved in a number of retail businesses that they classify under three divisions: Home Centre, Shopping Centre, and Petroleum. The Home Centre consists of building materials, hardware, animal health products, livestock feed, livestock equipment, and twine; the Shopping Centre consists of food, hardware, clothing, and a cafeteria; and the Petroleum Division consists of bulk fuels, propane, oil/lubes, cardlock, and a gas bar. Despite the fact that Rocky Mountain House is in a significant grain producing area of the province, RMHC has elected so far not to sell crop supplies. Sales, cost of goods sold, and gross margins for each division for 1995 are shown in Exhibit 2. Exhibit 3 shows the operating statement of RMHC for the same year.

EXHIBIT 1	Rocky Mountain House Trading Area

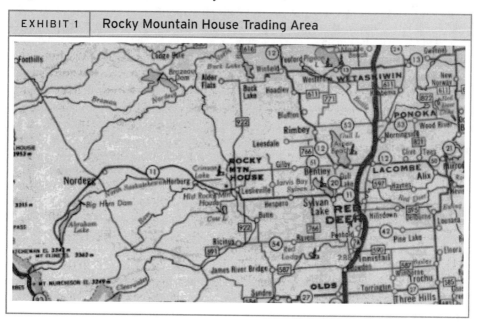

EXHIBIT 2	Product Line Breakdown		
	Home Centre	Shopping Centre	Petroleum
Sales	$ 4 620 000	$ 11 044 000	$ 2 550 000
Less: Cost of goods sold	$ 3 536 000	$ 8 418 000	$ 2 294 000
Gross margin	$ 1 084 000	$ 2 626 000	$ 256 000
Less: Operating expenses	$ 931 000	$ 2 106 000	$ 189 000
Contribution	$ 153 000	$ 520 000	$ 67 000

EXHIBIT 3	Operating Statement
Sales	$ 18 214 000
Less: Cost of goods sold	$ 14 248 000
Gross margin	$ 3 966 000
Less: Operating expenses	$ 3 226 000
Contribution	$ 740 000
Less: Indirect interest expense	($ 96 000)
Less: General overhead	$ 432 000
Savings	$ 404 000
Patronage dividends from federated co-ops	$ 683 000
Retained savings	$ 1 087 000

In 1995, RMHC received patronage dividends of $683 000 from Federated Co-operatives Limited in Saskatoon, the large wholesaling co-operative owned by several hundred local co-ops like RMHC across Western Canada. Like most other local co-ops, RMHC used Federated Co-op as their main source of supply for all products they sold. The patronage dividend they received from Federated was based on a percentage of purchases. In the same year, RMHC allocated $614 000 in patronage dividends to local owners. This, together with current savings, left RMHC with retained savings of slightly more than $1 million. This represented funds the organization could use for future expansion.

PETROLEUM DIVISION

The petroleum division of RMHC has always been a tough business. Margins in the petroleum division are much lower than in other areas of the company largely due to intense competition and the commodity-type products being sold. In the Rocky Mountain House trading area alone there are six major oil companies competing for a total fuel market of approximately 26.9 million litres. Exhibit 4 lists the major petroleum companies with facilities in Rocky Mountain House and their approximate fuel sales.

Most of the 26.9 million litres of petroleum sold in the Rocky Mountain House trading area went to commercial accounts. Commercial accounts purchased 18.3 million litres in 1995 in contrast to 6.1 million litres to farm accounts and 2.5 million litres to consumers. Although precise market shares were not known, Milt estimated that Co-op and Esso were

EXHIBIT 4	Competitive Petroleum Suppliers

	Estimated Litres
Co-op	5 900 000
Esso	7 500 000
Shell	4 000 000
Petro-Canada	3 500 000
Turbo	3 500 000
Husky	2 500 000
Total	26 900 000

EXHIBIT 5	Approximate Market Shares by Type of Account

	Farm	Commercial	Consumer	Total
Co-op	34%	17%	30%	23%
Esso	31%	27%	27%	28%
Shell	13%	15%	16%	15%
Petro-Canada	6%	17%	4%	13%
Turbo	12%	13%	13%	13%
Husky	4%	11%	10%	9%
	100%	100%	100%	100%

the major petroleum suppliers in the area followed by Shell, Petro-Canada, Turbo, and Husky. Exhibit 5 shows approximate market shares for each company by type of account.

RMHC currently sells four product lines in petroleum: bulk fuels, propane, oil/lubes, and gas bar (self-service pumps at the Shopping Centre). Sales, cost of goods sold, and gross margins for these products in 1995 are shown in Exhibit 6. Exhibit 7 shows the petroleum department expenses for the same year.

Like most petroleum suppliers in the area, RMHC sells five types of petroleum products: premium gasoline, regular gasoline, clear diesel, marked gasoline, and marked diesel. Exhibit 8 shows 1995 sales of the five products in each of the major markets while Exhibit 9 shows current pricing for each product in each major market. Marked gasoline and marked diesel are dyed purple to identify them as tax-exempt because they are used for off-road purposes and not subject to normal fuel taxes. At the moment, this means marked fuels sell for approximately $0.09 per litre less than clear fuels, which are intended for on-road use and subject to a road tax. The prices established by RMHC are very similar to other petroleum suppliers in the area. Only Turbo and Husky sell petroleum at lower prices than other companies in the area and, in both cases the differences are very small.

Margins on petroleum products do not vary by type of product, but do vary by type of customer. Current margins in the farm market are $0.049 per litre; in the commercial market $0.034 per litre; and in the consumer market $0.063 per litre.

EXHIBIT 6	Financial Summary for Petroleum Products				
	Fuels	Propane	Oil/Lubes	Gas Bar	Total
Sales	$ 2 016 000	$ 41 000	$ 126 000	$ 367 000	$ 2 550 000
Cost of goods	$ 1 829 000	$ 34 000	$ 106 000	$ 325 000	$ 2 294 000
Gross margin	$ 187 000	$ 7 000	$ 20 000	$ 42 000	$ 256 000

EXHIBIT 7	Petroleum Department Expenses
Depreciation	$ 5 600
Utilities	$ 500
Insurance	$ 4 900
Repairs and maintenance	$ 9 000
Taxes and licences	$ 4 600
Total standby costs	**$ 24 600**
Employee benefits	$ 18 000
Staff discounts	$ 1 600
Training	$ 1 800
Salaries and wages	$ 99 000
Uniforms	$ 1 500
Total staff costs	**$ 121 900**
Advertising and promotion	$ 5 600
Delivery trucks	$ 29 000
Other expenses	$ 7 900
Total operating costs	**$ 189 000**
Contribution	$ 67 000

In the petroleum end of the business, RMHC deals with three main types of customers: farms accounts, commercial accounts, and consumers.

At the moment, RMHC has about 350 farm accounts which purchase 2 086 000 litres of fuel. Although the average farm account purchases about 6000 litres of fuel each year, some purchase much larger amounts and many purchase much smaller amounts. The largest RMHC farm account purchases nearly 20 000 litres of fuel a year. Farms in the RMHC trading area are somewhat smaller than typical Alberta farms. A very high proportion of these farms have livestock as their principal operation.

Commercial accounts represent the major proportion of RMHC petroleum business. At the moment, RMHC has 175 commercial accounts which together purchase approximately 3 113 000 litres of fuel and range in size from 5000 litres per year to as much as 300 000 litres per year. The average commercial account buys 18 000 litres. Exhibit 10 provides a breakdown of commercial accounts into various types of businesses.

EXHIBIT 8	Petroleum Sales by Market (in Litres)			
	Farm	Commercial	Consumer	Total
Premium gasoline			16 500	16 500
Regular gasoline	200 000	1 173 000	666 500	2 039 500
Clear diesel		1 154 000	63 000	1 217 000
Marked gasoline	949 000	50 000		999 000
Marked diesel	937 000	736 000	_____	1 673 000
Total	2 086 000	3 113 000	746 000	5 945 000

EXHIBIT 9	Petroleum Prices by Market		
	Farm	Commercial	Consumer
Premium gasoline			$ 0.540
Regular gasoline	$ 0.495	$ 0.480	$ 0.500
Clear diesel		$ 0.390	$ 0.420
Marked gasoline	$ 0.403	$ 0.390	
Marked diesel	$ 0.300	$ 0.300	

EXHIBIT 10	Types of Commercial Accounts
Type of Account	Percentage
General business	29%
Loggers	11%
Truckers	18%
Construction	17%
Oil company contractors	22%
Institutional	3%

The final category of customer is individual consumers, who currently purchase 746 000 litres of fuel. About 80% of consumer sales are through the gas bar at the Shopping Centre and the remaining 20% are through the cardlock system, described below.

Although all three types of accounts (farm, commercial, and consumer) can use the cardlock system, it is very popular among commercial accounts. The cardlock system allows approved buyers to have 24-hour access to bulk fuels at the main RMHC petroleum outlet. To obtain fuel, the buyer inserts a card into a metering device which then pumps the requested amount of a certain type of fuel into the user's tank. The user's name and the amount of the purchase are recorded electronically for future billing. Use of this system is growing very rapidly among farm and commercial accounts because of convenience and cost savings. The price of fuel purchased through the cardlock is generally $0.008 per litre less than bulk delivery. Although RMHC has a good, very clean cardlock operation, there are two problems that make it less than ideal. One problem is the fact that currently it does not sell marked gasoline and does not have the capability of adding this product into the existing system. This undoubtedly prevents some potential customers from using the RMHC cardlock. Another problem with the cardlock is that access to the facility is a little more difficult than some customers would like.

At the moment, the marketing program used by RMHC is fairly similar to that used by other petroleum suppliers in the area. In 1995, less than $6000 per year was being spent on advertising petroleum products. Most of this was for ads placed in local papers highlighting special deals on oils and lubricants (see Appendix A for a sample ad). In addition to advertising, a substantial amount of selling is done by Milt on farms, at the offices of commercial accounts, and on the phone. Milt maintains contact at least four times a year with most customers, and more often with larger customers. Some very large customers are contacted on a weekly basis. In addition, he spends a considerable amount of time calling on prospective customers. Milt's philosophy is that regular contact with prospects will put him in contention for their business if there is ever a reason for a customer to switch. History shows this to be a good strategy, as RMHC has picked up a number of new customers each year when they became dissatisfied with their present supplier. Customer loyalty in petroleum, however, is very high. Milt figures that less than 10% of customers change suppliers each year. Milt also follows the practice of driving the delivery truck himself on occasion so he can have more contact with customers.

Frank and Milt have long thought that the success of RMHC in the petroleum business was due to a number of factors:

- The company provides excellent service. All people working for RMHC are topnotch individuals committed to providing good service. In addition, the company prides itself on clean, modern facilities and prompt attention to detail. Any customer who needs fuel can expect to receive it the same day an order is placed. RMHC currently spends more than its competitors on staff training.

- Co-op products are quality products produced under strict quality control measures.

- Patronage refunds provide customers with "cash back" at the end of the year based on their volume of business. For many customers this is a real incentive to do business with a co-op.

- The company has an excellent highway location in Rocky Mountain House. This provides excellent visibility in the community.

- RMHC offers a very wide range of products making "one stop shopping" possible for customers.

UNITED FARMERS OF ALBERTA

United Farmers of Alberta (UFA), like RMHC, is a member-owned co-operative. UFA has approximately 30 outlets in Alberta in which they sell petroleum and a complete line of farm supplies. In addition, they operate approximately 90 outlets in which only petroleum products are sold through bulk plants, cardlocks, and gas bars. UFA has shown considerable growth in recent years through very aggressive marketing. This growth has come from an increase in the number of retail distribution points as well as an increase in the volume sold through existing outlets.

Recently, UFA was granted a development permit to build a farm supply facility in Rocky Mountain House. The permit allows UFA to construct a facility that contains: a 204 square metre building, bulk petroleum plant, gas bar, cardlock, and farm supply distribution facility. It is expected that UFA will sell a complete line of both crop and livestock farm supplies through this facility. It is also expected that UFA will construct a cardlock facility that is larger than any other in the area and will sell a compete line of fuels.

The entry of UFA into this market has the potential of causing significant problems for RMHC for a number of reasons:

- UFA is a co-op like RMHC and therefore very similar in structure and philosophy. As a result, they might be considered a good alternative for many current RMHC customers.

- The fact that they are building a complete farm supply outlet might be attractive to many current RMHC customers who would like to purchase crop supplies where they buy petroleum.

- UFA's facility will be much newer than that of RMHC. This is of particular concern for the cardlock.

- UFA currently has a number of commercial accounts on the fringes of the RMHC trading area. This gives them a foothold into the market.

- UFA has demonstrated a willingness in similar situations to enter new markets in a very aggressive manner. Often this entails aggressive pricing, introductory advertising in local media, a direct mail campaign targeted to larger potential customers, and special introductory deals.

- UFA traditionally supports its marketing efforts with a high level of excellent service. This includes the availability of skilled technical experts who can answer questions and help customers make informed buying decisions, attention to detail in all aspects of the business, and frequent sales calls (either by phone or in person) with key customers.

DECISION

Although at first Frank was not overly concerned about the situation, as he considered it in more detail, he began to worry about the effects it might have. RMHC had worked hard over the last ten years to build a strong customer base and some of this investment in time and marketing dollars appeared to be at risk. To determine the seriousness of the situation, and to develop some plans to counteract it, Frank called a meeting with Milt for early the next week.

The meeting began by Frank raising the issue of what impact the entry of UFA might have on RMHC. After some discussion, the two men agreed that if RMHC did nothing to soften the impact, it was conceivable they could lose a significant portion of both their farm and commercial business, especially the larger accounts that were more price-sensitive. Although it was hard to come up with specific numbers, they felt that up to a quarter of their present volume might be at risk. What was even more alarming was the fact that RMHC had three very large commercial customers who each purchased 300 000 litres of fuel a year.

Losing these people alone would result in a very large sales decline. Although these large commercial accounts had been with RMHC for a number of years, and Milt provided a high level of personal service through almost weekly contact, it was conceivable they could switch allegiance if they perceived greater value in an alternative supplier.

Given the seriousness of the situation, they then began to discuss alternative courses of action they might pursue to counteract the problem. A number of possibilities were identified and briefly discussed:

1. The first idea that came to mind was to pursue a preemptive pricing strategy. Under this strategy, RMHC would begin immediately cutting prices and margins to existing customers. The idea behind this strategy, of course, was to solidify business relationships with customers to the point that it would make it very difficult for UFA to be successful in taking customers from RMHC.

2. A second strategy they discussed was to match UFA's promotional programs dollar for dollar and engage in a substantial amount of local advertising and direct marketing themselves. Although neither Frank nor Milt had a precise idea of what UFA would spend entering the Rocky Mountain House market, they felt $30 000 was not an unrealistic amount. They considered stressing two main points in the promotion: their excellent staff and their outstanding record of providing patronage dividends. Frank envisioned ads and direct mail pieces with pictures and human interest stories about the staff as well as charts showing the steady growth in patronage dividends over the past few years.

3. Another idea they considered was to develop a program in which the rate of patronage dividends would vary by department. Under such a scheme it would be possible for the petroleum division, for example, to announce a patronage dividend of 8% where some other division's dividend might decline to 3%. They felt this might be particularly effective in the short run to meet a competitive challenge.

4. Yet another alternative they were considering was to get into the fertilizer and ag chemical business. On the assumption that some RMHC customers might be attracted to UFA because they had a complete line of crop and livestock supplies, this might provide existing customers with enough reason to stay with RMHC. It would, however, be a major investment for RMHC in a business they knew little about. Frank estimated it would require an investment of approximately $600 000 in facilities and working capital. In addition, two new full-time people would be required to run the business and work with farm customers. An additional five seasonal employees would be needed for a couple of months each year to help during peak sales seasons. Total additional labour costs would amount to approximately $150 000 plus another $50 000 in administrative costs. Margins on fertilizer were typically in the 15 to 20% range on products that sold for an average price of $250 per tonne. Although an average farmer in the Rocky Mountain House trading area currently used only 25 to 30 tonnes of fertilizer a year, use appeared to be growing fairly rapidly as more farmers started using fertilizer and those already using fertilizer were increasing application rates. Ag chemicals were not widely used in the Rocky Mountain House trading area, so this would be considered a break-even business which simply provided a complementary service to farmers who purchased fertilizer. Presently there are three fertilizer suppliers serving the 1200 farmers in the Rocky Mountain House trading area. One of these suppliers is a large

independent farm supply outlet specializing in crop inputs while the other two are smaller operations, one of which is the local Esso dealer.

5. The final alternative Frank identified was to move up construction of a new bulk petroleum facility. The current facility was old and starting to show its age. Of particular concern was the fact that the cardlock system had reached its capacity and could not add a tank and pumping system for marked gasoline. Frank knew that the new UFA facility would be "state of the art" and have ample capacity for the present and for future expansion. Although Frank hoped to get another five years out of the present facility, he felt one option was to invest immediately in new facilities so they would be ready at least by the time the UFA facility was built. A new facility, which would include a new bulk plant, an expanded sales area, and a new and expanded cardlock, would cost $300 000 to construct.

Frank and Milt concluded the meeting wondering what to do. They agreed to consider the options more fully and do some real thinking about the consequences of each option and then meet again in a week to make a decision.

Appendix A

Rocky Mountain House Co-op Ad

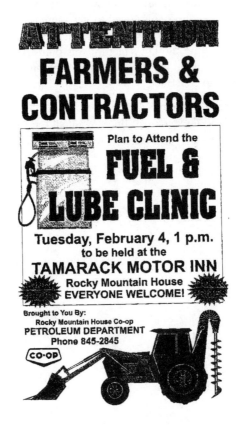

Executive Training Inc.

Tom Funk

"This could cost upward of $400 000 before I get my first customer," thought Tom Jackson, president and owner of Executive Training Inc. (ETI). It was early September 2004, and he was reflecting on his idea of starting Executive Training Inc., a new service using online delivery of training programs. ETI was a successful firm providing marketing and sales training for agricultural companies, but Tom was wondering if the time was right to introduce a major new product line. Since ETI's inception in 1982, all training programs had been conducted in face-to-face, classroom-type settings. ETI was very good at this traditional method of delivery, and had a number of long-term, highly satisfied customers.

Given the rapid expansion of Internet use, Tom's idea was to add online program delivery to his existing business. To further explore the idea, he commissioned a market research study and prepared initial cost estimates of the product launch. As he reviewed this information, he was concerned about the high initial investment. He wondered whether the market was really ready for this approach and if and how he should proceed.

EXECUTIVE TRAINING INC.

Tom Jackson established ETI, located in Milton, Ontario, in 1982 to provide marketing and sales training programs for agribusiness firms. The agribusiness industry included those firms that provided farmers with products (e.g., equipment, fertilizer, seeds, etc.) and services (e.g., crop management practices, dairy herd management, etc.). Over the 17 years the company had been in business, revenues grew from just under $100 000 in the first year to $1 200 000 in 2003. In addition to Tom, ETI employed three full-time trainers and one full-time administrative assistant.

ETI's product line consisted of programs in marketing and sales. All the programs were custom designed and offered to clients in both Canada and the United States. Current clients consisted of both large and small agribusiness firms in the seed, chemical, machinery, animal health, and feed industries.

A typical ETI program was three days in duration and normally held at a central location such as a hotel or a company's training centre. Although participants included middle and senior management, most were sales representatives. The usual number of participants at a program varied from 15 to 25.

Although ETI programs were custom designed for individual clients, they were built around standard course modules. The customization usually consisted of changing the mix of course modules used and some cosmetic changes such as use of the client's logo on visual materials.

Two three-day ETI programs were very popular and accounted for nearly 75 percent of the company's revenue. The first program, Principles of Agri Marketing (PAM), was targeted at sales reps and was designed to provide basic marketing skills. As in all ETI programs, the method of instruction consisted of lecture/discussions and case studies. PAM topics normally included (1) Marketing Strategy Planning, (2) Financial Analysis for Marketing Decisions, (3) Marketing Products and Services, (4) Building a Marketing Mix, and (5) Customer Buying Behaviour.

The second program, Strategic Agri Selling (SAS), was also targeted at sales representatives and designed to develop basic selling skills. In addition to lecture/discussions and case studies, this program involved role-playing sales situations. SAS topics normally included (1) Preparing for a Sales Call, (2) Opening a Sales Call, (3) Probing for Information, (4) Presenting Features and Benefits, (5) Handling Objections, (6) Closing the Sale, and (7) Follow-up Service.

THE ONLINE OPPORTUNITY

ETI had always relied heavily on computer technology in developing and presenting programs. It was one of the first training companies to adopt computer-generated graphics in the late 1980s when this technology was first developed. More recently, Tom experimented with digital video in presentations. For years the company used analogue video in taping role-plays for subsequent analysis and discussion.

In July 2003, Tom attended an American Marketing Association conference on the use of online educational programs. Although the conference was designed mainly for university people who might want to start teaching online, Tom immediately recognized that this approach might be appropriate for the type of training programs his company conducted.

Online educational programs utilized the Internet as a delivery mechanism. Instead of face-to-face lectures, narrated PowerPoint presentations were used to deliver conceptual material. Various conferences were designed in chat rooms to allow participants to discuss cases or exercises. Assignments were completed using word-processing programs and sent to the instructor as attachments. Tom was absolutely amazed at the versatility of this approach and began to think about how he might use this approach at ETI.

In October 2003, Tom signed up for a four-week online training program, Achieving Exceptional Customer Satisfaction, offered by the Ontario Agricultural Training Institute (OATI). During this course, Tom really began to appreciate the power of online delivery. Although the course only attracted eight participants, that was a sufficient number for Tom to see the ability of online delivery to facilitate participant interaction. Each week the participants were given case studies to read and discuss, and it was common for a hundred or more interactions among the eight people. Not only were there numerous interactions but also, in Tom's opinion, the quality of the interactions was superb. In addition, Tom was very impressed with the quality and quantity of individual feedback provided by the instructor. Based on this experience, Tom became convinced that the online method of delivery was a viable alternative to more traditional methods.

After completing the OATI course, Tom began to investigate the feasibility of adopting this approach for ETI. He started to assemble information on the costs associated with online delivery as well as the potential market for this product. He began by reviewing what was currently available on the Internet.

THE ONLINE EDUCATION INDUSTRY

Based on the online education industry review, Tom was amazed at the number of websites and course offerings on the Internet. He made the following summary notes:

- eLearners.com (www.elearners.com) provided extensive information for people considering learning online. It listed more than 24 000 online and distance learning courses and 2400 distance and e-learning degree and certificate programs offered by 2400 firms, ranging from universities, to community colleges, to consulting firms, to specialists in training in a variety of areas. He noted that no firm was focused on agribusiness.

- Globewide Network Academy (www.gnacademy.org) was a non-profit organization that listed distance learning opportunities throughout the world. Their catalogue contained 23 862 courses and 2511 programs.

- World Wide Learn (www.worldwidelearn.com) provided a directory of online courses ranging from online MBA programs to art courses. There were more than 300 marketing courses listed on the site from universities, community colleges, training firms, and publishers such as Harcourt and McGraw-Hill.

- University of Phoenix (www.phoenix.edu) was probably one of the most recognized online universities and had considerable experience in the online education market.

- National Agri-Marketing Association (www.nama.org) provided current news, events, and company information for professionals in the North American agribusiness market. No online courses were listed on the site but various local chapters listed talks and seminars dealing with a wide range of topics, most of them technical in nature.

COST INFORMATION

Because online training was a new concept, cost information was difficult to estimate. Based on information gleaned from a number of sources, Tom developed the following cost estimates:

- Course development costs could range anywhere from $30 000 to $50 000 for a single course. This included the development of teaching materials, software development, and programming. Once a course was developed it would cost at least $10 000 each year to update material and technology.
- Getting involved in online training would require more administrative support than ETI currently had available and this would cost an additional $50 000 each year.
- Because of the method of delivery, instructors for online courses could be retained on a per course basis. Hiring the type of people required would probably cost ETI $150 per hour of instruction time. Tom estimated that it would take approximately 30 minutes per student per week of an instructor's time to provide basic instruction and feedback. Higher levels of individual feedback would require much greater instructor involvement, perhaps as much as one hour per student per week.
- Several Internet providers were willing to support online training. Their fees for hosting a course were in the vicinity of $15 per week per participant. This included Internet access as well as some technical support for participants.
- The cost of teaching materials varied a great deal depending upon the subject matter. Tom felt that $15 per participant per week would be a high estimate.

MARKET INFORMATION

Although Tom had been involved in the training business for many years, online training was so new that he did not have a feel for this market. Consequently, he retained the services of Kelso Marketing Research to conduct a telephone survey of 50 randomly selected agribusiness organizations in Canada and the United States. The main objectives of this research were to (1) determine the size of the market for training in general, (2) determine the type of training currently undertaken, and (3) determine the likely demand for online training.

Summary results of this study are presented in Appendix A.

THE DECISION

Armed with the cost and market data, Tom started to think about how he might expand his business to include online training. It was fairly apparent that the major short-term opportunity would be in sales training. Most agribusiness companies used sales training for their employees and there appeared to be some dissatisfaction with existing programs.

Tom thought his first product would be a six-week introductory sales training course targeted at new sales reps. He thought this course could be offered on both a public and private basis. The public course would be scheduled to run eight times a year and people from any company could enroll. This would result in a group of participants from different companies. The private courses would be sold to individual companies and customized to some extent to meet their specific training needs.

Both the public and private courses would contain essentially the same content as the current three-day sales training courses offered by ETI. Lectures would be in the form of narrated

PowerPoint presentations. ETI would develop a number of video clips showing parts of sales calls that could be critiqued and discussed by participants in online conferences. An instructor who would monitor the discussion in the conferences would provide feedback. Participants would be expected to devote five hours a week to the course. This made one week of online experience more or less equal to one-half day of face-to-face training.

Marketing the courses was a major consideration. ETI had not done much marketing in the past because there was a lot of repeat buying by satisfied clients. Moreover, word-of-mouth was an effective method in getting new clients. Tom knew he would have to develop an effective marketing program in order to be successful with the new online venture. Ideally, the online courses would be sold to new clients so as not to cannibalize clients from existing face-to-face courses.

The marketing program for the online product could be designed using one or more approaches. One method was to hire one or more full-time salespeople who would use a combination of telephone and personal contact with prospects. A full-time sales rep would cost ETI approximately $100 000 annually including all benefits and expenses.

A second method was direct mail. A professionally prepared direct mail piece could be designed and mailed to prospects for approximately $20 a contact. This included all the design work as well as the costs of distribution. Tom noticed that many companies were using CDs in direct mail. The advantage of a CD was its ability to demonstrate how the online learning system actually worked. Adding a CD to the direct mail would increase costs to approximately $25 a contact and would result in a one-time production cost of $30 000 for the CD.

A third method was to use media advertising. The most logical publication to use was *Agri Marketing* magazine (www.agrimarketing.com), a monthly publication. Sales and marketing executives in virtually all agribusiness companies received this magazine. One full-page colour ad in this publication costs $6000.

Finally, the Internet was an obvious medium to use for the new product line. The question of what should be done or how it should be done was not clear.

Regardless of the communication media used, a key issue was how to position the new product. Tom was not sure how to deal with this issue, but felt the marketing research would provide some insight.

In addition to developing a communication program for the online product, another key issue was to establish a price. Normal industry practice was to establish prices on a participant-per-day basis. Tom noted from the research results that the average price paid per day per participant was $500, or $1500 for a three-day course. He felt that this might not be appropriate for online training, and other alternatives could be considered. While the research indicated that many respondents expected to pay a lower price for an online course, they also said that among the problems they faced with training were the time required for training, that people were away from their work, the costs associated with travel, and so on. Tom felt that the opportunity existed to price these courses higher to position them as a better alternative. He was considering a price of $2000 or even $2500 for the courses, but needed to consider the whole pricing issue further.

With all this in mind, Tom wondered if this was the right move for ETI at the present time. Online training seemed like the way of the future, and if he could get established in the area before competition, he would have a real advantage. On the other hand, was the time really right for this move? Was the market ready to accept a fairly radical departure from current practice? Given the initial investment of about $400 000 for marketing and course development, would it pay off?

Appendix A

Market Research Summary

The objectives of this research were to determine the size of the market for training in general, the type of training currently undertaken, and the likely demand for online training. In total, 50 companies representing different sectors of agribusiness were interviewed in Canada and the United States. Company names were randomly selected from a listing of 2500 agribusiness firms found in the annual *Marketing Services Guide* published by *Agri Marketing* magazine. It was believed that the 2500 companies encompassed virtually all agribusiness organizations in North America. The survey consisted of three sections: Section A focused on characteristics of the individual companies, Section B identified the various training programs currently used by these companies, and Section C was designed to gain information on how people perceived online training and whether or not they saw this as a viable alternative to more traditional methods.

Section A

The first section focused on the companies themselves in terms of what they did, how large they were, and the number of employees participating in training programs. The purpose of this section was to get some idea of market composition and size.

How many employees does your company have?

Each company was asked to provide data on the number of people they employed. The responses from the sample companies varied greatly with the smallest having ten employees and the largest having 85 000 employees. The average company in the sample employed 410 people, with 10 percent being involved in sales and marketing. All sales and marketing employees receive some training over the course of a year.

What business is your company involved in?

Respondents were then asked to list the type of business they were involved in. Possible responses were feed, seed, fertilizer, agricultural chemicals, farm equipment, financial services, and grain handling. Tabulation of the results revealed a good distribution among all of these sectors.

Approximately how many sales and marketing employees have access to computers and the Internet at home and at work?

Respondents were asked to provide the number of sales and marketing employees that had computer access at home or at work. Results showed that 64 percent provide computer access to all of their sales and marketing employees, another 12 percent provide computer access to more than 50 percent of their sales and marketing employees, while the remaining 24 percent provide computer access to less than 50 percent of their sales and marketing employees. These statistics decreased slightly when respondents were asked to give the number of employees who also had access to the Internet at home or at work.

Section B

The purpose of this section was to identify the different training programs currently in use. Information such as the styles of teaching, length and frequency of the course, cost, amount of feedback provided, and level of satisfaction were explored.

What are some internal and external training programs that you have provided to your sales and marketing employees on either an individual or group basis over the last two years? What are some of the characteristics of these programs?

The main types of training programs used by companies were, in order of popularity:

- Sales Training
- Product Training
- Marketing Training
- Time Management

The majority of programs appeared to be customized to the needs of the individual companies. Only a small percentage of the programs were generic. Almost all of the programs were purchased from external suppliers as opposed to being provided in-house. The sample companies listed a large number of external suppliers.

Respondents were also asked to state the methods of instruction used in training courses. The most common methods included:

- Lecture
- Video
- Case

Most of the training programs were one, two, or three days in length. The remaining programs were all less than one week in duration. Most of the courses were held either annually or biannually.

The range in the costs of these programs was from $3000 to nearly $30 000. The cost per participant per day varied from a low of $250 to a high of $600. The average was $500 per participant per day. These costs included:

- Fees and expenses paid to the training supplier
- Travel, food, and accommodations for participants
- Facilities for the program

The costs do not include the value of time away from work for program participants.

Not surprisingly, the number of participants in each course varied greatly. In most companies, all sales and marketing people took some training each year. As a result, the number of potential participants can be directly linked to the number of people employed in sales and marketing.

Most respondents confirmed that their training courses provided some feedback. This feedback took many forms, including individual follow-up by the trainer, tests, and role-play sessions. All respondents stated that feedback was something they valued a great deal and was an area that needed considerable improvement.

The data showed that while most respondents felt that training programs were effective, many stated that there was definitely room for improvement.

Are there other programs that you would like to see? How would they be structured?

When asked to list any training programs they would like to see, most people responded by saying that they would like to see more customized programs related to their company, products, and people. Virtually all respondents stressed the fact that sales training programs were the highest-priority training activities in their companies.

In your company, what are the biggest problems you have faced with the training of employees?

This question was asked to determine limitations with traditional methods of training. The most frequently cited responses to this question were:

- Time required to do training and have people away from their work
- Costs associated with travel, lost production, and the training program itself
- Finding training programs that meet the needs of the individual
- Identifying the skills that require improvement
- Finding time to complete the training and getting everyone into one central location
- Lack of ability to measure the impact of training on an individual or group basis
- Lack of individual feedback to participants during and after a training program

Section C

The last section of the questionnaire was designed to gain information on people's perceptions of online training. This information included awareness, benefits, concerns, and price.

Prior to this interview, have you ever heard of or have you used online training?

Two-thirds of the respondents confirmed they had heard of online training while 20 percent stated they had heard of and actually investigated online training. Only 8 percent of the respondents stated they were currently using online training.

Where did you hear about online training?

The most common ways people had become aware of online training were:

- Internet
- Magazines and newspapers
- Universities
- Training suppliers
- Colleagues
- Other companies

List the benefits you think online training might provide your company.

The most significant benefits identified were:

- Lower costs
- Increased convenience
- Can learn at own pace
- Flexible to needs and schedule
- Superior feedback and interaction

List any concerns you think you might have with online training.

The most significant concerns identified were:

- Not enough interaction with other participants or the instructor
- Motivating trainees to actually do the program
- Participants may not have the required technology or feel comfortable with this technology
- Difficulties in monitoring performance
- May be hard to provide good feedback

Assuming that online training in sales and marketing were available at a reasonable price, would your company be interested in trying this method of delivery?

In response to this question,

- 12% stated that they definitely would try online training;
- 20% stated that they probably would try online training;
- 36% stated that they may or may not try online training;
- 28% stated that they probably would not use online training;
- 4% stated that they definitely would not use online training.

*Would you expect this type of training to be less expensive,
as expensive as, or more expensive on a per-student basis than
traditional training?*

Nearly 72 percent of the respondents felt online training would be less expensive than traditional training, another 20 percent felt that online training would cost the same as traditional training, and the remaining 8 percent felt online training would be more expensive.

Dillon Controls, Ltd.

James E. Nelson and Mark S. Johnson

"The choices themselves seem simple enough," thought Jac Dillon, "either we enter the U.S. market in Pennsylvania and New York, we forget about the United States for the time being, or we do some more marketing research." Dillon was president of Dillon Controls, Ltd., located in Brantford, Ontario. The company was formed in 1980 and, after a slow start, had grown steadily to its present size of 25 employees and annual revenues of about $1.6 million. About 2% of these revenues came from sales to U.S. accounts.

THE AQUAWATCH SYSTEM

Dillon Controls' product line centred around its AquaWatch System, a design of computer hardware and software for the monitoring and control of pressurized water flows. Most often these water flows consisted of either potable water or sewage effluent as these liquids were stored, moved, or treated by municipal water departments.

The system employed an AquaWatch microprocessor installed at individual pumping stations where liquids are stored and moved. Often, stations were located many kilometres apart,

This case was written by Professor James E. Nelson and doctoral student Mark S. Johnson, University of Colorado. It is intended for use as a basis for class discussion rather than to illustrate either effective or ineffective administrative decision making. Some data are disguised. Copyright © 1990 by the Business Research Division, College of Business and Administration and the Graduate School of Business Administration, University of Colorado, Boulder, Colorado, 80309-0419. Reprinted with permission.

linking geographically dispersed water users (households, businesses, etc.) to water and sewer systems. The microcomputer performed a number of important functions. It governed the starts, stops, and alarms of up to four pumps, monitored levels and available capacities of storage reservoirs, checked pump capacities and power consumptions, and recorded pump flows. It could even measure amounts of rainfall entering reservoirs and adjust pump operations or activate an alarm as needed. Each microcomputer could also be easily connected to a main computer to allow remote control of pumping stations and produce a variety of charts and graphs useful in evaluating pump performance and scheduling needed maintenance.

The AquaWatch System provided a monitoring function that human operators could not match in terms of sophistication, immediacy, and cost. It permitted each individual substation to control its own pumping operations; collect, analyze, and store data; forecast trends; transmit data and alarms to a central computer; and receive remote commands. Alarms could also be transmitted directly to a pocket-sized receiver carried by one or more operators on call. A supervisor could continually monitor pumping operations in a large system entirely via a computer terminal at a central location and send commands to individual pumps, thereby saving costly service calls and time. The system also reduced the possibility of overflows that could produce disastrous flooding of nearby communities or contamination of potable water.

Dillon Controls personnel would work with water and sewage engineers to design and install the desired AquaWatch System. Personnel would also train engineers and operators to work with the system and would be available 24 hours a day for consultation. If needed, a company engineer could be physically present to assist engineers and operators whenever major problems arose. Dillon Controls also offered its clients the option of purchasing a complete service contract whereby company personnel would provide periodic testing and maintenance of installed systems. The contract called for clients to pay Dillon for all direct costs of the service plus 15% for overhead.

An AquaWatch System could be configured a number of ways. In its most basic form, the system would be little more than a small "black box" that monitored two or three lift station activities and, when necessary, transmitted an alarm to one or more remote receivers. An intermediate system would monitor additional activities, send data to a central computer via telephone lines, and receive remote commands. An advanced system would provide the same monitoring capabilities but add forecasting features, maintenance management, auxiliary power backup, and data transmission and reception via radio. Prices to customers for the three configurations in early 1991 were about $1500, $2800, and $4800.

AQUAWATCH CUSTOMERS

AquaWatch customers could be divided into two groups—governmental units and industrial companies. The typical application in the first group was a sewage treatment plant having some 4 to 12 pumping stations, each station containing one or more pumps. Pumps would operate intermittently and—unless an AquaWatch or similar system were in place—be monitored by one or more operators who would visit each station once or perhaps twice each day for about a half-hour. Operators would take reservoir measurements, record running times of pumps, and sometimes perform limited maintenance and repairs. The sewage plant and stations typically were located in flat or rolling terrain, where gravity could not be used in lieu of pumping. If any monitoring equipment were present at all, it typically would consist of a crude, on-site alarm that would activate whenever fluid levels rose or fell beyond a preset level. Sometimes the alarm would activate a telephone dialling function that alerted an operator some distance from the station.

Numerous industrial companies also stored, moved, and processed large quantities of water or sewage. These applications usually differed little from those in governmental plants except for their smaller size. On the other hand, there was a considerably larger number of industrial companies having pumping stations and so, Dillon thought, the two markets offered about identical market potentials.

The two markets desired essentially the same products, although industrial applications often used smaller, simpler equipment. Both markets wanted their monitoring equipment to be accurate and reliable, the two dominant concerns. Equipment should also be easy to use, economical to operate, and require little regular service or maintenance. Purchase price often was not a major consideration—as long as the price was in some appropriate range, customers seemed more interested in actual product performance than in initial outlays.

Dillon thought that worldwide demand for these types of systems would continue to be strong for at least the next ten years. While some demand represented construction of new pumping stations, many applications were replacements of crude monitoring and alarm systems at existing sites. These existing systems depended greatly on regular visits by operators, visits that often continued even after new equipment was installed. Most such trips were probably not necessary. However, many managers found it difficult to dismiss or reassign monitoring personnel who were no longer needed; many were also quite cautious and conservative, desiring some human monitoring of the new equipment "just in case." Once replacements of existing systems were complete, market growth would be limited to new construction and, of course, replacements with more sophisticated systems.

Most customers (as well as non-customers) considered the AquaWatch System one of the best on the market. Those knowledgeable in the industry felt that competing products seldom matched AquaWatch's reliability and accuracy. Experts also believed that many competing products lacked the sophistication and flexibility present in AquaWatch's design. Beyond these product features, customers also appreciated Dillon Controls' knowledge about water and sanitation engineering. Competing firms often lacked this expertise, offering their products somewhat as a sideline and considering the market too small for an intensive marketing effort.

The market was clearly not too small for Dillon Controls. While Jac Dillon had no hard data on market potential for the United States, he thought that annual demand there could be as much as $30 million. In Canada, the total market was at least $4 million. Perhaps about 40% of market demand came from new construction while the rest represented replacements of existing systems. Industry sales in the latter category could be increased by more aggressive marketing efforts on the part of competitors in the industry.

DILLON CONTROLS' STRATEGY

Dillon Controls currently marketed its AquaWatch System primarily to sewage treatment plants in Canada as opposed to industrial companies. Approximately 70% of its revenues came from Ontario and Quebec. The company's strategy could be described as providing technologically superior equipment to monitor pumping operations at these plants. The strategy stressed frequent contacts with customers and potential customers to design, supply, and service AquaWatch Systems. The strategy also stressed superior knowledge of water and sanitation engineering along with up-to-date electronics and computer technology. The result was a line of highly specialized sensors, computers, and methods for process controls in water treatment plants.

This was the essence of Dillon Controls' strategy, having a special competence that no firm in the market could easily match. The company also prided itself on being a young, creative company, without an entrenched bureaucracy. Company employees generally worked with enthusiasm and dedication; they talked with each other regularly, openly, and with a great deal of give and take. Most importantly, customers—as well as technology— seemed to drive all areas in the company.

Dillon Controls' strategy in Canada seemed to be fairly well decided. That is, Dillon thought that a continuation of present strategies and tactics should continue to produce good results. However, an aspect that would likely change would be to locate a branch office having both sales and distribution functions somewhere out west, most likely in Vancouver. The plan was to have such an office in operation within the next few years. Having a branch office in Vancouver would greatly simplify sales and service in the western provinces, not to mention increase company sales.

Beyond establishing the branch office, Dillon was considering a major strategic decision to enter the U.S. market. The North American Free Trade Agreement, which came into effect in 1989, was prompting many Canadian companies to look southward. Among other things, the agreement eliminated all tariffs on computer products (such as the AquaWatch System) traded between Canada and the United States. In addition, Dillon's two recent visits to the United States had led him to conclude that the market represented potential far beyond that of Canada and that the United States seemed perfect for expansion. Industry experts in the United States agreed with Dillon that the AquaWatch System outperformed anything used in the U.S. market. Experts thought that many water and sewage engineers would welcome Dillon Controls' products and knowledge. Moreover, Dillon thought that U.S. transportation systems and payment arrangements would present few problems.

Entry would most likely be in the form of a sales and service office located in Philadelphia. The Pennsylvania and New York State markets seemed representative of the United States and appeared to offer a good test of the AquaWatch System. While the two states represented only 12% of the U.S. population, they accounted for almost 16% of U.S. manufacturing activity. The office would require an investment of some $200 000 for inventory and other balance sheet items. Annual fixed costs would total upwards of $250 000 for salaries and other operating expenses—Dillon thought that the office would employ only a general manager, technician, and secretary for at least the first year or two. Each AquaWatch System sold in the United States would be priced to provide a contribution of about 30%. Dillon wanted a 35% annual return on any Dillon Controls investment, to begin no later than the second year. At issue was whether Dillon could realistically expect to achieve this goal in the United States.

MARKETING RESEARCH

To estimate the viability of a U.S. sales office, Dillon had commissioned the Browning Group in Philadelphia to conduct some limited marketing research with selected personnel in the water and sewage industries in the city and surrounding areas. The research had two purposes: to obtain a sense of market needs and market reactions to Dillon Controls' products and to calculate a rough estimate of market potential in Pennsylvania and New York.

Results were intended to help Dillon interpret his earlier conversations with industry experts and perhaps allow a decision on market entry.

The research design itself employed two phases of data collection. The first consisted of five one-hour interviews with water and sewage engineers employed by local city and municipal governments. For each interview, an experienced Browning Group interviewer scheduled an appointment with the engineer and then visited his office, armed with a set of questions and a tape recorder. Questions included:

1. What procedures do you use to monitor your pumping stations?
2. Is your current monitoring system effective? Costly?
3. What are the costs of a monitoring malfunction?
4. What features would you like to see in a monitoring system?
5. Who decides on the selection of a monitoring system?
6. What is your reaction to the AquaWatch System?

Interviewers were careful to listen closely to the engineers' responses and to probe for additional detail and clarification.

Tapes of the personal interviews were transcribed and then analyzed by the project manager at Browning. The report noted that these results were interesting in that they described typical industry practices and viewpoints. A partial summary from the report appears below:

> The picture that emerges is one of fairly sophisticated personnel making decisions about monitoring equipment that is relatively simple in design. Still, some engineers would appear distrustful of this equipment because they persist in sending operators to pumping stations on a daily basis. The distrust may be justified because potential costs of a malfunction were identified as expensive repairs and clean-ups, fines of $10 000 per day of violation, lawsuits, harassment by the Health Department, and public embarrassment. The five engineers identified themselves as key individuals in the decision to purchase new equipment. Without exception, they considered AquaWatch features innovative, highly desirable, and worth the price.

The summary noted also that the primary use of the interview results was to construct a questionnaire that could be administered over the telephone.

The questionnaire was used in the second phase of data collection, as part of a telephone survey of 65 utility managers, water and sewage engineers, and pumping station operators in Philadelphia and surrounding areas. All respondents were employed by governmental units. Each interview took about ten minutes to complete, covering topics identified in questions 1, 2, and 4 above. The Browning Group's research report stated that most interviews found respondents to be quite cooperative, although 15 people refused to participate at all.

The telephone interviews had produced results that could be considered more representative of the market because of the larger sample size. The report had organized these results about the topics of monitoring procedures, system effectiveness and costs, and features desired in a monitoring system:

> All monitoring systems under the responsibility of the 50 respondents were considered to require manual checking. The frequency of operator visits to pumping stations ranged from monthly to twice daily, depending on flow rates, pumping station history, proximity of nearby communities, monitoring equipment in operation, and other factors. Even the most sophisticated automatic systems were checked because respondents "just don't trust the machine." Each operator was responsible for an average of 15 stations.

Despite the perceived need for double-checking, all respondents considered their current monitoring system to be quite effective. Not one reported a serious pumping malfunction in the past three years that had escaped detection. However, this reliability came at considerable cost—the annual wages and other expenses associated with each monitoring operator averaged about $50 000.

Respondents were about evenly divided between those wishing a simple alarm system and those desiring a sophisticated, versatile microprocessor. Managers and engineers in the former category often said that the only feature they really needed was an emergency signal such as a siren, horn, or light. Sometimes they would add a telephone dialer that would be automatically activated at the same time as the signal. Most agreed that a price of around $2000 would be reasonable for such a system. The latter category of individuals contained engineers desiring many of the AquaWatch System's features, once they knew such equipment was available. A price of $5000 per system seemed acceptable. Some of these respondents were quite knowledgeable about computers and computer programming while others were not. Only four respondents voiced any strong concerns about the cost to purchase and install more sophisticated monitoring equipment. Everyone demanded that the equipment be reliable and accurate.

Dillon found the report quite helpful. Much of the information, of course, simply confirmed his own view of the U.S. market. However, it was good to have this knowledge from an independent, objective organization. In addition, to learn that the market consisted of two, apparently equally sized segments of simple and sophisticated applications was quite worthwhile. In particular, knowledge of system prices considered acceptable by each segment would make the entry decision easier. Meeting these prices would not be a major problem.

A most important section of the report contained an estimate of market potential for Pennsylvania and New York. The estimate was based on an analysis of discharge permits on file in governmental offices in the two states. These permits were required before any city, municipality, water or sewage district, or industrial company could release sewage or other contaminated water to another system or to a lake or river. Each permit showed the number of pumping stations in operation. Based on a 10% sample of permits, the report had estimated that governmental units in Pennsylvania and New York contained approximately 3000 and 5000 pumping stations for waste water, respectively. Industrial companies in the two states were estimated to add some 3000 and 9000 more pumping stations, respectively. The total number of pumping stations in the two states—20 000—seemed to be growing at about 2% per year.

Finally, a brief section of the report dealt with the study's limitations. Dillon agreed that the sample was quite small, that it contained no utility managers or engineers from New York, and that it probably concentrated too heavily on individuals in larger urban areas. In addition, the research told him nothing about competitors and their marketing strategies and tactics. Nor did he learn anything about any state regulations for monitoring equipment, if indeed any existed. However, these shortcomings came as no surprise, representing a consequence of the research design proposed to Dillon by the Browning Group some six weeks ago, before the study began.

THE DECISION

Dillon's decision seemed a difficult one. The most risky option was to enter the U.S. market as soon as possible. There was no question about the vast market potential of the United

States. However, the company's opportunity for a greatly increased bottom line had to be balanced against the threat of new competitors who were, for the most part, larger and more sophisticated than Dillon Controls. In fact, a friend had jokingly remarked that "a Canadian firm selling microprocessor controls in the United States would be like trying to sell Canadian semiconductors to the Japanese."

The most conservative option was to stay in Canada. Of course, Dillon Controls would continue to respond to the odd inquiry from the United States and would continue to fill orders that the company accepted from U.S. customers. However, it would not seek this sort of business in an aggressive fashion. Nor would it seek representation in the United States through an agent or distributor. The latter option put Dillon Controls out of the picture as far as controlling sales claims, prices, product installation, service, and other important aspects of customer relations was concerned.

In between the two extremes was the option of conducting some additional marketing research. Discussion with the Browning Group had identified the objectives of this research as to rectify limitations of the first study as well as to provide more accurate estimates of market potential. (The estimates of the numbers of pumping stations in Pennsylvania and New York were accurate to around plus or minus 20%.) This research was estimated to cost $40 000 and take another three months to complete.

Nickel Belt Paving

Justin Funk and Tom Funk

Frank Lawson parked his pick-up truck on his driveway late one night after a hard day at his company, Nickel Belt Paving. Walking up to his front door, and pulling out the day's mail, he found the usual collection of advertisements, magazines, and personal letters. One letter in particular was from his good friend and cousin Don in Calgary.

Frank and Don had gone through grade school together and started a small paving company in their hometown of Hamilton, Ontario. Although they had a successful business, over the years they had spent many hours together in heated debates about how a business should be run. Frank had little patience for Don's laissez-faire attitude when it came to running a business, while Don argued that Frank's fear of losing control, and his tendency to overwork himself, would eventually burn him out before he turned 40. Frank always stood by the motto, "If you want something done right, you need to do it yourself." Although Don respected Frank's view, in 1980, after 15 years in business together, they mutually agreed to go their separate ways.

In the early 1980s, Don moved out west and started his own paving company. He had always dreamed of retiring and buying a cattle ranch. After 20 successful years in business, he sold his company and did just that—he bought a ranch and now lives the life he always dreamed of. In 1982, Frank moved to Sudbury, Ontario, and set up his own paving company, Nickel Belt Paving.

NICKEL BELT PAVING

Today, Nickel Belt Paving is a small, but very successful business. For over 20 years Frank has managed to build a reputation in the community and many would argue he *was* Nickel Belt Paving.

Frank, now in his early 60s, is the sole owner of the business. Unlike Don, Frank is the first to arrive at work, usually around 6:00 a.m., and is always the last to leave. He will often arrive home at 9:00 or 10:00 o'clock at night. Frank doesn't look like your average business owner; in fact, you might mistake him for one of the crew. He shows up to work in his coveralls, boots, and helmet, and works in the blazing sun with his team—shovelling, grading, and rolling. He is a very "hands-on" boss.

Frank's wife, Martha, runs the office. She handles the accounting, payroll, and marketing functions of the company. She is responsible for making decisions on things Frank doesn't care too much about. Computers, couriers, and office supplies are all her choice. If asked, Frank would not know the difference between a fax machine and a photocopier. Over the years, Martha has become quite familiar with the technical side of paving, but she knows when it comes to this side of the business, her input is not required. She is, however, always quite willing to share her opinions on people, employees, and the overall welfare of the business.

Frank's oldest son, Peter, 35, who began working with Frank when he was 18, is Frank's right-hand man. Peter shares his father's ambition, and lately Frank has been looking to Peter more and more for information, advice, and leadership. Although Peter is happy in his current role, he looks forward to having his opportunity to take charge.

Frank's youngest son, Mitchell, 27, went to university and studied landscape architecture. He works in Nickel Belt's office as an estimator and company representative. He is the one who helps generate new business, submits bids, and oversees large projects. Frank often seeks Mitchell's advice when it comes to buying materials and pricing jobs. In the winter time, when the snow arrives and the paving season is over, Mitchell joins Peter and Frank in snow plowing. This is a major part of Nickel Belt's business.

Frank has two other sons, John, 33, and Joe, 30, who are not involved in the company at all. They never really showed an interest. After working on the crew for a few summers in high school, they both decided it was not the career for them.

Elisabeth, 24, is Frank's youngest child and only daughter. Elisabeth works with Mitchell and Martha in the office and handles reception and other administrative duties. She answers the phone, receives packages, and helps her mother schedule different jobs for the crews. While Elisabeth enjoys her job, she is formally trained as a teacher and is waiting to get full-time work.

Nickel Belt employs twenty other people who make up three different work crews. Next in line to Peter is Rick, who has been Frank's loyal employee since he and Don owned their company together in Hamilton. While Rick helps manage the crews, he always knows where his responsibility ends. Over the years Rick has learned to respect the fact that Frank is in charge; Rick simply follows orders. The other nineteen workers drive trucks, lay pavement, operate heavy machinery, and landscape. For the most part, they are all long-term employees. Turnover is not a big issue for Nickel Belt. Those who are fired, or who leave on their own accord, usually do so because they cannot work up to Frank's expectations. Those who stay are treated very fairly and are rewarded for their hard work and loyalty.

THE BREAKDOWN

As Frank walked into his house, he thought to himself, "What a long day it's been." In the middle of the workday, another loader[1] broke down. This would make three in less than a month.

Martha asked him, "What's the matter, Frank?"

He replied, "Another loader broke down today . . . and with two already in the shop for repairs! These XTR loaders are giving me a real headache." He grabbed a drink out of the refrigerator, sat down, and began shuffling through the mail.

Frank added: "This will seriously delay our project. Unless we get a loader back from the shop tomorrow, we're going to have to rent one. I was going over the numbers with Mitchell, and he agreed that if we have to rent for a long time, it's going to destroy any profit we hoped to make on this job."

Frank took a sip of his drink, wiped his forehead and continued, "And what makes it worse is that Sellers guy won't get back to me. I've left him message after message—at his office, on his cell phone—and no reply. I've told him how important this is and if we don't get a loader back soon, we're going to be in big trouble."

Jim Sellers was the sales representative for the local XTR dealership. He sold Frank the three loaders that are now in for repair. At the time of the sale, he had done a good job of presenting the features and benefits of the new machines, and promised if anything ever went wrong, he would be there to deal with it. Even though the XTR machines were priced a little higher than most other brands at the time, this didn't matter much to Frank because he liked having machines that were widely regarded as being the best. He also enjoyed dealing with Jim. At one time, Frank had been a little irritated at Jim when he learned that some of his competitors, who purchased similar machines, received a somewhat better deal than he did.

Frank generally had good experience with the local XTR dealer. Until recently, they always provided good service. Two months ago, Frank noticed they were expanding into new product lines. At that time, Frank was somewhat surprised when he received a brochure highlighting new products designed for the agricultural market and an invitation to a demonstration at the Canada Outdoor Farm Show. Frank thought this was strange since he had nothing to do with farming, or agriculture in general.

Martha sat down beside Frank and said, "Well then, you probably don't want to see this," as she handed him a brochure for XTR's newest model. Stapled to it was Jim's business card with a handwritten message reading, *Isn't she a beauty?*

Frank did not hold brochures in very high regard. He did not think you could learn anything from a brochure. Rather, he liked to hear what people who actually used different products had to say about them. Frank and Don would often exchange thoughts on these

---

[1]A loader is a piece of construction equipment, similar to a tractor, with a large shovel on the front. It is used to move heavy materials from one location to another. The average loader costs $100 000.

types of matters. Don had owned XTRs and was very happy with them. Furthermore, when visiting Don one winter, Frank was able to try one. Frank also enjoyed attending machinery trade shows in the off-season. Once a year, he and Martha would fly to Las Vegas where North America's largest construction trade show and auction was held. This was a good way for Frank to evaluate new equipment while giving Martha a vacation at the same time. Sometimes he would actually make a purchase while he was there. At the most recent convention, Frank noticed the new XTR loader was chosen as the Mid-sized Machine of the Year.

Martha continued, "Jim dropped this off to Elisabeth today. He then went back and spoke with Rick. I have no idea what it was about. He left before I came back from the post office."

"You mean he was in the office today? And he didn't try to get in touch with me?" Frank began to show a little bit of frustration. "And he left this?" gesturing towards the brochure. "The nerve of that guy."

Martha replied, "Well, you did tell him you were interested in buying a new machine."

"But that was over a month ago. Since then, we've had two of his lemons in for repairs. And then today . . . ." Frank huffed, "I'm going to bed. I'll deal with this in the morning."

Frank was considering buying a new machine because he had a lot of projects scheduled over the next few months that would place considerable demands on his current equipment. His initial reaction was to purchase the new XTR model because it had increased its horsepower and fuel efficiency, but he was also seriously considering TigerCat equipment, a brand he used extensively in his early days. There were other machines on the market, such as the Japanese imports Sumitomo, Matsui, and Komatsu, but Frank didn't know much about these brands and generally preferred to buy North American-made equipment.

THE NEXT DAY

The next day, Frank arrived at the shop, early as usual, and took a look at the day's schedule, knowing full well he would fall way behind by losing another loader. Frustrated, he took out the phonebook and began searching for machinery rental companies. About a half-hour later, Rick arrived.

"Morning, Frank. How's it going?" Rick asked.

"Was Jim Sellers here to see you yesterday?"

"Yeah," Rick replied. "He came to tell me two of your loaders would be ready tomorrow."

"He told *you* this?" Frank asked.

"Yes," answered Rick.

"Did he say what was taking so long?" Frank asked.

Rick replied, "Yeah, he said they were installing some new gadget. I think it allows you to locate and track your machines from a computer or something like that. It's some new fancy service they offer—in case your machines are stolen or if you want to find out where they're currently working."

"I know where my machines are. They're with me most of the day. And I know where they are right now, and they're not doing much good!" Frank exclaimed.

XTR had recently established a new program to retrofit all older machines with new GPS microchips, allowing them to be tracked by satellite. It was a way for managers to locate machines during the course of a workday, or recover them in case of theft.

"I've been trying to reach that guy for three days now and he hasn't returned my calls, but he comes in and talks to *you*? Unbelievable. What else did he say?"

Rick replied, "He said he would stop by next week with one of their new XTRs. He wanted me and Peter to check it out."

"Oh," said Frank. "I see."

When Elisabeth arrived at the office, Frank asked her to phone Brookfield rentals and have a loader delivered to their work site as soon as possible. He also told her if Jim Sellers phoned or stopped by, to have him get in touch right away.

By this time, Frank was running late. He needed to get to the job site and coordinate the crew so they could get other things done before the rental arrived. If Frank disliked anything worse than broken machinery, it was watching workers standing around and doing nothing while on the clock. As Frank walked out back of the shop, he was startled from behind by Chuck Hustead, a sales representative for TigerCat equipment and a good friend of Mitchell's.

"Morning, Frank! How's it going?"

"It's okay, Chuck," Frank said as he continued walking towards his truck, arms full of plans, tools, and keys. "What can I do for you?" he asked.

"I was talking with Mitchell the other day and he mentioned you had some breakdowns with your XTR's. Not good! Those things are garbage. I don't know why you chose them in the first place. Anyway, I wanted to show you this brochure on our new TigerCat Claw, the newest model in our line of loaders."

"Thanks, Chuck, leave it with Elisabeth and I'll have a look at it later," Frank replied as he started loading up his truck.

"Take it with you, Frank. You can read it on one of your breaks."

"Right," said Frank as he took the brochure and hopped into his oversized white pick-up truck.

"And when you get back to the office, be sure to log onto our website. www.TigerCatMachines.com, slash models, slash claw, dot html. Okay? It has a neat flash plug-in that takes you through all the different configurations. Point and click and you can build your own machine. It's really cool. But it has a lot of multimedia content, so you should have a broadband connection and at least a 2.8 GHz processor to run it correctly. What type of Internet connection do you have?"

Frank just looked at Chuck. After thinking to himself for a brief second he said, "I better go. I'm late for work. Talk with you later, Chuck."

As Frank started the ignition on his truck, Chuck began to say something else, but the loud rumble of the diesel engine drowned him out.

"Sorry," said Frank over the noise of the engine. "Gotta go." He then drove off to the job site.

On his way to the site, Frank thought how much he liked TigerCat equipment. He had owned some of their earlier models before he bought the XTRs. He never had an issue with them, they were nice looking, and he knew several other construction companies that used them. He made a note on a scrap of paper to call Bob Daniels, a good friend and owner of a local construction company, to see what he thought about the new TigerCat Claw.

Frank regarded Bob as an expert in construction, and he often consulted with him on issues relating to business, equipment, and construction in general. Over the years they had done a lot of business together and developed a solid personal and business relationship.

ON-SITE DELIVERY

Frank arrived at the job site to find Peter directing the crew and keeping everyone busy. Frank was pleased. When Peter asked Frank where he had been, Frank replied, "Tied up."

About an hour later, a loader arrived on-site. Frank noticed the delivery truck was not from Brookfield, but rather from Sudbury Heavy Equipment, a new dealership located in town that sold Robinson machines. Robinson was a European line of construction equipment, newly reintroduced in Canada.

Out of the delivery truck stepped a young man, no older than Elisabeth.

"Mr. Lawson," he said.

"Yes," replied both Peter and Frank at the same time. They looked at each other and smiled.

"Frank Lawson?" asked the young man again.

"That's me. You're not from Brookfield," Frank responded.

"No, sir. My name is Dave Crawford, from Sudbury Heavy Equipment. I was in your office talking with your daughter Elisabeth the other day and she mentioned you were having some trouble with your loaders. I know you've been working really hard to get this project done, so I thought I would let you borrow one of our new Robinson models. I thought it would give you a chance to see how it worked, and also help out your unfortunate situation. I hope this is okay."

"Well, thank you very much Dave. I appreciate the gesture."

"No problem, Mr. Lawson. You can have it until the end of the week if you would like. When you are finished, give me a call and I'll personally come out and pick it up."

"That's great. I'm looking forward to giving it a whirl," said Frank.

"Elisabeth said you might be anxious to try it out. She hinted you enjoy working with equipment hands-on. I think that's very admirable. Apparently your appreciation of hard work really pays off. I've heard a lot of great things about you and Nickel Belt Paving. You actually did my grandmother's driveway many years ago. She remembers you well."

"Well, we always try to do a good job," said Frank. "Thanks for the loaner. I'll take good care of it."

"No doubt," said Dave. "I'll be in touch with you in a few days. Is there a good time to call?"

Frank replied in a somewhat joking voice, "Well, you might be asleep. I usually don't get done work until late. Probably not till 9:30."

"I'll call you at 9:30 in two days," responded Dave in an enthusiastic tone.

"Alright," said Frank in a pleased voice.

LATER THAT NIGHT

When Frank arrived home that night, he phoned Elisabeth and asked her how she knew Dave Crawford. If she was dating someone, he wanted to know about it. Even at 24, she was still his little girl.

Elisabeth told Frank, "He dropped by the office a couple of days ago looking for you and I told him you were out working. I said you're always working." She smiled, and then continued, "He then told me he was talking with Bob Daniels and Bob told him you had some breakdowns with your XTRs. He then asked if he could leave his card and follow up in a few days."

"Okay," said Frank.

"This morning, before I had a chance to phone the rental company, he called. I guess he was driving around last night and noticed another loader being taken away on a flatbed. He wanted to know if there was another problem, and if you received any of your other machines back from the repair shop. I told him you had another breakdown and needed to rent one this morning. That's when he offered to bring one of his loaders to the work site, free of charge. I checked with Mitchell, and he said you probably wouldn't be interested because you were going to buy a TigerCat, but when I asked Mom she said to give it a try. I hope that was okay."

"Yes, dear. That was perfect."

Later that night, Frank called Bob Daniels to get his opinion on the new Robinson machine. Bob mentioned to Frank that he was looking at the Robinson line himself, but had some doubts because it was so new to the North American market and had yet to be thoroughly tested and proven. He also commented that he felt the XTR, TigerCat, and Robinson machines were all about the same in both price and quality.

TWO DAYS LATER

Two days passed, and Frank still hadn't heard from Jim Sellers, not even to follow up on the brochure he dropped off. Elisabeth mentioned that Chuck had sent several emails to the office with links to a website.

Frank spent much of the evening working with the new Robinson machine himself to get a true feel for it. He liked the way it handled and the way it looked; however, he was a little confused by all of the electronic equipment in the cabin. He also wondered how expensive it might be to repair because it was an import.

Later that night at 9:30, Frank's phone rang. It was Dave Crawford. Frank told him how much he appreciated the nice thing he had done.

Dave replied, "I'm glad I could be of some help, Mr. Lawson. It was my pleasure. May I ask what you thought of the machine?"

Frank replied that it had performed very well. He was impressed.

Dave said, "Well, that's great. If you are ever interested in Robinson machinery, please feel free to give me a call. I'll be happy to meet with you any time."

Frank replied, "Well, I might just do that. But what happens when the Robinson machine breaks down? Will I have the same trouble I'm having now?"

Dave told Frank that Robinson machines had an excellent service policy. If a machine broke down, Sudbury Heavy Equipment would bring a loaner to the site on the same day for as long as it was needed.

Dave said, "I know how important it is for you to limit your downtime. We recognize machine repairs are a fact of life, but we promise to stand by our products. Our goal is to help you be efficient, not just sell you a machine. Our guarantee is one way we can do this."

Frank like what he heard.

On his drive home, Frank though what a nice thing Dave had done. He was slightly concerned that he had little experience with Robinson equipment. He would have to ask Peter and Rick what they thought.

The next morning, Frank arrived at the office very early. He began looking through all of the different brochures he received from Jim and Chuck. He then went out back and looked at the Robinson loader, still on loan. A little later, Jim Sellers showed up.

"Hey Frankie! Sorry about your machines. We'll get them back to you ASAP, I promise. We've been having a little trouble installing all these new GPS tracking devices, but the parts just came in and they'll be installed in your machines later today. I thought you might want to get this all done in one shot, you know, so you wouldn't have to bring them back later for the retrofit. And listen, I know I haven't been the best at getting back to you, but getting all these new devices installed in *all* my customers' machines has kept me running. And now I have all these new farmer customers. By the way, have you decided what you want to do with that new XTR model?"

"I certainly have, Jim," Frank replied.

Toronto Door & Trim

Donna Bernachi, John Blackie, and David S. Litvack

INTRODUCTION

Gerry, accompanied by his friend John, was waiting around inside his newly leased building in Markham, Ontario, surveying the layout (see Exhibit 1).

"What do you think? Isn't it great? I like it more than the old building in Scarborough where I was for two years. It has the same amount of warehouse space, but it is better laid out. I can now use a forklift instead of doing everything by hand. This really saves me time. At the front there is an office and a service counter where I can deal with the contractors, and there is a large empty area in front of the counter."

"Gerry, it looks bigger than the old place."

"That's right, it is larger than the one I had in Scarborough, and of course, more expensive. The rent here is an additional $1500 per month. I'm either going to have to sell more doors or else cut costs to be able to afford this place. I thought that if I used the whole building for warehousing then I could sell doors to more contractors. But the dividing walls in the front are well-built and would be expensive and difficult to move.

EXHIBIT 1	Layout of New Building

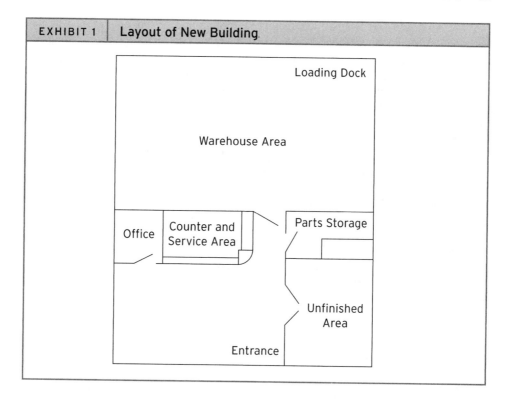

A contractor friend of mine estimated that the cost would be around $15 000 to remove the walls and renovate the area. What do you think, John?"

"Well, it looks like the front area was used as display space by the former tenant," John replied. "Maybe you can use the area to show contractors what products you offer. Or, instead, concentrate on selling your doors retail and bid on a few jobs from the larger contractors in Toronto."

Gerry responded, "The retail market has some interesting possibilities. A lot of people renovate their homes themselves, especially now during this recession. John, you've just finished your MBA—you could probably come up with some good ideas. What would you do with the extra space?"

TORONTO DOOR & TRIM

Toronto Door & Trim was started by Gerry Brown in January of 1992 as a wholesale business selling interior doors, wood trim, and casements to small contractors who build residential homes and small apartments. The product line offered consists of three categories:

1. Standard interior doors and accessories (door handles, hinges, etc.)

2. Specialty doors: French doors (solid wood and bevelled glass); closet doors (mirrored, sliding, etc.)

3. Wood mouldings and trim (required to finish the interior of residential and commercial buildings)

The doors are sold to small contractors in Toronto and surrounding areas. The new location is quite attractive, situated on the outskirts of the city across from a major nursery, which has a large clientele. It is easily reached by highway; a convenience for the customers since they can avoid travelling through the congested downtown traffic.

Gerry buys the doors and frames separately. He assembles the doors in the frames and sells them pre-hung to small contractors. This extra service saves the contractors installation time on the job site. He also offers measurement on site, delivery, and credit for the return of leftover products. According to Gerry, it is this high level of service that differentiates him from his competitors. This service and the quality products offered are what he feels have made him successful to date.

The current gross margin on products is 33%. Gary estimates products sold to large developers would yield gross margins of about 20% to 25%, and that retail gross margins would be 60% to 75%. (Exhibit 2 shows the income statement and the cost and selling prices of various doors.)

Although Toronto Door & Trim was opened during the recession period, Gerry's familiarity with the contractors in the area has contributed to the company's success to date. Before opening this business, he worked as a salesperson for a wholesaler of building products for ten years.

EXHIBIT 2	Income Statement

Income Statement

	Standard	Specialty	Trim	Total
Sales Revenue	$850 000	$50 000	$300 000	$1 200 000
COGS	600 000	25 000	175 000	800 000
Gross margin	250 000	25 000	125 000	400 000
Other expenses				375 000
Net income				$25 000
Total assets	$400 000			
Total debt	$265 000			

Note: Other expenses include the wage Gerry pays himself.

Price List

	Cost	Wholesale	Retail
Standard interior door	$60	$75	$80
Closet door (sliding mirror)	$70	$105	$125
French door (oak and bevelled glass)*	$120	$225	$260
French door (oak and stained glass)	$230	–	$500

*Available from supplier of bevelled glass doors. Retail price includes finishing door.

The staff consists of two employees who assemble the doors, and one commissioned salesperson who deals directly with the contractors. Most of the sales and marketing is done by Gerry himself. Should he decide to enter the retail market, an extra employee to serve at the counter would be necessary, and this would cost an additional $400 per week. He might also need to advertise to create some awareness.

CUSTOMERS

Most of the sales of Toronto Door & Trim are to the small contractors involved in building small apartments and residential developments. These contractors look for quality products at low prices and expect a high level of service from Gerry and his staff. However, price is the main determining factor when making a purchase.

Targeting the larger contractors, who build large apartment and row housing developments, is a feasible way for Gerry to increase sales. These customers have some similarities to his current market. However, low price becomes even more important with the larger contractors as does prompt delivery and the installation of precuts. These customers can be quite demanding at times, and they constantly seek ways to reduce costs.

The retail market consists of homeowners who are doing their own home renovations or are acting as their own contractor. Aside from quality products at a reasonable price, this group seeks service, advice, and a wide selection of products. Installation would be offered on an as-required basis.

COMPETITORS

Competition on the wholesale side of the business consists of both large warehouse-style stores and smaller specialty stores. Lumberyards such as Beaver Lumber are currently serving the retail market. They can sell doors at a competitive price because their volumes are high, but they do not offer a very wide selection of products. In the Scarborough and surrounding area there are about 15 companies other than Toronto Door & Trim that specialize in or offer doors as part of their product lines as industrial distributors to smaller contractors.

Entry barriers into this industry are minimal as a result of relatively low capital requirements to start operations, simple technology, and a relatively modest level of expertise and skills required.

INDUSTRY

Wholesale

This industry's activities have always closely followed cyclical trends in the level of new housing construction as well as interest in do-it-yourself and contracted renovation projects. Studies have shown that the small size and urban market dependency of most companies in this industry make it especially vulnerable to competitive market forces. The ability to give close personal attention to customers' needs, especially in urban centres, is important to a firm's success.

The recession, which started in 1991, brought an abrupt decline in the number of new housing starts. As fewer homes are built, fewer contractors need Gerry's products. However, at the same time, the potential for the retail market to remain unchanged during recessionary times exists as an interest in do-it-yourself or contracted renovations is sparked. Renovations can give your home a new look at a lower cost than buying a new home (see Exhibit 3).

EXHIBIT 3	Renovations Help Take Up the Slack

New kitchens and bathrooms will make up a large part of building activity over the next year. Renovation spending is on the rise, several construction forecasters predicted recently, although the outlook for housing starts across the nation remains bleak.

Peter Anderson, principal of Toronto-based Anderson & Associates, called 1993 the "worst year in this [business] cycle in terms of housing starts." He said about 150 000 new homes will probably be built this year, followed by some recovery in 1994, with a high of 168 000 forecast. Renovations are expected to increase this year and next, but figures are deceiving, Anderson said. He explained that this is because so much renovation work forms part of the so-called underground economy—cash payments permit both homeowner and builder to avoid the goods and services tax.

Canada Mortgage & Housing Corp. (CMHC) said last week that it projects a 3.5% increase in renovation spending to $17.5 billion in 1994 from $16.8 billion this year. But a recent study by the Canadian Home Builders' Association said at least 45% of all building and renovation activity takes place in the underground economy and is not reported.

Current low interest rates are a major factor in the upswing expected in renovations, Anderson said. "People are refinancing their five-year mortgages, and with the rates [expected to be at] about 8% next spring instead of 12% in 1988, there's financing room for those thinking about redoing their kitchens or bedrooms," the real estate analyst told the recent CanaData construction forecasting conference.

Demographics may also work in favour of renovators. As people get older and their children grow up, they are more likely to make improvements to their homes. Anderson estimates about 60% of houses in Canada are more than 15 years old.

Gerry Proulx, CMHC's chief economist, agreed that as housing starts and sales of existing homes begin to increase next year, renovation activity should also rise. "Home sales tend to boost the renovation market because many improvement projects are done shortly before and immediately after a house is sold," he said. This represents at least a glimmer of hope for the construction industry, which has been devastated by the collapse of the real estate market in the late 1980s.

The Canadian Construction Association estimated that 120 000 workers have lost their jobs in the past five years. Anderson said homeowners will fuel the renovation market, not work on multiple units. He added that as more people switch to working at home, he sees a niche for home-office building or refurbishing.

EXHIBIT 3	Renovations Help Take Up the Slack (continued)

David Ellis, vice-president of Royal LePage Appraisal & Consulting Services, said there may be some renovation work in commercial real estate as well. "You need to keep your tenants happy or they won't stay," he said. "This bodes well for the renovation and retrofit markets, but it will be offset by the fact that 50% of office space has been built in the last ten years."

Source: *Financial Post*, October 6, 1993, p. 14.

Retail

The retail market is served in two ways: by large warehouse-type stores and high-end specialty stores. Nothing really exists to serve the segment between these two types of stores. The main renovation seasons are in the fall and spring. The industry does experience price competition.

The aging population is expected to present large opportunities in all retail sectors. As children leave the home, homeowners find that they have more funds available for home renovations.

Another factor affecting this industry is the slow recovery from the current recession. Large numbers of job losses over the past few years have caused consumers to tighten their purse strings. Buyer confidence is slow to return and this is hampering the recovery.

QUESTION

John sat staring at the information he had gathered about Toronto Door & Trim, wishing he had paid more attention during his marketing courses. If you were John, what recommendations would you make to Gerry?

Ontario Rutabaga Council

Jane Funk and Tom Funk

In June of 2004, Smithfield Communications was retained by the Ontario Rutabaga Council (ORC) to develop a new promotional campaign for Ontario rutabagas. This was a fairly unusual account for the medium-sized agency that specialized in agriculture. The average Smithfield client had a promotional budget of $4 million. The firm's clients included a number of organizations in the fertilizer, chemical, feed, and seed industries. They also handled a few industrial accounts, the largest of which was the $6 million Warren ("Windows to the World") Window account.

The agency was established in 1972 by Simon Smithfield, a former sales representative for Massey Ferguson. Smithfield had started by working with equipment accounts, but as the business prospered and the staff expanded, the firm moved into other areas of agribusiness and industrial products. The agency remained fairly conservative in its approach. Smithfield's own specialty was slogans, but the real agency emphasis was on "quality" promotion designed to inform customers. Though Smithfield himself had no formal marketing training, he was a great believer in hiring account executives with a marketing background because he recognized that ad executives couldn't work in a vacuum.

"We have to work on behalf of the client! We have to look at their strategy or help them develop one. Otherwise, they may as well toss their money down a rat hole for all the good a flashy ad campaign will do! What's more, we gotta have the guts to tell them their ideas stink! We owe them that honesty!"

This philosophy was still at work at Smithfield though Simon had retired. Every junior account employee was thoroughly versed in the philosophy and history of the company.

Though the agency dealt mainly with agribusiness accounts, Smithfield had never been in favour of hiring only those with an agricultural background. As Simon often said, "Too narrow-minded! If he grew up on a hog farm in Simcoe, then basically he thinks he has the last word on hogs! In this business you need a wide range of experience and a quick, open mind."

Most of Smithfield's junior ad people came right out of university. One of the latest additions was Ted Banner, a graduate of the Ontario Agricultural College. Ted had been with Smithfield for two years. He learned fast and was quite ambitious. To date, his greatest success had been the brochure for Farnum Feed. On the basis of his past performance, Smithfield executives felt he was ready to take on the ORC account.

Ted realized this was his big chance. The ORC account was expected to increase to around $300 000 for 2004/05 and he planned to make the campaign a real landmark. First, however, he knew he must do his homework, so he began studying all the background material he had collected on the ORC.

RUTABAGA INDUSTRY IN CANADA

Canadian rutabagas were originally used as feed for sheep that were bound for New England markets in the mid-1800s. In those days, rutabagas were called turnips. The sheep buyers themselves tried the vegetable and ordered more for their own consumption. These early turnips were a far cry from the sweeter tasting turnip developed in the 1930s and known as the Laurentian. This variety became known officially as rutabaga in 1967. The rutabaga is large and globular in shape, with yellow flesh and a purple top. Usually it is waxed to preserve it during shipping and storage. Rutabagas vary in size from one to three pounds and cost anywhere from 40 to 60 cents a pound.

Ontario is the centre for Canadian rutabaga production, although some Canadian competition comes from Quebec and P.E.I. The Ontario industry supports 130 growers, plus a number of shippers and packers. In 2001, the farm value of rutabagas in Ontario was $5.9 million, making it the eighth highest for vegetables grown in Ontario. Rutabagas reach the consumer by way of the following channel: Farmer —> Packer —> Shipper —> Wholesaler —> Supermarkets and Fruit and Vegetable Stores.

A large share of the Ontario rutabaga crop is shipped to the United States; in fact, rutabagas account for approximately 15 to 20 percent of the value of all fresh and processed vegetables exported to the United States from Canada. Rutabagas are also grown in the United States, but Ontario rutabagas are considered superior. Since there is no tariff on rutabagas, Canadian rutabagas compete effectively in price with those grown in the United States.

PAST PROMOTIONAL EFFORTS

Although the ORC had coordinated promotional programs on behalf of rutabaga producers for many years, its efforts were hampered by small budgets that often varied significantly from year to year. For example, last year, the ORC had a $60 000 promotional budget while the year before it was over $100 000. They used their budget, mainly in the United States, to promote rutabagas to homemakers as a unique and different vegetable. In the United States, most rutabagas are consumed south of the Mason-Dixon Line and east of the Mississippi River and the ORC felt that the main competition in this area was white turnips and turnip greens; hence, their program of differentiating the rutabaga.

To formulate their promotional program, the ORC hired the advertising agency of J.B. Cruikshank Ltd. This agency prepared a promotion mix consisting of magazine ads, press releases for radio, a TV video, and a video for high school family science teachers. All of this was developed around the persona of "June Conway," the fictional resident home economist for the ORC.

The magazine ads appeared in *Woman's Day* and *Family Circle* magazines during the months of November (the beginning of the holiday season in the United States, which is the peak period of rutabaga consumption) and April (the end of the turnip season in the United States). These full-page ads stressed new uses and recipe ideas, and featured a sample recipe and picture. They mentioned but did not stress nutrition, and they included a free write-in offer of a rutabaga recipe book. The agency reported that this phase of the program had received a "reasonable response" of 1000 requests per month.

Other aspects of this promotional program included press releases for radio and a short TV video. The agency hoped the radio releases would be aired in the late morning or early afternoon on women's shows. The television video, produced at a cost of $48 000 and entitled "Everything You Wanted to Know About Rutabagas—But Didn't Know Who to Ask" was distributed upon request to cable TV channels for use at their convenience. The agency felt "this scheduling gave the video excellent exposure without requiring the ORC to pay for air time." The film highlighted the growing of rutabagas and their nutritional value, and included attractive recipe ideas. In addition to this, a new video entitled "The Ontario Rutabaga in the Kitchen" was distributed to high school family science teachers.

The TV video, like the magazine ads, included a write-in address for recipes, but response here was not as high as for the magazines. Mr. Cruikshank explained, "This doesn't indicate less interest, but rather that TV viewers are less likely to copy an address down and mail for more information than those who see advertisements in a magazine or newspaper." Mr. Cruikshank further reported that "by use, the video appears successful. All ten prints are booked well in advance." He encouraged the ORC to increase the number of video copies and increase the number of high school videos available. Council member Fred Hunsberger supported this idea, especially increasing the number of high school videos available. He felt that "we have to let those kids know what a good value tur—*rutabagas* are. If we get them early on, we've got them for life."

CURRENT SITUATION

ORC President, Clyde Carson, was not as excited about Cruikshank's suggestion as was Fred. He had recently seen a publication entitled "Report on the New England Market for Canadian Rutabagas" which documented a decline in rutabaga consumption in that area. Further research revealed that per capita, rutabaga consumption had been declining for the past 20 years, and growers were reducing their acreage or leaving the industry altogether. Clyde presented these depressing statistics to the ORC and suggested a new "marketing strategy" like that discussed at a seminar he had recently attended. As expected,

Clyde ran into heavy opposition from other council members who did not understand what a marketing strategy was and who were more interested in increasing their production levels. Fred Hunsberger had been particularly adamant about keeping their current promotional program:

> Clyde, we're already telling 'em about all the vitamins and offering free recipes. Now what woman wouldn't jump at a free recipe? And that June Conway is a mighty fine woman! The way she talks about those rutabagas just makes my mouth water. And the kids are sure to like the video. I sure would have been pleased to see videos when I was in school! That TV cable film is doing the job too. Booked solid all last year. It looks real classy to have our own TV film. Just a fluke that consumption is down. People don't know when they're well off these days. You wait! The old values will come back soon and people will see that turnips—uh—rutabagas are good solid food!

Clyde persevered and finally got the council to agree to a large-scale study of the North American rutabaga market. The project was funded mainly by the Ontario Ministry of Agriculture and involved two stages. The first stage was to obtain rutabaga awareness and usage information from 2000 Canadian and 6000 U.S. households. More detailed information was obtained in the second stage on usage, attitudes, and preferences from 300 households in Canada and 800 in the United States. Based on the report, Clyde was able to convince the ORC that a drastic overhaul was needed. The first thing they did was to find a replacement for J.B. Cruikshank Ltd., the ad agency responsible for "Everything You Always Wanted to Know About...." Fred Hunsberger had insisted that Smithfield Communications be hired as a replacement because "That's a classy outfit! I knew old Sim when he was with Massey and I'll never forget his big 'Keep Pace with Case' campaign. That's what we need. A catchy slogan! It will turn the tide in a few weeks. Look at the milk people. My grandkids won't stop singing 'Drink Milk, Love Life.' Drives me crazy but they say it sells the milk. Why not tur—*rutabagas* too? Of course, we'll keep June Conway."

Clyde didn't argue with Fred, though he privately felt that perhaps Smithfield Communications was not the best choice and questioned the usefulness of a slogan. Fred, on the other hand, thought that Smithfield Communications' familiarity with agriculture would be an asset. The two men planned a meeting with Ted Banner, the Smithfield Communications manager assigned to the ORC account.

RESEARCH PROJECT RESULTS

Ted Banner sat at his desk in the office of Smithfield Communications. In front of him were various documents and folders containing background and past promotional programs of the ORC. On top of the pile was a manuscript entitled "Consumer Analysis of the North American Rutabaga Market," the report that presented the results of the large-scale survey done in 2003. Ted knew that this report had to form the basis of his recommendations to the ORC. In preparation for his initial meeting with Clyde Carson and Fred Hunsberger, Ted looked through the report and summarized the main points.

Common Product Names

The report revealed that the product is called by many different names including rutabaga, swede, swede turnip, and turnip. In the United States, 78 percent of consumers referred to the product as a rutabaga compared to only 20 percent in Canada.

Awareness and Frequency of Use

Consumers were placed in one of six categories depending on their awareness and frequency of rutabaga use. These results are shown in Exhibit 1.

The first category is relatively small and contains people who are not aware of rutabagas. The second category contains people who are aware of rutabagas but never purchased one. This group is relatively small in Canada but large in the United States. The third group contains people who have not purchased a rutabaga in the last 12 months. These are probably "lapsed users" who have discontinued use of the product. This is a relatively small group.

EXHIBIT 1	Rutabaga Market Segments, United States and Canada	
Market Segments	Percent of Canadian Households	Percent of U.S. Households
Non-user, not aware	11	14
Non-user, aware	16	40
Lapsed user (not used in past year)	8	14
Light user (less than 4 times a year)	23	19
Medium user (5 to 12 times a year)	25	9
Heavy user (more than 12 times a year)	16	3

The last three groups are classified as current rutabaga users and account for 64 percent of Canadian consumers and 31 percent of U.S. consumers. The heavy user segment accounts for 16 percent of Canadian consumers but only 3 percent of U.S. consumers.

User and Non-User Profiles

Analysis of the above groups in terms of demographic characteristics revealed some distinct profiles. In Canada, rutabaga usage tends to be highest among older consumers, consumers who live in rural areas and small communities, French-speaking Canadians, families whose female head is either a homemaker or retired, and families whose male and female head have less education. U.S. results are very similar, with rutabaga usage being highest among older consumers, lower income families, families whose male and female heads have less education, single person households, and African-Americans.

Vegetable Purchase Criteria

Consumers in the study were asked to rank six possible purchase criteria. The highest ranking criteria were quality, nutritional value, and taste preference. Price and time needed to prepare the vegetable were of some but lesser importance. Rutabaga users consistently ranked price higher than taste preference. Non-users ranked taste preference ahead of price.

Consumers in both countries responded to a series of statements designed to measure attitudes toward a number of issues related to vegetable and rutabaga usage. The following attitudes emerged:

- Consumers feel they are eating about the right quantity and variety of vegetables, but a sizeable group think they should eat more and a greater variety. This is particularly true for the non-user segment.

- Rutabagas are not considered expensive in relation to other vegetables, but consumers stated that large price increases could cause some reduction in consumption.

- A large percentage of consumers increased their purchases of rutabagas when on special. Most consumers felt that rutabagas were seldom "featured" items at their stores.

- Most consumers felt that rutabagas are not conveniently located, nor attractively displayed, and frequently not available at their stores.

- A large percentage of consumers felt that rutabagas are generally too large for the size of their families. They indicated an interest in pre-sliced, ready-to-cook rutabagas or, especially in the United States, ready-to-serve rutabaga casseroles.

- Most consumers judge product quality by external appearance and many felt that the rough, black, or brown spots on the exterior of the rutabaga indicated inferior quality.

- Many consumers commented on the difficulty of preparing a rutabaga.

- Most consumers have little information on the nutritional value of rutabagas and would like more.

Reasons for Non- and Lapsed Users

Both non-users and lapsed users listed not liking the taste as the main reason for non-use. The second most frequent reply given by non-users was that they didn't know how to cook or prepare them. Lapsed users listed several secondary reasons: too much trouble to prepare, too hard to cut, poor quality, and prefer more nutritious vegetables.

Purchase and Use

Rutabaga users were asked about their purchase and use of the product. Their responses indicated the following:

- Approximately one-half of all users decide to purchase the product after entering a store.

- Almost all purchases are made in supermarkets.

- The most popular methods of preparation are boiled and mashed.

- Less than 30 percent of all users serve the vegetable raw.

- The vegetables consumers consider close substitutes for rutabagas are carrots and squash.

- Most consumers consider the rutabaga as an ordinary everyday dish.

- Over 80 percent of all current users indicated that they were using rutabagas just as often or more often than five years ago.

- Most consumers obtain recipe ideas from magazines and newspapers.

TED'S REACTION

After thoroughly studying the background information and the research report, Ted knew that the problem he faced was far more complex than he imagined. His telephone conversations with Clyde Carson indicated that Carson was aware of the severity and complexity of the problem, but Carson hinted that other council members expected a "magic cure-all" along the lines of the famous "Keep Pace with Case" campaign of a few years ago. Ted knew he would need to call on all his tact as well as his past marketing background in order to come up with a promotional campaign for the ORC. His first task, however, would be to develop a set of marketing strategy recommendations based on the research report he had just read.

Marketing-in-Focus, Inc.

H.F. (Herb) MacKenzie

In the fall term of 2002, Donna Mason was considering what she would like to do after completing her undergraduate business degree. She was in the last academic year of study at an eastern Canadian business school. She was at one time considering going into the family furniture business with her two older brothers, but the closer she came to graduation, the less attractive this option seemed. She had applied to several consumer goods companies for a marketing position, and she was confident that at least one would result in a job opportunity. However, Donna's first choice was to open her own small consulting firm, Marketing-in-Focus, Inc.

Donna first started to think seriously about consulting after talking to one of her marketing professors. He told her that there was a dramatic increase in demand for marketing consulting in recent years. Donna decided to do some investigating on her own, and she found an article in *Consultation* titled "The Management Consulting Profession: An Empirical Description" by Terry L. Maris. The article stated that a higher percentage of consultants serviced the manufacturing sector than any other sector.

As she continued her search, Donna found that there was little published information that would help her decide where opportunities might exist, although she found a lot of information in trade magazines related to consulting. Specifically, Donna wanted to know who in companies made the decision to hire a consultant, what types of consulting were most commonly needed, what criteria were used to decide which consulting firms were selected, and most importantly, whether companies preferred to use large consulting firms or if they would consider using small independent consulting firms such as the one she wished to start. Donna decided to conduct her own marketing research.

MARKETING RESEARCH STUDY AND RESULTS

Donna decided that she would focus specifically on manufacturing firms with 20 or more employees, located in principal cities within a two-hour drive from where she hoped to operate her business. Following a search of *Scott's Directories* for that region, she was able to identify 681 firms. She randomly chose 100 of these firms for her research sample. Donna divided the sample into four equal groups, and convinced three of her friends to each conduct 25 telephone surveys for her. She did the first 25 surveys herself to ensure that there were no problems with the questionnaire. Among the 100 companies chosen for the study, 7 had gone out of business or had disconnected telephones and could not be located by company name, 6 were abandoned by interviewers after a minimum of three callbacks, and 5 refused to cooperate.

Among the 82 firms that cooperated, only 30 used management consultants (36.6%). The average number of employees among these firms was 274; those firms that did not use consultants averaged only 67 employees. There was one firm included in the sample that employed 2300 people, and another that employed 1100 people. All other respondent firms had less than 1000 employees. If the two largest firms were dropped from the sample, the average number of employees of companies that employed management consultants was 173.

Exhibit 1 provides the questions Donna asked in her survey, along with a summary of respondent answers.

EXHIBIT 1	Survey Questionnaire and Summary Results

Question 1

Has your firm used the services of an external consultant or consulting firm within the past three years?

Yes	30	(Go to Question 2)
No	52	(Go to Question 8)

Question 2

Who in your firm decides which external consultant or consulting firm is to be hired?

Title	Responses	Percent
President/CEO	17	(30.4)
Vice-President	8	(14.3)
COO/General Manager	12	(21.4)
Director	3	(5.4)
Controller	3	(5.4)
Manager	11	(19.6)
Owner	2	(3.6)

EXHIBIT 1	Survey Questionnaire and Summary Results (continued)

Question 3

For what reasons has your firm hired an external consultant or consulting firm within the past three years?

Purpose for Hiring	Responses	Percent
Human resources	16	(33.3)
Operations issues	11	(22.9)
Computers	5	(10.4)
Technical issues	4	(8.3)
General management	4	(8.3)
Strategic planning	4	(8.3)
Marketing / sales management	2	(4.2)
Reorganization	2	(4.2)

Question 4

Please indicate the importance of choice criteria by circling your response to each question.

	Not Very Important				Very Important
When your firm chooses an external consultant or consulting firm, how important is their experience in your choice?	1	2	3	4	5
When your firm chooses an external consultant or consulting firm, how important is their past performance in your choice?	1	2	3	4	5
When your firm chooses an external consultant or consulting firm, how important is the reputation of the individual who will be managing the project in your choice?	1	2	3	4	5
When your firm chooses an external consultant or consulting firm, how important is the reputation of the firm in your choice?	1	2	3	4	5
When your firm chooses an external consultant or consulting firm, how important is it that the individual be recommended to you in your choice?	1	2	3	4	5
When your firm chooses an external consultant or consulting firm, how important is it that the firm be recommended to you in your choice?	1	2	3	4	5
When your firm chooses an external consultant or consulting firm, how important is price or fees in your choice?	1	2	3	4	5
When your firm chooses an external consultant or consulting firm, how important is the size of the firm in your choice?	1	2	3	4	5

EXHIBIT 1	Survey Questionnaire and Summary Results (continued)

Criteria	Mean Response
Experience	4.57[a]
Past performance	4.40
Reputation of individual	4.40[b]
Reputation of firm	4.00[b]
Individual recommended	3 .57
Firm recommended	3.50
Prices/fees	3.47[b]
Size of firm	2.00

a. Significantly different from the next-highest mean, p <.10.
b. Significantly different from the next-highest mean, p <.05.

Question 5

Are there any other criteria that your firm uses when choosing an external consultant or consulting firm? If *yes*, what are they?

Criterion	Responses
Personality fit	4
Appropriate expertise	3
Fit with organization culture	2
Availability / flexibility of hours	1
Presentation	1
Diagnostic ability	1
Government subsidization	1

Question 6

Consider the last external consultant or consulting firm your company hired. Did your company choose a small, independent consultant or one of the large management consulting firms such as Ernst & Young or PricewaterhouseCoopers? *Also:* If your company considered a second alternative, how would you describe that second alternative?

	Only Alternative	Second Alternative
Small, independent firm	9	7
Larger management consulting firm	6	8

EXHIBIT 1	Survey Questionnaire and Summary Results (continued)

Question 7

Consider the last external consultant or consulting firm your company hired. What criteria did you use to evaluate their performance?

Criterion	Responses
Accepted by client people	8
Experience with consultant	5
Practical recommendations	4
Results on time	4
Maintained good relationship	4
Met objectives	3
Ability of client to carry on	2
Flexible schedule of consultant	2
Ethics of consultant	1
Involvement of consultant	1
Organized approach to project	1
Walked client through process	1
Cost control	1

Question 8

Can you tell me why your firm has not used an external consultant or consulting firm within the past three years?

Reasons	Responses	Percent
We had no requirement	17	(37.0)
We have in-house expertise	9	(19.6)
Head office decision	9	(19.6)
We are too small	8	(17.4)
They are too expensive	3	(6.5)

African Market Square Inc.

Donna Stapleton and Dr. Zainab Jerrett

Zainab Jerrett sat at her kitchen table in her home on University Avenue, St. John's, Newfoundland and Labrador, Canada. She stared in shock at the letter dated January 10, 2005 that she just received from a business consultant with Metro Business Opportunities (MBO). In July 2004, Zainab submitted the first draft of her business plan for African Market Square Inc. to MBO for approval of the Self-Employment Benefit Program. The plan was approved and she received 10 weeks of support under the program to finalize her business plan for submission and approval of an additional 42 weeks of support. With the help of a business consultant, Zainab finalized her business plan and on Tuesday, October 2, 2004, submitted it to MBO management for approval and recommendation that she receive the remaining 42 weeks of support. On the same day, she also submitted a copy of her business plan to Business Development Bank of Canada (BDBC) to get approval for a small business loan. In early November 2004, MBO management submitted the plan to Human Resources and Skills Development Canada (HRSDC) for final approval. BDBC evaluated the business plan and approved the business loan subject to MBO/HRSDC awarding the 42 weeks of Self-Employment benefits. Zainab had been patiently waiting since

November to get the final word that everything was fine and to start to receive the needed money.

Zainab could not believe what she had just read; she was turned down to receive the additional 42 weeks of support as MBO believed that there was little market for her products. She was also unable to receive the business loan from BDBC because they felt she would not have adequate income to meet the loan payments without the 42 weeks of income support. Zainab wondered why it had taken this long for someone to say that her business was not viable or competitive. As she sat there, many questions raced through her head. What could she say or do to get the financial support to run her business and pay for the inventory that was arriving on a daily basis from many African countries? Was management at MBO correct that her business did not have adequate market potential to survive and grow? Zainab was convinced that there was adequate market for her products. How could she convince officials at MBO that she knew her market and had completed an adequate market assessment?

THE BUSINESS DESCRIPTION

Zainab Jerrett owned and operated African Market Square Inc. which she started on November 27, 2004 as a home-based business that bought a variety of products directly from producers in Africa and sold them primarily to consumers in Canada and the United States via the Internet and through face-to-face sales. The focus of the business was to sell African products to individual consumers and to other businesses and retailers for resale. The company hoped to capitalize on the increase in online shopping by North American consumers by selling the African products via the Internet. In addition to the website, www.africanmarketsquare.ca, Zainab also displayed products at trade shows, during related presentations, and to potential buyers through personal visits or personal contacts. The company also had an online catalogue on its website, as well as copies of its printed catalogue which not only displayed pictures of the African products in the company's inventory, but also provided a description of each product; when, how, and where it was made; who made it; and the traditional and modern ways of using it.

The products sold by the company were produced by hand. Thus, although the products were carefully handcrafted and were good quality, many were not mass-produced. When handmade products were reproduced, they tended to vary slightly. Many African producers still lacked the financial resources to establish businesses that enabled them to produce their products on a large scale.

African Market Square Inc. products were imported from Africa to North America, resulting in high shipping costs that increased the retail prices. Unfortunately, often the shipping costs were priced from Africa to Montreal, Quebec, or Halifax, Nova Scotia, in Canada and Zainab then had to arrange additional shipping from these Canadian locations to St. John's, Newfoundland and Labrador at an extra cost. To reduce shipping costs for its imports, African Market Square Inc. shipped product samples from Africa to North America by sea, and by air using registered post, ordinary post, and courier services. Zainab also searched for shipping agencies that provided efficient but relatively low shipping costs for importers.

The company provided access to international markets for many local producers in Africa. Zainab knew that many financial institutions and countries in Africa provided financial assistance to producers or small-scale businesses if those producers had access to international markets. Eventually, Zainab hoped that purchases made by her company would enable African small-scale producers to establish their own factories and manufacture their products in large scale.

THE ENTREPRENEUR - ZAINAB JERRETT

Zainab grew up in Africa but was now married to a Canadian and living in St. John's. Not only did she grow up in Africa, she was also considered a specialist in African folklore, economy, and development. For six years (1986-1992), Zainab was involved in teaching and conducting research in African culture, economy, and development at the University of Maiduguri, Nigeria, and in 1998 she completed a Ph.D. in Folklore at Memorial University of Newfoundland, in Canada. Her doctoral study and research led her to conduct academic studies and field research in African folklore, including African music, folk arts and folk crafts, food, clothing, jewellery, hair care and body care products, and African customs. As a result, Zainab had diverse knowledge of African societies, African products, and Africans' ways of life. She used her knowledge of Africa and African culture to identify and buy quality African products directly from producers in Africa. During Zainab's doctoral study and research she combined her studies in African culture with studies in North American culture by being actively involved in studying and conducting library and field research in North American folklore. Living in North America since 1992 and studying North American folklore had furnished Zainab with an in-depth knowledge and understanding of Canadian and American culture, trends, and values. Furthermore, Zainab had university-level teaching experience in both Africa and Canada.

Zainab's formal education in Canada also included a Post-Graduate Diploma in Information Technology, which she obtained at Memorial University of Newfoundland in 2000. From the IT program, Zainab learned how to design, create, and manage professional and business websites. For her IT-term course projects, Zainab designed, created, and set up two websites for retail stores. She also acquired hands-on knowledge and experience in ecommerce, technical support, project planning, computer programming, publishing and document management, and in creating business databases and multimedia presentations. The IT study and work-term experiences provided Zainab with knowledge and skills in ecommerce, web designing, desktop publishing, business planning, and small business operations, which she applied in her business.

Zainab also had some valuable and unforgettable work experience in Africa that prepared her to operate her own business. Throughout her teenage years and her early twenties, Zainab combined schooling and trading in order to earn some money for herself and her mother. She used to prepare snack foods to sell at local markets in Nigeria and she worked for her mother in her retail business, selling goods at home and in local markets.

MARKETING RESEARCH

The planning and background research on the viability of her business started in 1994. Since that time, production and market research had been conducted on the demographic, economic, cultural, and social relevance, and viability of this business. The production surveys and ethnographic research were conducted among the producers in Africa to find out the types of products they produced that can be marketed in North America, and at the same time provide them with income revenue. As well, consumer and market surveys were conducted in Canada and the United States to find out the kinds of African products that are high in demand in North America, and if there was enough demand to support such a venture.

Research in African Products

The primary research Zainab conducted in Africa relevant to her proposed business was ethnographic studies of various aspects of African folklore or culture. The ethnographic studies involved observations and interviews. This research was completed in the 1980s and 1990s as part of her Masters and Doctoral studies. Zainab conducted interviews with individuals and groups who were either makers of African music, arts and crafts, clothing, and jewellery, or were producers of African foods, including spices. She also conducted research at libraries, museums, and archives in Africa where she obtained relevant information on African culture. This primary and secondary research in African folklore provided her with in-depth knowledge and understanding of the types of products produced in Africa that can be marketed in North America.

Research on the Potential Market for African Market Square Inc.'s Proposed Products

For her primary research on the potential market for her proposed business, Zainab designed and created a Consumer Survey questionnaire in June 2004. (See Exhibit 1 for a copy of the questionnaire.) The survey questionnaires were distributed in Ontario and in Newfoundland and Labrador, from June 2004 to September 2004. Zainab gave 60 copies of the survey to a professor at Memorial University of Newfoundland, and the professor administered the surveys to her students. The professor's class comprised students from Newfoundland and Labrador, other provinces in Canada, China, Africa, and the United States. Zainab and her research assistant also administered the surveys to several people, including Newfoundlanders, Asians, Americans, and Africans living in St. John's.

EXHIBIT 1	CONSUMER SURVEY QUESTIONNAIRE

Selling African Products in Canada and the US: A Market Survey of Consumers' Experiences and Opinions

A Canadian Business is planning to sell unique African products in Canada and the U.S. Your opinion matters a great deal to the company. Please tell us what you think by filling out this questionnaire. The products which the company plans to sell include: unique Western-inspired African clothing, organic spices, 100% natural body care and hair care products, unique African jewelleries, essential oil, African arts and crafts, contemporary African music on CD and Video, contemporary African movies on DVD and video, and African educational books.

   Your opinions, comments, and suggestions will be used to help the company make an informed decision in its effort to provide a variety of rare and unique products made in Africa to consumers in North America.

   All information will be treated as confidential.

EXHIBIT 1	CONSUMER SURVEY QUESTIONNAIRE (continued)

QUESTIONNAIRE

1. Gender: Male ☐ Female ☐
2. Age: under 18 ☐, 18-24 ☐, 25-34 ☐, 35-49 ☐, 50-64 ☐, 65 or older ☐
3. Ethnic or racial identification (optional): Black ☐, White ☐, Chicano or Hispanic ☐, Member of the First Nations ☐, Asian or Pacific Islander ☐, Middle Eastern ☐
4. How many times did you buy African products at retail stores in North America?
   Never ☐, once ☐, a few times ☐, many times ☐
5. If you have bought African products at store(s) in North America, which store(s)? Please check all that apply:
   Sears ☐, COSTCO ☐, Wal-Mart ☐, Zellers ☐, Future Shop ☐, Other ☐
6. If you have never bought African products in North America, is it because African products are not readily available in stores in North America?
   Yes ☐, No ☐
7. Would you recommend that African products be sold to consumers in North America?
   Yes ☐ No ☐
8. If you recommend that African products be sold to consumers in North America, which of the following varieties of African product would you be interested in buying? Please check all that apply:
   African arts and crafts ☐, clothing ☐, jewellery ☐, music on CD, Video and cassette ☐, movies on DVD and Video ☐, educational books ☐, organic spices ☐, natural body care and hair care products ☐, essential oil ☐
9. Which methods of selling African products in North America will you prefer? Please check all that apply:
   In retail stores ☐, online ☐, mail order ☐
10. Do you have any specific African countries in mind that you would like to see their products sold in North American markets?
    Yes ☐ No ☐
11. If your answer to question number 10 is yes, please list the names of those African countries.

    _____

    _____

12. If you would like to make further comments or suggestions on the plan to sell African products in North America please do so: _____

    _____

Thank you for your time and effort.

As well, Zainab's friend took dozens of surveys with her to Toronto and administered them to Africans and non-Africans living in Toronto. As of September 30, 2004, 220 people had filled out the survey questionnaires.

Zainab also conducted interviews (in person and by phone) with individuals and groups. She carried out informal conversations with individuals and groups whom she met at social occasions. She searched through *Yellow Pages* and made telephone calls to several retail stores in both Canada and the United States to find out if there were any businesses that sold African products at present and if they would be interested in carrying African products in the future. (See Exhibit 2 for a copy of the Retail Survey questionnaire.) She also gathered market and consumer information related to her business through the Internet and she studied relevant books, journals, and magazines.

EXHIBIT 2	RETAIL SURVEY QUESTIONNAIRE

Selling African Products in Canada and the US: A Survey of Retailers in Canada
A Canadian company with direct contact with producers and manufacturers in Africa is seeking to sell or supply unique, authentic and high quality African products to retailers in Canada and the US. The products which the company plans to sell include:

- Western inspired African Clothing.
- Organic Spices.
- Natural body care and Hair Care Products.
- Unique African Jewelleries.
- African Arts and Crafts.
- Essential Oils.
- Contemporary African Music on CD and Video.
- Contemporary African Movies on DVD and Video.
- African Educational Books.
- Other African Products.

Your opinion matters a great deal to the company. Please tell us what you think by filling out this questionnaire. Your opinions, comments and suggestions will be used to help the company make an informed decision in its effort to provide a variety of rare, unique and good quality products made in Africa to consumers in North America.

All information will be treated as confidential.

QUESTIONNAIRE

1. Your Name: _____

_____

2. Company Name and Address: _____

_____

3. Phone Number: _____

4. E-mail Address: _____

P.T.O.

EXHIBIT 2	RETAIL SURVEY QUESTIONNAIRE (continued)

5. Web Site URL/Address: _____

4. Do you sell African Products in Your Store? Yes ☐ No ☐

5a. If your answer to question number 4 is No, would you like to be supplied with African products? Yes ☐ No ☐

5b. If your answer to question number 4 is Yes, do want to be supplied with additional African products? Yes ☐ No ☐

6. If you would like to be supplied with rare, authentic and high quality African products, which of the following categories of African products would you be interested in buying? Please check all that apply:

   Western Inspired African Clothing ☐, Traditional African Clothing ☐, African Arts And crafts ☐, African Jewelleries ☐, Contemporary African Music on CD, Video, and Cassette ☐, Contemporary African Movies on DVD and Video ☐, African Educational Books ☐, Organic Spices ☐, Natural Body Care and Hair Care Products ☐, Essential Oils ☐, Other African Products ☐.

7. If you want to be supplied with African products that are listed in question 6, please list those African products here: _____

   _____

8a. Do you want to sell African products in your store and be paid a commission?

   Yes ☐ No ☐

8b. If your answer is Yes, Please list those African products here (see question 6 for a list of products/items): _____

   _____

9. Do you have any specific African countries in mind that you would like to buy/sell their products? Yes ☐ No ☐.

10. If your answer to question number 9 is Yes, please list the names of those African countries.

   _____

   _____

11. If you would like to make further comments or suggestions on the plan to sell African products in North America please do so: _____

   _____

Thank you for your time and effort.

Zainab believed that her research in African folklore, and her primary and secondary information collected on the North America market, showed that the proposed business fit well into the overall economic, social, and cultural trends. On the producers' side, the research showed more and more Africans were working either as individuals or as co-operatives to produce varieties of quality products that were valuable to North American consumers, but they did not have access to international markets, especially North American markets. The consumer surveys and market research showed that as a result of globalization, growing multiculturalism, risk and cost of travel, demands for African products by Africans in the Diaspora, as well as by other cultural groups in North America, had increased greatly and continued to increase. However, despite their high demand, many African products were still rare finds in North America. The research also revealed that online shopping by North American consumers was a growing trend. This was due to the fact that more people in North America had computers with access to the Internet. Today, people tend to take advantage of the comfort, safety, and convenience of online shopping by ordering products. These were growing opportunities that African Market Square Inc. hoped to tap.

MARKET SEGMENTS

Zainab identified several consumer and business market segments that she believed were customers for the products to be sold by African Market Square Inc. The benefit that African Market Square Inc. provided to these potential market segments was the ability to purchase a variety of rare, unique African products at competitive prices, without having to travel to Africa, something that was currently lacking in the marketplace.

Segment 1: Consumers Interested in Unusual and Unique Products

Based on the results from the consumer surveys, Zainab believed that one major market segment for her business was the high percentage (over 80%) of potential consumers in North America who were interested in unusual, unique, and educational products that were not easily available in North America, particularly African products. A majority of respondents to the surveys and interviews indicated that they were interested in buying a variety of African products if the products were made available to them either in retail stores, online, or through mail order at competitive prices. This segment of potential customers comprised males and females, teenagers, adults, seniors, people from various races and ethnic backgrounds, and from low and high income levels. Many of the individuals in this group were young Canadians and Americans, students and non-students. They considered African products to be unique and different from the products they were used to buying at retail stores in Canada and the United States. Some of the potential customers in this segment were educated adults who had either travelled to Africa on vacation, had worked in Africa, or had African students as their friends and classmates when they were in school. They have, in some ways, come in contact with Africans and African culture and were, therefore, interested in buying things from Africa. Also in this category of potential customers were those Canadians and Americans who were interested in buying African products mainly because of their quality, value, and affordable price. They wanted to buy African products for themselves and as gifts to others. Zainab anticipated consumers interested in unique and unusual products would be the largest segment of African Market Square Inc. customers.

Segment 2: Africans Living in North America

A great number of potential customers from Zainab's surveys and experience were Africans living in North America. As a result of civil wars in a number of African countries and economic hardships in Africa, there was an unprecedented influx of African immigrants into Canada and the United States, especially since the 1990s. According to the 2001 Canada census figures, the total population of immigrants from Africa in Canada was 282 600. Many of the immigrants came to North America either to escape from civil wars in their countries or to search for better opportunities for themselves and their families. Most of these refugees and asylum seekers were educated people, but they came to North America with nothing other than the clothes they were wearing. They left everything they had: African clothing, food items, arts and crafts, educational books, and music. While living in Canada or the United States, the refugees cannot travel back to Africa to bring all the things they need, partly because of their refugee status and partly because it would cost them a lot of money to ship things from Africa. From Zainab's consumer surveys of African immigrants living in North America, and from the interviews she has had with some of the immigrants, most of them said they were interested in buying African products, but they have never bought any African products in North America because of availability.

Some of the potential customers in this category were African students studying in Canadian and American universities and colleges. The 2001 Canada census revealed that the population of non-permanent residents from Africa was 22 085. Since 2001, the population of non-permanent residents from Africa in Canada and the United States has increased because there are more youths from Africa now studying in universities and colleges in Canada and the United States, especially those whose education was disrupted in their homeland as a result of either political instabilities or civil wars. Many were now living in either Canada or the United States with their parents or relatives. The African students that Zainab either interviewed or surveyed said they felt homesick or nostalgic. They wanted to eat the foods that they were used to in Africa (at least occasionally), to listen to African music, wear African clothing, and have African arts and crafts to give as gifts to their Canadian and American friends. But there were very few retail stores in Canada and the United States where they could buy these African products. And if the students tried to import these African products on their own, the cost of importing them would be very high, even if they imported in small quantities. Furthermore, it would take weeks for the imported products to arrive in Canada and get cleared through Canada Customs. Also, the products were sent back to the originating countries by Canadian and American customs if they were imported without all the supporting documentation. When an African student was going to his/her homeland for holidays (which rarely happened), he/she received a lot of phone calls and email messages from other African students studying in Canada and the United States, asking him/her to bring them something from Africa (foodstuffs, clothing, and music, for example). Quite often, an African student travelling to Africa for holidays declined requests to bring African products because he/she did not want to be held up by Customs and Immigration officials at the airports of departure and entry.

Segment 3: Canadians and Americans of African Descent

African-Canadians and African-Americans who were not African immigrants but had their ancestral roots in Africa were potential customers for African Market Square Inc. Until the early 1990s, a number of Canadians and Americans of African descent used to go to Africa either to work or to visit as tourists. They bought African products and brought them back home as souvenirs and keepsakes to remind themselves of their African heritage. However, as a result of civil wars and other social problems in Africa, relatively few African-Canadians and African-Americans currently went to Africa either to work or for vacations. They were, however, still proud of their ancestral roots and wanted to buy African products if made available to them in North America.

Segment 4: Retailers Who Sell Specialty Gift and Craft Items

Retailers in Canada and the United States who sell items that were considered to be either exotic or unique were identified as potential customers of the business. These included retailers who sell items that were in demand by individuals or groups from particular cultural or social backgrounds. African Market Square Inc. was a potential supplier of African products to these specialty gift and craft retail stores. Also, major retail stores such as Costco, Wal-Mart, and Zellers were potential customers as these major retail stores bought gift and craft products in large quantities.

COMMUNITY PROFILE

African Market Square Inc.'s primary area of operation was to be St. John's. The company would sell African products to consumers in St. John's and other places in Newfoundland and Labrador using various marketing strategies, such as participating in trade shows, advertising its products through local electronic and print media, and through word of mouth. Also, African Market Square Inc. would supply African products to specialty gift and craft stores and retail stores in St. John's and other areas in the province.

As of April 1, 2004, the population of Newfoundland and Labrador was 518 955. In 2001, total population of blacks in Canada was 662 215. Out of this number, 845 blacks were living in Newfoundland and Labrador. The number of blacks living in Canada in general, and in Newfoundland and Labrador in particular, had increased because most of the individuals and families who fled from their war-torn countries in Africa and came to Canada as refugees settled in Newfoundland and Labrador.

African Market Square Inc. sold African products to consumers in Canada and planned to sell to the United States. Therefore, its trading areas were not limited to St. John's, or to the province of Newfoundland and Labrador. Thus, the secondary trading areas consisted of other provinces in Canada, and the United States. The total population of potential customers in Canada and the United States was huge. In 2001, the total number of immigrants and non-immigrant residents from Africa living in Canada was 304 680 (immigrant population: 282 600; non-permanent residents: 22 085). Canada's population estimates on April 1, 2004, was 31 825 416. The results of consumer surveys conducted by Zainab in Newfoundland and Labrador, and in Ontario, in June and July 2004 were very encouraging. The results showed that 100% of the respondents were interested in buying African products if the products were made available in North America either in retail stores or online. The great demand for African products by those surveyed suggested that among Canada's population of approximately 30 million people, a majority of them might be interested in buying African products occasionally, especially if the products were unique, valuable, met Canadian and international safety, packaging, and labelling standards, and were readily available at an affordable price.

The population of Newfoundland and Labrador had been declining. As well, family income was relatively low, compared to that in other provinces in Canada. According to the 2001 census, the number of families in Newfoundland and Labrador in 1991 was

77 295. But, the number dropped to 70 440 (–8.9%) in 2001. Median family income in Newfoundland and Labrador in 2000 was $59 466. It was second to the lowest in Canada. According to a release from the Labour Force Survey of Friday, July 9, 2004, the employment rate in Newfoundland and Labrador fell 0.3% from May 2004 to June 2004. This caused some concern because a decline in Newfoundland and Labrador population combined with relative low income would cause a decline in customers for African Market Square Inc. However, recently there had been some growth in the Newfoundland and Labrador economy. The growth in the economy would likely provide more jobs to Newfoundlanders and Labradorians, and increase consumers' spending. Also, the growth in Newfoundland and Labrador economy would reduce out-migration and attract new residents.

COMPETITION ANALYSIS

In January 2005, there were no direct competitors in the St. John's area. Specifically, there was not a single business in all of Newfoundland and Labrador that imported African products directly from Africa. Only one store in St. John's had sold African food products in the past, but now it did not (Auntie Crae's Food Shop, a specialty food store). In Canada and the United States there were relatively few stores that sold African products. The specialty stores that sold African products through point-of-sale purchases were usually small corner stores or retail shops that sold multi-ethnic or multicultural products, which included African products. Usually, such stores sold only one or two varieties of African products, and in limited quantity. The stores that sold African products solely online were few in North America. Usually the websites were for a few of the specialty stores that sold their products mainly through point-of-sale purchases.

Competitors' Strengths and Weaknesses

Only a few of the businesses that sold African products had websites. Some of the websites either could not be displayed or the products displayed on the websites had no price listing. Most of the websites were poorly designed and did not contain specific information on the individuals or groups that made the products; the countries, regions, states, and communities where the products were made; and how they were made. This type of information was important to some customers. Most websites did not provide information on the traditional and modern ways of using the products.

Many of the businesses sold their products through point-of-sale displays; that is, in street shops and corner stores. As a result, their businesses were known only to people in their communities, and to a few tourists. Most of the stores that sold African products sold "African-inspired" products that were made in the United States, Canada, India, Asia, or the Caribbean and claimed that the items were African products. Another competitors' weakness was the fact that the businesses sold only a limited quantity of African products along with products from many other countries. As well, their pricing was not competitive; it was either too low or too high. eBay.com, eBay.ca, and Amazon.com were three online businesses with professionally designed websites. However, African products were rarely sold on these websites.

Online African Market Square Inc.'s Competitive Advantage

In contrast to its competitors, African Market Square Inc. sold a variety of unique, authentic, and high-quality African products, not African-inspired products, to consumers anywhere in North America. African Market Square Inc. products were bought directly from the producers in Africa. The company planned to increase the variety of African products sold as the business grew.

African Market Square Inc.'s website enabled customers to easily browse, view items, select what interested them, and safely purchase products. The website also provided information on each product in the company's inventory: what the product is, who made it, where and when it was made, how it was made, as well as the traditional and modern ways of using the product. Customers who were not comfortable with the idea of providing personal information on the Internet had the option to print out the company's mail order form from the company's website, fill it out, and mail it to the company. Also, customers were able to place orders by phone. All African Market Square Inc. customers' orders, whether online, through mail order, by phone, or by fax, were processed expeditiously.

African Market Square Inc. was committed to providing quality African products at favourable prices to consumers, establishing fair trading relationships with the local producers in Africa so as to enhance their economic advancement, and offering excellent service to its customers.

MARKET ESTIMATE

In the first year in operation, African Market Square Inc.'s total sales were projected to be $68 820. This was based on estimated $16 300 total retail sales of African clothing, $20 400 total retail sales of African arts and crafts, $1950 total retail sales of African educational books, $3090 total retail sales of African spices, $2580 total retail sales of African music, and $24 500 total retail sales of miscellaneous African products, including African jewellery, natural essential oils, natural body care products, and hair care products. Based on Zainab's June to August 2004 market surveys, it was estimated that the sales of African products in both Canada and the United States accounted for less than 1% of products that were sold in North America. Zainab believed her business could secure the projected level of sales ($68 820) in the first year of operation based on the size of her identified target markets.

Zainab's secondary research showed that consumers in Canada spent billions of dollars every year on clothing, arts and crafts, spices, educational books, music and jewellery, and other products. A survey report on retailers' total operating revenue in 2002 published on Statistics Canada's website revealed that despite fierce competition and declining prices for some retail goods, retailers in Canada achieved a robust year, with total operating revenue reaching $344 billion, a gain of 6.6% over 2001. Zainab's research also revealed that there was growth in non-store retailing. According to Statistics Canada, in 2001 the total operating revenue for non-store retailers was over $10 billion. Out of that total, the operating revenue for electronic shopping and mail order business was approximately one-third. More consumers in North America purchased items through electronic shopping and mail order shopping in 2001.

Another table provided on the Statistics Canada website contained the Statistics Canada annual report on retail trade, by provinces and territories, from 1999 to 2003. The table showed Newfoundland and Labrador had a relatively high volume of retail trading, compared to four other provinces and territories in Canada, namely Prince Edward Island, Yukon, Northwest Territories, and Nunavut. The province with the highest retail trade was Ontario; the lowest retail trade was in Nunavut.

The financial projections for African Market Square Inc.'s business were based solely on retail sales of items. They did not take into consideration wholesale transactions projected to take place with other retailers. Zainab planned to aggressively target retailers to carry her products, and it was envisioned that this could account for large sales transactions and a large volume of sales. However, only her own estimated retail transactions had been used in the projections to provide a very conservative estimate of sales. If, however, accounts with small local businesses were secured, the actual sales volume would be increased.

To get a feel for how realistic her sales projections were, Zainab thought it would be useful to consider how many transactions she would need to attain to reach her sales target. To estimate the number of transactions, she assumed that the average customer would make a $20 purchase with the business. This would translate into 3441 separate transactions over the first year of operation and equated to an average of 67 transactions a week. Zainab was confident this transaction level was attainable. In fact, Zainab expected that she would achieve more than 67 transactions and that many customers would spend more than the $20 figure. She also believed that, as more people became aware of her business, sales would grow and she conservatively estimated sales for years two and three to be $89 466 and $96 348, respectively.

Zainab believed in her business concept and in her ability to make African Market Square Inc. a success. She just needed the employment support from Human Resources and Skills Development Canada and the small business loan from Business Development Bank of Canada to give her business a financial boost. She wondered what she should say and do now to convince the experts that her business had adequate market potential and could achieve the identified sales targets.

Agro Seeds

Tom Funk

Tom Wilson, marketing manager for Agro Seeds, was faced with the problem of increasing his company's sales and profits in the highly competitive Ontario seed corn market. One option under active consideration was a strategy to increase the company's share of the market for silage corn seed. Although this would be a smaller market than the market for grain corn seed, he felt the silage market offered good potential for his company. He knew, however, that he would have to build a strong case for this course of action to gain top management approval.

BACKGROUND

Farmers can grow corn for two very distinct purposes: grain corn, in which only the ear or grain is harvested, and silage corn, which is harvested by cutting the entire plant. Grain corn is either stored on the farm in bins and subsequently fed to livestock, or sold to local grain elevators. Silage corn, on the other hand, is stored in silos and fed directly to livestock on the farm. Silage corn does not enter commercial markets. In the past, with the exception of lower priced silage blends, seed companies have not sold separate silage varieties; the same varieties are used by farmers for both grain and silage corn.

There is a substantial difference in the number of acres planted to grain versus silage corn in Ontario. At the present time, approximately 2 100 000 acres of corn is harvested as grain corn compared with roughly 500 000 acres harvested for silage. Over the past several years the acreage of grain corn has been increasing at a 2% annual rate, while the acreage of silage corn has been declining at a rate of about 1% each year. It is not known whether this trend will continue. All major seed companies concentrate their research and marketing efforts on grain corn because of the larger size of this market.

Two types of dealers distribute seed corn to customers: store dealers and farmer dealers. Store dealers are farm supply outlets that sell crop supplies such as fertilizer and agricultural chemicals. Many of these retailers like to have a complete line of crop supplies so they also carry seeds from one or two seed companies. Farmer dealers are farmers who supplement their income by also selling seeds. Agro Seeds has approximately 175 dealers in Ontario. While some are large volume outlets, most are relatively small and serve a limited number of customers. Most Ontario farmers would be no further than ten miles from an Agro Seeds dealer. A company sales force of five people coordinates the selling activities of dealers. Dealers receive a 15% commission on the seed they sell.

The average price of seed corn is $120 per unit and ranges from $80 per unit to $180 per unit. Higher prices are charged for better performing varieties and varieties with special traits like resistance to certain insects and diseases, while lower prices are charged for poorer performing or discontinued varieties. In general, varieties mainly used for silage sell at the low end of the price range, while varieties mainly used for grain sell at various prices within the entire range. Each unit of seed plants approximately three acres. Direct production costs for seed are approximately $45 per unit regardless of whether it is for silage or grain.

The seed corn industry in Ontario is very competitive. There are seven companies competing for a total market estimated to be no larger than $100 million per year. The leading company in the market, Pioneer, is estimated to have over 50% of the market. NK and Dekalb each are estimated to have approximately 15% of the market, while Agro Seeds' share is thought to be about 7%. Management at Agro Seeds estimates that Pioneer will continue to maintain a dominant position in the market in the foreseeable future, and that the market shares of smaller companies will change only as a result of mergers.

SILAGE PRODUCTION

Farmers who are in the beef or dairy business often find it advantageous to raise silage corn for feeding to their livestock. In many cases, they would raise both grain and silage corn on their farms. Generally, they would follow the same management and cultural practices for each crop, including using the same seed varieties. A very common attitude among farmers and seed companies has been that if a variety is good for grain production, it is also good for silage production. As a result, farmers may spend considerable time selecting a grain corn variety, and then use the same variety for their silage corn.

The performance of a grain corn variety is relatively simple to assess. Basically, farmers are concerned with yield, normally measured in bushels or tonnes per acre. After harvesting the crop, a farmer simply measures the amount of grain sold or put into a bin from a certain number of acres to determine yield.

Measuring the performance of silage varieties is not as straightforward. As in the case of grain corn, many farmers estimate yield by observing how full the silo is after harvesting a certain number of acres. Although this gives a measure of volume, it does not measure protein or energy, the two factors important in subsequent feeding. These can only be measured by taking samples of the silage to a laboratory for feed analysis. Relatively few farmers take the time to have this sort of analysis carried out. Instead, they fall back on the rule of thumb stated earlier that a good grain corn variety is also a good silage corn variety.

For many years, the Ontario Corn Committee has operated a variety-testing program in which they scientifically measure corn variety yields and publish the information for farmers to use in making purchase decisions. At the present time, the only measures of performance assessed in this program are related to grain corn production. Several scientists, as well as some farmers, are advocating the incorporation of silage performance measure in this program, but to date this has not been done. The yield information generated through this program is published in a booklet and circulated to most corn growers in Ontario. It is also available on the Ontario Corn Committee's website. This information is widely used by farmers in making variety selection decisions.

SILAGE STRATEGY

Tom Wilson felt that Pioneer's current dominance of the total seed corn market would make it very difficult for Agro Seeds to increase market share if the company continued to concentrate on seed for grain production. He reasoned that it might be much easier to gain share by targeting the silage producer with hybrids having high silage performance attributes, and, therefore, avoiding direct competition with the market leader. Several reasons seemed to support this strategy:

- No market leader existed in the silage market.

- A silage strategy would allow Agro Seeds to differentiate itself from competition.

- Recent field data indicated that some Agro varieties had better silage performance characteristics than competitors' varieties.

- There appeared to be a substantial product use overlap in the sense that many farmers grew both grain and silage corn. As a result, the silage strategy might allow the company to gain new customers initially by selling them silage varieties, and then later, trying to sell them Agro grain varieties. Such a "back door" approach would avoid head-to-head competition with Pioneer, NK, and Dekalb in attempting to get new customers.

The primary measure of silage performance the company decided to use was harvestable energy or TDN (total digestible nutrients). Crop scientists at many universities supported this approach. Their research has proven that grain yield is not the most suitable measure of silage performance because it has been consistently found that the highest yielding varieties often have lower levels of energy.

The research department at Agro Seeds had been developing and testing both their own and competitive silage varieties for some time. Currently, the company has six varieties that produce a significantly higher level of TDN than most competitive varieties tested. Two varieties, in particular, yield over 8000 pounds of TDN per acre compared with the best Pioneer variety that yields only about 7600 pounds of TDN per acre.

Under the so-called "silage strategy," the company would attempt to maintain current sales in the grain corn segment, while directing growth efforts at the silage segment. Implementation of the strategy would require additional resources for promotion, field-testing, and program coordination. Tom estimated that he would need an additional $250 000 per year for promotion and one full-time person to coordinate the strategy at approximately $100 000 per year. Field testing expenses were hard to estimate, but probably would be in the neighbourhood of $250 000.

MARKET RESEARCH

To provide information to help decide whether or not to pursue the silage strategy, Tom commissioned a market research study of silage growers in Ontario. The study involved interviewing a random sample of 400 farmers from all areas of the province. The sample was geographically balanced to ensure that the major silage producing regions were represented in the proper proportion. All interviews were conducted on the telephone.

The basic purpose of the marketing research was to assess the viability of the silage seed strategy. In addition, the research was designed to provide information to further develop the strategy if it was determined to be sound. Specific objectives of the research were to:

- Determine the size of the corn silage seed market in terms of number of buyers and number of acres.
- Determine the decision-making process used by farmers in buying silage seed.
- Determine basic attitudes farmers have about corn silage seed.
- Determine possible segments that exist in the corn silage seed market.

The major findings of the study are shown below:

- Current market shares for grain corn and silage corn seed were estimated to be:

	Grain Corn	Silage Corn
Pioneer	48%	49%
NK	17%	17%
Dekalb	16%	13%
Agro Seeds	7%	6%
All others	12%	15%

- Approximately 70% of the farmers growing silage corn in any year also grow grain corn in the same year.
- The total number of Ontario farmers growing silage corn is 6800. The average farmer who grows silage grows 73 acres per year.
- Farmers tend to make their decision concerning which varieties to plant in the fall and early winter months. Actual orders are placed with seed dealers in the early winter.
- High yield of feed per acre is the most important reason cited by farmers for growing and feeding corn silage. Other reasons given were source of energy and source of protein.

- Most farmers indicated that they planned to grow the same amount of silage corn in the future as at the present time. A small percentage said they planned to grow less silage corn in the future compared to the present time.

- Approximately 35% of all silage growers change seed varieties from one year to the next. Beef producers are more likely to switch than dairy producers. Many farmers who switch varieties stay with products produced by the same company.

- Over 60% of farmers who grow both grain corn and silage reported using the same varieties for both.

- Approximately one-third of all silage growers reported having their silage analyzed for its feeding value. More dairy farmers than beef farmers have this type of analysis done. Almost all farmers who have feed analysis done use the information to balance rations. Only about 5% use the results to aid in silage variety selection.

- The information sources used by farmers in selecting a silage variety, together with the percent of farmers rating each as either useful or very useful, are shown below:

	Percent Rating Source as Useful
Own experience	93%
Other farmers	92%
Seed company information	84%
Ontario Corn Committee trial results	84%
Seed dealer recommendations	82%
Seed company test plots	80%
Farm magazine ads	66%
Radio ads	24%

- The study also generated some interesting results in terms of market segmentation. Based on cluster analysis of the results, four segments emerged. Exhibit 1 shows a detailed profile of the four segments in terms of demographics, buying behaviour, and attitudes.

EXHIBIT 1	Silage Segment Profiles			
	Segment 1	Segment 2	Segment 3	Segment 4
Average age	Youngest	Middle Age	Oldest	Middle Age
Farm size	Larger than average	Average	Smaller than average	Smaller than average
Silage acres	Larger than average	Slightly less than average	Average	Slightly less than average
Grain acres	Larger than average	Average	Smaller than average	Smaller than average
Size of dairy operation	Above average	Average	Smaller than average	Smaller than average
Size of beef operation	Above average	Average	Average	Smaller than average

EXHIBIT 1	Silage Segment Profiles (continued)			
Buying and Use Behaviour				
Adoption behaviour	Innovators and early adopters	Early adopters and early majority	Late majority and laggards	Early and late majority
Brand loyalty	Lowest level	Low level	Highest level	Average level
Timing of purchase	Latest	Early	Earliest	Early
Main source of information	Ontario Corn Committee Report	Ontario Corn Committee Report	Ontario Corn Committee Report	Seed dealers
Measure of performance currently used to evaluate silage varieties	Performance indicators such as TDN and protein levels determined from feed analysis	Visual estimates of volume	Most don't evaluate the performance of silage varieties	Most don't evaluate the performance of silage varieties
Attitudes (measured on a scale of 1 to 10 where 1 = strongly disagree and 10 = strongly agree)				
Different varieties have different levels of protein	9.2	8.8	5.1	4.2
There is quite a bit of difference among varieties in the energy they produce	9.1	8.8	5.3	4.8
If there were more silage testing, I would use it to choose my silage variety	7.8	9.3	4.2	4.0
Presently no seed company has reliable silage performance information	6.0	5.8	6.1	5.5
The energy of corn silage comes mainly from the grain	6.6	6.3	9.1	5.3
The best grain variety makes the best silage variety	6.7	6.8	9.5	5.6
When I plant my corn I know which fields will be harvested for silage	9.4	7.7	4.3	9.5

EXHIBIT 1	Silage Segment Profiles (continued)			
A tall corn variety usually makes the best silage variety	4.7	5.6	6.1	6.7
Total tonnes per acre is the only reliable method to evaluate silage varieties	4.2	5.4	6.8	6.9
Most lower-priced varieties perform about as well as silage as higher-priced varieties	4.2	4.8	5.8	9.3
I think I could do a better job evaluating my silage corn	8.3	9.3	5.4	4.5
I would use performance information on silage varieties if it were available	9.0	9.1	4.8	4.4
Segment Size				
Percent of all silage growers	10%	45%	20%	25%
Average silage acres	92	78	72	62
Agro Seeds' share of silage seed	6%	6%	4%	14%

Milton Quality Inn

Joe Barth and Nashrin Bhimji

It was September 2002 and Shamim was deep in thought as she looked out the window of the Quality Inn as the steady stream of traffic on Canada's busiest highway, the 401, passed by. Milton had changed dramatically in the past eight years. The population of the town had almost doubled due to the new housing developments. Competition was intensifying. When Shamim had first purchased the hotel, the closest competitive hotel was 20 kilometres away. Today, there were 6 hotels within a 20-kilometre radius. Shamim realized that she desperately needed a strategic plan that would build on the property's success and sustain her competitive advantage within the town of Milton.

BACKGROUND

Shamim had purchased the property in 1994 after a trust company had foreclosed on the mortgage. The property in Milton, Ontario, is visible and easily accessible from Highway 401, in the heart of "Escarpment Country." The hotel was approximately 30 kilometres west of the Toronto Pearson International Airport and within close proximity to skiing, world-class golfing, Rattlesnake Point, and other major tourist attractions and recreational activities.

Shamim had bought the property with the intention of turning it around, and had realized that it would be both an operational and financial challenge to do so. The property had been neglected for years. The rooms needed to be refurbished and redecorated. The mattresses were approximately 14 years old, and the case goods (furniture) were over 10 years old. The carpet, wallpaper, bedspreads, and drapes all needed to be replaced.

Shamim knew that it was imperative that she become affiliated with a nationally recognized chain and, after much research, she decided on Choice Hotels Inc. Choice Hotels would be able to provide the establishment with access to an international central reservation system. It would also increase the property's exposure through international marketing campaigns, and increase national exposure through print and TV ads as well as corporate sponsorships. Choice Hotels would also provide support with respect to the implementation of effective local marketing strategies. Shamim had to decide on which brand within the Choice Hotels chain would be the best fit. She was torn between the Quality Inn and the Econo Lodge brand. She decided to be associated with the Quality Inn as that brand targeted corporate clientele in the middle market. Econo Lodge, on the other hand, targeted low- to mid-market destination travellers.

She shook her head and smiled just thinking about how much she had accomplished; however, it was not enough. She had decided on branding the hotel as a Quality Inn, but more improvements were required. These included major renovations and guestroom refurbishing since the hotel did not meet all of the quality and capital standards required by the franchising company.

Money had been in very short supply at the time. Through hard work, a hands-on management strategy, and the elimination of a number of managerial positions, Shamim took the business from a deficit position and turned it into one with a positive cash flow. She then promptly re-invested into the major renovations required to meet the franchising standards.

The hotel now qualified to become a Quality Inn. The property had been upgraded to an attractive, competitive hotel and the guests were content, for the time being.

LOCATION

Milton was a small town, with a population of approximately 32 000 people. In the past, the town had experienced little, if any, growth due to an inadequate water supply and sewage facility. The surrounding area was quiet and the natural landscapes had been preserved. As mentioned, the hotel was approximately 30 kilometres west of the Toronto Pearson International Airport and within close proximity to skiing, world-class golfing, major tourist attractions, and recreational activities. Milton also boasted a healthy industrial sector with large corporations such as Sobeys, Johnson Controls, Karmax, and various large government offices.

The proximity to a major highway, being a principal destination point between Toronto, Burlington, Oakville, and Kitchener/Waterloo, as well as being easily accessible to companies within the industrial park have proven Milton to be an exceptional location. There were also a number of tourist attractions in the local area, such as Rattlesnake Point, Kelso Ski Resort, and the Renaissance Festival that have contributed to recognizing Milton as a destination point by travel agents and tour operators. Milton was immediately adjacent to the Niagara Escarpment, which was recently designated by the United Nations as a "World Biosphere," and offered hiking, skiing, rock climbing, nature exhibits, and various other outdoor activities at a number of parks and conservation areas. The area was very picturesque and had a number of banquet facilities and museums, as well as craft and antique shops. Mohawk Casino was less than ten minutes away and also provided both tourists and those that were on business a venue to relax and be entertained while in Milton.

Recently, a large water main and increased sewage capacity have spurred a massive growth in Milton that has attracted subdivision developers as well as created a demand for large office space. The town was projected to grow by 50.8% over the next five years, and to double in size in 11 years. Magna International, a manufacturer of parts and components for the auto industry, recently announced plans to construct a 600 000 square foot factory; Parker Hannifin began construction on a new plant across the street from the hotel as well. A new outlet centre would be completed by the year 2005, boasting Home Hardware, Wal-Mart, Silver City theatre, and various outlet stores.

FACILITIES

The hotel was a 74-room facility. The building itself was built in two parts, with the main portion being approximately 25 years old and the addition being 15 years old. The Hotel offered 64 standard rooms and 10 rooms that were classed as "executive suites." At the time, the executive suites had a queen-size bed and a living room area. In reality, this room-type offered little improvement over the standard room. The amenities offered within the hotel included an outdoor pool, restaurant, lounge, and several meeting rooms.

During the first six years, Milton Quality Inn had enjoyed a competition-free market-place within which to operate. However, over the past year, competition had increased substantially with the development of four new hotels within a 20-kilometre radius. Shamin was concerned with the amenities that were offered by these properties. Each hotel had an indoor pool, full-service restaurant, room service, high-speed Internet access, business centre, and fitness centre. Shamim contemplated renovating again in order to position the hotel to meet a changing competitive and market-driven environment.

Milton Quality Inn's competitors included a Holiday Inn Select, Holiday Inn Express, Motel 6, Marriott Residence, and Marriott Courtyard. Holiday Inn Express opened in the summer of 2000 and the Motel 6 opened in June of 2001. The Holiday Inn Select had just opened and The Marriott was to come online in May of 2002. The increase in available rooms had created a negative effect on the Milton Quality Inn's average daily rate, RevPAR (revenue per available room), and occupancy percentages.

With two Holiday Inns and two Marriotts within 15 minutes of Milton Quality Inn, Shamim wondered if she should consider re-branding the hotel to project a stronger corporate image. Recently, the Quality Inn brand had changed its marketing strategy to targeting "the family" more than the corporate traveller. She considered several options but was leaning toward the Ramada Inn brand.

The existing restaurant seated just over 100 people, and at the time it was not leased out and was simply left idle. Shamim had decided that she was great at selling "sleep." She did not have any experience in the restaurant or catering business and felt that leasing out the restaurant would prove to be an advantage in the long run. There were four meeting rooms, the largest of which could hold 98 people. Fax and photocopying services were available through the front desk, and secretarial services were provided when requested. The hotel rented audio-visual presentation equipment from a local rental company upon request and the rental fee was posted directly to the guest's account without an additional service charge.

THE CHOICE INNS' FAMILY OF BRANDS

There were 15 properties under the Choice Hotels umbrella within a 50-kilometre radius of the Milton Quality Inn and this caused concern with respect to the central reservation system. The fact that all of these properties were situated within a relatively small area forced them to compete with each other, and at times against their own brand. For example, when a potential guest called the reservation centre and did not specify a specific establishment but only the destination, the agent provided them with a choice of two properties that were closest to their request under the Choice Hotels umbrella. (Refer to Exhibit 1 for a list of Choice Hotels properties in the area, along with room rates.)

EXHIBIT 1	Choice Hotels' Properties within a 25-mile Radius		
		Rates ($)	
Properties		Low	High
Quality Inn, Milton		79.00	199.00
Quality Inn Airport West, Mississauga		94.00	179.00
Quality Hotel & Executive Suites, Oakville		129.00	195.00
Quality Hotel - Airport, Mississauga		84.00	270.00
Comfort Inn, Brampton		90.00	165.00
Comfort Inn, Burlington		70.00	149.00
Comfort Inn, Cambridge		92.00	137.00
Comfort Inn - Airport West, Mississauga		84.00	179.00
Comfort Inn - Downsview, North York		95.00	149.00
Quality Suites - Airport, Toronto		99.00	210.00
Quality Hotel And Suites - Airport East, Etobicoke		65.00	209.00

Source: *World Wide Hotel Directory 2001,* Canadian Edition.

THE RAMADA INNS

There were seven Ramada properties within a 50-kilometre radius of the Milton Quality Inn. When a guest called the Ramada reservation system, they would only be given the option of the Ramada brand.

MARKET SEGMENT

Milton Quality Inn's customer base comprised 70% business travellers and 30% transient or vacation travellers. The average occupancy rate hovered at 57%.

Due to the fact that the hotel was visible from the highway, Milton Quality Inn also received a large number of "walk-in" guests. Signage along the highway had been recently upgraded and was now in colour. It provided notice for potential customers to exit when travelling west. Eastbound signage on the highway was not adequate due to the Ministry of Transportation signage specifications, and it was imperative that other options be considered. Walk-ins were generally guests that were too tired to keep driving or had to stop due to poor weather conditions, or who came because accommodations in the surrounding area were booked.

The peak season was in the summer months, particularly from May until the beginning of October. The shoulder months ran from the end of October through April. Most customers were frequent guests who visited Milton for business and stayed from Monday through to Thursday. Generally, they were consultants or contract employees doing work in the area (e.g., CP Rail employees). Other guests frequented the hotel while annually attending sporting events or visiting the variety of local tourist attractions, such as the Renaissance Fair or Hot Air Balloon Show.

The central reservation system had also been quite effective with respect to first-time visitors. Guests that were considered to be destination travelers—who came to the area for specific events such as weddings, golf tournaments, sporting events, or other recreational activities—made the majority of these reservations. They generally stayed up to two nights and used the central reservation system toll-free number to make their reservations.

CORPORATE RELATIONSHIPS (BUSINESS STATUS)

Milton Quality Inn had cultivated a number of long-term relationships with local area businesses over the past several years. Corporate clients negotiated special corporate rates, and had set up account features that were tailored to meet their specific requirements, such as preferred room types and lists of designated billable items. Milton Quality Inn had associations with companies such as CP Rail and a number of construction companies. These firms booked standard rooms for extended periods of time in order to lodge work crews who were working in the area. In addition, arrangements were made with companies such as Karmax and Parker Hannifin to accommodate upper management. It, therefore, had been imperative that the hotel offered two tiers of corporate room rates. It could be argued that you could not be all things to all people, however, given the location of the hotel and the nature of the clientele, it had been beneficial to target two different market segments.

The ADR (average daily rate) for fiscal 2002 was $56.36 and the RevPAR was $38.76. This compared unfavourably with the majority of operations within the Choice Hotels chain whose numbers were $81.44 and $52.16, respectively. Milton Quality Inn's total revenue for fiscal 2002 was just over $1 million. Financial details are provided in Exhibit 2.

EXHIBIT 2	Projected Income and Cash Flow Statements		
	Projected		
	2002	2003	2004
Number of Rooms	74	74	95
Days of Operation	365	365	365
Room Nights Available	27 010	27 010	34 675
Occupancy Rate	57%	60%	62%
Room Nights Sold	18 582	19 325	25 313
Average Daily Room Rate	$56	$59	$78
Room Revenue	1 047 000	1 132 832	1 974 414

EXHIBIT 2	Projected Income and Cash Flow Statements (continued)		

	2002	2003	2004
REVENUES			
Room Revenues	$1 047 000	$1 132 832	$1 974 414
Restaurant Revenues	0	0	0
Conference Rooms	32 000	33 280	55 000
Restaurant Lease (1)	0	0	60 000
Telephone	42 442	47 442	63 745
Misc. Revenue	4 000	4 160	5 800
Total Revenues	**1 125 442**	**1 217 714**	**2 158 959**
EXPENSES			
Accounting/Legal	3 000	3 000	10 000
Advertising	7 500	9 000	10 000
Property Business Taxes	76 360	78 000	98 000
Bank & Credit Card Charges	7 000	7 500	9 500
Franchise Royalties (2)	62 000	68 000	156 000
Insurance (3)	7 600	8 000	10 000
Miscellaneous	1 000	1 000	2 000
Mortgage Interest (6ii) (6iii)	98 000	94 000	172 000
Office Expenses	1 300	1 400	2 000
Repairs & Maintenance	10 000	1 000	5 000
Management Fee (4)	48 000	48 000	48 000
Supplies & Linen	48 000	52 000	62 000
Small Bus. Improv. Loan Int. (6i)	24 000	22 000	17 000
Telephone	9 000	11 000	14 121
Utilities	76 000	78 000	98 000
Wages & Benefits (5)	175 000	180 000	260 000
Total Expenses	**653 760**	**661 900**	**973 621**
NET INCOME BEFORE DEPREC.	**471 682**	**555 814**	**1 185 338**
LESS;			
MTG. PRINC. REPAYMENT	106 666	106 666	186 666
SMALL BUS. IMPROVEMENT LOAN PRINC.	60 000	60 000	60 000
CONSTRUCTION COST		550 000	1 650 000
ADD;			
SMALL BUS. IMPROVEMENT LOAN	0	0	0
RENOVATION LOAN (2ND MORTGAGE)	0	600 000	600 000
OWNER'S CONTRIBUTION	0	600 000	600 000
NET CASH FLOW BEFORE TAXES	**305 016**	**1 039 148**	**488 672**

EXHIBIT 2	Projected Income and Cash Flow Statements (continued)

Notes to Exhibit 2.

1. Restaurant lease with franchise commencing Jan. 1995: 1995-1997– $5000 per month.
2. Franchise royalties have been discussed with Ramada Inn, who would be paid $22 000 per year.
3. Insurance rate has been quoted.
4. Ms. Bhimji will be paid $48 000 per year management fee and serve on-site as general manager.
5. Four permanent full-time and three permanent part-time front desk staff
   One permanent full-time and one permanent part-time night auditor
   One permanent part-time maintenance person
   Six permanent full-time and five permanent part-time housekeepers
   One seasonal full-time and one seasonal part-time housekeeper
6. (i) Renovation project cost S.B.L $300 000
   (ii) First mortgage for $1.6 million dollars at prime + 0.75
   (iii) Second mortgage for $1.2 million dollars at prime + 1
7. Owner's contribution $1.2 million dollars at 0 percent.

The ten rooms currently classed as "executive suites" were in high demand and were constantly sold out in the summer months. It was unfortunate that the hotel was not able to capture more of the upscale market that used executive suites.

MANAGEMENT

Shamim oversaw the hotel with a combined staff of approximately 11 people, which included assistant managers and a housekeeping supervisor. She assessed daily sales, occupancy rates, and analyzed labour costs to determine if staff were performing to their expected potential. Employees were formally evaluated every three months due to the high turnover rate within this industry. Monthly sales and expenses were evaluated to determine whether individual departments were reaching their targets.

Comparisons between the budget and actual interim profit and loss statements were made to determine better strategies to improve on these figures. This also pinpointed which departments required revamping or further control.

Shamim strived to keep standard procedures in place and ensured that full-time staff were given the opportunity to advance and travel. This entailed training employees on a new Point-of-Sale Program. For those staff members who did not have any prior computer training, a training manual was put together that familiarized them with the keyboard and basic function keys before learning the hotel program.

Shamim also regularly reviewed the accounts payable and receivable. Maintaining a high standard of quality was very important; therefore, she inspected guestrooms on a rotating schedule to ensure that this standard was met.

As a leader, it was very important for her to be able to motivate others through innovative incentive programs so that they would strive to perform to the best of their ability and be able to achieve their goals.

THE DILEMMA

It was imperative that the hotel offered the necessary amenities and facilities that its competitors already delivered and which its customers came to expect, such as high-speed Internet access. Shamim realized that if customer needs were not met, they would stay elsewhere. She contemplated adding new suites, renovating the lobby, and/or adding a fitness centre. (Exhibit 3 provides information on the "hotel of the future.") Shamim also wondered if she should consider re-branding the hotel to project a stronger corporate image.

EXHIBIT 3	The Hotel of the Future

- Communication centre
- Employee/management relationships will demand a respect for differences
- Rational user of scarce resources
- Compete primarily using the "purpose of visit" formula
- An extremely secure and healthful haven
- Pricing activities will be driven less by inflation and more by broad-based demand/supply conditions reflecting the capacity control environment
- Technology dependent, focusing upon the time, information, and convenience needs of the traveller
- Personal encounters with the guest will be highly customized with high performance expectations
- Less human resource dependent with higher skill level expectations per employee
- The hotel cost structure will be less labour intensive but with a higher cost per unit of input

Shamim realized that she had to move quickly. She arranged meetings with the mayor, the director of development, several individuals that made reservations for their managers, and with the director of the Milton Chamber of Commerce. The purpose of these meetings was to make these key individuals realize that she was determined to provide the business community with what it needed. By openly communicating with them, she would be provided with the information to steer her in the right direction to satisfy their needs. Shamim understood that Milton was a small town and that business was about relationships. She wanted the town to feel involved and be able to provide suggestions. Shamim wanted them to feel a part of the project; she understood that this was important to succeed in such a close-knit community.

BACK TO THE PRESENT

Shamim had just finished a telephone conversation that disturbed her. A local real estate agent had informed her that a group of investors had just bought a piece of land with the intention of building a Holiday Inn. The land was situated less than two kilometres from the Milton Quality Inn.

Over the next few days Shamim made several phone calls to find out more about the situation. It was rumoured that construction would not begin until the end of 2003, and that the hotel would provide suites, a fitness centre, and a swimming pool. Shamim realized that she had time to react and maintain a competitive advantage, but she had to move quickly.

"Greener Pastures": The Launch of StaGreen™ by HydroCan

Anne T. Hale

Stone Age Marketing Consultants was founded five years ago by Cari Clarkstone, Karen Jonestone, and Robert Sommerstone. Their target clients were small, startup firms as well as medium-sized firms looking to expand operations. Their newest client, HydroCan, had a meeting scheduled for the following afternoon and the three founders were discussing the results of their market analysis. HydroCan was a startup company that was obtaining patents in both the United States and Canada for a new type of lawn-care product. Since the company was made up of four agricultural engineers and a financial accountant, they were in need of marketing advice concerning their new product, StaGreen™. This product, when applied to most types of grass, enabled the root system to retain water longer, thus reducing the need for both extra watering and frequent fertilizing. They were anxious to take this product to market; however, they desperately needed answers to several questions, including which segment to target, how to position their new product, and what type of launch strategy they should use. They approached Stone Age Marketing Consultants approximately four weeks ago with their needs. The marketing consultants had analyzed the markets, costs, prices, and communications options. Their last task was to formulate a comprehensive strategy for the launch of StaGreen.

Prepared by Anne T. Hale, formerly Visiting Assistant Professor of Marketing, Faculty of Business, University of Victoria, Victoria, British Columbia, as a basis for class discussion. Copyright © 1996 by Anne T. Hale. Reprinted with permission.

INITIAL MEETING WITH HYDROCAN

During the initial meeting between HydroCan and Stone Age, the engineers outlined the product and its potential benefits. The product was very similar in appearance to most brands of common lawn fertilizer. In fact, StaGreen was classified as a chemical fertilizer, but with one very important difference. Its primary benefit was its effect on the root system of most of the common types of grasses used for lawns. The small pellets attached to roots and attracted and retained moisture. Extensive laboratory testing demonstrated that StaGreen reduced the need for manual watering on most types of grass by up to 40%. Obviously such a product would have high demand. The first question that HydroCan needed addressed was what market to target initially with this product. Gary Gillis, CEO of HydroCan, wanted to target the consumer lawn and garden market as their initial target segment. Carla Humphreys, on the other hand, was more inclined to target the commercial lawn and garden market. Since these two markets required very different launch strategies, selecting the appropriate segment was the primary concern. And, due to the fact that both Mr. Gillis and Ms. Humphreys were extremely biased toward their position, the consultants knew that they would have to present strong reasons to support their recommendation. To make this task manageable, they divided the research and analysis along the following lines: Cari Clarkstone was to investigate the viability of a consumer launch, Karen Jonestone was to investigate the viability of a commercial launch, and Robert Sommerstone was to obtain all necessary financial information.

THE CONSUMER MARKET

In 1995, Canadians spent nearly $2.3 billion, at the retail level, on gardening. This figure includes $945 million for grass (both sod and seed), trees, and plants, $620 million on lawn maintenance (fertilizers accounting for 52% of the total), and $815 million on hand tools, pots, window boxes, books, magazines, landscaping services, etc. In other words, gardening is big business in Canada. Lawn care is, however, a highly seasonal business, with 70% of sales occurring in the second and third fiscal quarters (i.e., April to September).

According to Cari Clarkstone's research, if HydroCan was to target this segment, they would be competing primarily with fertilizers. The consumer fertilizer market is extremely competitive, with the top two firms, Scotts Co. and Ortho Chemicals, controlling approximately 50% of the total consumer market. Both firms are headquartered in the United States (with divisional offices in Canada), and both have extensive international operations. The market share leader is Scotts Co., with their two powerful brands, Turf Builder® and Miracle-Gro® (acquired in May of 1995 from the privately held Stern's Group). Turf Builder is a slow-release fertilizer that reduces the number of applications required for a healthy lawn. This slow-release technology is relatively new—having been available to the consumer market for less than two years. Slow-release simply means that the fertilizing chemicals are released gradually over a number of months. Thus one application of slow-release fertilizer could last for a maximum of two years (although most manufacturers recommend applications every year).

Turf Builder is priced slightly lower than most Miracle-Gro products, which are advertised as maximum-growth products, and not specifically (i.e., exclusively) aimed at lawn care. Ortho's products are priced competitively with Turf Builder—their added value comes from the inclusion of pesticides within the fertilizer that prevents most common lawn infestations. See Exhibit 1 for pricing information on the major branded fertilizer products.

EXHIBIT 1	Competitor Prices for the Consumer Market	

	Size(s)	Retail Prices(s)
Scotts Turf Builder	10 kg	$24.50
Scotts Turf Builder	25 kg	$59.99
Scotts Turf Builder	5 kg	$14.75
Miracle-Gro–plant/crystals	200 g	$ 8.50
Miracle-Gro–lawn/garden	2.5 kg	$12.95
Miracle-Gro–liquid	1 L	$ 7.99
Ortho (with pesticide)	10 kg	$23.99
Ortho (with pesticide)	30 kg	$68.79

Market research has shown that four out of ten consumers in this market have no concrete brand preferences. They rely heavily on in-store advertisements and sales staff for information and recommendations. Many consumers cannot recall a brand name or a manufacturer of fertilizer. The product with the highest brand-name awareness is Miracle-Gro; however, most associate this brand name with their plant foods rather than their lawn fertilizers. Because of consumer behaviour and attitude toward this product category, most manufacturers relied on a strong push strategy.

Most lawn care products are sold by three distinct types of retailers: discount stores, such as Canadian Tire, Wal-Mart, and Sears; specialty stores, including nurseries; and home improvement stores. The discount stores, who buy direct from manufacturers, place strict requirements on their orders and expect price concessions and special support. Marketing expenses for both Scotts and Ortho went up by approximately 10% between 1994 and 1995, with the bulk of the increase devoted to promotions to discount retailers. This indicates the relative importance of this channel—it is estimated that 60% of all consumer fertilizer sales are made in discount stores, compared to approximately 30% of sales being made in specialty stores and 10% of sales being made in home improvement stores. Discount stores have, in fact, been spending millions in renovations in order to accommodate larger lawn and garden areas within their stores. The same is true with home improvement stores, such as Home Depot, which has 21 locations in Canada.[1]

Specialty stores, the vast majority of which are nurseries, tend to be independently owned and thus much more numerous. While the 9 top discount chains across Canada control over 89% of all sales from discount stores, the top 50 specialty garden stores account for less than 28% of all sales from this store type. The most recent research indicates that there are over 1000 specialty garden stores in Canada. Most of these stores purchase from large horticulture wholesalers, and receive little, if any promotional assistance from the major manufacturers. Home improvement stores are growing in numbers, and tend to be large, powerful chains, such as Home Depot. While these stores do not represent a large portion of current sales, they are expected to grow in importance. Like discount stores, home improvement stores buy direct from the manufacturers and require price concessions and promotional support.

The large manufacturers of fertilizer products generally spend approximately 20% of sales on marketing activities. The bulk of this money goes toward the sales force, selling in general, and trade promotions. Due to the three different channels in which their product is sold, most fertilizer manufacturers recognize the importance of a strong sales force. In terms of trade promotions, they provide in-store literature, displays, and sales training—especially to the large discount stores and the home improvement stores. Less important is advertising. Miracle-Gro is the most heavily advertised brand on the market, and Scotts generally spends 4% of sales on advertising (which probably accounts for the high brand-name awareness). Scotts advertises TurfBuilder, but only during the early spring when demand for lawn fertilizers is at its peak. Most companies run their advertisements for their existing brands and any new brands they may be launching during the spring and early summer months. Thus, advertising expenditures are generally at their highest in March, April, May, and June, and zero at all other times. Only Miracle-Gro is advertised year-round, with different messages at different times of the year. For example, Miracle-Gro advertises its benefits for house plants during the winter months, and its benefits for fruits, vegetables, and flowers during the spring and summer months.

THE COMMERCIAL MARKET

The commercial market consists primarily of Canada's 1800 golf courses, but also includes commercial properties such as office complexes and apartment buildings. The most lucrative market, however, are golf courses. Currently under fire for being a major source of groundwater pollution, due to the high and frequent levels of fertilizers used to keep courses green, most owners are actively looking for ways to cut both water and fertilizer usage. Course owners spend, on average, $300 000 to maintain their golf course during the year, of which 42% represents water usage costs and 24% represents fertilizer purchases. For extremely large, complex courses, this figure can run as high as $800 000, and for smaller inner-city public courses, as low as $104 000. Tests have indicated that StaGreen™ will reduce water usage by one-half and fertilizer usage by one-third. This is the primary reason why Ms. Humphreys was so adamant that the company select the commercial market as its primary target.

The game of golf has been enjoying a renewed popularity after a drastic decrease in participation during the 1980s. The growing number of public courses with reasonable fees, the continued aging of the Canadian population, and the development of better equipment have all contributed to this growth in popularity. It is estimated that the number of golf courses will increase by 22% to 2200 within five years. Most golf courses are independently owned and operated. Only 4% of all courses are owned by a company that owns more than one course. Courses are dispersed throughout Canada, but British Columbia, and Vancouver in particular, boast the highest number of courses.

Currently, golf courses purchase maintenance supplies from wholesalers who specialize in products uniquely designed for the type of grasses used. Manufacturers of these fertilizers tend to be small firms, or divisions of the larger chemical companies. The market share leader in golf course fertilizers is Sierra Horticultural Products, a subsidiary of Scotts Co. Scotts purchased Sierra in 1993, and it represents only about 2.2% of Scotts' total sales. Their biggest competitor in Canada is Nu-Gro Corporation, an Ontario-based horticultural products company founded in 1992. Unlike the firms competing in the consumer lawn maintenance market, these firms spend only about 9% of sales on marketing activities. These firms engage in little advertising, preferring to spend their marketing funds on sales calls to golf courses. They provide free samples of their products to non-users and try to build solid, long-lasting relationships with course owners. They know that it takes a tremendous selling effort to get a golf course owner to switch brands. If satisfied with their current brand, many course owners are unwilling to risk switching to a new product that may not perform as well. Since the condition of the course is the most important attribute in a consumer's selection of a course to play, course owners tend to be highly brand-loyal.

Course owners, however, have two overriding concerns. The first concerns the growing public debate on the groundwater pollution caused by golf courses. Heavy use of fertilizers and constant manual watering results in a chemical buildup in nearby reservoirs. In fact, according to the U.S. Environmental Protection Agency, golf courses are the major source of groundwater pollution in the United States. More and more negative publicity, in the form of newspaper and magazine articles, has resulted in golf course developers being denied permits to construct new courses. Thus, addressing the issue of groundwater pollution is a major concern with course owners.

Their second problem is that of shrinking profits. While golf is growing in popularity, and more courses are being built to accommodate demand, the actual number of golfers that can be accommodated on any one course cannot be expanded. With some courses engaging in green-fee price wars, profit margins for many of the public courses have become strained. Thus, while loyalty may play a role in fertilizer purchases, these difficult problems will also influence purchase behaviour.

Estimated to be about one-eighth the size of the golf course market is the balance of the commercial lawn care market, consisting of apartment and office complexes. Their needs are much less complex than those of golf courses, resulting in purchasing behaviour that mirrors that of the consumer market. Little concrete information is available concerning the number of office complexes and apartment buildings, although estimates have put the total figure around 2900, of which 16.5% represent multiple holdings by one corporation. These commercial real estate property firms spend a disproportionate amount on lawn maintenance—they account for nearly 26% of the total dollars spent in this sector of the commercial maintenance market. This sector of the commercial market tends to purchase in bulk through wholesalers—generally the same wholesalers who service the specialty stores in the consumer market.

HYDROCAN

HydroCan was incorporated nearly one year ago. They have leased their production facilities, and have purchased and/or leased all of the equipment and machinery necessary for use in the production of StaGreen. Their production facility has the capacity to produce 180 000 kilograms of StaGreen per month. The owners of HydroCan have suggested a quality/value-added pricing strategy. They believe that they have a superior product that will save the end user both time and money, due to the reduced need for fertilizer products and manual watering. The founders of HydroCan outlined their ideas for the launch year marketing strategy for both the consumer and the commercial lawn-care markets.

If HydroCan elects to target the consumer market, they will package StaGreen in a 10-kilogram bag, which market research indicates was the most popular size with consumers. They will set their price to trade (i.e., wholesalers and retailers) at $22.50, with their variable costs representing 52% of sales. On average the large discount stores and home improvement stores take a 25% markup on lawn maintenance products. The smaller specialty stores take a larger markup of 35%. Wholesalers (if used) take a 15% markup. Fixed production costs include $700 000 in annual rental (for the site and equipment), general and administrative expenses of $80 200, research and development expenses of $20 650, and miscellaneous expenses of $12 350. Distribution costs (including freight, warehousing, and storage) represented a significant yearly expense due to the seasonal nature of demand. Production of StaGreen would be continuous year-round; however, sales would be highly concentrated in the months of April through September. This means that the company would have relatively high distribution costs, estimated to be $426 000 per year. Not yet included in any of their financial statements are the salaries for the four founding partners of HydroCan. They would like to earn $50 000 per year (each), but are willing to forgo their salaries in the launch year.

Their marketing budget has been set at $555 000, and HydroCan has suggested this amount be allocated to the various tasks, as shown in Exhibit 2. Seasonal discounts are price discounts offered to retailers and wholesalers as an incentive to purchase well in advance of the peak selling season. HydroCan plans to offer these discounts, estimated to be 20% off the trade price for each bag purchased, to wholesalers and retailers in the months of November and December as a method to reduce warehouse and storage costs. The displays will cost approximately $250 each (which includes promotional materials, such as brochures), and will be furnished to discount stores, home improvement stores, and as many nurseries as possible. The sweepstakes is used to increase awareness and interest in StaGreen. Consumers will have the chance to win several valuable prizes including a year of free lawn maintenance, lawn and garden equipment and supplies, and other related prizes.

EXHIBIT 2	Allocation of Marketing Budget for Consumer Market Launch
Marketing Task	Total Expenditure (estimates)
Seasonal discounts	$225 000
In-store displays	$ 92 000
Magazine advertising	$104 000
Newspaper advertising	$ 84 000
Sweepstakes	$ 50 000

In terms of the sales force, HydroCan has planned on hiring 20 sales reps at an average cost of $25 000 per rep (salary and commission). The sales reps will be responsible for selling the product to the various channels as well as offering sales training seminars.

If HydroCan elects to target the commercial market, then the size of the product will be increased to a 50-kilogram bag, which they will sell to wholesalers or end users at a price of $150. Because they would be charging a slightly higher price under this option, variable costs as a percentage of sales drop to 40%, resulting in a relatively high contribution margin of 60% of sales. Wholesalers, who generally sell directly to the commercial users, take a 15% markup. Fixed expenses will remain nearly the same as for the consumer market option, with the exception of marketing and distribution costs. None of the promotional activities, such as displays, seasonal discounts, sweepstakes, or advertising will be used in the commercial market. Instead, the size of the sales force will be increased to 30 to handle the lengthy sales calls necessary to golf courses. In addition, $100 000 has been set aside for free samples to be distributed to potential customers by the sales force. Finally, distribution costs decrease if the commercial market is chosen because demand tends to be slightly less seasonal. Thus costs for freight, warehousing, and storage decrease to $225 000 under this option.

THE DECISION

The three founding partners of Stone Age Marketing Consultants were in the conference room discussing the results of their research and analysis. As Karen Jonestone pointed out, "A strong case can be made for both target markets! Each has its own advantages and limitations." Rob Sommerstone countered with the fact that HydroCan was a startup business. "Their financial resources are extremely limited right now. They cannot increase their production capacity for at least two years, and if they hope to acquire expansion capital to increase their total capacity, they need to show a profit as early as possible." Cari Clarkstone was considering a more creative solution—targeting selected parts of either or both the consumer and commercial markets. Before the group could begin to assess the viability of HydroCan and its product, StaGreen, they had to decide on which market to target and how to position StaGreen in that market, and then they had to develop a viable marketing strategy for the launch year. The final pressure for the group was the fact that HydroCan needed to launch in February—just prior to the peak selling season; thus, the consultants knew there was no time to acquire additional market research. The decision had to be based on the information at hand.

Note

1.   *Maclean's,* April 22, 1996, pp. 62–63.

MN Design

Andrei Craciun and Christopher A. Ross

It was the summer of 2002 when Mr. Malo observed that the revenues of his company were increasing, but that the gross profit margin was decreasing. This observation prompted Mr. Malo to undertake a review of his company, MN Design, in order to ensure its long-run survival and success. MN Design produced and marketed booths (also called kiosks) to companies that exhibited at trade shows. The trade-show industry was changing and competition was becoming increasingly intense. As part of his review, Mr. Malo wondered if he should continue aiming at all market segments, or if he should focus on only one of them. He was also considering several other options but did not know whether or not they were appropriate given the present situation of his company and the market.

THE COMPANY

It was in 2000 that Mr. Malo and his partner, Mr. Costello, incorporated MN Design with offices in Montreal. In the early stages of the firm's operation, Mr. Malo would

Andrei Craciun, research assistant, and Christopher A. Ross, professor, John Molson School of Business, Concordia University, wrote this case. It is partly based on a student report that was submitted in the fall of 2002. It is to be used for discussion purposes only. It is not designed to illustrate either effective or ineffective handling of an administrative or commercial situation. Some of the information in this case has been disguised but essential relationships have been retained. Copyright © 2005. This case was made possible through the financial support of the Institute for Cooperative Education, Concordia University. Reprinted with permission.

seek an order for a booth and the partners would together undertake its construction. They normally did everything from start to finish, but would sometimes hire a few people to help them manufacture the booths (paint, glue, etc.). At its peak, MN Design had up to seven workers, including students, assembling booths. As the company grew, each of the partners assumed different responsibilities. Mr. Costello focused on designing and constructing the booths while Mr. Malo focused on business development and selling. Selling was his passion, according to Mr. Malo, and, in fact, he had been a successful salesperson for the past 25 years or so.

In order to develop the business and increase sales, Mr. Malo's strategy was to attend several trade shows. At these shows, he waited until there were no customers around a booth and then approached the person in charge—sometimes the company president or the vice-president of marketing. He identified himself as a booth builder and subsequently tried to sell his product. He found that many of the companies had special needs but had no idea where to find a booth builder. After listening carefully to his customers' demands, Mr. Malo met with Mr. Costello and explained to him what the customer expected. Mr. Costello then designed the booth and MN Design presented the drawings to the customer. The product could be subsequently modified depending on the customer's feedback on that initial drawing. Once the customer was satisfied, the final design would then be put into production. It took about four to six weeks for a smaller booth (between 100 and 600 sq. ft.) to be designed. Construction normally took between one and two weeks. Larger booths obviously took more time to build.

THE PRODUCT

The company designed booths both for clients who demanded highly customized projects as well as for clients whose main concerns were practicality and durability. MN Design's main focus, however, was on clients where uniqueness of design was the main benefit sought. This focus resulted in price increases, which tended to alienate some segments of the market. In designing a booth, major considerations were reduced weight, ease of transportation, and minimal set-up time.

Unlike many competitors who focused on standardized products, MN Design was flexible enough to be able to adapt to different customer needs. Thus, many projects were somewhat distinct. MN Design aimed at creating and developing booths with an image that was consistent with the customer's product or service. Exhibitors also wanted booths that were personalized and which incorporated their ideas. In order to portray the image and identity of the client, the company designed and coordinated the entire exhibit, including lighting, customized drapery, booth furnishing and accessories, as well as material handling.

The exhibitor was responsible for transportation services as well as space reservation, floor plan development, and market research. Exhibitors also customized event signage, such as banners and signs to attract potential clientele. Finally, exhibitors were in charge of installing and dismantling the booths. A significant number of clients preferred "turn-key" projects, however, which meant that MN Design also installed the booths at the show. Examples of booths are shown in Exhibit 1.

EXHIBIT 1	Examples Of Booths Made By MN Design

THE INDUSTRY

There were two kinds of trade shows: public trade shows, open to the general public, e.g., camping, recreational vehicles, wedding and home shows; and buyer trade shows, open to businesses that were looking to purchase new product lines or to improve their existing product lines. Buyer trade shows were much more numerous and the exhibitors also spent more on the booths in order to impress the visitors who were potential buyers. According to Mr. Malo, most exhibitor companies participated in between 6 and 30 buyer shows, compared to only a few public shows, per year. Accordingly, MN Design targeted only buyer trade shows.

Since 1997, an increasing number of trade show promoters had begun to use the Internet to provide more information on their services, participating exhibitors, and registration. Recently, too, more exhibitors were using the Internet and other innovative technologies in their booths, in order to increase the effectiveness of their communication. Oftentimes, included in the exhibitor's information were detailed descriptions of the firms' booths, locations within the trade show, and what was unique about the products or services displayed. These trends offered great exposure to the exhibitors.

The events of September 11, 2001 had a negative impact on attendance, and on exhibit and sponsorship sales for most trade shows. But, as the impact of September 11 subsided, there were other factors that could potentially have a negative impact. These included the growth of mergers and acquisitions, downsizing, and changing channels of distribution/supply chain shifts. These changes reduced the number of exhibitor prospects, attendees, and buyers. Major manufacturers were also developing preferred vendor relationships with smaller component manufacturers. There was also growing key account selling to major buyers, as well as shorter product development and life cycles. All of the preceding factors could potentially reduce the need to participate in trade shows.[1]

In Canada, there was a lack of consistent and reliable data on the industry. In 1998, however, U.S. data showed that attendees were no longer looking to trade shows to simply discover what was new on the market, but rather to actually try out the new technologies. In 1995, attendees spent an average of 7.8 hours at a trade show visiting all exhibits. By 2002, the average time spent by an attendee at a trade show had increased to 8.4 hours. Attendees reported that product accessibility was the most important criterion, since they attended in order to compare a number of products in one location. Designers, therefore, followed this trend by designing booths recognizable for the ease with which products could be tested.[2] Furthermore, it was reported that 91% of trade shows attendees believed trade shows to be their principal means of acquiring information for making their final decision.[3] Eighty-three percent of trade show attendees were the final decision makers or the influencers of the purchase.[4] Average traffic density had decreased in the last few years because show organizers were much more successful in selling exhibit space than in increasing attendance at the shows.[5] (Industry statistics are presented in Exhibits 2 and 3.)

---

[1] Skip Cox, "Growing Your Event in a Rapidly Changing Business Environment," Exhibition and Convention Executives Forum, Washington, D.C., 2002.

[2] "*Tradeshow Week*," August 24, 1998.

[3] "Power of the Exhibitions 1," Center for Exhibition Industry Research, 1993.

[4] www.exhibitsurveys.com/trends.htm.

[5] Skip Cox, ibid.

EXHIBIT 2	Recent Trends in Trade Show Attendance

Year	Average Hours	Total Buying Plans	Net Buying Influences	Traffic Density
2002	8.4	54%	83%	**2.3**
2001	8.9	53%	83%	2.1
2000	9.6	56%	83%	2.2
1999	9.2	57%	83%	2.5
1998	8.8	62%	84%	2.6
1997	8.4	61%	85%	2.6
1996	8.6	63%	85%	2.7

Source: http://www.exhibitsurveys.com/trends.htm. Accessed 13th Aug, 2004.

Glossary

Average Hours:	Amount of time an average attendee spends visiting all exhibits
Total Buying Plans:	Percentage of attendees planning to purchase one or more exhibited products within 12 months of the show
Net Buying Influences:	Percentage of attendees who can recommend, specify, or make a final purchasing decision for one or more products exhibited
Traffic Density:	Number of attendees occupying every 100 sq. ft. of exhibit space (excluding aisle space) throughout the show's run

EXHIBIT 3	Trends by Industry, 2002

Trends	Average Hours	Net Buying Influences	Total Buying Plans	Traffic Density	Potential for New Contacts
Hi-Tech	8.6	84%	56%	2.8	86%
Retail	7.7	86%	57%	1.6	86%
Medical	6.3	78%	57%	2.1	93%
Mfg/Ind	8.9	83%	42%	2.1	88%
All Shows	8.4	83%	54%	2.3	79%

Glossary

Average Hours:	Amount of time an average attendee spends visiting all exhibits
Total Buying Plans:	Percentage of attendees planning to purchase one or more exhibited products within 12 months of the show
Net Buying Influences:	Percentage of attendees who can recommend, specify, or make a final purchasing decision for one or more products exhibited

EXHIBIT 3	Glossary (continued)
Traffic Density:	Number of attendees occupying every 100 sq. ft. of exhibit space (excluding aisle space) throughout the show's run
Potential for New Contacts:	Percentage of the average exhibit's visitors who have had no contact with that company within the previous 12 months

Note: *The Trade Show Trends Report* is based on results of audience surveys conducted by Exhibit Surveys Inc. of Red Bank, NJ, for 47 trade shows held in 2002. Each survey was administered by mail or Internet shortly after the show. In most cases, exhibit personnel are excluded from the sample. Surveys typically obtain response rates of 10 to 35 percent.

Source: Sequeira, Ian and Nancy I. Gordon, "Are Trade Shows Really Worth It?" *Exhibit Surveys*. (ND)

Financially, exhibitions accounted for a large percentage of business marketing expenditures. Studies showed that the size of trade show budgets was second only to the direct selling budgets in the market mix.[6] Exhibitions accounted for such large expenditures because they were said to effectively achieve objectives such as the generation of sales leads, the introduction of new products, and the taking of sales orders. Sixty-five percent of salespeople rated trade show leads as the highest among all leads obtained through promotion.

There were about 450 trade shows each year throughout Canada, representing a vast array of industries. The local demand was expected to grow as Montreal became increasingly popular with trade show organizers.[7] Nationally, the physical size of trade shows was expected to continue growing because of exhibitors' desire to increase booth size, so as to increase their visibility. However, the number of exhibiting companies was expected to decrease due to consolidation in virtually every industry.[8] Overall, demand was expected to increase by 2% every year until 2004.

THE CUSTOMERS

For some trade shows, the promoters of the show were the ones who purchased the booths. Exhibitors then simply purchased a spot, which included the booth, in the show. With this arrangement, the booths were relatively standardized regarding design, colour, and size.

As a general rule, exhibit booth suppliers accepted any booth contract, as long as what the customer requested was within their manufacturing capability, and provided a reasonable margin of profit. Since MN Design preferred customizing booths, the company focused on those shows where the exhibitors desired customized booths. While there were many industries participating in a great number of both national and international trade shows, there was no generally accepted way to segment the market. MN Design segmented its customers into three groups: unique design seekers, convenience design seekers, and technology seekers.

Unique design seekers were clients who sought uniqueness and quality designs in their booths in order to effectively differentiate themselves from the competition at trade shows. They needed and wanted a booth that was far beyond the standardized booths used by competitors. Each booth must possess one-of-a-kind characteristics. It must convey to the public the timely thought process of both design and construction of the designer. In order to keep

---

[6] Skip Cox, "Making the Case for Trade Shows," *Advertising Age*, June 1996.
[7] Alain Duhamel, "Montréal intéresse les organisateurs internationaux," *Les Affaires*, 2 February, 2000, p. 43.
[8] TV interview of Darlene Gudea, Editor of *Tradeshow Week*.

up-to-date with the current industry trends, the order frequency of customers within this segment tended to be higher. The clothing industry was a good example of this segment. This industry was one of the most sought after by exhibitor suppliers, inasmuch as clothing designers, because of their trade, inherently looked to differentiate themselves from fellow designers and, therefore, had a greater willingness to spend more to do so. The higher expenditures included more attractive, thus more expensive, materials, intricate lighting, and complex, modern architectural designs. The Montreal clothing industry comprised about 455 manufacturers. Customers in this segment attended predominantly the fashion trade shows, which included clothing, leather, and footwear companies exhibiting their products.

Convenience design seekers were highly price-conscious. They sought ease of assembling and transportation, durability, quality, and reliability of suppliers. They purchased less frequently since their requested booths were highly standardized. They had less need to keep up with the design trends of the industry. Such consumers were known to purchase booths that they expected to last from two to five years, reinforcing the long-term vision of the companies. Examples of such clients included manufacturers or distributors in the dental and chemical industries. Overall, all customers in this segment sought practicality and conservative designs, as the attendees at these trade shows were generally less fashion conscious.

Technology seekers included all companies in need of booth designers that were capable of providing them with the latest technological breakthrough. The electronic industry represented the largest number of customers in this segment. The lifetime of their booths was shorter because of their desire to be innovative and move in accordance with changes in technology. These manufacturers/distributors were more or less price conscious. Exhibit 4 shows the segmentation of the market.

EXHIBIT 4	Market Segments				
	SEGMENTS				
	Unique Design Seekers			Convenience Design Seekers	Technology Seekers
INDUSTRY	Clothing	Leather	Footwear	Chemical Dental	Consumer Electronics
BENEFITS SOUGHT	Uniqueness	Uniqueness	Uniqueness	Standardization	On-time delivery
	Customization	Customization	Customization	Practicality	Technological capacity
	New ideas	Image	On-time delivery	Easy set up	Image
BOOTH LIFE SPAN	1-2 years	1-2 years	1-2 years	2-5 years	$\frac{1}{2}$-$1\frac{1}{2}$ years
No. OF COMPANIES IN MTL AREA	455	76	36	378	140

EXHIBIT 4	Market Segments (continued)				
	NUMBER OF FIRMS IN EACH REVENUE RANGE ($)				
	Unique			Convenience	Technology
	Clothing	Leather	Footwear	Chemical Dental	Consumer Electronics
100K-499K	79	12	6	25	18
500K-999K	54	14	8	40	10
1M-2.99M	110	19	10	92	36
3M-4.99M	51	9	7	42	21
5M-9.99M	79	10	4	62	18
10M-24.99M	63	10	0	51	15
25M-49.99M	14	2	1	56	13
> 50M	5	0	0	10	9

Source: www.criq.com, 2002.

In general, companies that participated in trade shows began their search for a booth supplier three to six months prior to the actual date of the exhibition. They needed this lead time in order to conduct the proper supplier search, design the booth, and construct the final product. With increasing use of the Internet, exhibitors and suppliers were beginning to consummate transactions electronically. Furthermore, exhibitors often repeated their purchase from the same supplier. Thus, there was a great deal of customer loyalty. This loyalty was an advantage to the chosen supplier but it worked against suppliers who were seeking new business

About 90% of MN Design's customers were Canadian firms, and the rest were U.S. customers. Of the Canadian customers, about 50% were located in Montreal, and the rest were distributed across Canada. About 65% of MN Design's customers were fashion firms, while 25% of its customers came from the chemical and dental segments, and the rest from consumer electronics. For the fashion segment, the peak demand for booths was in the summer, for the chemical industry it was in the spring, and the consumer electronics industry had its peak demand in the winter. For a list of customers of MN Design as of June 2002, see Exhibit 5.

THE COMPETITION

Reports from the United States suggested that one of the biggest competitive threats to trade show promoters was the corporate or private show. There were no statistics kept on this phenomenon but it was generally felt that growth had been significant over the last five to ten years. In addition, while a few years ago only large companies, such as Oracle, Computer Associates, and SAP sponsored private events, currently smaller mid-cap companies were also producing their own events. Some large companies attracted as many as 10 000 attendees who spent four to five days listening to company representatives who

EXHIBIT 5	Customer List of MN Design

Active Customers

April 2002	May 2002	June 2002
Cartise Int'l	Billabong Canada	Artex Fashions
Distex	Distex	Billabong Canada
Modextile	Modextile	Picadilly Fashion
Pino Furs	Selection A & S	Rudsak
Rudsak	Pino Furs	

Total Customers

June 2002

Artex Fashions
Billabong Canada
Caribbean Pacific
Cartise International
Casa Bawa Import
Casa Wear
Connaissance Virtuelle
De Capra International
Distex
Encino Electronics
Groupe Arc Design
Groupe Vezina et Associes
Modextile
Oblik 2000
Pantouffle
Picadilly Fashions
Pino Furs
Rudsak

focused on their own products. Private events included private trade shows, user groups, technical conferences, mobile marketing (truck exhibits, road shows, mall tours, campus tours), product seminars, etc. These private events competed with trade shows for the marketing budget and also competed with trade shows for attendees.[9]

There were 14 competitors in Montreal vying for market share, plus an additional four big competitors who already owned a large portion of the market for booths. Design firms ranged from one-person freelance operations to large multi-disciplinary firms. In Canada, a firm with 20 or more people was considered large. In this market, EDI and GES were the main players among all producers in the booth trade.

GES: This company was owned by VIAD Corp. and had helped VIAD achieve sales of $1.7 billion for the year 2001. GES did not sell, but rented its booths. Despite an estimated income increase of 16.8%, the company's sales were expected to grow at a slower rate of 8.3%. GES dated back to 1966. Formerly Panex Show Services, it was purchased by VIAD in 1995 and renamed GES Canada. In the United States, GES Exposition Services was the largest company within its industry. It employed 1400 employees worldwide.

---

[9] Skip Cox, ibid.

GES Canada was present in four Canadian cities: Toronto, Calgary, Edmonton and Montreal. In 1996, GES had 75% of the Montreal market. It had been rated the top Show Service Contractor in Canada since 1984. The company had a 100 000 square foot facility in Toronto, which was its head office. In 1998, it purchased Ainsworth Trade Show Electrical, which was later renamed Showtech Power and Lighting. This company was Canada's leader in electrical and mechanical services for trade shows in six of Canada's largest cities.

In Montreal, the operations were split into two distinct organizations. Clarkson-Conway specialized in hotel shows and Exposervice Standard specialized in shows occurring at Place Bonaventure, the Palais des Congrès, and the Olympic Stadium, Montreal's largest venues for hosting trade shows.

EDI: Expo Design International had the largest reach of all competitors with four Canadian offices (Quebec, Montreal, Toronto, and Vancouver), as well as seven U.S. offices, and one in Mexico. This was one of the only competitors with an office in Las Vegas, the capital of conventions and trade shows.

EDI was started in Montreal in 1986 and quickly grew. It was best known for its Profilex system. When EDI built a kiosk, the walls and many other vertical surfaces were covered with PVC slats that allowed those working in the booth to affix anything by hanging it off the raised edge. Customers could, therefore, customize their kiosks depending on their situational needs. It was the largest competitor to offer a standardized product. It was possible to order the booth online and all pre-made packages included carpet, lighting, signs, accessories, and set-up of the booth. Its focus was on functionality.

Archex Displays: Archex was based in Montreal and was part of the global network of Octanorm Service Partner International. This allowed them to provide services all over the world and to travel with their clients. This company focused on creating intricate designs that had a high quality of craftsmanship. Their designs tended to be more extravagant and reflected the industry of the company. It created designs that were lightweight and easily set up by one person. It also included carrying cases.

Presentation Design Expositions: This company was also part of Octanorm Service Partner International. They had been in Montreal for 25 years. They provided truly standardized booths. The packages included the Express, the Pro Pop Up and the Go System. Presentation Design Expositions also offered digital printing and lamination. This company focused on practicability.

Nomadic Displays: This was a large international competitor with two manufacturing facilities in the United States and Ireland. They had direct sales offices in the United States, London, and Frankfurt. They prided themselves on product quality and customer service. They had a 24-hour hotline where customers could track their order. They also included a lifetime warranty on their product. This company offered modular frames that could be molded into different shapes. The set-up was quick and efficient and the materials used were compatible with other Nomadic products. They stressed quality of products.

Salco Stand Design Communication Inc.: This company started in Montreal in 1985. It specialized in portable stands and large format printing. Its main target was trade shows. The sister company was Philing Expo. As a result of the pairing of these two companies, Selco offered the Para-Graf and the Para-Post, both of which were deployable stands. The idea with Selco was the one-stop supplier. Customers got the stand and also benefited from the graphic capabilities of the firm. This company was attempting to create an international presence by expanding its business.

Other Competitors: Other competitors included those who specialized in certain aspects of booth building and contracted out the other tasks to partner companies. An example would be Production Design Associates based in South Carolina. Their history included lighting for numerous presidential campaigns as well as conventions around the world.

PROMOTION AND SELLING

MN Design sold directly to exhibitors and this created a personal relationship with them. However, Mr. Malo was the only salesperson working for MN Design and he thought that this prevented the company from acquiring additional leads.

He attended 12 trade shows in 2002 and was able to gain 33 customers. The estimated number of trade shows in Canada was 450 so Mr. Malo thought that it might make sense for MN Design to hire additional salespeople, who would each cost MN Design between $40 000 to $50 000 annually. This cost was the sum of $25 000 to $30 000 base salary and a percentage from sales that could range from 7% to 10%.

The only other promotional tools used by the company were a brochure and Mr. Malo's cold calls. The folded brochure was approximately 8.5 by 3.6 inches. It was relatively easy to lose and did not exude an impression of professionalism.

Usually, Mr. Malo made numerous cold calls a few months before important shows, such as the MAGIC[10] Show in Las Vegas. The success rate of this strategy was 6% (30% return the phone call, and of those, only 20% become customers of MN Design). Some other sources of clients came through referrals from actual or previous clients.

PRICING AND FINANCE

As a rule of thumb, MN Design and its competitors priced according to the size of the booth, as shown in Table 1.

Table 1	Competitive Pricing of Booths by Company in Dollars				
	COMPANY				
SIZE	MN Design	GES**	EDI	Archex	Nomadic
10 X 10 ft.	$ 10 000	$ 700	$2000 to $12 000	$2000 to $4000	$4000
10 X 20 ft.	$20 000	$1400	$24 000	$10 000 to $20 000	$8000
20 X 20 ft.	$30 000	$1800	$40 000 to $50 000	$30 000 to $40 000	$15 000 to $100 000
** Rental price per show					

The latest financial statements for MN Design are shown in Exhibits 6 and 7. Mr. Malo was able to identify that the average revenue per client was about $15 000. With a gross profit margin that was decreasing and net profit margins of only 6%, Mr. Malo felt that the cost of materials was too expensive or, alternatively, that the prices of the booths were too low for the quality of materials.

---

[10] This was the largest men's apparel trade show in the world. It was held annually in Las Vegas.

EXHIBIT 6	MN Design Income Statements for the Years 2001-2002 Ending June 30th	

	2002	2001
Gross Profit		
Revenues	$489 000	$255 651
Cost of Sales	310 515	123 596
Gross Profit	178 485	132 056
Expenses		
Salaries	$90 720	$57 647
Travel	14 000	15 544
Car	15 600	12 563
Electricity	1 820	790
Telecommunications	1 800	1 877
Insurances	4 400	664
Rent	6 360	5 856
Maintenance	7 200	3 091
Office	2 400	1 835
Training	NA	1 575
Honoraries	4 350	2 733
Depreciation	4 800	3 011
Financial	6 269	2 347
Total Expenses	$159 759	$109 533
Net Income		
Income before taxes	$18 726	$22 523
Tax on income expense	2 435	3 196
Net Income	16 291	19 327
Income		
Beginning of period	$15 784	$ (3 543)
End of period	$32 075	$ 15 784

Source: Company files.

THE FUTURE

Mr. Malo was concerned about the future of MN Design and had begun thinking of possible actions that would maintain the sales growth of the company and increase its profitability. He started by setting a few financial objectives: 1) generate sales of $800 000 to $1 000 000 by December, 31st, 2003, and 2) increase the contribution margin to 50% over the following two years.

EXHIBIT 7	MN Design Balance Sheet as of June 30, 2002

ASSETS

Current Assets

Chequing Bank Account	$ 2 774.68
Accounts Receivable	18 444.32
Total Current Assets	21 219.00
Inventory Assets	3 765.00
Capital Assets	15 555.64
Other Assets	1 132.43
TOTAL ASSETS:	$41 672.07

LIABILITIES & EQUITY

Current Liabilities

Accounts Payable	$ 1 309.72
Corporate Taxes Payable	3 196.00
Vacation Payable	3 838.00
Total Receivable General	1 173.42
Total - Quebec Minister of Finance	2 008.60
GST Owing	4 433.88
QST Owing	5 018.45
Total Current Liabilities	$20 978.07
Loans from owners	2 377.45
TOTAL LIABILITIES:	$23 355.45

Equity

Retained Earnings - Previous Year	$ 15 783.59
Current Earnings	2 527.96
Total Owners Equity	$ 18 316.55
TOTAL EQUITY:	$ 18 316.55
TOTAL LIABILITIES & EQUITY:	$ 41 672.07

Source: Company files.

He thought that with the firm's small market share and its overhead costs, it would be unsound to target segments where competition relied heavily on price. He believed that since mass production was reserved for giants such as GES or EDI, the advantage of MN Design would be its ability to customize each design to individual customer needs.

In addition, he assumed that both the fashion and electronics industries would be prepared to pay for unique designs that would stand out during trade shows and that the frequency of repeat purchase with both would be higher due to the need to keep up with the trends. The clothing industry alone represented 43% of the market for booths, and Mr. Malo thought that the addition of the leather and footwear segments would allow MN Design to reach 10% more. As a result, Mr. Malo felt that he should target the segments where uniqueness was the prime benefit sought by the customers. He was concerned about relying too much on these industries, however, because an increasing number of the manufacturers were moving offshore.

Mr. Malo acknowledged that customers generally endured an unduly lengthy process when deciding to invest in trade shows. Particularly with respect to trade show displays, Mr. Malo learned that not only were the exhibitors concerned with purchasing booths that differentiated them from competitors, but he also recognized that whether the client had purchased a brand new booth, or simply needed an old one removed from storage, on-time delivery was of utmost importance.

The main inconsistency lay with the low to medium price strategy and the product offering. MN Design served two types of segments: price-sensitive customers, who preferred standardized products, and those who were less price sensitive. Mr. Malo was, therefore, thinking of raising the prices and focusing exclusively on the price inelastic segment, especially in the fashion industry. He was considering a 20% increase in prices. With a possible increase in prices, there was the risk of losing existing customers, but Mr. Malo thought that unlikely, as he knew that once satisfied, the probability that the customer would re-purchase MN Design booths was 99%.

Mr. Malo thought that another way to improve sales was to create a more comprehensive brochure. With a presentation folder, Mr. Malo wanted to display MN Design's corporate philosophy as well as clear examples of his work. As customer relations were one of the strengths at MN Design, he felt that a more elaborate presentation of the company by an efficient salesperson would increase the potential for sales. He estimated the cost of this promotional effort as shown in Table 2.

Table 2	Cost of Promotional Effort		
240 presentation folders with embossed logo:			
Folders = $5.48 per pack of 5		$306.88	
Die		$105.00	
Embossing		$200.00	
			$ 611.88
Information sheet about the company:			
Paper = 125 x $1.50 per sheet		$ 187.50	
			$ 187.50
Case Studies: (Examples of booths built)			
3 case studies x 125 copies each = 375 pgs			
Colour copies of studies		$450.00	
Infography: 4 hours at $50/hr		$200.00	
			$ 650.00
		Subtotal:	$1449.38
		Tax:	$ 217.40
		Total Cost:	$1666.79

Mr. Malo also thought of creating a website. MN Design would then be able to show-case its entire project with dynamic pages, which would allow him to change content, images, and text. This would cost around $15 000. An increasing number of companies were surfing the Internet when searching for information so MN Design could benefit from using this tool, as it would be accessible to potential clients from any location. The website would be a constant advertisement and relay to customers the firm's capability to keep up-to-date with changes in technology.

Mr. Malo forecasted the following sales and expenses for the year 2003. Research indicated that if he called 30 prospects per show only 2 became customers. With 12 shows × 2 customers, Mr. Malo estimated 24 new customers for 2003. Based on 2002 figures, there were 33 customers, so Mr. Malo predicted that he would serve 33+24 = 57 total customers in 2003. Each customer spent on average $15 000 on MN Design's products, so 57 customers × $15 000 = $855 000 in sales.

He noted that the selling expenses and the marketing expenses did not fluctuate significantly over the years 2001 and 2002, so he assumed that they would be the same for 2003; i.e., 2% of the revenue for marketing activities and 3.5% of the revenue for selling expenses. Based on these assumptions, he calculated the following:

1. 2% of sales expected in 2003 for marketing: $855 000 × 0.02 = $17 100
2. 3.5% of sales expected in 2003 for selling expenses: $855 000 × 0.035 = $29 925

    Therefore, Mr. Malo's expected budget for expenses was $17 100 + $29 925 = $47 025.

He calculated three possible outcomes for the year 2003 as shown in Table 3. The forecasted sales potential was $855 000. He assumed that:

1. The average revenue per client was $15 000.
2. The average variable cost per client was $9410 ($310 515 / 33 customers in 2002).
3. The 57 clients remained constant and that COGS does not fluctuate as a result of pricing changes.
4. COGS: 57 customers at an average variable cost of $9410 = $536 370.

Table 3	Probable Revenue and Profit for 2003		
	Best Outcome: 20% sales increase	Medium Outcome: No change in sales	Worst Outcome: 20% sales decrease
Annual Sales	$1 026 000	$855 000	$684 000
Cost of Goods Sold	$ 536 370	$ 536 370	$ 536 370
Gross Margin	$ 489 630	$ 318 630	$ 147 630

THE DILEMMA

At this point, Mr. Malo was wondering what he should do. Should he try to follow all the suggested strategies at the same time? Should he pursue one at a time and, if so, how should he prioritize his actions? He wanted to be clear about his priorities so that he could implement them early in 2003.

Therm-eze

William A. Preshing and Denise Walters

Mr. Mark Tanner, a successful Canadian entrepreneur, purchased the Canadian rights to manufacture and distribute a reusable chemical heating pad named Therm-eze. The product—a vinyl bag containing chemicals that produced a constant level of heat—had a variety of therapeutic uses, including treatment of muscle injuries and relief from arthritic pain. The task facing management was to develop a strategy for Therm-eze in a market that had not changed in a number of years.

THE COMPANY

Mr. Tanner owned the Tanner Company, which operated three businesses in western Canada—a peat moss company, a mini-warehouse operation, and a landfill site. While attending a new business seminar, he met the inventor of Therm-eze and, after considerable investigation, paid $250 000 for the Canadian manufacturing and distribution rights. Mr. Tanner also obtained a patent on the product in Canada which would last 17 years.

This case was written by William A. Preshing, now Professor Emeritus, University of Alberta, and Denise Walters. Copyright © William A. Preshing. Reprinted with permission.

THE PRODUCT

Therm-eze consisted of a vinyl bag containing a sodium acetate solution and a small stainless steel trigger. Activating the trigger caused the solution to crystallize, producing a predictable and constant level of heat. Since the concentration of the sodium acetate solution could be varied, the pad was available in two temperature settings: 117 and 130 degrees Fahrenheit (47 and 54 degrees Celsius). The pre-set temperature could not be exceeded. The pad gave off heat at its pre-set temperature for about 20 minutes, then started to cool but still produced enough heat to have therapeutic value for up to three hours. Use of the felt cover, which came with the pad, prevented rapid heat loss. The pad could be prepared for reuse by immersing it in boiling water for fifteen minutes or auto-claving it in a chemical (but not a steam) autoclaving unit. An autoclaving unit acted in a similar manner to a pressure cooker. The pad could be reused hundreds of times until the vinyl wore out.

The Therm-eze pads could be marketed in rectangles of various sizes (8" × 18", 8" × 8", 4"× 4") and in the shape of a mitt. The vinyl bags, which would be produced by an outside contractor, were stamped from a die and could be made in virtually any size and shape at an average cost per bag of $0.50. Each die cost about $1000 (which would be paid for by the Tanner company). It could be made in less than three weeks, enabling the company to respond quickly to changing market demand. The sodium acetate solution would be purchased from an Ontario supplier at an average cost per bag of $1. Tanner Company obtained an inventory of 150 000 triggers, on consignment from the inventor, which did not have to be paid for until the pads were sold. The triggers were required to "start" the Therm-eze pad the first time it was used. The inventor had guaranteed to provide a future supply of triggers at a cost of $1.50 per unit. The felt covers and packaging were available from local suppliers at a cost per bag of $0.75.

The filling and sealing process was simple and neither labour nor capital intensive. This work would be done in the mini-warehouse to maintain quality control. One welder and three unskilled workers could produce 150 pads per hour or 22 000 per month. The combined wages of the welder and three workers would be $37.50 per hour. The company had purchased two welding machines, one as back-up in case of mechanical failure. As production needs increased, new welding machines could be purchased for approximately $7500 each.

THE MARKET

Shortly after obtaining the rights to Therm-eze, Mark Tanner hired Richard McKay at a salary of $40 000 per year as the marketing manager. He had extensive sales experience, including the introduction of a number of new products to the Canadian market. Mr. McKay's first assignment was to conduct an analysis of the market potential for Therm-eze.

Because of Therm-eze's versatility, it could be sold in three broad segments: (1) the medical treatment market, (2) personal warmth (e.g., seat cushions, survival clothing, hand warmers), and (3) heating of inanimate objects (e.g., food service, industrial equipment). After evaluating these market segments, Mr. McKay felt the medical treatment segment had the greatest potential for the immediate future, and he collected further information on this segment.

THE MEDICAL TREATMENT MARKET

The application of heat was a well-known treatment for relief from pain and increased mobility in cases of arthritis and traumatic joint or muscle injury. This market can be divided into two segments: the institutional and the home market.

Within the institutional market, there was a number of market sub-segments including active treatment hospitals, auxiliary hospitals, nursing homes, and physiotherapy and chiropractic clinics. Mr. McKay estimated that the total annual usage for these facilities would be 29 232 units. He arrived at this estimate by phoning 20 hospitals in the Calgary and Edmonton areas and asking how many of these types of pads would be ordered each year. On average, 24 pads were used by each hospital. Using Statistics Canada data he found there were 1218 hospitals in Canada and then projected the annual usage rate at 29 232.

Mr. McKay felt that the home use market would be reached primarily through retail pharmacies and secondarily through medical and surgical supply stores. There were about 2700 such outlets in Canada, and he estimated demand through them at 189 000. This estimate was based on a telephone survey of 25 retail pharmacies and 10 medical supply stores. He explained the product to each respondent and asked how many they might sell in one year. On average, the respondents said they would sell 70 units each year. Based on this information, Mr. McKay estimated that the total home use market was 189 000 pads annually.

As well, Mr. McKay felt that three market trends indicated a positive future for Therm-eze. Heat had been underutilized as a means of treatment because of the problems with burns, electrical shocks from heating pads, inconvenience, and high cost. Therm-eze, with its unique design and features, could surmount these problems. Secondly, the mean age of the Canadian population was rising and the "baby boom" generation was now approaching retirement. As people got older, the incidence of arthritis and other associated disorders would increase, leading to a more extensive personal use of Therm-eze. Finally, as more people became fitness-conscious and participated in physical activities, athletic injuries that could be treated with heat would also increase.

COMPETITION

No new products had been introduced in the industry in recent years and market shares were stable among competing firms. Therm-eze would compete with four existing products: electric heating pads, hot water bottles, instant hot packs, and reusable hot packs. Mr. McKay prepared a competitive analysis for these products (Exhibit 1). The companies producing these competing products were divisions of large multi-product firms, such as 3M and Johnson and Johnson, fabricated rubber manufacturers, and electrical goods manufacturers.

Electric heating pads applied controlled heat over large areas of the body. The pads could cause burns, especially in older patients with decreased skin sensitivity. There was a slight electric shock hazard with the pads and, as they required electricity to operate, were not truly portable.

Hot water bottles were portable and inexpensive, but less convenient to use. The temperature was hard to regulate and heat was lost quickly, requiring frequent refilling. As with electric heating pads, there was some danger of burns or scalding from hot water.

Instant hot packs worked on an exothermic chemical reaction principle. A larger bag contained water as well as a smaller bag full of chemicals. When the entire bag was crushed the chemicals were released and combined with water to produce heat. These

EXHIBIT 1	Competitive Analysis					
Product Type	Safety	Temperature Control	Selling Price	Heat Retention	Portability, Convenience	Weight, Pliability
Electric Heat Pad	Burn & shock possible	Controlled even	$10+	Indefinite	Fair, needs electricity	Fair
Hot Water Bottle	Burn possible	Uneven	$4+	15-25 min.	Fair, needs refilling	Poor
Instant Hot Pack	Burns, toxic	Uneven	$2+	10-20 min.	Good	Poor
Reusable Hot Pack	Good	Good	$30	35-40 min.	Fair, needs reheating	Fair
Home Pack	Good	Low Heat	$1.50	15-25 min.	Good	Fair
Therm-eze	Good	Good	$20	2-3 hours	Good	Very Good

packs were easy to use and were inexpensive. However, they gave off uneven heat that could cause burns and the chemicals were often toxic. They were not reusable.

Reusable hot packs were of two types: institutional and home use. The institutional market leader was the Hydropack, a canvas pack filled with gel that was heated in a steam or hot water autoclave. The pack was wrapped in towels and applied to the patient. The main advantages of the pack were control (it was available in different sizes and the temperature could be regulated by proper heating) and long equipment life—in excess of 20 years. The disadvantages were the high initial cost, specialized heating equipment that was required, higher laundry bills (due to use of towels), and inability to produce "dry" rather than "moist" heat.

The home use packs contained chemicals that were activated by hot water or steam. They were portable and provided a controlled temperature, but the heat output was lower and lasted a shorter time than Therm-eze.

Therm-eze had features that made it superior to all these products. It was truly portable, easy to use, and did not require specialized equipment. The temperature was absolutely controlled to reduce the possibility of burns, there were no toxic chemicals involved, and the pad produced therapeutic heat levels for two or more hours.

Based on his assessment of the competitive products, Mr. McKay felt that with a good marketing program Therm-eze could achieve a market share of up to 50%. However, he knew that this was a "guesstimate" at best, and the actual market share obtained might be quite different. In particular, he was concerned about the need to change traditional patterns of use.

FOCUS GROUPS

To initiate some ideas as to how to market the product, Mr. McKay conducted five focus group sessions. The five focus groups consisted of three groups of consumers who were likely users (e.g., people suffering from arthritis, people in extended care facilities, and physiotherapists). In each session people were shown a sample of the product and asked about its uses, important features, suggested selling price, and where it should be sold. Selected results from the focus groups are provided in Exhibit 2.

EXHIBIT 2	Summary of Focus Group Discussions

The summary is grouped into three categories:

(1) consumers as users (particularly the arthritic and home market); (2) the institutional market (extended care facilities and hospitals); and (3) the physiotherapy group (personal and sports-related use).

1. The Consumer Market

Key Uses
a. Substitution for other sources of heat.

b. Apply heat to ease the pain.

c. Arthritic users indicate that the pain is so substantial they will try anything on the market to seek relief.

d. Arthritic users tend to be sensitive to the word arthritic, thus anything that indicates relief will catch their attention. This is true with respect to advertisements, packages, discussions on talk shows, meetings with other arthritics, word-of-mouth, etc.

e. Major use occurs at any time, but there was substantial interest in the fact that the product could be used in the night without significant preparation.

Key Product Features
a. Portability and controlled heat.

b. Variable temperature at purchase time (product line question).

c. Flat product—very useful when user is lying down.

d. Product durability.

e. Reusable, therefore, only pennies per use.

f. Length of time heat lasts, particularly when covered in a towel, was viewed to be very positive.

g. Product could be packed in a suitcase or purse and used when travelling (in a car, plane, etc.).

h. Product is safe to use (unlike the hot wax treatment for arthritis).

i. Product is flexible and can be shaped to meet the user's needs.

j. The product does not leak (unlike a water bottle).

Price
a. Arthritics were prepared to spend in the order of $20 retail for the product, and many indicated they would consider more than one product.

b. The group indicated a warranty would be critical to initial purchase decision.

c. Some felt a towel cover could be provided for an additional sum.

EXHIBIT 2	Summary of Focus Group Discussions (continued)

Outlet

a. The majority of the group felt the product would be best suited to availability in a drug store or a department store. The great advantage of the department store was the implicit guarantee provided by the store as a part of their retail policy.

2. The Institutional Market

The discussion with people in the extended care facilities indicated that they received treatment from the central physiotherapy units. In addition, many were arthritic and indicated they would like to have such a product in their room for use during the night. A major factor in the new product is safety and reliability with respect to temperature control. This is particularly significant for older people because of a reduction in sensitivity to temperature on their skin (they tend to like heat that is too strong and thus harmful to the skin).

The major entry would be through the purchasing activity of the institutions. Individual pads may be acquired but payment would be personal. Price is thus a major factor for older people on restricted incomes.

Product acquisition varied greatly depending on whether the individual worked in a private clinic or in a hospital. The distinctions were also made by nurses who attended a focus group earlier. That is, the staff who use the product are important to the decision, but the central purchasing group also assumes a key role. It was indicated that the *major* factor in the minds of central purchasing people in the institutions was the ability to show cost effectiveness and advice was given to use this part of the presentation to individual buyers for institutions. The private clinics indicated they also consider cost effectiveness and would look at the new product as the supply of existing heating pads was used up.

3. Physiotherapists

The focus group with physiotherapists indicated that they spend substantial amounts of money on heating pads and are looking for cost effective products.

Use

a. Useful where heat is the treatment medium.

b. Use in emergency cases of hypothermia.

c. Do not use in cases of inflammation or where internal bleeding may be present. Use in cases of inflammation after an initial treatment period where ice was used as the treatment medium.

d. Good potential for treatment of seniors because of temperature control, which is essential due to poor circulation.

e. Good potential for in-home use after physiotherapy treatment program.

EXHIBIT 2	Summary of Focus Group Discussions (continued)

Benefits

a. Convenient.
b. Cost effective.
c. Safety due to constant temperature (point made was that heat is damaging; ice will not damage the skin because the person will stop using the ice due to the cold).
d. Warranty is essential to remove product liability from the user, particularly the user in private clinics. In essence, they indicated a need to guarantee treatment time and product life.

INITIAL MARKETING IDEAS

Based on his analysis of the market, competition, and focus group results, Mr. McKay developed a preliminary marketing plan for Therm-eze. He felt that the product could have a retail price of $20, which was in line with the price consumers appeared willing to pay for a reusable pad with Therm-eze's features. Retailers would probably expect a margin of 25% on retail selling price.

Successful marketing of Therm-eze in both the institutional and home markets probably required acceptance by the medical profession. In the institutional market, the physician must order heat treatments before there would be a demand for the pads. The home user often bought products on the basis of a doctor's recommendation.

Existing competitive products were marketed through three distributors. Canadian Hospital Products was the only Canadian company that distributed to the institutional market. The company prided itself on carrying Canadian-made products. Northern Medical was a national distributor that would distribute the pad to pharmacies and surgical supply stores. In Quebec there was resistance to a product distributed from outside the province, and because of this, a Quebec distributor would be chosen. All three distributors would require margins of 15% on their selling price. Mr. McKay considered adding three salespeople to push the distribution of the product; each salesperson would be responsible for servicing either the home, institutional, or Quebec market. Salary and travel expenses for each salesperson were estimated at $30 000 per year.

Mr. McKay was uncertain about advertising but knew that the institutional market could be accessed on two levels: through the doctors and other paramedical personnel, and through advertising aimed at purchasing agents for hospitals, nursing homes, and clinics. Considering the home market, promotional considerations would include the type of packaging and the product literature enclosed, as well as the type of advertising that would best reach the home market, which is primarily composed of older people.

Based on the information he had collected, Mr. McKay began preparing a marketing plan for Therm-eze. He was optimistic about the success of the venture and looked forward to presenting the plan for approval to Mr. Tanner.

Protocase

*Sherry Finney, Doug Lionais,
and Jacqueline Lalanne*

Adam Kehoe and Simone Meijer, marketing and sales employees at Protocase in Sydney, Nova Scotia, left a staff meeting in February 2005 with a challenging task at hand. Steve Lilley, President of Protocase, had just announced that he wanted to double the company's sales in the next six months. Market analysis had revealed that increased sales potential existed for the company and up to this point, Protocase had been realizing an annual average sales growth of 100 percent. Lilley now thought it was time to raise the bar. Further, he believed that this objective could be achieved by targeting electrical and mechanical researchers. Kehoe and Meijer now needed to determine the appropriate marketing tactics.

COMPANY BACKGROUND

Steve Lilley, a mechanical engineer, founded Protocase in October 2001. Protocase manufactured steel boxes or enclosures for low-volume manufacturers and product developers. Lilley had developed many prototypes himself over the years and knew of the difficulties in finding customized cases in order to complete the design.

Protocase had a team of 14 individuals who contributed to different stages of product development. Six employees graduated from Cape Breton University (CBU), two of whom were Simone Meijer and Adam Kehoe. Meijer graduated from CBU with a BBA in tourism marketing in 2002 and had been with Protocase since graduation. Kehoe completed a BBA degree in marketing in 2003 and joined the Protocase team in January 2004. Lilley functioned as the president and CEO; however, because it was a relatively small but growing business, he was directly involved in the day-to-day operations. Other employees included a manufacturing manager, an office administrator, three mechanical technologists, and six manufacturing personnel. The company had a group benefit plan and a small bonus/incentive program. Staff turnover wasn't an issue; however, the company did have difficulty finding qualified mechanical technologists. For the past several months, they had been trying to recruit a technologist with no success.

All employees worked well together, and Meijer and Kehoe attributed much of their success to the company culture. Staff were willing to work after normal working hours, if necessary, and make personal sacrifices. Meijer and Kehoe were excited to be working for a young, growing company like Protocase and felt that the long hours sometimes required were worth it. Sales had been steadily increasing; however, the growth had not come without its challenges. Access to capital had been an issue in the recent past.

THE PRODUCT AND PRODUCTION PROCESS

A prototype in the electronic devices industry was an early stage product design, often used for testing and test marketing before beginning mass production. Typically, electrical and mechanical engineers developed the prototypes, and they needed an outer casing to complete the design (Exhibit 1). Protocase offered a solution.

EXHIBIT 1	Protocase Enclosures

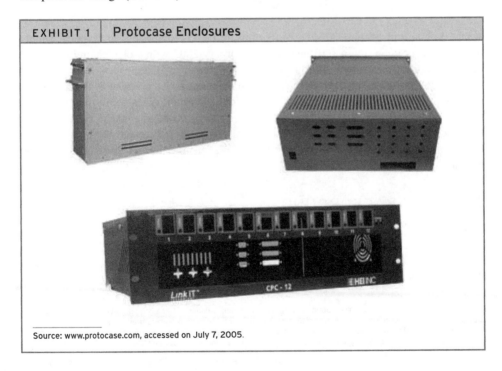

Source: www.protocase.com, accessed on July 7, 2005.

The production process usually began with Meijer or Kehoe responding to an online inquiry sent to the company website. Once they did the groundwork on the pricing, if there was any design work required, they passed the project over to a mechanical technologist. The customers determined the type of enclosure required usually by one of two methods. The first was to choose a common enclosure design (Exhibit 2). These were off-the-shelf products that required no customization. The second method was for the creation of a fully customized enclosure (Exhibit 3). Both methods involved using computer-aided design software (CAD). If the customer was unfamiliar with the software or did not have the software capabilities, then one of Protocase's mechanical technologists would accommodate the customer by designing the enclosure in-house. The enclosure itself was manufactured from steel or stainless steel.

One aspect of Protocase's positioning was its ability to provide the customized product in a very short timeframe. The manufacture of the enclosures had a two-to-three day turn-around from the time all the information was received from the customer until the time it was shipped. Each enclosure was customized to meet the exact specifications of the customer and Protocase was able to perform all aspects of the design including powder coating, installing self-clinching fasteners, and silk-screening.

In most cases, the majority of communication during the production process occurred by email. The customers sent original specifications and, after a phone consultation, the production process began. The customer was then sent emails when the product entered the production line, and when the product was shipped. The email with the shipping information also included a reference number that allowed the customer to track the package. After the customer received the product, a follow-up call was made a day or two later to see if the customer was pleased with the product.

CURRENT CLIENT BASE AND FUTURE MARKETS

Protocase had approximately 400 customers; 85 percent were in the United States, one was in the United Kingdom, and the rest were in Canada. Of its Canadian customers, the majority were based in Quebec. Alberta, British Columbia, and Ontario, in that order, were the next most lucrative markets. In the United States, Florida and California represented its largest markets among the 40 states where Protocase had customers. Organizations such as Boeing, IBM, three divisions of NASA, UCLA, Stanford University, and MIT had all purchased enclosures from the company. While Protocase had done work for many large companies, however, the majority of its business was with companies similar in size to itself. About 65 percent of Protocase's sales represented repeat business, and the average order size was approximately $500. Since inception, the company had experienced continuous sales growth and most recently, its annual sales reached $1.5 million. With respect to market potential, Meijer and Kehoe were uncertain and really couldn't predict how large the actual market was; their uncertainty was primarily because they did business with so many different kinds of manufacturing companies.

In all cases, Meijer and Kehoe dealt directly with electrical or mechanical engineers and over time, they came to realize that they had unique characteristics. It was their impression that engineers really didn't want to be "marketed to." As well, they felt that while the typical engineer completely understood his or her prototype and what was to be contained within the enclosure, the engineer really didn't understand the enclosure production process.

EXHIBIT 2	Protocase Common Enclosure Designs

Common Enclosure Designs

Step 1: Select box type.

Two-piece　　　　　　U-shaped　　　　　　Rack-mount

Step 2: Select box size (X, Y, and Z).

 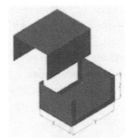 

Step 3: Specify cutout shapes and locations on each face.

Step 4: That's it! Your enclosure will be shipped in days.

Source: www.protocase.com, accessed on July 7, 2005.

EXHIBIT 3	Protocase Fully Customized Enclosures

Fully Customized Enclosures

For your fully customized enclosure requirements, it's simple and fast . . . send us your CAD drawing and one of our technical representatives will review your drawing and contact you within hours. Once accepted, your order will be shipped in days.

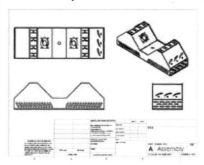

Step 1: Send us a CAD file of your customized enclosure. One of our CAD technicians will review it within hours.

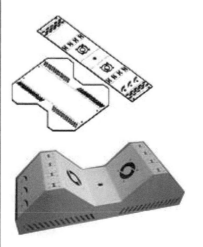

Step 2: Once the order is approved, the job enters our manufacturing queue. Seen here is a computer rendering of the flattened enclosure.

Step 3: The completed order is ready for shipment within days.

Source: www.protocase.com, accessed on July 7, 2005.

Meijer and Kehoe came to the conclusion that they had to adjust the communication and marketing process so they could provide the tools for the engineer to inform him/herself, and once educated, he/she would be prepared to discuss the design and purchase of the enclosure. Meijer and Kehoe also decided they needed to adapt their promotion and put most of their emphasis on Internet marketing. According to Lilley, "engineers are natural leaders online. We like to go sit in front of computers to search and find things." [1] Finally, the customers also seemed to prefer email communication to an actual phone conversation. Many times Meijer or Kehoe would try to call a customer but never seemed to be able to get the individual on the phone. Emails, however, seemed to get an almost immediate response.

The other interesting observation made by Meijer and Kehoe was that most Canadians appeared hesitant to switch suppliers. When Protocase first started, the common question they were asked by potential customers was "who else uses your product?" Because they were a

---

[1] Procter, S. "C.B. Firm Makes Its Case," *Chronicle Herald*, July 31, 2005, p. A12.

new company, it was more difficult for them to enter the market; they had no track record. U.S. companies, though, appeared more willing to try a new enclosure supplier, at least once. Because it was only a small expenditure, most were willing to take the risk. Sometimes, however, it was difficult to sell to the larger businesses because they wanted their suppliers to be qualified and pre-approved before being placed on an approved supplier list. In many instances, Protocase was not large enough or established enough to be considered. Customers in the past who wanted to buy from Protocase but couldn't because of approved supplier criteria would get approved suppliers to buy from Protocase and resell the product to them.

Lilley decided Protocase should target university researchers. The university researchers of interest consisted mainly of engineers, physics students, and PhDs who concentrated on the electronics field. Protocase already had 15 to 20 university clients and most of these were acquired through a postcard campaign or through its website. Over 50 percent of the university engineers Protocase served were repeat purchasers; and, while they might only order a couple of times a year, the orders had a very attractive profit margin. Meijer and Kehoe had found that most of the time, the doctoral students made the decision about the enclosure and they typically had a budget for their project. The researcher target market was primarily located in the United States as U.S. universities generally had larger funds allocated to research than Canadian institutions. Through their research efforts, they had compiled a list of 16 Canadian engineering universities and the top 50 U.S. engineering universities. They had not directed any marketing efforts towards these schools. One consideration with the university market, though, was that many universities had their own metal fabrication shops that could produce enclosures. Using a university metal shop meant, however, that the researcher was required to draw out the sketch, deliver it to the metal shop, and explain the design.

Protocase also felt that by targeting student researchers, they could secure long-term customers. Potentially, the students would continue to purchase from Protocase when they joined the workforce. As an example, Protocase had done work for the MIT Lincoln Lab, which is affiliated with more than 100 spin-off companies. Many of the MIT engineering students looked to these companies for employment. Protocase needed to determine a method that would allow it to maintain contact with these students once they entered the workforce.

THE COMPETITION AND POSITIONING

While there were competitors in the enclosure manufacturing industry, Protocase believed that there was really no one offering the same level of service and quality that it did. Because developers of prototypes generally required only one enclosure, mass producers were not interested in the limited protocase market. As a result, there was a need for a company like Protocase that specialized in customized enclosures for product developers as well as for low volume manufacturers.

Some of the biggest players in the industry were Hoffman, Hammond, Eurobex, and E-machine Shop. Despite the fact that these companies would perform enclosure customization, most of their business came from their off-the-shelf units. As well, their turnaround time on the delivery of a customized unit could not compare with Protocase's—three days from start to finish. Meijer and Kehoe believed that their products were superior in quality, and they promoted to their customers that "they could take care of all their enclosure needs . . . don't worry about it." Protocase sold on overall value and, while its customers were not overly price sensitive, the company believed that prices must be fair. They also strived for and achieved a very quick response rate of 24 hours on all inquiries.

Another source of competition was metal fabrication shops, but the metal fabricators were not specialized in providing enclosures for prototypes. Therefore, the prototype developer would have to go to the metal shop to explain the enclosure specifications. Furthermore, metal shops often would not provide the prototype developer with all the services that were needed to complete the casement, such as attachments, painting and/or decaling, and labelling. Finally, the turnaround time for the metal shops tended to be much longer than that offered by Protocase. One-unit orders for customized enclosures took the back seat to larger quantity and more profitable orders. Even in consideration of the delays, using a local metal shop seemed to be attractive to some customers in the Canadian market. Meijer and Kehoe suspected that it was because the developer believed he/she could have more control over the production of the protocase. They also wondered if there was perhaps an assumed level of risk associated with ordering the enclosure online.

One challenge that Protocase did face was the shipping costs to send products to the United States. This increased the cost, but Meijer and Kehoe felt that their quality and quick service made up for it. Many of their customers were willing to pay the premium. Over the past couple of years, shipping rates had remained fairly stable.

PAST PROMOTION AT PROTOCASE

Past marketing efforts at Protocase were a shared effort between Meijer, Kehoe, and, sometimes, Lilley. Being a small and growing business, though, meant that periodically they had to abandon promotional planning in favour of negotiating and closing sales. Meijer and Kehoe did not work with an established marketing budget. Instead they discussed their ideas with Lilley and, if it was felt that there was one that had potential, Lilley gave the okay. Since business inception, the company had tried several marketing tactics.

Website

Protocase's website (www.protocase.com) was designed for two types of customers: product developers and low volume manufacturers. Each target market had its own link to enter the site. On the site, the customer was able to receive a quote, place an order, email questions, download templates, and look at sample enclosures and other items that could be added to the enclosures. The website also provided a brief overview of the company and the history of the industry. Although many clients used the Protocase website, only 3 to 5 percent actually placed their orders on it. Most customers preferred to phone, fax, or email their initial specifications to receive a quote. Approximately 80 percent of the customers became aware of Protocase either through the website or through Google AdWord advertising. Protocase measured unique visitors to its website, meaning they are counted only once, regardless of how many daily visits made to the website. In February 2005, there were approximately 5000 unique visitors and this directly translated into 10 to 12 new customers for the month.

Google AdWords

Google AdWords was a Google service that connected companies to potential customers worldwide. Protocase would bid on a word it believed a potential customer would be searching on Google. If it won the bid when the customer Googled the word, a Protocase ad would appear, with a direct link to the Protocase website, above or to the right of the search results as a sponsored link. Protocase is only charged if the link is clicked. Kehoe and Meijer felt that being in the top three positions was most beneficial. The top three positions were the closest to the top of the webpage results. It is possible to bid on several key words in order to improve position. As well, with this kind of advertising, the purchaser can set its own budget. Currently, Protocase had established a budget of approximately $2000 per month. However, if it desired, it could increase this amount significantly to improve its position in search results.

Postcards

Advanced Circuits, a Protocase customer, produced printed circuit boards (PCB), components often used in the production of electrical prototypes. Meijer and Kehoe knew that some of Advanced Circuits' customers could be potential Protocase customers, and, as a result, they pursued an arrangement with Advanced Circuits that allowed Protocase to include a postcard with each order Advanced Circuits sent to its customers. Approximately 12 000 postcards were sent out in a two-month period, costing about $2000. The company figured that this campaign accounted for a 10 percent increase in its customer base.

Magazines

Protocase had also advertised in magazines. However, Meijer and Kehoe believed that because Protocase was a young company, it needed to establish its brand first. They both felt that the magazine ads would be more beneficial to companies that were already established and were introducing a new product or service. Ads cost anywhere between $3000 and $10 000 per ad, per issue, and tracking revealed no apparent response.

Tradeshows

Protocase had participated in one tradeshow in March 2003, in San Jose, California. The show was called PCB West and was targeted to those interested in printed circuit board (PCB) design. It seemed to Meijer that those in attendance were more interested in circuit boards and weren't necessarily thinking about enclosures at that time. The tradeshow did allow for an opportunity to arrange a meeting with potential customers to demonstrate the enclosure. However, it was costly, totalling approximately $15 000 for the booth, display, and travel. As well, because they had no brand awareness, they felt that it wasn't as beneficial as it could be for a more recognized company.

Personal Selling

In the past, Lilley had travelled to various places in Ontario and Atlantic Canada to promote the enclosures. Prior to his trips, he would arrange meetings with companies to demonstrate his product. However, Lilley felt that personal selling was not the most appropriate method to promote the enclosures given the average value of each sale. Travelling required considerable time and money.

Telemarketing

In the past, Protocase had also used telemarketing to promote its product. Employees would telephone companies to introduce them to the enclosures, but it was often difficult to speak to the person who would be interested in the product—usually an engineer—and they would typically have to speak with an administrative assistant instead. Also, if they were actually able to speak to the engineer, it was difficult to explain the enclosures and the value that could be added to the prototypes. Prospects were found by browsing the Internet. While not necessarily abandoned forever, Protocase was not conducting any telemarketing in February 2005 and had no immediate plans to do so.

FUTURE PROMOTION

Meijer and Kehoe knew that certain tactics had been more successful than others, and they really needed to sit down and perform a thorough analysis. In addition to what had been done in the past, however, they had some other ideas.

Given the importance of their website, they believed it needed revamping. They envisioned online tutorials that would introduce engineers to the basics of silk-screening, enclosure design, self-clinching fasteners, CAD templates, etc. Additionally, they were working on the concept of "Protocase Designer," a free CAD-based downloadable enclosure design application that would put the power of design in the hands of their clients. It was anticipated that Protocase Designer would work by having clients progress through the following stages: selection of standard enclosures, selection of cut-outs and fasteners, real-time price calculation online at the website, and, finally, online order placement. The projected development budget for this application was $60 000.

Meijer and Kehoe also believed that more could be done through electronic media to maintain relationships with past and future clients (e.g., electronic newsletters, a website project-of-the-month competition, etc.). Neither of them had the technical expertise to maintain a website, however. Someone would need to be hired that would have a combination of computer engineering as well as electronic marketing skills. This could cost anywhere between $40 000 and $50 000.

Meijer and Kehoe were also considering attending the Consumer Electronics tradeshow. At this show, engineers had the opportunity to showcase their prototypes. Meijer and Kehoe felt that this particular type of show was more attractive as engineers who had already gone through the development process attended it. This group of show attendees represented future market potential. Another possibility was to attend the tradeshow aspect of an academic conference targeted toward electrical/mechanical researchers. Associated costs were uncertain, but it was expected that they would be similar to costs of attending past tradeshows.

Although Meijer and Kehoe were responsible for the promotional planning and implementation, they also had other responsibilities such as managing sales. They did most of the communicating with the customers during the production process, and they were responsible for taking orders from the customers, ensuring that the product was delivered, and following up with phone calls. The customer relationship management interfered with the time they would have liked to allocate to the planning function. To date, they had also not done any kind of public relations work because they just didn't have the time. There really needed to be a dedicated management position to the marketing function.

THE TASK

Meijer and Kehoe were pressed for time and they had to determine a way for Protocase to target university researchers. They were aware of the success of the promotional tools that were used in the past, but were unsure of the appropriate direction that Protocase should take to focus on this market. Lilley's goal was to double sales for the company in the next six months. This was ambitious, but given the company's recent growth, Meijer and Kehoe felt it was possible. There was little time to waste; they immediately needed to identify the most appropriate promotional mix for this market.

Wilderness Newfoundland Adventures

Cori-Jane Radford and H.F. (Herb) MacKenzie

It was a beautiful January morning in St. John's, Newfoundland, and Stan Cook Jr. was staring out of his office window, contemplating the 1999 promotional strategy for his family's ecotourism business, Wilderness Newfoundland Adventures (WNA). He was supposed to meet with his father on Friday to discuss it. It was already Tuesday, and time was short. Many advertising and promotional items should have been placed by now. Stan Cook, Sr. would be expecting a progress report. Stan, Jr. decided to review the 1998 promotional strategy to see which items should be continued, and which should be changed or dropped for 1999.

WNA'S PRODUCT

WNA offers single- and multi-day tours, including kayak day (approximately eight hours), half-day, and sunset trips. As well, they offer weekend tours, multi-day combination-activity tours, multi-day single-activity tours, and on-site and off-site equipment rentals. Tours include instruction and interpretation on sea kayaking, mountain biking, hiking, canoeing, orienteering, outdoor camping, and wilderness survival skills. WNA offers a comprehensive program for beginner, intermediate, and expert paddlers, and adventurers of all ages.

WNA tours are all-inclusive. The adventurer is supplied with all food, camping equipment, sporting equipment, and safety gear. Participants only bring appropriate clothing and a backpack. WNA covers all sections of non-consumptive adventure tourism and caters to the traveller who is attracted to these activities. WNA also specializes in outdoor excursions that are modified for its clients.

WNA has been focusing recently on products that are thought to have national and international potential and are "market-ready." Sea kayaking is one of these products. According to the Canadian Recreation Canoe Association, sea kayaking is the fastest-growing paddling activity, with an annual growth rate of 20%. Many areas of Newfoundland are ideal for this activity. Newfoundland is an island with over 10 000 miles of fascinating coastline, dotted with caves, waterfalls, sea stacks, and arches. Icebergs are abundant from May through July, and thousands of humpback and minke whales visit from late June to mid-August.

WNA mainly uses two-person, ocean-going kayaks for all trips. These kayaks are very stable and seaworthy, and all use rudders to steer. The area that the Cooks picked to run their day trips, Cape Broyle, is beautiful and quite calm. Rarely has anyone ever fallen out of a kayak, although it has happened in knee-deep water when participants were pulling the kayak up on the beach. The guide-to-participant ratio is 1:6, one guide kayak (single-person kayak) to every three participant kayaks. WNA's guides are all trained in safety, rescue, and first aid techniques. Sea kayaking in these circumstances is not difficult; people of all ages and fitness levels can participate. In fact, WNA has taken an 84-year-old grandmother on one of the day trips.

HEADQUARTERS

After searching for three years, WNA decided to locate its operations in Cape Broyle, about 50 minutes south of St. John's on the province's Avalon Peninsula. The area has natural beauty (soaring cliffs, caves, waterfalls, varied topography), nature attractions (icebergs, bird sanctuaries, caribou herd), protection from the wind (7-kilometre fjord), an abundance of marine life (whales, seals, otters), proximity to a large urban population (St. John's), an historic property (85-year-old community general store), and cultural distinction (Irish Heart of Newfoundland). WNA believed this spot to be a world-class area for sea kayaking, mountain biking, and hiking, and an ideal location for its site.

WNA has become the first adventure travel and ecotourism operator to utilize the opportunity that Newfoundland and Labrador offers with its unique culture and history. WNA has leased a heritage building for $150 per month in Cape Broyle. The building is suitable for barbecues and dinners for groups of up to 30 people. Together, the adventure tours and facilities highlight the cultural and historical identity most tourists and visitors welcome, and provide a unique and memorable experience.

SHORT SEASON

Newfoundland has a relatively short summer. Therefore, WNA has a short season to generate revenue. WNA presently has 12 two-person kayaks, but is considering purchasing 4 more for the 1999 season. Newfoundland's summer extends from late June until mid-September. Kayaking in May and early June is beautiful, but it can be cold and uncomfortable. Late September is a great time to paddle, but the tourist trade usually drops off. As well, once children are back in school, local people lose interest in summer activities. To counter this seasonal disinterest, WNA has contacted local high schools, and has encouraged them to take their students on kayaking field trips. Biology and physical education teachers were the targets of this promotion. Biology students were invited to take a close-up look at the marine life in Newfoundland's waters, and physical education students were invited to participate simply for exercise. This promotion was relatively successful; four of twelve schools participated in 1998. On average, schools have the potential to take at least two classes of students.

TRIP BREAKDOWN

WNA's day trips run from May until early October. People can book any day they wish, but a trip is cancelled if fewer than four people book in advance. An equal number of tourists and local adventurers participate in the shorter trips. During the peak whale and iceberg period, WNA runs a 5-day kayak trip; a 7-day kayak and mountain bike trip; a 14-day kayak, mountain bike, and canoe youth trip; and several "kayak weekends." In 1998, the number of participants for each of these types of trips was 12, 10, 12, and 16, respectively. Extended trips are made up entirely of tourists who come from all over the world, including Japan, Germany, the United Kingdom, the United States, and other parts of Canada. These trips often involve other areas of the province, such as Trinity Bay, Notre Dame Bay, and Terra Nova National Park. These trips begin when participants arrive at the St. John's airport, where they are met and then taken to the appropriate trailhead.

Tourists book reservations for these excursions months in advance, often by calling the WNA toll-free number. The provincial travel guide, WNA's webpage, the television program *The Great Outdoorsman,* and the Outdoor Adventure Trade Show seem to be the routes of discovery to WNA for international tourists. As well, wholesalers in both Ontario and the United States have expressed an interest in representing WNA to their markets. These wholesalers take WNA's price and mark it up 10–15% before advertising it to their customers. This requires limited marketing by WNA, and is a relatively stress-free option, although unpredictable. These wholesalers usually market trips to different locations each year.

WNA markets sea kayaking packages to both potential tourists and visitors who come to the province. This forward strategy provided WNA with an early introduction in the industry, and allowed it to become the premier adventure travel and ecotourism company in the province.

COMPANY BACKGROUND

In 1970, Mr. Cook introduced commercial canoeing to Newfoundland. He provided all-inclusive canoeing trips that averaged five to ten days in length. These trips included instructions on canoeing operations, trout fishing, camping skills, and orientation with maps and compass instruction. The focus of the trips was placed on acquisition of life skills that are indigenous to outdoor experience. Cooperation, self-reliance, and appreciation of the great outdoors were main priorities with Mr. Cook. He guided and instructed both children and adults of all skill levels throughout the 1970s and early 1980s.

During the 1980s, Mr. Cook received numerous international inquiries about his abilities to coordinate and handle groups interested in canoeing and camping in Newfoundland. After joining the Marine Adventures Association of Newfoundland and Labrador in the late 1980s and becoming its secretary/treasurer, he noticed the interest that the province was generating for adventure travel. Mr. Cook believed that it was economically feasible to expand his current canoeing school, which was focused on the local provincial market, to encompass a larger, yet specific, international market interested in adventure travel and ecotourism. This would not only include the usual training in canoeing and portaging skills, but would also utilize the world-class sea kayaking and mountain biking opportunities that existed in the province and had not been properly marketed.

In 1995, Mr. Cook changed the company name from Stan Cook Enterprises to Wilderness Newfoundland Adventures, symbolizing the new focus on international business. The expanded product line was promoted to new target markets, and the business and Mr. Cook's reputation soon enhanced the Newfoundland and Labrador tourism industry.

Besides Mr. Cook, the company involved two other members of his family, and a number of seasonal workers. Stan Jr. was responsible for the daily operations of the business. He had an undergraduate business degree, and was available to manage the business during the earlier and later parts of the season when his father was still teaching physical education at one of the St. John's high schools. Much of the success of WNA can be attributed to its first marketing plan, developed and implemented by Stan Jr.

Mr. Cook's daughter, Cori-Jane Radford, started working with WNA in the spring of 1996, when she assumed responsibility for marketing. This allowed Stan Jr. to get more involved with daily operations, and to address issues that had previously been ignored. Many of the marketing ideas implemented during 1997 and 1998 were her creation. In September 1998, however, Cori-Jane decided to get her MBA, and her involvement with the business diminished.

During the summer of 1998, WNA had five seasonal employees. There were three full-time guides and one part-time guide ($10/hour), and a junior guide ($7/hour). The full-time guides averaged 40 hours of work per week, the part-time guide averaged 15 hours of work per week, and the junior guide averaged 30 hours of work per week. All guides had specific outdoor qualifications before they were hired. Before being given responsibility to lead trips, all guides had a one-week training program, followed by a weekend expedition with Mr. Cook and Stan Jr. Guides were hired on the basis of their qualifications, personality, and knowledge of the history and culture of Newfoundland. (See Exhibit 2 for an indication of a guide's duties on a typical day or overnight trip.)

For 1999, WNA plans to increase the number of seasonal employees, and it will also attempt to increase the length of the season. This is an attempt to increase revenues and to market itself as a destination in the shoulder seasons (spring and fall) as well. However, this strategy directly hinges on the ability of WNA to attract larger volumes of out-of-province travellers. WNA wishes to expand further into the international adventure market. To achieve this goal the company needs a larger workforce, and perhaps a full-time marketing and salesperson.

This person would be expected to take the marketing responsibilities from Stan Jr. so that he can concentrate on other important matters. As well, this person would be responsible for generating individual sales, both locally and internationally. The 2-day sea kayak trip sells for $250, the 5-day trip is $625, the 7-day combo trip (sea kayak / mountain bike) is $875, and the 14-day youth combo is $980.

ADVENTURE TRAVEL AND ECOTOURISM IN NEWFOUNDLAND AND LABRADOR

The tourism industry in Newfoundland and Labrador has evolved to the point where traditional markets are being segmented into highly specific niche markets, such as soft and hard adventure, and ecotourism. However, in Newfoundland and Labrador, the ecotourism segment of the market is still in its developmental stages, with few quality operators. This category of tourism is particularly beneficial to the province, due to its careful use of the environment, and the tendency of nature-oriented travellers to spend more money during their vacations than recreational travellers.

Adventure travel is defined as a leisure activity that takes place in an unusual, exotic, remote, or wilderness destination, and is associated with high or low levels of activity by the participants. Adventure travellers expect to experience varying degrees of risk, excitement, or tranquillity, and to be personally tested or stretched in some way. Adventure travel is participatory, informative, interesting, unique, and in addition to excitement, it offers a wide range of challenges in an outdoor setting. A trip might be devoted to one activity or a combination of activities. The duration can be from several hours to several weeks.

Non-consumptive tourism uses the natural habitat without removing any of its resources (consumptive tourism removes resources, e.g., hunting or fishing). Non-consumptive adventure tourism can be subdivided into three areas: soft adventure, hard adventure, and ecotourism. WNA is most concerned with soft adventure and ecotourism but can offer participants hard adventure if they so desire. All three types of adventure tourism take place outdoors, involve travel to a particular natural attraction and some level of physical activity, and focus on activities that offer new or unusual experiences. Though these types of adventure tourism differ in degree of physical exertion, it is possible that all three can be combined into a single tour package.

Soft Adventure Travel

Soft adventure travel focuses on providing a unique outdoors experience or "adventure." However, it involves only a minor element of risk, little physical exertion, and no skill. It involves less physically demanding activities. All ages and fitness levels can participate.

Hard Adventure Travel

Hard adventure travel combines a unique experience in an outdoor setting with excitement and a degree of risk. It frequently demands physical exertion, a level of skill, and it often requires that the participant prepares or trains for the experience.

Ecotourism

Ecotourism is purposeful travel that creates an understanding of the region's culture and natural history, while safeguarding the integrity of the ecosystem and producing economic benefits that encourage conservation. An ecotour can be either soft adventure or hard adventure, but not both.

THE APPEAL OF ADVENTURE TRAVEL AND ECOTOURISM

Adventure travel and ecotourism form one of the world's fastest-growing tourism sectors. It holds appeal for travellers who are no longer happy with traditional vacations. Members of these groups look for the things that adventure travel and ecotourism offer: excitement, risk, unique experiences, education, and fun.

Analysts believe that the worldwide demand for adventure and ecotourism vacations will continue to grow well into the twenty-first century, with increasing demand each year. Currently, growth in this sector is leading the whole Canadian tourism industry, and it is actually outperforming the Canadian economy.

Newfoundland and Labrador is in a good position to profit from the increased demand for adventure travel and ecotourism. The province offers pristine environments, wildlife, unique flora and fauna, and exotic, challenging experiences. Almost every region of the province is trying to develop a variety of activities or products to draw visitors. However, the adventure travel and ecotourism business is highly seasonal with few operators open all year. Despite its potential, Newfoundland and Labrador attracts a small fraction of the North American market. Clearly, there are opportunities for growth in this business. This task is not easy because international competition has kept pace with the growth in demand. Today, consumers can choose from the wide variety of appealing activities and experiences available in many countries.

WNA believes its success in the international marketplace depends on both the quality of the experience it provides and how that experience is marketed and managed. The future success of Newfoundland and Labrador adventure travel and ecotourism will depend on how well operators are provided with tools to address challenges with informed, effective action.

TARGET MARKET FOR ADVENTURE TOURISM

The target market includes travellers interested in visiting a specific place to engage in a new or unusual participative experience. This group of tourists has different product needs that change on a seasonal basis. Many market researchers believe the single most significant trend that will determine the nature of demand for the adventure product will be the aging baby boomers. They are wealthier, not as interested in the hard "roughing-it adventure," have less time, and yet still seek new experiences.

Some interesting statistics about adventure travellers are:

- There are 30 to 40 million Americans that are potential candidates for an adventure trip of some kind.

- There are 787 000 potential adventure tourism clients in the United Kingdom. Thirty-five percent of British vacationers seek adventure and are looking for an active holiday where they can get in touch with their daring adventurous side.

- The outdoor sports segments, totalling 1.3 million people, represent potential for adventure travel.

These potential adventure travellers fit the following three main profiles.

Casual Adventure Travellers

These are the entry-level adventurers, experimenting with new and challenging outdoor activities. They take short trips (one or two days) to get a "taste of adventure." This market affords the greatest growth potential in the short term. Also, there is little difference between these travellers and the touring urban-based tourists. Therefore, the opportunity to attract city-touring visitors for short excursions is good, due to their closely related desires.

Committed Adventure Travellers

These travellers form the most affluent segment. They are fitness-conscious, in the middle- to upper-income brackets, 30 to 55 years old, well-educated, and live in urban centres. They demand and are willing to pay for quality accommodations.

Expert Adventure Travellers

These are the adventurers who are on their way to mastering a sports-related skill or knowledge about a topic (e.g., wildlife), and for whom the motivation for a trip has shifted from general growth and exploration to the fine-tuning of a particular skill. This market tends to be younger, has less disposable income, and is more inclined than other groups to "rough it."

COMPETITION

It is important for WNA to understand and cultivate its target market and to know its competition. The main competition for WNA is not within the province. Since this province has very few quality operators, the real competition is coming from operators outside Newfoundland and Labrador who are offering similar travel experiences. Many of these operators are very good and have much to offer. Therefore, WNA is working hard to create better products. By monitoring its larger international competitors, WNA has been trying to improve its products, providing better value and, hopefully, attracting more customers.

The major competition for all adventure travel and ecotourism customers comes from outside Canada. Worldwide consumer demand for unique experiences and intriguing packages is fuelling international competition. However, current market opportunities support WNA's products. WNA remains highly competitive with its current pricing strategy, service quality, product uniqueness (i.e., sea kayaking with whales and icebergs), wilderness environmental appeal, and current currency exchange rates.

1998 PROMOTIONAL ACTIVITIES

Stan Jr. and Cori-Jane generated all of the ad concepts and material and created the 1998 media plan (see Exhibit 1). Cori-Jane created the physical displays and then had films produced by the printer. This is quite inexpensive compared to hiring a marketing firm, although it is time-consuming. Stan Jr. had limited involvement with the graphic design, but his involvement has been increasing due to Cori-Jane's decreasing involvement in the business.

EXHIBIT 1	WNA Media Budget, 1998

Media	Date	Company	Form of Ad	Cost
TV	07/28/98	The Great Outdoorsman	Half-hour television show	$ 7 500.00
Radio	06/30/98	OZ-FM	60 × 30 sec. spots (2 weeks)	$ 1 750.00
	07/31/98	OZ-FM	60 × 30 sec. spots (2 weeks)	$ 1 750.00
	08/31/98	OZ-FM	60 × 30 sec. spots (2 weeks)	$ 1 750.00
Print	12/29/97	St. John's Visitor's Guide	1/4-page ad–full colour	$ 575.00
	01/15/98	NewTel Communications	Yellow Pages–1/8-page ad–1 colour	$ 1 200.00
	04/30/98	NFLD Sportsman	1/6-page ad–full colour	$ 400.00
	05/03/98	NFLD Sportsman	1/6-page ad–full colour	$ 400.00
	06/07/98	NFLD Sportsman	Full-page ad–full colour–accompanying story	$ 1 300.00
	12/29/97	Provincial Travel Guide	1/4-page ad–full colour	$ 1 500.00
	04/30/98	St. John's Board of Trade	Front cover	$ 1 200.00
	03/31/98	Sterling Press Printers	Small brochure–full colour	$ 1 350.00
Sales promo	06/04/98	Gift certificates	25 half-day trips for 2	$ 2 500.00
Signage	05/02/98	Highway signage	Three 12' × 8'	$ 500.00
	04/26/98	WNA van signage	Full-colour, 4 sides	$ 500.00
Trade show	06/01/98	Kinetic Marketing	NFLD Sportsman Show, St. John's–Booth	$ 600.00
	02/14/98	National Event Management	Outdoor Adventure Show, Toronto–Booth	$ 2 000.00
				$ 26 775.00

Print Advertising

Newfoundland Sportsman Magazine

Newfoundland Sportsman magazine is a 70-page, full-colour, glossy magazine. This magazine prints 20 000 copies every two months. It has approximately 5000 subscribers and the other copies are distributed to retailers and news stands all across the province. This magazine is published in Newfoundland and marketed to adults interested in the outdoors. Most readers are between the ages of 18 and 55, and include both men and women in approximately equal numbers. Both consumptive and non-consumptive approaches are represented in this publication. In 1998, WNA placed three ads in this magazine. Two were 1/6-page ads, placed for recognition, and the third was a full-page, full-colour advertisement that appeared facing an article written by the magazine on sea kayaking, and, in particular, on WNA.

Newfoundland Travel Guide

Newfoundland Travel Guide is a 200-page, colour brochure created by the provincial Department of Tourism. Interested potential tourists from all over the world contact the Department to request information. The *Guide* is then delivered free-of-charge to anyone expressing an interest in visiting the province. A new guide is published each year, listing accommodations, events, attractions, tours, and services.

All businesses relating to the tourist industry receive a free 100-word listing under their appropriate heading. As well, the Department provides pages in the publication for business that wish to purchase ad space. Rates for 1999 are double the 1998 rates.

Brochures

WNA has produced two brochures. A small brochure (see Exhibit 2, which displays the front and back of the brochure) was created to advertise WNA's sea kayaking cruises,

EXHIBIT 2 | WNA 1998 Brochure

although WNA was planning on changing its prices for 1999 to $100 per person for full-day cruises, and $65 per person for half-day and sunset trips. This was targeted at the local population and the tourists visiting the St. John's area. These brochures are placed throughout St. John's, in tourist chalets, hotels, motels, restaurants, and any stores that will accept them. These are two-sided, full-colour, high-quality brochures. They are printed on cardboard-type paper, cut to $3\frac{1}{3}$"× 8".

WNA's larger brochures are mailed to people interested in extended trips. This brochure was created and printed in 1996. In order to keep the brochure up to date, there is a pocket inside the back cover that allows WNA to insert current prices and updated information. This brochure was expensive to produce, but most adventurers have been impressed by it.

Radio Advertising

OZ-FM (94.7) is a St. John's radio station that reaches approximately 182 000 people over 12 years of age each week. The target market for OZ-FM is 18-to-49-year-old adults with active lifestyles, from all socioeconomic classes.

WNA ran three sets of 30-second ads throughout the summer. The duration of each set was two weeks. In conjunction with the advertisements, WNA arranged to have six pairs of free gift certificates given away on the radio during the Friday "morning drive" time slot. OZ-FM's morning drive is called the *Dawn Patrol,* and has three radio personalities. WNA invited all of them to participate on a free day trip. This proved to be a great idea, as, when they gave away the free passes, they were able to make first-hand and favourable comments about sea kayaking. In fact, they continued to promote WNA and sea kayaking with personal comments throughout all of the radio advertising campaigns.

Television Advertising

The Great Outdoorsman (TGO) is a half-hour Sunday night television program on the Life network (carried all over North America). The program host, John Summerfield, and his two-man crew travel all over the world seeking different types of adventure. John was interested in sea kayaking with whales and icebergs, and contacted Stan Jr. after meeting him at a trade show. In July 1997, TGO came to St. John's and filmed a show. The shooting went extremely well, and both John and WNA received considerable praise. John enjoyed Newfoundland so much that he decided to return to film another show with WNA (never before had he done two shows with the same company, with the same product). The Great Outdoorsman and his crew returned in July 1998 and filmed another show. This show aired in October 1998, and was scheduled for two repeats during 1999.

WNA has received many benefits and much recognition from these shows, although they were very expensive. WNA paid the air travel, accommodations, and meals of the TGO team for four days and three nights, a total of approximately $2500. As well, there was a $5000 fee payable to TGO to participate in its show.

Internet

WNA first created its website (www.wildnfld.ca) in the spring of 1997. It enlisted a small local Web-design firm to assist in developing its online personality. The site gets updated about twice a year (before and after the regular season). WNA is currently investigating e-commerce, hoping to take both bookings and payments over the Internet.

Signage

St. John's is the end of the line when driving east on the Trans-Canada Highway (TCH), as it is the most easterly city in North America. The TCH is the most-used route into the city and many local businesses have signs along it, advertising to incoming motor tourists.

WNA decided to strategically place three signs. The first was placed along the TCH with all the other signs. The second was put on a highly used arterial within the city. The final sign was placed along the Southern Shore Highway. This highway follows the coast from St. John's, south past Cape Broyle, and then it loops back along St. Mary's Bay to the city, a route called the Irish Loop. The signs were designed by Stan Jr. and Cori-Jane, and were painted by an art student at Stan Sr.'s high school.

Additional signage was placed on a company van. WNA leased a forest-green Ford AeroStar in April 1998 ($500/month). This van is used for pickup and delivery of clients, shuttle of equipment, and transportation for the guides to and from the various sites. The van is only used for 16 weeks during the summer. It requires gas about twice a week, and costs $60 per fill-up. Cori-Jane thought that WNA should take advantage of the vehicle's visibility around St. John's and that it should be incorporated in the promotion strategy. She hired a local business that specializes in auto advertising to put WNA's logo and other information on all four sides of the vehicle. The final product was quite impressive, and a number of people commented that they had seen the "Green WNA Machine" around town.

Sales Promotions

In 1998, WNA gave away 25 pairs of "Half-Day Sea Kayak Adventures for Two" gift certificates to different individuals. Some people won them on the radio, while other tickets were given to local celebrities or other prominent people. WNA wanted to get people to try sea kayaking and thought this would be a good idea, although only 11 pairs were redeemed over the summer.

Trade Shows

The Newfoundland Sportsman Show, sponsored by *Newfoundland Sportsman* magazine, is the largest show of its type in the province. It is a consumer retail trade fair with its primary focus on the outdoor industry. Many types of land, air, and marine activities are represented, and it attracts 8000 to 14 000 interested consumers.

A new trade show, the Outdoor Adventure Sports Show (OASS), has been held in February in Toronto, Ontario, for the past two years. At the OASS, attendees can try climbing the Pyramid wall, test-ride mountain bikes on a demo track, and canoe or kayak in an indoor pool. As well, outfitters from all over North America show what their province/company/activity has to offer the willing adventurer.

Attendance at the 1998 OASS included 23 320 people, with 62% either making an adventure purchase there or expressing an intention to make such a purchase as a result of the show. This attendance was 120% over the 1997 attendance, and it is expected to continue to grow for some time. WNA has participated both years. This show provides a venue for WNA to reach clients for their longer-duration adventures. These people will specifically come to Newfoundland for an excursion with WNA. Travelling, accommodation, and meal expenses amount to approximately $2000 for two people to attend OASS.

Other Methods

Excluding trade shows, the majority of WNA's personal selling has been informal. Mr. Cook and Stan, Jr. attend many local events, sporting rallies, and other activities that attract adventure-minded people. As well, WNA encourages its summer employees to promote sea kayaking on their own time by giving them a $10 bonus for every customer they bring on a full-day kayak trip, and a $5 bonus for every customer they bring to half-day or sunset trips. This encourages the guides to get a group of friends together to go out kayaking. (At the beginning of the summer, each staff member also receives three free day passes for family and friends.)

In their first two years of operation, WNA had a difficult time attracting local customers. Due to unfamiliarity with sea kayaking, many people were very nervous. The only information people had accumulated previously was on the dangerous sport of river kayaking. River and sea kayaking are completely different sports, with very differently-shaped vessels and different objectives. Now that people have heard of sea kayaking, they are starting to differentiate WNA from other local outfitters by both reputation and value.

St. John's is becoming a popular tourist destination. An increasing number of businesses and associations are holding annual conferences in the oldest city in North America. Exhibit 3 presents a list of conferences planned in 1998 to come to St. John's in the summer of 1999.

EXHIBIT 3	Upcoming Conventions and Events, St. John's, 1999	
Date	**Convention**	**Delegates**
May 10-13	Canadian Association of Principals	550
June 1-5	Co-operative Housing Federation of Canada	700
June 11-14	Canadian Council for the Advancement of Education	250
June 13-20	Canadian Corps of Commissioners AGM '99	400
June 17-20	Air Cadet League of Canada	150
June 23-27	CAMRT/CSDMU Joint Meeting	500
July 5-9	Canadian Orthopedic Association	700
July 11-16	Offshore Mechanics and Arctic Engineering	400
August 21-26	Canada Employment & Immigration Union	325
September 19-22	Risk & Insurance Management Society	500
September 27-30	Workers' Compensation Commission	100
October 1-3	International Association of Business Communicators	300

Source: Department of Economic Development and Tourism.

Finally, WNA is considering the possibility of hiring a salesperson. So far, little thought has been given to what the salesperson would do, how he or she would be compensated, and exactly what criteria would be important in hiring an appropriate person.

Public Relations

WNA has attempted to take advantage of free publicity. Stan Jr. has invited several local reporters to participate on a free day trip in return for writing articles on WNA. So far, two reporters have participated, and both have written very positive articles on their experiences. The first appeared in *The Evening Telegram* (St. John's). It was a full-page article, accompanied by five full-colour photos. The second appeared in *Mount Pearl Pride.* Mount Pearl is a smaller city that borders St. John's. Again, it was a full-page article with full-colour photos. WNA received many phone calls following the printing of these articles.

CONCLUSION

Before making any decisions with respect to the 1999 promotional strategy, Stan Jr. decided to review the summary of responses to the customer satisfaction surveys collected in 1998. Every person that participated on a day, half-day, or sunset trip between May 24 and September 6, 1998, filled one out. The summary of responses is provided in Exhibit 4.

EXHIBIT 4	WNA Customer Satisfaction Survey Results, Summer 1998

Age	Total	Sex	Total	Trip	Total
10-19	48	Male	332	Full day	360
20-29	309	Female	388	Half day	180
30-39	239	Total	720	Sunset	180
40-49	76			Total	720
50-59	28				
60+	20				
Total	720				

How Did You Like Our Staff and Service?

		Guides			
Friendly	Ratings	Total	Knowledgeable	Ratings	Total
Dissatisfied	1	0	Dissatisfied	1	0
	2	0		2	0
	3	0		3	0
Satisfied	4	11	Satisfied	4	15
	5	33		5	28
	6	73		6	55
100% satisfied	7	603	100% satisfied	7	622
Total		720	Total		720

EXHIBIT 4	WNA Customer Satisfaction Survey Results, Summer 1998 (continued)

Physical Product

Food	Ratings	Total	Equipment	Ratings	Total
Dissatisfied	1	0	Dissatisfied	1	0
	2	0		2	0
	3	4		3	9
Satisfied	4	14	Satisfied	4	12
	5	32		5	33
	6	68		6	70
100% satisfied	7	602	100% satisfied	7	596
Total		720	Total		720

How Do You Feel?

Would You Return?	Ratings	No. of People	Recommend Us to Others?	Ratings	No. of People
No	1	0	No	1	0
	2	0		2	0
Maybe	3	38	Maybe	3	30
	4	66		4	69
Definitely	5	616	Definitely	5	621
Total		720	Total		720

Where Did You Hear About Us?	No. of People	What Influenced You to Try Sea Kayaking?	No. of People
Brochure (large)	10	Advertising:	148
Brochure (small)	99	Brochure	45
Gift certificate	11	Travel guide ad	8
Other	7	Sign on road	8
Phone book (Yellow Pages)	32	OZ-FM ad	44
Radio	66	Television show	24
Referral (word of mouth)	175	Mount Pearl Pride	19
Repeat customer	53	Alpine Country Lodge recommendation	15
Television: The Great Outdoorsman	19	Always wanted to try sea kayaking	33
Travel Agency	5	Dept. of Tourism recommendation	13
Website	23	Familiarization tour	20
Magazine:		Family recommendation	26
Newfoundland Sportsman	35	For the adventure	15
Provincial Travel Guide	68	Free invitation	10
St. John's Visitor's Guide	12	Friend of the Cooks	22

EXHIBIT 4	WNA Customer Satisfaction Survey Results, Summer 1998 (continued)

Road sign:

Harbour arterial	31	
Trans-Canada Highway	19	
Southern Shore Highway	17	

Trade show:

Newfoundland Sportsman	33
Outdoor Adventure Show	5
Total	720

Friend recommendation/ going with friends	112
Good reputation	44
Group from work going	55
Guide recommendation	35
Hotel recommendation	22
New experience	10
OZ-FM Dawn Patrol recommendation	55
Received gift certificate	16
Repeat customer	53
Wedding day activity	10
Won on the radio	6
Total	720

Overall Satisfaction with Your Excursion

Overall	Ratings	Total
Dissatisfied	1	0
	2	0
	3	0
Satisfied	4	8
	5	24
	6	96
100% satisfied	7	592
Total		720

Stan Jr. has a tremendous amount of planning to do and decisions to make over the next few days. How successful has the 1998 promotional campaign been? What items should be retained for 1999, and what items should be changed or deleted? How should WNA set its promotional budget? Stan Jr. knew his father would want answers to all of these questions at their Friday meeting.

ABS Global (Canada) Inc.

Tom Funk, Justin Funk, and Steve Fried

Steve Fried, newly appointed general manager of ABS Global (Canada) Inc. (hereinafter referred to simply as ABS), was faced with the monumental task of rebuilding market share and revenue for his company. By 1999, ABS had captured 8% of the dairy artificial insemination (AI) business in Canada. However, in the winter of 2000, Select Sires, a direct competitor, successfully recruited the ABS Ontario Sales Manager and four service technicians, resulting in a sales loss of over one-third of current Ontario dairy business. By June 2002, when Steve was appointed general manager, only a fraction of this lost business had been recovered. It was up to Steve to determine how to do this in the highly competitive AI market. One possibility being considered was the introduction of a new service called Reproductive Management System (RMS), developed by ABS Global and currently being successfully implemented in the U.S. market. Steve felt this might give him the edge he needed to significantly increase sales and profits. There were, however, a number of issues that needed to be sorted out prior to moving in this direction: Would the Canadian market be receptive to this system? Was the market for this system large enough to justify the added costs? How should ABS price the system? And what type of promotional strategy would be required for a successful launch?

THE ONTARIO ARTIFICIAL INSEMINATION INDUSTRY

Much of the success of a dairy operation depends on reproduction. Dairy cows produce milk only after giving birth to a calf, and the amount of milk they produce depends on their genetic makeup. So, being able to get cows with superior genetics pregnant in a timely manner is a high-priority activity for dairy producers. This can be done in two ways. Either the dairy producer can use a bull to mate with his cows, or he can use artificial insemination. Appendix A entitled *Fundamentals of Reproduction in Dairy Cattle* provides background on some of the issues and technology important for understanding this case. Readers not familiar with this industry should read this appendix before proceeding.

First introduced to the Ontario dairy industry in the early 1950s, AI has become a widely accepted tool for genetic improvement. AI has allowed Ontario dairy workers to obtain semen from the best bulls around the world at reasonable prices for selective breeding in their herds. The combination of improved genetics, herd health, nutrition, and livestock management over the years has impacted the production, efficiency, and profit of all dairy breeds. For example, the average Holstein cow in the 1950s produced approximately 3600 kg of milk in a typical 305 day lactation period; by 2001 this had increased to nearly 9000 kg of milk in 305 days.

The use of AI has reached maturity in Ontario. In fact, of the 366 825 dairy cows and 197 000 heifers, approximately 75% are bred using AI. The number of dairy semen units inseminated in Ontario in 2001 was approximately 846 000. At an average retail price of $25 per unit, this made the value of dairy semen sales in Ontario approximately $21 000 000. Fees for insemination and related services generated an additional $9 000 000, making this a $30 million per year provincial industry.

In 2001, the retail value of a unit of semen ranged from a low of $5 for young unproven sires to a high of $75 for top proven sires. As the system of selecting and sampling bulls has become more reliable, and information on bulls is transmitted globally, genetic uniqueness has been minimized, and semen is approaching commodity status. While it was not unusual to pay over $500 for one unit of semen 20 years ago, today the choice is so broad, and competition so fierce, that anything over $75 per unit is virtually unheard of.

Artificial insemination service is delivered to Ontario dairy herds in two ways—technician services and owner insemination. Approximately 75% of the 846 000 units or 630 000 inseminations are delivered through technician services, while the remaining 216 000 inseminations are performed by owners.

Technician services are provided by the major semen suppliers on a pay per use basis. Almost all technicians are exclusive to their respective employer, and are hired under a variety of compensation programs including full salary with benefits, salary plus commission, or full commission. Semen producers provide a toll-free number customers can call when they identify one of their animals is "in heat" (estrus) and requires insemination. The technical service rep arrives at the farm and inseminates the animal for a fee that encompasses the cost of the semen plus a breeding fee. It is the responsibility of the herd owner or manager to determine when the animal is ready to be inseminated and make all necessary arrangements; the technician is only responsible for the act of insemination. Although breeding fees vary between companies, a rule-of-thumb figure is $10 per insemination.

Not every insemination results in a pregnancy. The main reason for lack of success is the cow is not ready to be bred because she is not estrus. An industry rule of thumb is it takes an average of two inseminations to produce a pregnancy. Therefore, at a cost of $25 per dose of semen, plus $10 insemination fee, the average out-of-pocket cost of achieving a pregnancy is $70 using artificial insemination. The real cost could be a lot higher because a delay in getting a cow pregnant includes the cost of supporting the cow while it is not producing milk.

Generally when a customer contacts a company to inseminate his cows, the customer will purchase the majority of his semen (approximately 70%) from that same company. With the increasing commodity nature of semen, the real value is seen in the service that is provided; relationships between the customer and the company (or technical service rep) have become a larger determining factor in semen purchases over the years.

Some dairy producers have trained to perform artificial insemination in their own operations. There are several reasons why a farmer may wish to breed his own cows:

- The herd is in a remote location and tech service is unavailable or substandard.

- The added convenience and flexibility of having a semen storage tank on their own farm and purchasing semen from a variety of suppliers.

- The savings of the $10 per cow insemination fee. Note, however, that the average cost of training and equipment for storing semen would be in the area of $1500, excluding semen purchases. All of this could be amortized over several years.

- A belief that they can achieve a higher pregnancy rate than the technician because they have a vested interest in the result. Experience, however, has shown that much of the time tech specialists can achieve significantly higher pregnancy rates than producers.

Few technological breakthroughs in the field of AI have been achieved in the past two decades. Some changes have been made in the processing and packaging of semen to improve sperm motility and fertility of the product, but outside of this, the fundamental product is the same as it was 50 years ago. Many organizations are investing in R&D projects designed to give them a competitive edge: projects such as sexed semen, freeze dried semen, and bulls that have been genetically modified to produce "female" sperm cells only. Although research is ongoing, major breakthroughs are at best three to five years away.

The globalization of the industry has resulted in a smaller genetic pool providing the majority of the young sires for all organizations. Ultimately, product differentiation opportunities become limited as all competitors offer similar genetic value at similar prices. This lack of new technology and declining genetic differentiation creates an environment where the competitive fight for new business is narrowed down to a discounting battle and/or a focus on service.

There are eight companies selling semen to Ontario dairy farmers. These companies, together with a brief profile of each, are shown in Exhibit 1.

With 75% market share, it's obvious that Semex Alliance is the dominant provider in the market. This full-service company is the result of a recent merger of Western Ontario Breeders, Eastern Ontario Breeders, and United Breeders. ABS, Alta Genetics, and Select Sires are all about the same size and offer similar products and services. All other companies are very small.

EXHIBIT 1	Artificial Insemination Companies in Ontario

Company	Profile	Services	Estimated Ontario Market Share	Estimated Dairy Semen Units
Semex Alliance	• Canadian company • Member-owned co-operative • Over 50 years in business • International sales • Profit sharing with provincial partners	• Technicians • On-farm service for owner insemination • Provincial young sire program + benefits • Genetic mating program • Consultation	75%	630 000
ABS & St. Jacobs ABC	• ABS is a subsidiary of Genus plc. (UK publicly traded firm) • ABS manages all marketing and business for St. Jacobs ABC • St. Jacobs ABC domestic farmer-owned co-operative	• Technicians • On-farm service for owner insemination • National young sire program + benefits • Genetic mating programs • Consultation	5%	42 000
Alta Genetics	• Alberta company • Privately owned with a Dutch parent company	• Technicians • On-farm service for owner insemination • National young sire program + benefits • Genetic mating programs • Consultation	6%	50 400
Select Sires	• Canadian distributor for U.S. parent based in Plain City, Ohio • Parent company is a U.S. co-operative	• Technicians • On-farm service for owner insemination • Genetic mating programs	5%	42 000
Foundation Sires	• Canadian company • Farmer-owned partnership	• On-farm service for owner insemination	2.5%	21 000
Browndale Specialty Sires	• Domestic company • Privately owned	• On-farm service for owner insemination through Foundation Sires	1%	8 400
Genex	• U.S. distributor	• On-farm service for owner insemination	2.5%	21 000
Genervations	• French company • Canadian managed	• On-farm service for owner insemination	2%	16 800
Others	• Imported and independents		1%	8 400

ABS GLOBAL (CANADA) INC.

ABS Global (Canada) Inc. is a wholly owned subsidiary of ABS Global Inc., based in DeForest, Wisconsin. ABS Global Inc. is the breeding division of Genus Plc., based in Crewe, U.K. and publicly traded on the London Stock Exchange. ABS Global Inc. achieved sales in excess of U.S. $110 million in the fiscal year ending March 31, 2002, making them the largest revenue generating global semen supplier. Net profit exceeded U.S. $15 million.

In Canada, ABS operates in a joint venture with St. Jacobs ABC, a Canadian co-op with 2 200 members. ABS is contracted to perform bull housing, semen collection, distribution, and marketing for St. Jacobs. This arrangement provides St. Jacobs ABC with a global sales and distribution outlet and ABS with a domestic presence and image.

ABS first entered Canada in 1961 in Manitoba and has continued to grow over the past 40 years. Initially, the focus was the western Canadian beef market, but over the years, ABS has expanded into the dairy market in the rest of Canada. Today, the company operates in all provinces with a central housing, collection, and distribution centre in Elmira, Ontario.

ABS began building their 100% commissioned technician force[1] across the province and by 1999 had reached a point of approximately 8% market share, or 66 000 semen units in sales. Much of their business was with smaller herds. A major setback in the ABS development plan occurred in March 2000 when Select Sires, a U.S.-based organization establishing in Canada, successfully recruited the ABS Ontario Sales Manager as well as a core group of technicians in southwestern Ontario. Overnight, ABS lost 4 key technicians, over 24 000 semen units, and approximately $384 000 in gross revenue. This loss has never been fully recovered.

The key issue facing ABS was how to operate a profitable business in a competitive, mature market. Current sales were unsatisfactory to support the investment in the existing infrastructure. ABS was faced with two options: (a) increase sales volume, market penetration, and profit in a sustainable fashion, or (b) downsize the infrastructure to meet the minimal needs of current sales and "milk the cow" for profit.

In March 2002, ABS Global made a management change in Canada signalling a corporate initiative to gain back the market they had lost, and to grow the business to a position of strength and profitability. Steve Fried was appointed general manager, and new dollars were committed to make investments in developing the strategies and securing the people that would achieve the goals. Several new employed salespeople were added at this time.

REPRODUCTIVE MANAGEMENT SYSTEM

The U.S. dairy industry has experienced significant change over the past ten years, with rapid decline in the number of herds producing milk, and equally rapid growth in the number of cows milked per herd. Today, the United States is approaching the 80/20 rule, namely 20% of the herds produce 80% of the milk. Most recent numbers from the United States Department of Agriculture (USDA) indicated that 21% of the nation's

---

[1]While ABS charged producers $10 for each insemination, technicians received $7.50 of this fee. In the case of ABS, this was the only compensation they receive.

largest dairies (100 or more milking cows) milk 70% of the nation's cows, and produce 75% of the nation's milk. USDA estimates also showed that the number of larger herds was growing at an annual rate of 10% and the number of animals in these herds was growing at an annual rate of 3%.

The increase in herd size has changed many management issues for dairy producers. At the present time, the leading cause of culling or replacing cows in larger U.S. herds is reproductive inefficiency. This makes the value of a pregnancy substantial. A great deal of research has been conducted in the U.S. to determine exactly what the value of a pregnancy is to the average U.S. dairy producer. One of the most comprehensive and industry supported models is the Cowval model included in Dairy Comp 305, a data management software program designed exclusively for use in dairy operations. The model determines the net present value of a cow, taking into account factors such as future production, stage of lactation, reproductive status, and age. Also considered are herd reproductive performance measures, heifer replacement costs, cull animal value, milk price, marginal feed cost, and culling rates. A recent study released on 30 commercial dairy herds using the Cowval model determined the value of a pregnancy ranged from $394 to $795 with an average of $618. Another study conducted at the University of Florida concluded that the economic value of a 1% increase in the pregnancy rate for a herd was approximately $10 per cow per year.

ABS Global has led the U.S. industry in responding to the needs of dairy workers through the development of RMS. RMS is a comprehensive, team-oriented approach to improving reproductive performance in client herds. Operated by ABS reproductive specialists, it includes, but is not limited to:

- Daily inspection of all animals eligible for insemination
- Insemination of all animals showing signs of estrus
- Maintenance of farm breeding records
- Regular meetings with veterinarian, nutritionist, herd owner, and herd manager— becoming a part of the reproduction consultation team
- Utilization of synchronization programs to maximize insemination opportunities with eligible animals
- Packaged pricing of products and services which, in the most advanced cases, may mean charging per pregnancy, and not per insemination

In essence, the RMS specialist takes ownership of reproductive performance within the herd, and in return the dairy worker commits to using 100% ABS products to meet his/her reproductive and genetic needs. This approach differs significantly from the two AI delivery systems in use in Ontario at the present time where the owner/manager has all the responsibility of managing the AI program, and too often tries to "fit it in" an already full schedule.

Record keeping and data analysis are critical components of success within an RMS program. There are a variety of herd management software programs on the market with the most popular being Dairy Comp 305 (DC305). Ontario Dairy Herd Improvement (DHI), the provincial milk recording body, has the exclusive provincial marketing rights for the Canadian version of DC305. Although herd data information is automatically available to any herd enrolled in DHI, less than 10% of Ontario milk producers utilize DC305.

ABS Global has a technical service department consisting of five nationally recognized veterinarians who conduct certification programs for prospective RMS specialist candidates. The tech service department is not only committed to RMS growth in the United States, they are dedicated to training and systems launches in many other parts of the world, including Canada.

RMS has been a successful marketing tool for ABS Global, Inc. because the results are measurable and positive. Recent research conducted by ABS Global tech services on over 60 000 dairy cows determined that the average pregnancy rate[2] in these RMS herds ran 10% over the national average of 13%. At an average value of $618 per pregnancy, a 5% increase in the pregnancy rate is significant and creates exceptional value for RMS.

WHAT TO DO?

Steve knew he only had two options to grow ABS's market share to a respectable level and restore profitability for the company. The first was to "slug it out" with existing competitors and attempt to regain lost business selling semen in the conventional manner. The second was to create differentiation by introducing the RMS service and picking up a number of new medium and large producer accounts. Steve's preference was for the latter option, but it would have to provide a reasonable chance of being successful before he could justify such a significant change in how the company did business, let alone the dollars and risks involved in providing such a high level service.

Market Research

Steve was not sure the Ontario market was ready for RMS. Although RMS was starting to achieve considerable success in the United States, the smaller herd sizes in Canada were a concern. To help him assess market potential, Steve commissioned a telephone survey of 100 dairy producers with herds greater than 75 cows. The survey was designed to determine:

- A profile of mid-to-large dairy operations in Ontario
- The reproductive management practices of progressive Ontario dairy producers
- Producer reaction to the ABS Reproductive Management System

Key findings of this research are shown in Appendix B.

In general, Steve was encouraged by the findings of the marketing research. He was especially pleased to see that 28% of those interviewed said they definitely or probably would try RMS, and only 6% said they definitely would not try RMS. He was also pleased to see the fairly widespread adoption of synchronization methods among medium and large dairy producers. He was somewhat surprised to see the high percentage of dairy producers doing insemination procedures themselves instead of using a technician.

---

[2]Pregnancy rate is a widely used measure of reproductive efficiency. It is calculated by dividing the number of cows confirmed pregnant by the number of cows eligible to be bred in the three week cycle. For example, if there were 20 cows eligible to be inseminated, 10 of which were detected in heat and inseminated, and 5 became pregnant, the pregnancy rate would be 25%. Other measures of reproductive efficiency are conception rate (number of cows pregnant divided by the number of cows inseminated), and calving interval (number of months between the births of calves).

To further assess the potential of the RMS opportunity, Steve searched for information on the size and structure of dairy herds in Ontario. Information from Dairy Farmers of Ontario revealed there were 1080 dairy farms in Ontario with a herd size greater than 75 cows. (See Exhibit 2.)

EXHIBIT 2	Number of Dairy Farms in Ontario				
Farm Size	1998	1999	2000	2001	2002
< 75 Cows	5463	5063	4723	4362	4136
> 75 Cows	787	857	949	964	1080
Total	6050	5920	5671	5326	5216

Pricing RMS

A major issue was how to price RMS. One option was to charge the same fee for semen and insemination services as was done at the present time, but require the purchaser to commit to dealing exclusively with ABS for some defined period of time. All synchronization drugs and other supplies would be billed separately.[3] This was the approach used in the United States. Although it had the advantages of being simple and low cost to the producer, Steve wondered if it might not be undervaluing the benefits of RMS.

A second alternative was to charge a per cow per day fee that bundled semen and insemination. The fee being considered was somewhere in the neighbourhood of $0.20 to $0.25 per cow per day. At $0.20, for a 100 cow herd, this would cost the producer $7 300. Steve liked this pricing option because it was more in keeping with the RMS concept and would be unique in the industry. Once again, all synchronization drugs and other supplies would be priced separately.

A third approach was to establish a retainer fee arrangement with producers. Here, ABS would develop a full implementation plan with each dairy producer and then establish an annual fee to execute this plan. It would be based on the number of female animals in the herd, but would be quoted to the producer as a fixed amount payable in equal monthly installments. Steve was not sure of the amount, but felt something in the order of $80 to $90 per cow per year would be appropriate. The producer would still need to purchase the required synchronization drugs.

The fourth approach was to charge on the basis of results, not effort. This would be a novel approach, but might be attractive to many dairy producers. Under this approach, ABS would only extract a fee when there was a pregnancy. Of course, this would shift the risk to ABS, but could be a powerful way to demonstrate the value of the service. If this approach were used, Steve felt an appropriate fee per pregnancy would be somewhere in the neighborhood of $85 to $95. Given that the value of a pregnancy was over $600 and RMS had the ability to increase the pregnancy rate by 10%, Steve thought this would be an acceptable fee.

---

[3] ABS could not sell synchronization drugs because they required a prescription and ABS did not have a veterinarian on staff. A good estimate of the cost of these drugs to a dairy producer was $3 per female cow per year.

Steve thought there might be other pricing approaches, but these were the main ones he was considering. Not only was he unsure which to use, but he was also unsure as to the actual fees to charge. He felt there was a fine line between pricing too high and restricting uptake, and pricing too low and not capturing the value created by RMS.

Developing Demand

Steve felt a big issue he faced was developing demand for RMS. Although relatively small, his target market contained over 1000 Ontario dairy producers scattered over a fairly large geographical area. All of these producers were already using AI services and, for the most part, there was a fairly high level of satisfaction with current AI companies and services. Steve had his work cut out for him.

In considering how to communicate with his target market, Steve realized he had a number of approaches that could be used—traditional advertising, public relations, direct marketing, sales promotion, and personal selling. Although budget was an issue, he did not want to make this a key constraint, at least initially. If he found the ideal communications program cost more than he could justify, he would have to make adjustments. But, his primary goal at first was to develop an ideal communications program.

Steve was not sure whether he should use traditional advertising. There was a number of possible publications he could use for this purpose, but all were fairly expensive and it would not be possible to target just medium and large producers using this approach. The *Ontario Milk Producer* was a good example of the type of publication that could be used. This was a monthly publication of the Dairy Farmers of Ontario, so it reached all dairy producers in the province. Its circulation also included approximately 2500 others—primarily veterinarians, nutritionists, bankers, and government officials. A full-page ad in this publication costs $2500 per issue. A one-page insert in the publication costs $2750. Designing the ad itself would cost an additional $10 000. If he used media advertising, Steve wondered what the ads would look like and what message would be used.

In addition to paid advertising, Steve thought the novel RMS concept would generate a lot of media attention and could be the focus of articles in dairy publications or features on farm television and radio programs. He also knew this was not guaranteed and would require substantial effort to achieve. Steve's good friend, Chris O'Rourke, had a small marketing services firm that specialized in this type of activity. Chris told Steve an annual budget of $9500 would be appropriate to prepare articles and pursue publicity opportunities.

Steve wondered about participating in agricultural trade shows. There were approximately five events in Ontario each year attended by a significant number of dairy producers. Examples of these trade shows included the Canada Outdoor Farm Show, the International Plowing Match, and the Royal Agricultural Winter Fair. The out-of-pocket cost of attending a trade show was approximately $7500 per show. In the past, ABS participated in many of these events, but in recent years cut way back because they felt the expenditure was not as productive as other promotional activities.

Steve was a big proponent of direct marketing. Over the years, ABS had built a good database of dairy producers in Ontario and devoted considerable effort to making sure it was as up-to-date as possible. In addition to producer names and mailing addresses, the database also contained information on email addresses, telephone numbers, and herd sizes. This additional information was available for about 70% of dairy producers. ABS used the database three or four times each year to mail promotional material. The cost of direct marketing varied tremendously depending on the approach used. Simply mailing a letter or small promotional piece could be as inexpensive as $1 per contact. A more elaborate brochure could cost up to $5 per contact to produce and mail plus $10 000 for design.

ABS had not used outbound telemarketing in the past, but Steve was not ruling this approach out. With his database of producers, he felt he could use telemarketing in a number of possible ways: lead generation and announcing events were just two he had in mind. Outsourcing telemarketing services could be fairly expensive. Most professional telemarketing firms specializing in business-to-business contacts had rates of $60 per hour for outbound calling. With an average flow rate of three completed calls per hour, the cost of a contact would be approximately $20. Steve had not ruled out the possibility of setting up a telemarketing unit within ABS, however, he felt initially it would be best to hire an agency that specialized in this activity.

Steve was not sure the role sales promotion would play in his communication plan. Like most agricultural companies, ABS already used a number of sales promotion tools such as hats, pens, and rain gauges. It was not clear how these tools might be used in launching the new RMS. Steve had noticed a growing use of things like contests in launching new products. He felt a clever promotion might capture a lot of attention and perhaps aid in speeding up adoption of RMS.

Steve felt there also was a great need for personal contact with targeted producers. At the present time, ABS had three sales reps in Ontario—one covering central and eastern Ontario and two in southwestern Ontario. These reps were responsible for making on-farm calls to maintain current business and attract new business. They also supervised technicians in their area and made sure inseminations were performed in a timely manner. The existing sales people were "stretched to the limit" and not necessarily the right people to sell RMS. As a result, Steve was contemplating hiring new reps who would be totally dedicated to selling RMS to medium and large producers. Each rep would cost ABS approximately $100 000 in salary and expenses. An RMS rep would be responsible for finding new clients and setting them up on RMS. Although much of the "selling" that would be done by an RMS rep would be one-on-one, it would also be possible to organize farmer meetings where approximately ten producers would come to a central location for a meeting and dinner. At the meeting, the RMS rep would explain how RMS worked and answer any questions. After the meeting, the guests would be treated to a nice lunch or dinner depending on the time of day. This would be a great opportunity to book appointments with individual farmers. The out-of-pocket costs of a farmer meeting were probably $25 for each producer that attended.

Additional Considerations

In addition to sales reps, there was also a need for RMS specialists who would deliver the service to clients. Examination of RMS in the United States revealed that one RMS specialist could handle 2500 cows and heifers. The annual cost of a specialist was approximately $90 000 in salary, travel expenses, and breeding supplies. Information maintenance per herd was estimated at $500 per year. Because of improved heat detection, the average number of inseminations required to produce a pregnancy declined to 1.8. There would also be an overhead charge of $200 000 from ABS Global, Inc. in the United States to cover training and administrative costs. The average cost of goods sold for a dose of semen was $3.50.

In addition to wondering how dairy producers would view RMS, Steve also wondered how veterinarians would view the new service. Would they see this as a valuable service for their clients, or would they view this as an infringement on their turf? Recently, a few veterinarians started to assume more of a consultancy role for some of their clients. Although Steve was not aware of any veterinary clinic that provided a similar, comprehensive reproductive management service, he knew that some were providing consulting expertise in this area and selling synchronization drugs.

With all of this information at hand, Steve was preparing to assess the attractiveness of this opportunity and make a recommendation. He had a number of decisions to make. Should he launch the new service? How should it be positioned? Which pricing option should he use? How should he communicate the new service to his market?

Appendix A

Fundamentals of Reproduction in

Dairy Cattle

Reproduction in the dairy industry is a complex issue that has significant impact on the profitability of the industry. Cows only produce milk after they have given birth to a calf, so it's critical for dairy producers to get cows pregnant at the desired time. Moreover, the amount of milk a cow can produce is related to her genetic makeup, so it's important to use semen from good bulls.

There are two methods that can be used to inseminate dairy cattle. The first is to use an on-farm bull. Of course, this is the method that has been used through the ages, and it works well. By nature, bulls can detect when cows are ready to be bred and then do the job. The cost of this approach to a dairy farmer is the cost of acquiring and maintaining a bull. Depending upon the genetics of the bull, this can result in a high or low cost.

The second method is to use artificial insemination. In this approach, semen from bulls with outstanding genetics is collected, frozen in vials, and then used to inseminate cows. A whole industry has developed around this concept. Although dairy farmers pay a fee for the semen and the insemination service, many times this is much less expensive than maintaining a bull on the farm. Moreover, it allows the producer a vast selection of sires that can be used in breeding.

In order to understand dairy reproduction, it's useful to start at the beginning. A heifer is a young female cow that has not been bred and given birth. In order for the heifer to produce milk, it must first be bred and deliver a calf. After giving birth to a calf, the cow starts to produce milk to feed the calf. In a commercial dairy operation, the calf is taken away from the mother and raised as veal, allowing the mother's milk to be collected and used for human consumption.

As in any species, cows have a reproductive cycle. When a heifer reaches sexual maturity, she releases an egg every 24 days (give or take a few days). If this egg is fertilized, after nine months she gives birth to a calf. If the egg is not fertilized, it takes another 24 days before she releases another egg and breeding can be attempted again. After giving birth, the mother produces milk for 305 days (lactation period) or approximately 10 months. At the end of 305 days, the cow stops producing milk and is said to be dry. After giving birth, a cow cannot be bred again for approximately 60 days, or two months.

The following chart shows the reproductive cycle of a heifer/cow pushed to the limit. After a heifer/cow is bred, it takes nine months for a calf to be born. Once a calf is born, the cow begins a ten month milk producing cycle. Two months into this cycle, the cow can be bred again and nine months later produces another calf. In the entire cycle, the cow is only

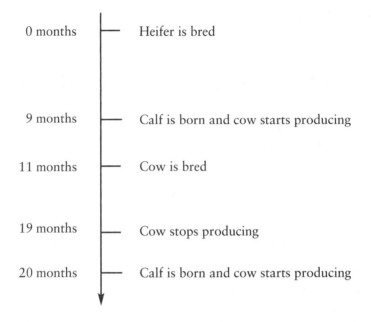

0 months	Heifer is bred
9 months	Calf is born and cow starts producing
11 months	Cow is bred
19 months	Cow stops producing
20 months	Calf is born and cow starts producing

dry one month between the time she stops producing milk and has another calf. As noted, this scenario where the cow produces a calf every 11 months (calving interval) and is dry only one month is the theoretical maximum. Calving intervals of 12 to 15 months are common.

A dairy cow that is not producing milk is not a productive asset. As a matter of fact, the cow becomes an expense because she must be fed and maintained even though she is not producing milk. As a result, it is a high-priority activity for a dairy farmer to get cows pregnant again as soon as possible.

When using artificial insemination, the most limiting factor in achieving a timely pregnancy is detecting when a cow is estrus or "in heat." Estrus or "heat" is the period of time that occurs every 24 days in sexually mature female cattle when they are receptive to mounting activity by bulls or other cows. In dairy, where artificial insemination is the means of breeding, the herdsman must recognize and interpret a cow's heat signals. Proper timing of artificial insemination is necessary to accomplish a high percentage of conceptions.

Although there are various ways to detect heat in dairy cows, the most reliable is called "standing heat." This happens when a cow allows other cows to mount her while she is standing. This occurs approximately 12 hours before the cow releases an egg. Because sperm need time in the cow's reproductive tract before they are capable of fertilizing the egg, insemination should be made several hours before ovulation or at the time of standing heat. Because the window of opportunity is short, proper heat detection in a timely manner is essential to achieving reproductive efficiency.

Recently, some new technology has been developed that can improve reproductive efficiency. Called synchronization, this allows a dairy producer to inject heifers or cows with hormones that will "force" them into estrus at a predetermined period of time. Although this can be a significant advantage, it is not totally reliable and adds expense and hassle for the dairy producer.

Appendix B

Key Findings of Marketing Research

Profile of Mid-to-Large Dairy Operations

- Of the 1080 herds over 75 cows, 22% were between 75 and 100 cows (average size 79 cows), 26% were between 100 and 150 cows (average size 118 cows), 41% were between 150 and 250 cows (average size 182 cows), and 11% were greater than 250 cows (average size 371 cows). This resulted in approximately 176 500 cows in the medium and large size herds, plus an additional 95 000 heifers resulting in an average of approximately 250 animals per year requiring insemination.

- On average, dairy producers with medium and large size herds expected to increase the size of their herds by 3% per year.

- In terms of delivery of AI services, 42% of herds used owner insemination exclusively, 28% used technicians exclusively, and 30% used a combination.

- Although 99% of herds used AI and only 1% used a bull for breeding, 31% used a bull for "clean up" purposes, especially during peak periods (planting and harvesting) when time was of critical importance to the farmer.

- 72% of herds use a synchronization program of one kind or another to enhance reproductive efficiency.

- 34% of herds use a computerized herd health management system.

Reproduction Management Practices

- By far the most common measurement of reproductive performance on Ontario dairy farms is calving interval in months. Over 70% of dairy producers indicated use of this measure. The calving interval range was from 12.4 to 15.5 months with a median of 13 months.

- Only 21% of herds reported using pregnancy rate as a measure of performance.

- The level of satisfaction with reproductive performance indicated that 23% of producers were somewhat dissatisfied, 41% were somewhat satisfied, 27% were satisfied, and 9% were completely satisfied.

- Dairy producers cited the following as factors affecting reproductive performance: 67% poor heat detection, 17% poor insemination skills, 27% timeliness of insemination, 32% semen quality, 44% poor nutrition in the herd, and 44% poor herd health.

- The level of satisfaction with synchronization programs indicated that 30% were dissatisfied, 16% were somewhat dissatisfied, 37% were somewhat satisfied, 15% were satisfied, and only 2% were completely satisfied.

Assessment of the Reproductive Management System

- Each producer was presented with the following concept of the new Reproductive Management System: *The company provides the farm with a Reproductive Specialist whose principal role is to manage the reproductive program. Using data management software, the current reproduction results are determined. Then, specialist and herd owner establish reproductive performance goals for the farm and a protocol to achieve the desired results. The specialist is responsible for all elements of the reproductive program to be performed on a daily basis including heat detection, insemination, and data management. The company guarantees that if all protocols are followed by both parties, the reproductive goals will be achieved. Payment for the service would be competitive to current costs of AI delivery and based upon one of the following options: included in the cost of insemination and semen, on a contracted/consultancy fee basis, or on a per pregnancy basis.*

- When asked to cite benefits they saw in the RMS concept, the following categories emerged:
  - 48% mentioned time savings
  - 41% mentioned an overall improvement in reproductive performance, especially improved pregnancy rates
  - 22% mentioned they would not have to do heat detection themselves
  - 20% mentioned the impact of goal setting on achieving improved performance
  - 17% mentioned cost savings by reducing veterinarian expenses
  - 14% mentioned improvements in data management

- When asked to cite concerns they saw in the RMS concept, the following categories emerged:
  - 65% mentioned a perceived high cost
  - 43% mentioned they didn't want to give up control of this important function
  - 28% mentioned bio-security problems with having someone else on the farm
  - 27% mentioned they felt the concept was unrealistic and would be unable to achieve better results
  - 24% mentioned they didn't understand how it would work or didn't believe it would work
  - 21% mentioned they were already doing a satisfactory job either themselves or with their vet and having another person involved would be unnecessary
  - 7% mentioned they were not in favour of using drugs for synchronization

- When asked their willingness to try the new concepts, the following results were obtained:
  - 11% said they definitely would try it
  - 17% said they probably would try it
  - 35% said they may or may not try it
  - 31% said they probably would not try it
  - 6% said they definitely would not try it

- The average herd size of those who indicated they would definitely try it was 125 cows and those who would probably try it was 111 cows.

- Producers who were more dissatisfied with current reproductive performance were much more likely to try the new service.

- There was no difference in willingness to try it based on whether an AI technician or the owner did the insemination.

- In general, younger producers with higher levels of education were more likely to try the new service than older producers with lower levels of education.

Key Benefits

The following is a verbatim list of statements made by producers when asked to cite benefits:

- Might be beneficial depending on how much it costs.
- Might be beneficial for some producers, but I'd rather do it myself.
- I hate doing heat detection and don't do a very good job, so this would be very useful to me.
- I don't have any problems in this area.
- This would take some of the pressure off me. If it were cost effective, it would increase the pregnancy rate and increase my profits.
- One other company approached me about this already. I heard they made a lot of mistakes. Maybe I should just do it myself.
- I can see where this might have merit, but I would need to see the recommended protocols and how they would fit into my operation.
- Sounds great for farmers who don't spend enough time doing it themselves.
- I can't see where this would have any benefits.
- I'm satisfied with how this is working on my farm. I don't want to hire someone to do what I'm already doing myself.
- I can see where this would be useful for herds where they are having problems. We seem to be getting along okay the way it is.
- I'm with my herd all the time, so I don't see much benefit in this type of program.
- If this doesn't cost too much I think it would be great because it would shorten the number of days open and reduce the culling rate.
- I hate the data collection side of things. Having this done for me would be a big benefit.
- I can see where this would reduce a number of headaches and help me do a better job of managing reproduction in my herd.
- This would be a great program for people who are too busy doing other things and are having problems.
- I think this would be a big help. The whole concept makes a lot of sense to me. I would still want to be involved in some ways.
- I already work closely with my vet, so this would not be that useful to me.

- I like the idea of setting goals and then working toward these goals.
- I might be interested in the consultancy side of the program, but I'd prefer to do the rest myself.
- I like the idea of a specialist doing this. This is a very complicated area.
- This sounds way too good to be true.
- Not very relevant to our operation. We have four families involved so we are very close to our herd.
- I'm always looking for ways to improve my performance. Reproductive management is something I don't know much about. I'd definitely be interested.
- Anything to help with heat detection would be an advantage.
- This would be great for farmers who don't have the time to do this on their own.
- It would be really helpful for problem herds.
- If it will save me time, I'd definitely be interested.
- I have my vet help with this, but at $150 per hour, this can get expensive. I'd like to know more about this.
- This would be great to save me a lot of time. I'm running the operation by myself and need all the assistance I can get.
- I really don't understand how this could work.
- Might consider it in the summer when we are busy in the fields.
- This is a great idea. I'm not good at heat detection but I understand how important it is to improving my profitability.
- I think there's great potential for this service. Using vets is so expensive.
- This could be very useful, but I would want to see how it works on other farms before I would commit myself.
- I think some companies are already doing this. I don't think it's a new idea.
- Hard to get the vet to come in a timely way, so this would be very useful.
- Anything that would improve the pregnancy rate would be great. Low pregnancy rates could be my biggest limiting factor.
- I think it's a little idealistic. Not sure I'd be interested.
- This is why I have children—they do all of this for me.
- I like the idea of having someone on-site looking after this for me.
- With a conception rate of 12.8, I'm already doing a good job. I doubt they could do better. (It's a good starting point for educating farmers about true benchmarks, though.)
- I'd give it a try if they guarantee results.
- Great if it would eliminate vet pregnancy checks.
- I like the idea that one specialist would take care of all the steps in reproduction—heat detection, data collections, and insemination.
- I like the data collection aspect of this.
- As my herd gets bigger, this makes more and more sense. I can't do everything.
- Improving the conception rate would really offset the cost of the program.

Key Concerns

The following is a verbatim list of statements made by producers when asked to cite concerns:

- I would not be managing my herd anymore. I would be giving all the responsibility away.
- I want to be involved as much as I can in my operation.
- I think this would cost a lot.
- I just can't picture how this would work.
- I don't like using synchronization techniques. I've never had good luck with them.
- I hate depending on someone else.
- I don't want to be needling my cows all the time. Maybe natural breeding is still best.
- The specialist would have to be around almost all the time if they were to do a good job in heat detection.
- I'd be worried about bio-security. I don't want someone coming on the farm that's been in all kinds of other barns.
- Sounds too good to be true.
- How is someone else going to watch for heat when they aren't here all the time?
- I may disagree with their decisions.
- I think this would cost too much to be worth it.
- I don't think I want to admit that someone else could do a better job than I do.
- Nobody knows my cows better than I do.
- I don't think reproduction is a big problem.
- I'm already using synchronization programs.
- How could one person do all of this for so many herds?
- My vet already does a lot of this for me.
- I can't see how this would work because the specialist would not be there much of the time. Observation is so important.
- What if I didn't get along very well with this person?
- My vet is my specialist.
- I want to be in full control.
- May cost more than a pregnancy is worth.
- To be effective the specialist would have to be here all the time.
- Sounds way too expensive to me.

EverLine Inc.

Andrei Craciun and Christopher A. Ross

INTRODUCTION

"Theoretically, this should have been our year . . . We have our references and testimonials, we are getting calls, but I just don't understand, there's something that we're missing . . . I don't know what it is . . . Everything is costing us more money and all we could do is decrease our price, and we still can't sell. We keep pumping money into the business and trying to make it work," said Melissa Desjardins, president of EverLine Inc., in February 2004.

Located in Toronto, EverLine Inc. manufactured inlaid synthetic field marking lines for natural athletic grass fields. Martin Desjardins, Melissa's uncle, had invented the product while Stephane Desjardins, Melissa's father, owned the business. In return for inventing the product, Martin Desjardins had exclusive rights to the Canadian market. Melissa, therefore, had focused her efforts on the U.S. market. After suffering financial losses in 2001, 2002, and 2003, Melissa had grown increasingly concerned about the

Andrei Craciun, research assistant, and Christopher A. Ross, professor, John Molson School of Business, Concordia University, wrote this case. It is partly based on a student report that was submitted in the fall of 2002. It is to be used for discussion purposes only. It is not designed to illustrate either effective or ineffective handling of an administrative or commercial situation. Some of the information in this case has been disguised but essential relationships have been retained. Copyright © 2005. This case was made possible through the financial support of the Institute for Co-operative Education, Concordia University. Reprinted with permission.

chances of success for the business. As a result, she decided to review the significant activities of the business over the last few years.

Stephane Desjardins was the youngest of three brothers. Martin, the inventor of synthetic marking lines, was the second son. The eldest was in the jewellery business and did not play any role in EverLine. Stephane had attended university in the United States and graduated with a B.A., minor in psychology. He was a creative person and, with 30 years experience, had extensive knowledge of the sports surfacing industry. In the past, Stephane had been involved with companies that provided artificial turf for golf, tennis, soccer, baseball, and football.

EverLine, incorporated in 2001, was Stephane's most recent company. He was the owner of EverLine Inc. but he was not involved with sales or production. He served, however, in an advisory capacity to Melissa. Two employees, Melissa and Sherri, her assistant, ran the company. Melissa, a B.Comm. graduate, officially became the marketing manager and president of EverLine Inc. in May 2002. Prior to EverLine Inc., Melissa was the marketing manager of a student pub at a well-known metropolitan university in Canada.

THE PRODUCT AND THE COMPANY

EverLine's inlaid synthetic marking lines were an environmentally friendly, low cost solution to repetitive, high maintenance field marking expenses. These synthetic grass lines were installed in *real grass* athletic fields as a permanent solution for defining perimeter and other field markings. The lines provided a high level of marking visibility in all types of lighting and weather conditions and were made of a synthetic yarn, which simulated the appearance of grass. The yarn, $2\frac{1}{2}"$ long, was made from polypropylene or polyethylene and was attached to a porous backing. Water drained through this porous backing with little hindrance. Graded sand surrounded each EverLine fibre in the same way that natural earth held a blade of grass. The synthetic tufted white line, about 4" wide, had two rows of green tuft on either side which blended in with the natural grass. In total, the product was $7\frac{1}{2}"$ wide. Grass grew into the green fibres, and the lines were anchored down securely into a 2" deep trench with 6" staples that were covered by grass and sand after the installation, thus becoming invisible. Figure 1 is an example of what the lines looked like after installation.

Figure 1	INSTALLED SYNTHETIC LINES

The company identified the benefits of using these lines as follows:

- ease of installation
- virtually maintenance free
- average payback of 1–3 years
- 10–15 year life span
- 5–year warranty against wear and UV degradation
- elimination of most recurring marking costs
- enhanced facility image
- visible lines from stands and field
- field can be mowed as usual
- installed wherever natural grass grows
- available in yellow, red, blue, and white

The use of this product cut costs associated with all recurring field lining expenses, such as the cost of paint and chalk, machinery (including maintenance and repairs), labour, storage of flammable paint, and so on. In addition, the use of these synthetic lines also eliminated traditional ways of marking and their associated major drawbacks such as seepage of toxins into the water table, lines washed away by rain, or bad calls by referees caused by less visible lines.

Applications included synthetic white and yellow lines for baseball, softball, soccer, and football fields. Other possible applications included delineation, campgrounds, walkways, military targets, aviation ground markers, park and recreation uses, cemetery paths and borders, skydiving targets, and so on. The product was patented in Canada, the United States, Europe, and Australia.

EverLine had the following mission statement in 2002:

> *To revolutionize the sports line marking industry by producing a technologically advanced and cost efficient alternative to existing line marking methods; to eliminate products such as paint and chalk (except for when and where necessary), and to become the industry leader with a FIFA[1] endorsement for soccer within 5 years.*

As soon as she had become involved with EverLine Inc. in May 2002, Melissa Desjardins formulated the company's objectives as follows:

1. Double market share in all targeted states each year for the first three years. (Sales from states outside the target market may occur due to national advertising, yet will not be actively pursued.)
2. Generate, at least, the sale of one football, soccer, and baseball field in each of the targeted states within the first year.
3. Become the market leader of athletic field marking in the United States within five years.

THE MARKET

Melissa had initially targeted the southern areas of the United States because the climate permitted year-round use of athletic fields. More specifically, she had targeted Florida, Mississippi, Louisiana, Alabama, Georgia, and Texas. She had also wanted markets that were located close to the manufacturing source in Georgia. She soon discovered, however, that the favourable climate for athletics also encouraged the rapid growth of weeds, which

---

[1] Fédération Internationale de Football Association

engulfed EverLine. Consequently, she began favouring states like Minnesota, for example, that were located further north where weeds and UV rays were not critical factors.

Melissa came across a survey conducted by the Sports Turf Managers Association (STMA) in February 2001, which collected budget data from turf managers for personnel, materials, equipment, and all other expenses (393 completed surveys were received, a 21.3% response rate).[2] She was able to estimate a conservative total of 524 660 fields, or 888 359 900 linear feet of potential athletic field lines in the United States. These figures did not include private outdoor facilities.

In estimating the market potential for EverLine in the US, Melissa assumed that half of the fields were not within her market; i.e., they did not have the budget, they were already synthetic, poor field conditions, etc. Thus, EverLine Inc. was left with 444 179 950 linear feet as the size of the potential market. Using an average retail price of US$2.58/linear foot, including infill, she determined that the total possible sales potential in the United States was $1 145 984 271 with a potential gross margin of $533 015 940 (47%). These figures did not include profit of approximately US$0.50/linear foot on the installation, since about 95% of customers installed the product themselves.

Another source of data collected in the STMA survey pertained to budget allocation by sports turf managers. In 2001, approximately US$2.5 billion was spent on materials, with another US$1.3 billion spent on equipment. Exact numbers regarding the expenditure on lining or costs associated with it were not, however, available.

She also noted that the number of college sports teams was generally stable, as most had been established for many years. Research had shown, however, that college sports departments were becoming increasingly unprofitable and were, therefore, cutting costs. Though this could be a threat to the synthetic grass industry, Melissa felt that EverLine had the potential to shine through as the cheaper alternative to constant painting or chalking costs, or to covering an entire field in synthetic grass.

Melissa also identified several developing market trends with the potential to affect EverLine Inc. These were as follows:

1. Cost efficiency: While synthetic grass opportunities were becoming increasingly popular, groundskeepers were constantly seeking low cost alternatives.

2. Permanency: Decision makers who were responsible for selecting field surfaces were increasingly looking towards more permanent solutions. The long-term cost savings of permanent lines were appealing to such buyers.

3. Environmentalists: The line marking industry had experienced a shift towards environmentally safe alternatives. For instance, certain states had banned the use of chalk as it had been linked to water contamination. Similarly, lime and some paint were increasingly being avoided for their harmful effects on the environment.

4. Soccer Growth: Soccer was becoming increasingly popular in the United States. According to the 2002 annual Harris survey on sports preferences, soccer was followed by 18% of the U.S. adult population compared to 10% in 1985. This was seen as an opportunity since there could be greater demand for lines with the increased installation of soccer fields. U.S. Sports Turf Management Survey attributed 301 695 acres to soccer fields, which was higher than any other sport, including baseball, softball, and football.

---

[2] Rich King, "The Sports Turf Manager and STMA," *Sport Turf Magazine*, February 2002.

Melissa had expected that the increasing popularity of soccer in the United States would generate demand for EverLine. Few soccer fields, however, had actually purchased the lines. For the year 2003, EverLine Inc. had sold its product to 2 football fields, 18 soccer fields, and 198 baseball fields. She subsequently discovered that the managers of quite a few of the soccer and football fields moved the lines a few feet each spring in order to allow the grass to rejuvenate itself. They were, therefore, reluctant to install permanent lines. Only 25 states had purchased EverLine, of which 9 had only purchased 2 each. The top 3 states that had adopted most of the lines were Minnesota (34 fields), Arizona (24 fields), and Wisconsin (16 fields). Table 1 shows all the states using EverLine for their baseball fields and the corresponding number of fields.

Playing fields varied in size. A baseball field had about 400 feet of lines, a soccer field had about 2200 feet of lines, and a football field had between 2000 and 5100 feet of lines, depending on whether or not the purchaser needed all the yard/hash lines. Melissa had observed that in the case of a baseball field, for example, the cost associated with the traditional way of marking was between US$1000 and US$1500 per year, whereas EverLine, installed, cost a maximum of US$1200 up front, but it was good for as long as 15 years (about US$80/year). Using traditional ways of marking a football field required an investment of about US$4500 to US$5000 per season, the same amount of money as a soccer field. Even though a football field had about twice as many lines as a soccer field, the soccer season was twice as long as the football season. This intense use explained the equal amount of money spent on line markings for both fields.

Although lining costs appeared not to be a priority for them, Melissa felt that her main focus should be on cities, because they controlled several fields and, therefore, placed larger orders. Schools and colleges, on the other hand, usually bought only one or two, if any at all.

Table 1		The Number Of Baseball Fields Using Everlines By State							
Minnesota	34	Massachusetts	10	Maine	6	Georgia	2
Arizona	24	New Jersey	10	Ohio	6	Illinois	2
Wisconsin	16	Connecticut	8	New Hampshire	4	Maryland	2
Texas	14	South Carolina	8	New York	4	Oregon	2
Kansas	12	Tennessee	8	California	2	Utah	2
Kentucky	10	Hawaii	6	Florida	2	Vermont	2
						Washington	2

BUYERS

There were two main groups with a vested interest in installing EverLine markings: the end-users—those who used the fields, and front-users—those who bought/maintained the fields. The end-users consisted of all athletes and spectators who used athletic fields. EverLine Inc., however, had focused its attention on the decision makers of the following:

- City Parks and Recreation Departments
- Schools—Mainly Colleges/Universities/High Schools

- Private Outdoor Athletic Clubs/Facilities
- Military Bases

Specifically, athletic directors, directors of parks and recreation, and managers/owners were the decision makers who were actively involved in the purchase of the product.

Melissa found that it was difficult to get buyers to switch from paint or chalk. She attributed this behaviour to the relatively high switching costs on the part of the buyer. Overall, field owners looked for several characteristics in any related product. These characteristics were as follows:

- natural look and feel
- physical security of sports players
- lines that stood up to wear and tear of normal sports uses
- attractive playing surface
- cost efficiency
- environmentally friendly marketing solutions

EverLine satisfied all of these requirements. For example, with growing environmental concerns, consumers sought to replace the harmful chemicals being used in today's field marking industry and EverLine offered a new choice to the market. Apart from enhancing the visibility of boundary lines and reducing the probability of a bad call by the referee, EverLine further reduced the need to routinely close the field for line marking maintenance.

Each of the organizations purchasing EverLine had a different approval process, but the majority had a specific individual who was responsible for field maintenance decisions. The final decision authority lay with the individual or board of supervisors having the budget/funding authority, such as the parks and recreation superintendent or athletic director. Before a purchase order could be issued or purchase agreement signed, the overseeing body had to approve the product and allocate the necessary funds.

Typically, the groundskeeper/superintendent had a large influence on the equipment and materials selected. He or she normally had the task of presenting the potential options or solutions to the decision makers. As part of the approval and bidding process, cities sometimes required several proposals from different companies. Being the sole source worked as both an advantage and disadvantage depending on the city. References and testimonials were almost always requested. These were important if a sale was to be made, as it was often taxpayer money that was being spent.

Melissa had also observed that the decision to order EverLine took up to one year from the buyer's initial contact with EverLine Inc. The reasons for this one-year turnaround included:

1. The purchase did not fit into the budget at that particular time. When this occurred, the supplying organization had to wait until the next budget was approved to see if money was available for a purchase, and that usually took about one year.

2. There was a certain perceived risk associated with the purchase, so the decision makers took their time to weigh all possibilities or risks associated with the purchase.

EverLine used the following criteria to identify target market states:

- states with a large amount of money spent in their parks and recreation
- departments compared to all the other states (Exhibit 1 shows spending on parks and recreation per state as of 2000.);
- size of the state, as well as population (Exhibit 1 also shows the population of each state as of 2002; Exhibit 2 shows the location of each state.);

EXHIBIT 1	Parks and Recreation Spending by State in 2000 ($ millions) and State Populations in 2002 (thousands)				
	$ mil	Pop.		$ mil	Pop.
Alabama	11	4 487	Nebraska	25	1 729
Alaska	9	644	Nevada	18	2 173
Arizona	37	5 456	New Hampshire	7	1 275
Arkansas	75	2 710	New Jersey	317	8 590
California	286	35 116	New Mexico	43	1 855
Colorado	59	4 507	New York	495	19 158
Connecticut	41	3 461	North Carolina	152	8 320
Delaware	48	807	North Dakota	9	634
District of Columbia		571	Ohio	132	11 421
Florida	144	16 713	Oklahoma	61	3 494
Georgia	128	8 560	Oregon	41	3 522
Hawaii	46	1 245	Pennsylvania	140	12 335
Idaho	21	1 341	Rhode Island	13	1 070
Illinois	141	12 601	South Carolina	56	4 107
Indiana	61	6 159	South Dakota	22	761
Iowa	18	2 937	Tennessee	116	5 797
Kansas	8	2 716	Texas	56	21 780
Kentucky	112	4 093	Utah	30	2 316
Louisiana	168	4 483	Vermont	7	617
Maine	10	1 294	Virginia	76	7 294
Maryland	173	5 458	Washington	64	6 069
Massachusetts	127	6 428	West Virginia	55	1 802
Michigan	125	10 050	Wisconsin	54	5 441
Minnesota	99	5 020	Wyoming	11	499
Mississippi	50	2 872			
Missouri	38	5 673			
Montana	14	909	**Total**	**4 049**	**288 370**

Source: U.S. Census Bureau, Statistical Abstract of the United States: 2003.

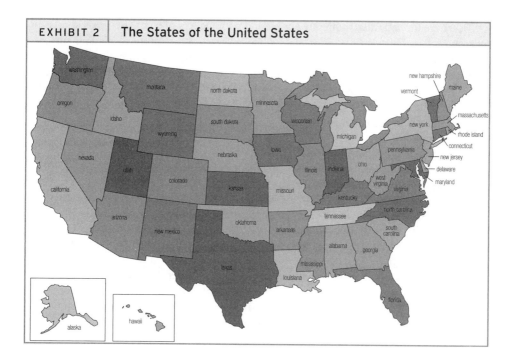

| EXHIBIT 2 | The States of the United States |

- states encountering rapid growth in the parks and recreation areas; and
- states with a high response rate to EverLine Inc.'s marketing attempts.

The ordering process was a fairly simple one. If a buyer in Minnesota, for example, wanted to purchase EverLine for a baseball field, he or she simply faxed the purchase order to EverLine. The product was then shipped from Georgia on pallets or in boxes via FedEx (ground service) or any other suitable carrier, with the required number of feet of product. Pegs, turf staples, and a blade that fitted a Ryan/Bluebird sod cutter were also sent. This cutter was used to make the trench into which the lines were laid. Customers deposited US$150 for the blade. EverLine returned this money when the customers sent back the blade. The company provided installation upon demand but, generally, most people found the lines easy to install.

COMPETITION

EverLine's product was unique; companies producing the same product were nonexistent. There were many players in the field marking industry, however. The closest competitors were the hundreds of manufacturers of painted and chalked lines, and the distributors in the athletic paint industry. The leaders were Pioneer Manufacturing, GameDay, Tru Mark, and AllState Athletic Supply. Diamond Pro was the leader in the industry for chalk, as well as Kromer and Line King for paint striping machines. Catalogue companies, such as M.A.S.A and Beacon Ballfields, were also competitors as they distributed a multitude of products including paint, chalk, and striping machines, which cost over US$12 000 (as well as $2000 for a clogged nozzle). EverLine's competitive advantage was its long-term cost savings and environmentally friendly characteristics. Other companies produced markers made of solid plastic.

EverLine Inc. was also indirectly competing with makers of synthetic-grass sports surfaces as well as hybrids (50% artificial—50% turf grass), and portable playing surfaces. This competition arose because EverLine could not be installed on synthetic fields. A fully lined football field in synthetic, however, could cost over $1 million, whereas EverLine cost a maximum of $20 000, thereby making EverLine more affordable. The leaders in the synthetic industry were General Sports Turf, Sportex, and Field Turf Inc. Exhibit 3 provides a brief description of some key competitors.

EXHIBIT 3	Competitor Profiles

Synthetic Turf Companies

1. General Sports Turf Systems
Date founded: 1994
General Sports Turf had experience in many areas of professional, collegiate, and amateur sports. Their backgrounds included construction management, sports facility development and management, revenue generation and enhancement, design-build delivery, and project financing. Their goal was to build the most professional, most reliable, most consultative company in the industry. They were well-known for their "Zero Tolerance" standards.

2. Evergreen Synthetic Turf LLC
Date founded: 1976
Evergreen Synthetic Turf LLC was the oldest owner-operated manufacturer of synthetic turf worldwide. The management team had over 100 years of combined experience and had produced over 50 million feet of turf. They had installed their products in over 50 countries including Russia, Greece, Ireland, and Brazil.

3. SportFields, Inc.
Date founded: 1997
SportFields, Inc. was a provider of turnkey synthetic turf and base systems. Its owners had been installing synthetic surfacing systems for more than 10 years. SportFields' owners were on-site during construction and for final customer inspection and approval. Every installation was backed by a manufacturer warranty and included inspections by the company's owners at six months to one year intervals after project completion to ensure that a high level of quality is maintained.

Source: *Athletic Management Magazine*, vol. XVI, No. 3, April/May 2004.

Paint/Chalk Companies

1. Kromer
Kromer Co. LLC specialized in building equipment for maintenance of athletic fields. The Kromer Athletic Field Machine (AFM™) was the only machine that applied dry lines, wet lines, groomed, conditioned, mowed, aerated, spread, sprayed, and cut and painted a line at the same time.

Source: http://www.kromer-afm.com/, accessed May 25, 2004.

EXHIBIT 3	Competitor Profiles (Continued)

2. Pioneer Manufacturing

Pioneer Manufacturing was the leader in the athletic paint industry. They sold paints for all kinds of natural grass fields and were also able to make customized designs in order to personalize a field.

Source: http://www.pioneer-mfg.com/, accessed May 25, 2004.

3. Tru Mark Athletic Field Marker

Tru Mark Athletic Field Marker produced athletic and sports field marker equipment and tools for striping and painting sports turf lines and spraying. Applications included football, soccer, and baseball field marking activities, youth association, high school, college, and parks and recreation. Tru Mark's line painting machines cost anywhere between US$1000 and 5000, not including any accessories or the paint itself.

Source: http://www.athleticfieldmarker.com/, accessed May 25, 2004.

MANUFACTURING

A one-time deal with a commission tufting company in Georgia had generated about 120 000 feet of lines. There had been a complete lack of quality control; however, the product had wavy lines, there were no rows of green tuft on the sides of the white line, etc. As a result, there was about 25% waste. Another problem was that Melissa did not know if the contracted plant was producing for anyone else. It was likely, she felt, that competitors could easily find out how to make the product from the tufting company. Because of these problems EverLine Inc. had started manufacturing the lines, on a contract basis, in a small factory in Toronto. Plans were moving ahead, however, for EverLine to do its own manufacturing.

PROMOTION

Melissa had thought of employing the following personal selling channels: sales representatives (manufacturer's agents), distributors, and licensees. She had planned that the sales representatives would function on a commission basis with all paperwork going through head office. They would not stock the lines but would receive a 15% commission on each sale. Distributors would purchase the lines in order to resell them. Finally, licensees would purchase exclusive rights to sell EverLine in a designated territory for approximately US$10 000 or more (depending on the population and potential facilities). This licence, in addition to the exclusive sales rights, would entitle the licensee to special privileges, such as purchasing the lines at a lower cost per linear foot, and full marketing support from head office. This support would include extra free brochures and videos, as well as CD-ROM listings of schools, parks and recreation departments, and private outdoor sport facilities in their state(s). They would also receive free exposure through EverLine advertisements. Licensees were to be imposed the highest sales quota. After trying several times in 2002 to obtain distributors and licensees, however, she was not happy with the results (she had one licensee and one distributor who were both unproductive) and ended up doing all the sell-ing, together with Sherri (trade shows, installations, phone calls, etc.).

Melissa also used a number of other promotional techniques, including brochures, a website, promotions, trade shows, ads in trade magazines, phone calls, and testimonials. The brochure used was a 3-fold, 9" by 12" glossy paper in colour. It briefly described the installation process and mentioned the benefits of using the product. It also had some tes-timonials and contact information.

The official EverLine Inc. website included a spreadsheet that allowed visitors to plug in cost per bag/gallon for chalk or paint, amount of linear footage marked, labour rates, length of season, frequency of paint applications (weekly, etc.), and paint yield, and then compare it with the cost of EverLine lines to discover the cost savings and payback period. (See Exhibit 4 for an example of payback analysis.) The website received a large number of hits, according to Melissa, and generated many leads. EverLine maintained a database of the email addresses of anyone who had inquired or purchased their product and sent them mass emails with information regarding special events, promotional sales, or news.

EXHIBIT 4	Payback Analysis

Sport:	Baseball
Months in Use	6
Applications/Week	1
Average Labour Rate ($/hr)	
300 ft. Painted per Hour	15
Paint Cost ($/gal)	10
Feet/Gal Yield (Paint)	300
Install with In-House Labour	Yes
Standard Field Markings/Size	Yes

Traditional Painting vs. EverLine
Linear Footage: 400

Annual Painting Cost:		EverLine:	
Material:	$347	Material 1st Quality:	$1400
Labour:	$520	Labour (if applicable):	$0
		Supervision (if applicable)	$0
Total:	$867*	Total:	$1400

***Does not include machinery or repairs**   **Payback in years:**   **1.6**

Remember, EverLine expected lifespan: 10–15 years!
Shipping is additional

When licensees and distributors purchased more than 25 000 linear feet of EverLine, they paid a discounted price per linear foot. When customers purchased between 5000 and 25 000 linear feet of EverLine, they received 10% additional free lines. Those who purchased more than 25 000 linear feet received either a reduced cost per linear foot or obtained 15% additional free lines. Additional promotional strategies included a sample of already installed EverLine in a container for the potential customer to touch and examine. There was also an unassembled two-foot sample, which the customer could install in an inconspicuous spot on the field next to a painted line in order to see the difference. Sample packages cost about US$10. One problem with this, however, was that EverLine Inc. did not know who demanded a sample package, and sometimes it was competitors who did. Melissa also felt that the use of this sample contributed to the one-year delay in purchasing because buyers often waited to see if the product held up. Melissa also provided special rebates and sales. For example, the advertised spring sale of 2004 offered a special price of US$1.00/ft of line.

EverLine Inc. had also installed lines for free or at a discounted price in order to increase awareness and to test the market. One example of this promotional effort was at a major university in California, one of two fields that used EverLine in California. The university, however, was not happy with the product. A distributor had sold it to them and he apparently misrepresented the product. He had told the university that EverLine was completely maintenance free, but because of all the sunshine, weeds flourished and there was some maintenance as a result. The university, as a consequence, did not want to be associated with the product. These promotional installations targeted schools that generate the most play time, visitors, and spectators.

Trade Shows

There were several well-known industry trade shows, including the Athletic Business Sport and Fitness Facility Expo, the National Recreation and Parks Association Expo, the National High School Athletic Directors Conference, the National Collegiate Athletic Directors Conference, and the Sports Turf Managers Association (STMA) Annual Convention. EverLine staff from head office regularly attended these trade shows with product samples and a $10' \times 10'$ booth displaying a real sod installation in order for potential customers to be able to see and feel an installed portion of a line. This was essential because of the high touch element of the product. This touching element gave customers who were hesitant to alter their natural field an understanding of the physical aspects of the product and eased their purchase decision process.

The following is a description of two trade shows.

The Athletic Business Sport and Fitness Facility Expo

This expo attracted about 3700 attendees, and allowed EverLine Inc. to reach three major markets: colleges/universities, military bases/installations, and parks and recreation/municipal centres. It was normally held in November in Orlando, Florida. Melissa got the most leads from this show (96 compared to an average of 30 to 40), but they did not generate any sales. A show booth ($10' \times 10'$ booth space) cost a total of US$1775. Travel and other expenses totalled CDN$800.

The National Recreation and Parks Association Expo

This expo attracted over 4500 attendees, including park and recreation facility designers, ground maintenance directors, park directors/superintendents, military recreation facility managers, landscape architects/park planners/specifiers/purchasing agents, college and university faculty in recreation departments, and recreation specialists/program managers. It ran in October in Tampa Bay, Florida. A show booth cost US$1700, and included a draped 8′ high back wall and 3′ side rails for in-line booths, a standard 7″×44″ booth ID sign, and some general hall security. Travel and other expenses were estimated to be CDN$1000, as hotel accommodations were required. Melissa and Sherri had targeted this show, but they never attended.

Magazines

According to Melissa, about 80% of the company's leads had come from trade magazines through a "bingo card" response system. Black and white ¼-page ads had been used in trade magazines such as *Athletic Business Magazine*, *National Recreation and Parks Association Magazine*, *Coach and Athletic Director Magazine*, *Recreation Management*, and *Government Recreation and Fitness Magazine*. A description of these communication vehicles follows.

Athletic Business Magazine

This magazine had a circulation of 42 025 and targeted high schools, colleges/universities, parks and recreation departments, YMCAs/YWCAs, military, stadiums/pro teams, sport architects, and consultants throughout the United States. In addition to the initial press release, Melissa had placed a ¼-page black and white ad for the July to December 2003 issues. This cost a total of US$7140. This magazine generated between 300 and 500 leads, but no sales.

National Recreation and Parks Association Magazine

This magazine had a circulation of more than 20 000 and targeted parks and recreation professionals and citizen board members involved with planning, developing, and operating parks and recreation facilities and programs. EverLine Inc. placed a ¼-page black and white ad for the July to December 2002 issues. This cost a total of US$4440. This magazine did not generate any leads at all.

Coach and Athletic Director Magazine

This magazine had a circulation of 48 745 (10 issues/year), and within this it reached 100% of colleges and 95% of the high schools in the United States. The target market was coaches (possible distributors/licensees) and athletic directors, who usually had the final say on purchases. EverLine Inc. placed a 2.25″ wide × 2″ high classified ad (end of magazine) with a brief description of the job opportunities with EverLine and contact information, in order to announce that EverLine Inc. was in search of distributors and licensees. This ad was placed in the May to December 2002 issues (May and

June issues are combined, and there is no July issue), and cost US$2400. It was not very productive.

Recreation Management Magazine

This magazine had a total circulation of 50 000 of which 12 500 reached city parks and recreation departments. It published 9 issues per year, and had an additional "buyer's guide" distributed in December. EverLine Inc. placed a ¼-page, 2-colour ad for the May to December issues (May/June, August/September, November/December issues were combined; July and October were separate). This cost a total of US$8624. The December buyer's guide cost an additional US$1960 for a ¼-page, 2-colour ad (second colour being green). In addition, EverLine Inc. had free listing under the "Grounds Maintenance —Line Marking Material" and "Line Markers/Stripers" sections. This magazine proved the most successful of all magazines, as EverLine got many leads along with free postcards that generated about a dozen sales.

Government Recreation and Fitness Magazine

This magazine was the forum for military and government recreation and fitness managers across the United States. For the month of June 2003, the total circulation was 9974. This magazine was published 10 times a year, and among its subscribers were the White House, state and local governments, and the Department of Defense. EverLine placed a black and white ¼-page ad.[3]

Melissa and Sherri also made phone calls to customers who had inquired about EverLine after attending trade shows, after visiting the website, after seeing an ad, and so on. According to Melissa, the phone is a very good way of closing a sale because the customer gets answers to all of the questions or doubts he or she may have. After a successful transaction, customers left feedback about EverLine in the form of testimonials. Some testimonials are included in Exhibit 5. Through "bingo card" responses from magazines, calls to the toll-free number, and inquiries from the website, tracking was done to determine how the customer had heard about EverLine Inc.

PROBLEM ANALYSIS

On her appointment as president of EverLine Inc. in May 2002, Melissa had anticipated a number of problems and had thought of potential solutions. These are outlined in Table 2.

PRICING AND FINANCES

In spite of Melissa's best efforts, however, EverLine had suffered losses in 2001, 2002, and 2003. Financial statements are provided in Exhibit 6. In an attempt to increase sales, Melissa had reduced the price from US$2.58 to US$1.00/$1.50 per linear foot.[4] By the

---

[3] http://www.ebmpubs.com/grf_web.html?grfcuris.
[4] Towards the end of 2003, US$1.00 was equal to approximately CDN$1.36.

EXHIBIT 5	Testimonials

"EverLine has saved us money on field lining and maintenance. Our fields look great and our teams are proud to play on them and host other communities. I would highly recommend this product to all athletic and recreation programs."

—Park and Recreation Director, Massachusetts

"EverLine has taken our soccer facility to a new level. We have received numerous compliments from visiting teams and positive reactions from recruits. It has definitely set us apart from the other teams in our league and in our region of the country! EverLine has also made our game day field preparation ten times simpler! It now only takes a few minutes the day of the game versus having to spend hours the day before!"

—Head, Men & Women's Soccer Coach, Kansas

"We just recently added our soccer programs and built new soccer fields. After crunching the numbers for the cost of labour, time, and material for painting the fields, it became very obvious to us that we would see considerable cost savings by installing the EverLine product. Once we decided to install the EverLine product on our soccer fields, it only made sense to us to also purchase the product for our baseball and softball fields. We feel we have made an excellent investment by having EverLine installed on all of our fields."

—Director of Athletics, Kansas

Table 2	Potential Problems and Possible Solutions

Problem	Solution
Potential buyers may perceive the permanent line as a liability to the security of players	Testimonials from tester installations will prove otherwise. Also hope to get endorsements to help increase credibility
Fear of vandalism on the field and of the resulting damages to EverLine	Possible partnership with a company offering fencing services; testimonials pertaining to the product's strength and durability
Fear of market saturation	Maintain relationships with clients to offer new products and to replace Everline after its expected life of 10 to 15 years
Competitor copying product	Patent protection
City budgets and purchase constraints	EDC financing program and guaranteed receivables at a cost of approx. 1.5%
Fields requiring different lining for different sports on the same field	Very rare occasion, usually for tournaments, but can use washable/removable paint for extra lines

EXHIBIT 6	Financial Statements

Statement of Income and Retained Earnings $

For the year ending	31 Dec. 2001	31 Dec. 2002	31 Dec. 2003
Revenue	280 422	365 550	268 126
Cost of Sales	151 574	203 304	151 912
Gross Profit	**128 848**	**162 246**	**116 214**
Expenses			
General & Administrative	302 422	183 510	318 410
Advertising	24 092	29 824	68 378
Total Expenses	**326 514**	**213 334**	**386 788**
Net Profit/(loss) before Taxes	(197 666)	(51 088)	(270 576)
Taxes	0	0	0
Net Profit/(loss) after Taxes	**(197 666)**	**(51 088)**	**(270 576)**
Retained Earnings: Beginning of Year	(76 452)	(274 118)	(325 206)
Net Profit(loss)	(197 666)	(51 088)	(270 576)
Retained Earnings: End of Year	(274 118)	(325 206)	(595 782)

Balance Sheet

As at	31 Dec. 2001	31 Dec. 2002	31 Dec. 2003
Assets (short term)			
Cash	23 170	34 134	30 192
Accounts Receivable	23 440	33 958	60 256
R&D, Tax Credits Receivable	0	72 930	73 942
Other Receivable	0	0	53 576
Inventory	41 400	41 400	173 280
Total	**88 010**	**182 422**	**391 246**
Assets (long-term)	32 484	47 990	72 818
Assets, Other			
Patent	90 382	114 228	173 804
Total Assets	**210 876**	**344 640**	**637 868**
Liabilities (short term)			
Accounts Payable	38 930	14 610	100 260
Deduction at Source Pay	6 656	0	0
Total	45 586	14 610	100 260
Liabilities (long term)			
Shareholder's Loan	419 410	635 236	1 095 382
Other Debt	0	0	18 008
Total	**419 410**	**635 236**	**1 113 390**

EXHIBIT 6	Financial Statements (continued)			
Equity				
Share Capital		20 000	20 000	20 000
Retained Earnings		(274 118)	(325 206)	(595 782)
		(254 118)	(305 206)	(575 782)
		210 876	344 206	637 868

end of 2003, the cost of producing one foot of line had fallen to between US$0.25 and US$0.30.

CONCLUSION

After reviewing the past three years, Melissa wondered what else she could do in order to stimulate sales in the United States. Sometimes, potential customers hung up on her when she said that EverLine was a Canadian company. She wondered if maybe the timing was not right with all the political issues that surrounded Canada's refusal to join the coalition forces in Iraq. U.S. businesses seemed to be reluctant to collaborate with Canadian businesses because Canada did not join the United States in Iraq. At other times she felt that people did not take her seriously because she was a woman. She wondered what she should do in order to turn things around.

Hannas Seeds

Tom Funk and Patricia Hannas

Patricia Hannas and Warren Stowkoski were engaged in a heated debate concerning the future direction of distribution at Hannas Seeds. Patricia, daughter of the founder Nicholas Hannas, and current president of the company, was a strong supporter of further development of the company's dealer distribution, while Warren, sales manager, was more inclined to favour direct distribution. As they sat in the company's head office in Lacombe, Alberta, Patricia commented, "Warren, I appreciate that direct distribution has a place in our company, but I cannot see building our long-term plans around this method of distribution. It's just too limiting in scope and would require hiring more people and incurring more marketing costs. In addition, it would take years to reach the volume objectives we have for the company." In reply, Warren commented, "I appreciate your point of view, Patricia, but further development of our dealer system will require more people, too. And, of course, it means we have to compensate our dealers for selling our product. This is a costly activity. And our dealers are always complaining about something. Just last week, a couple of dealers mentioned again that they were not adequately trained to provide technical advice to customers. And we are getting more and more complaints about not protecting dealer territories. It just isn't worth the hassle." And so the debate continued as Patricia and Warren argued the pros and cons of dealer versus direct distribution.

COMPANY BACKGROUND

In 1956, Nicholas Hannas purchased Lacombe Seeds, which was a retail store selling forage seed (alfalfas, clovers, and grasses) for use as hay or pasture to area farmers. Shortly after buying the company, Nicholas changed the name to Hannas Seeds and continued to operate in Lacombe. For the next 15 years, the company consisted of both a garden centre that supplied packaged seeds, bulbs, tools, and chemicals to local customers and a warehouse for forage seeds sold to central Alberta farmers. The marketing program during this period consisted in the distribution of forage seed price lists by mail or by customer pickup at the store. Advertisements were placed in the local newspaper during the busy spring season. Sales came from repeat customers, referrals, walk-in traffic, and telephone inquiries. Little or no effort was devoted to aggressively generating new business. The company did not own a delivery truck, so all sales were picked up by customers.

The 1970s were a time of significant growth for Hannas Seeds. Sale revenues and volumes increased substantially as a result of the well-established presence of Hannas Seeds in Lacombe, the continually expanding client base, and the absence of significant competition in the area. In 1973, a grain-cleaning and -processing facility was purchased in the Peace River region of northwestern Alberta and converted to a processing facility for creeping red fescue seed. Creeping red fescue was a primary component in packaged lawn grass mixtures sold for residential lawns, playgrounds, golf courses, and parks. The demand for creeping red fescue was substantial, so the purchase of this facility provided Hannas Seeds with the ability to produce and market a product that could be sold into world markets. During this period, there were only a handful of companies in the creeping red fescue market. Export sales were generated through the use of commodity brokers so there was no need to market one's own product. Brokers would approach a seller of creeping red fescue with a bid from a prospective buyer. If interested in selling one or more loads of seed, the seller would agree or counter the bid. Conversely, the seller may approach the broker first with an offer and the broker would then search for an interested buyer. The identities of both the buyer and seller remained undisclosed until a transaction was completed. As there were only a small number of fescue processors and exporters, demand tended to be greater than supply and the sellers could be assured that they would attain very attractive margins.

The successful entry of Hannas Seeds into the export market was accompanied by similar rapid growth in the domestic market. In the early 1980s, the company began developing a dealer network to complement retail sales. Despite this growth, marketing and sales efforts remained more or less the same as in earlier years with the exception of targeting golf courses, oil and construction companies, and parks and recreation departments, as well as the traditional farm customers. Occasionally an employee would be assigned the task of contacting potential customers by telephone, but this was never a sustained activity.

The retail side of the business continued to develop in the early 1980s although not at the same pace as in earlier years. Several new seed companies sprang up in Alberta, and large eastern Canadian seed companies also sought to establish a presence in the province.

Many of these companies entered the lucrative fescue market attracted by the possibility of attaining very high margins. Consequently, it was not long before the fescue market became saturated and margins declined accordingly.

Even with the entrance of new competition, Hannas Seeds did not alter its low-key approach to marketing. More advertising vehicles were used, such as radio, local newspapers, and the Yellow Pages, but there was no formal marketing program, nor was anyone hired or assigned to concentrate on marketing. The company continued to rely on its springtime mailing campaign to generate direct sales, and there was a small dealer network. Hannas Seeds dealers generally sold forage seed as a sideline to their existing farm or business operations and tended to order seed as they received orders from customers. Only a few dealers inventoried Hannas Seed products and attempted to sell them aggressively.

In the early 1990s, it became apparent that more effort should be devoted to marketing. In 1990 a Customer Appreciation Day was created on which customers were offered discounts on their forage seed purchases. That same year the company purchased a custom-designed display booth for use at various farm, turf, seed industry, and horticultural trade shows. Most competing seed companies had been attending such shows for years and it was felt that Hannas Seeds should establish its own presence at these shows in order to reach more prospective customers. More efforts were made to visit existing dealers in person as well as approach potential dealers. This was, however, not formalized into a job function and therefore not done on a regular basis.

An individual with a strong sales background was hired in the mid-1990s to focus on sales and marketing. In the last half of the 1990s, the company still was achieving some success in recruiting new dealers, especially in the eastern part of the province. At the same time, the number of customers who purchased directly from Hannas Seeds was increasing, although not as rapidly as dealer sales. In 2000, direct sales declined for the first time in many years.

FORAGE SEED BUSINESS

Forage crops were mainly used by farmers to produce hay and pasture for feed to livestock. The most common forage crops were alfalfa, clover, bromegrass, fescue, ryegrass, and timothy. Most of these crops were perennials, which meant that, once seeded, they would grow year after year. Even though this was the case, farmers usually reseeded every three or four years because after this period of time the forage crops started to lose vigour and production declined. Although Patricia was not sure how many pounds of forage seed were sold in Alberta each year, her best guess was approximately 8 500 000 pounds (1 pound = 0.45 kilograms) and that this had remained relatively stable for many years. The industry was hoping that the Canadian Seed Trade Association would start to collect and publish this type of information.

Although some seed companies developed their own proprietary lines of forage seeds, most accessed products from either public or private seed breeding organizations. Public seed breeders included universities and government agencies. The University of Alberta, for example, had an active forage seed breeding program. When they developed a new forage variety, they provided information about this variety to a number of seed companies and solicited bids from these companies. The company with the winning bid was then allowed to grow and distribute the variety and paid the developing organization a royalty. In addition to public institutions, there were a number of private seed breeders who developed varieties and provided them to seed companies on a similar royalty basis.

Most seed companies did not own seed production facilities. Instead, they contracted with farmers (seed growers) to produce seed on their behalf. The seed companies supplied seed growers with a small amount of the seed they wanted produced and then the growers multiplied this seed for the seed company under a contract. After the seed had been multiplied, it was transported to the seed company for cleaning and packaging under the company's brand name. In cases where more than one company had access to the same variety, seed companies often "traded" with each other. For example, if Hannas Seed had an excess supply of Alsike clover, they might sell some of this to a competitor who was short this variety.

There were a number of seed companies in the Alberta forage market. The seven most active are described here:

- Agricore, formerly the Alberta Wheat Pool, distributed forage seeds in all regions of Alberta through their system of grain elevators and local farm supply outlets located in most communities in the province. Agricore was estimated to have a market share of approximately 10%.

- Western Seeds out of Manitoba operated in central and southern Alberta, mainly through a dealer organization. Western Seeds had one sales rep in Alberta who spent most of his time managing the existing dealer organization and obtaining new dealers. The company experienced some growth in recent years by increasing their number of dealers. Hannas Seeds recently lost some dealer accounts to Western Seeds. Western Seeds was thought to have a 15% share of the forage market in Alberta.

- Peace Seeds was located in the Peace River region of Alberta and had its head office in Grande Prairie. Although primarily an exporter of creeping red fescue, Peace Seeds had a small dealer organization in northwestern Alberta and northeastern British Columbia. They did not have sales reps on the road, relying instead on telephone contact with their dealers. Their current share was thought to be about 5%.

- International Seeds was a Saskatchewan seed company that had developed some business in eastern Alberta. They were a division of a very large European seed breeding organization. Recently they created a division called Performance Seeds to set up a dealer organization in Alberta. Their estimated share of the market was 10%, but many thought it was likely to grow in the future.

- North American Seeds was an eastern Canada–based business with a division in Alberta. The Alberta division had a number of dealers, but also four sales reps who did a lot of direct business with larger farmers. They were probably the largest forage seed company in the province with an estimated share of 20%.

- Alberta Seed Company out of Edmonton sold in central Alberta. They sold only through a dealer organization and had approximately 10% of the market.

- Canada West Seed was owned by Continental Grain of Manitoba. They sold through independent dealers and their comprehensive network of grain elevators in many Alberta communities. In addition, they had five sales reps selling a complete line of seeds directly to large farm accounts. They currently had a market share of about 15%.

CURRENT OPERATIONS

By the end of the 1990s, three distinct divisions made up the operations of Hannas Seeds: the garden centre, international forage seed sales, and domestic forage seed sales.

The garden centre provided a wide assortment of competitively priced gardening products and accessories to Lacombe and area gardeners. Products included vegetable and garden seed, lawn grass seed, bird feed, horticultural supplies, ornamental concrete products, bedding plants, and nursery stock in a 167-square-metre retail store and a 93-square-metre greenhouse situated in downtown Lacombe. The garden centre accounted for approximately 5% of total company sales in fiscal year 1999/2000.

The international forage seed division exported high-quality creeping red fescue seed to the United States, Japan, and eastern and western Europe. This division accounted for approximately 65% of total sales in fiscal year 1999/2000.

The domestic forage seed operation provided a wide selection of competitively priced, high-yielding seeds to western Canadian farmers for use in the production of annual and perennial legumes and grasses. Although these products were sold throughout western Canada, the primary market was central Alberta. Domestic forage seed sales accounted for approximately 30% of total company sales in fiscal year 1999/2000. Exhibit 1 provides a list of all products sold by Hannas Seeds in the domestic market and their prices as of March 2000.[1] Patricia felt the real growth opportunities for Hannas Seeds were in this area of the business. Although the size of the forage seed market in Alberta was not growing, Patricia felt the company could increase its current 15% share of the market.

All the forage seed products sold by Hannas Seeds were non-proprietary varieties of annual and perennial legumes and grasses. These varieties were developed in public institutions such as agricultural universities and provincial and federal government research departments. Hannas Seeds acquired the rights to sell these products and contracted with Alberta seed growers to produce certain quantities of seeds which were cleaned and shipped to Hannas facilities for packaging and distribution.

Marketing and sales were under the direction of Warren Stowkoski. Warren had been with the company for six years but had extensive prior experience as a sales rep for BMW Canada. Although Warren's responsibilities were to manage both the company's direct and dealer sales of domestic forage seeds, time pressure meant that he spent most of his time working in the direct sales area of the company. Warren also attended a number of trade shows in Western Canada and industry meetings in both Canada and the United States. Patricia managed the company's modest advertising program, which averaged 2% of sales and mainly consisted of local newspaper and Yellow Pages ads.

Exhibit 2 shows the operating statement for the domestic forage division for the fiscal year ending July 31, 2000.

Direct Distribution

Hannas Seeds had been involved in direct distribution of forage seeds in the Alberta market since its inception. At first, distribution was through the retail store in Lacombe. Local farmers visited the store to purchase forage seeds, usually prior to or during the spring, summer, or fall planting seasons. This was an excellent method of reaching local farmers, but as Hannas Seeds wanted to expand outside the local area, other activities became necessary. In the early 1980s, the company started to advertise in community newspapers in

EXHIBIT 1	Hannas Seeds Retail Price List, March 1, 2000

Alfalfas	$/lb*	Wild Rye	
Alfalfa, Common No. 1	1.70	Altai wild rye, Common No. 1	6.75
AC Blue J	2.75	Altai wild rye, Prairieland	7.75
Algonquin	1.95	Dahurian wild rye, Common No. 1	2.15
Beaver	1.95	Dahurian wild rye, James	2.25
Hannas High Tech Brand	2.25	Russian wild rye, Common No. 1	2.50
Proleaf	2.50	Russian wild rye, Swift	(ask)
Rambler	2.20		
Rangelander	2.20	**Wheatgrass**	
		Crested wheat, Common No. 1	2.25
Clovers		Crested wheat, Fairway	2.75
Alsike clover, Common No. 1	3.10	Crested wheat, Kirk	2.75
Red clover, Common No. 1	0.90	Intermediate wheat, Common No. 1	1.90
Red clover, double cut	1.95	Intermediate wheat, Chief	1.95
Sweet clover, Common No. 1	0.70	Northern wheat, Common No. 1	17.95
Sweet clover, Norgold	1.25	Pubescent wheat, Greenleaf	2.50
White clover, Common No. 1	2.50	Slender wheat, Common No. 1	2.10
		Slender wheat, Revenue	2.25
Special Legumes		Streambank wheat, Common No. 1	11.00
Birdsfoot Trefoil, Common No. 1	2.50	Streambank wheat, Sodar	11.50
Birdsfoot Trefoil, Leo	2.75	Tall wheatgrass	2.75
Cicer Milk Vetch, Common No. 1	2.40	Western wheat, Common No. 1	8.95
Cicer Milk Vetch, Oxley	2.45	Western wheat, Rosanna	9.95
Bromegrass		**Special Grasses**	
Meadow brome, Common No. 1	3.25	Canada bluegrass, Common No. 1	2.95
Meadow brome, Fleet	3.95	Creeping foxtail, Common No. 1	2.70
Smooth brome, Common No. 1	0.90	Kentucky bluegrass, Common No. 1	1.95
Smooth brome, Carlton	1.30	Meadow foxtail, Common No. 1	2.70
Smooth brome, Manchar	1.95	Orchardgrass, Common No. 1	1.20
		Orchardgrass, Potomac	1.35
Fescue		Reed canarygrass, Common No. 1	3.50
Creeping red fescue, Common No. 1	1.70	Reed canarygrass, Palaton	3.75
Creeping red fescue, Boreal	1.75	Reed canarygrass, Rival	3.80
Hard fescue, Common No. 1	1.95		
Sheeps fescue, Common No. 1	4.25	**Timothy**	
Tall fescue, Common No. 1	1.25	Timothy, Common No. 1	1.25
		Timothy, Basho	1.75
Ryegrass		Timothy, Carola	1.75
Annual ryegrass, Common No. 1	0.60	Timothy, Champ	1.75
Italian ryegrass, Common No. 1	1.10	Timothy, Climax	1.75
Perennial ryegrass, Common No. 1	1.25		
		Special Seed	
*1 pound = 0.45 kilogram.		Fall rye, Prima	0.22
		Field peas	0.19

PRICES SUBJECT TO CHANGE WITHOUT NOTICE
HANNAS SEEDS
5039–49 Street, Lacombe, Alberta T4L 1Y2

areas up to 200 kilometres from Lacombe. The ads included a 1-800 phone number that prospective customers could use to obtain more information and place orders. Hannas Seeds also obtained a number of farmer lists it used for direct mail.

EXHIBIT 2	Domestic Forage Seed Division, Operating Statement, Period Ending July 31, 2000		
Gross sales			$2 462 000
Less: Discounts			$ 55 440
Net sales			$2 406 560
Less: Cost of goods			$ 1 625 000
Less: Delivery			$ 65 480
Gross margin			$ 716 080
Expenses			
Marketing manager		$ 75 000	
Office staff		$ 90 000	
Bad debts		$ 13 000	
Advertising and promotion		$ 52 000	
Direct marketing		$ 60 000	
Customer Appreciation Day		$ 15 000	
Travel		$ 30 000	
Division overhead		$ 200 000	
Total expenses			$ 535 000
Division profit			$ 181 080

In 1989, the company purchased a custom-designed display booth for use in various farm, turf, seed industry, and horticultural trade shows. Most competing seed companies had been attending such shows for years and it was felt that it was time for Hannas Seeds to establish its own presence at these shows and reach more prospective customers.

In 1990, an annual Customer Appreciation Day was created on which customers and prospects on the mailing list were invited to Lacombe for a one-day event where they could purchase forage seeds at a 10% discount. The day, usually scheduled for mid-March, also featured live entertainment, product seminars, and a great meal. Attendance at this event grew every year, reaching a peak of 250 in 2000. Company records indicated that approximately 33% of direct sales were made on this day. The event took a lot of staff time to organize and cost Hannas approximately $15 000 in out-of-pocket costs.

All of these efforts allowed Hannas Seeds to develop a direct marketing list of approximately 6000 customers and prospects by the year 2000. This list was used extensively: in 2000 Hannas spent approximately $60 000 on direct marketing activities, mainly direct mail. The direct distribution activities were carried out by Warren with the assistance of three office people who were all capable of assisting forage seed customers in person or on the phone.[2] These women would pass a "difficult" customer on to Warren when that customer required more technical information, had a complaint, or specifically asked to talk to "a man." Hannas Seeds also had a production manager who was responsible for all shipping and receiving. The office staff was responsible for maintaining the customer and prospect database. Warren enjoyed this part of his job, especially the customer contact.

Once an order was obtained, Hannas Seeds shipped the product to the customer. Because of the small volume purchased by each customer, shipping costs were relatively high at $0.10 per pound. Hannas Seeds paid the full cost of distribution to all direct customers except those who purchased and took delivery at a Customer Appreciation Day.

Direct sales of forage seeds in 1999/2000 were approximately 840 000 pounds. This was down about 50 000 pounds from the previous year.

Dealer Distribution

In the early 1980s, Hannas Seeds began to dabble in dealer distribution as well as direct distribution. Patricia felt this was an important step for the company to achieve significant sales growth.

There were four types of dealers available for seed distribution in western Canada: independent farm supply dealers, branches of large distribution companies, co-ops, and farmer dealers. Farm supply dealers varied in the type of product lines they carried. Some dealers carried a very narrow line such as fertilizer, seed, or feed, whereas others carried a broad product line including most of the items a farmer would need to purchase for his farm. Seed-cleaning plants often carried branded forage seeds to supplement their main business of cleaning grain for local farmers. In addition to the agricultural dealers, there were a few highly specialized dealers serving the oilfield and land reclamation markets.

Independent dealers were locally owned businesses that normally had one or two retail outlets. Although the number of independent dealers had been declining in Alberta, it was estimated that there were approximately 100 businesses in this category.

A growing percentage of farm supplies were sold by branches of large distribution companies such as Agricore, Continental Grain, and United Farmers of Alberta. With the exception of United Farmers of Alberta, the other large distribution companies had their own lines of forage seeds, making it difficult, but not impossible, for a company like Hannas to establish distribution in this channel. Each of the three major distribution companies in Alberta had approximately 50 retail outlets serving the province. Most of their retail outlets carried a full line of farm supplies.

Co-ops were farmer-owned retail outlets that operated much like independent dealers. Most co-ops had one or two retail outlets serving local farmers. Patricia and Warren felt there were probably 50 co-ops in their market area.

In an attempt to develop new sources of income, some farmers would become dealers for seed companies. Although some farmer dealers were very active in attempting to develop business, most were fairly passive, waiting for customers to contact them.

All forage seed dealers performed similar activities. They ordered supplies of forage seeds based on their sales forecast. Once received, these supplies were put in a warehouse for storage until purchased. This usually was done in the winter months as dealers prepared for the busy spring selling season. To the extent possible, they trained their inside and outside salespeople on forage seeds so they were able to advise customers on which varieties to purchase. If seed companies supplied them with point-of-purchase material, this was normally displayed in the retail store. With the exception of specialized seed dealers, most retailers did not make a special effort to push forage seeds; they simply attempted to answer questions and took orders.

Patricia took major responsibility for recruiting new dealers for the company and then Warren worked with the dealers once they were established. To date, Patricia had set up 37 dealers that carried Hannas Seeds products. Exhibit 3 shows a listing of all Hannas dealers. Exhibit 4 shows the sales of these dealers over the past four years.

EXHIBIT 3	Hannas Seeds Dealers			

Name	Product Line	Ownership	Other Brands Carried	Years as a Dealer
Agri Farm Supplies	General farm supplies	Independent	0	5 to 9
Alberta Agro Services	Fertilizer dealer	Independent	2	Less than 5
Alberta Ranch & Farm	General farm supplies	Independent	2	Less than 5
Alberta Seed Cleaning	Seed-cleaning plant	Independent	2	10 or more
Aylmer UFA	Feed dealer	Branch	0	Less than 5
Bruce Seeds	Seed dealer	Independent	2	5 to 9
Cedarview Co-op	General farm supplies	Co-op	1	10 or more
Clarence Seed Cleaning	Seed-cleaning plant	Independent	1	10 or more
Dartmouth Supplies	General farm supplies	Independent	0	10 or more
Drumbo Co-op	General farm supplies	Co-op	1	Less than 5
Eccles Co-op	General farm supplies	Co-op	2	10 or more
Eyckville Fertilizer	Fertilizer dealer	Independent	0	10 or more
Fowler Farm & Ranch	General farm supplies	Independent	0	10 or more
Francesville Agri Supplies	General farm supplies	Independent	1	Less than 5
Grimsby UFA	General farm supplies	Branch	1	Less than 5
Harry Krabbe	Farmer	Independent	0	Less than 5
Harvard Fertilizer	Fertilizer dealer	Independent	1	10 or more
Hi Tech Agro	Fertilizer dealer	Independent	1	10 or more
John Krug	Farmer	Independent	0	5 to 9
Laroche County Supply	General farm supplies	Independent	1	5 to 9
Lawrence Seed Cleaning	Seed-cleaning plant	Independent	1	10 or more
Len's Feed Store	Feed dealer	Independent	0	10 or more
Lloyd's Seed Cleaning	Seed-cleaning plant	Independent	1	5 to 9
Muller Feed Mill	Feed dealer	Independent	0	10 or more
Parkview Fertilizer	Fertilizer dealer	Independent	0	5 to 9
Philip Reynolds	Farmer	Independent	0	5 to 9
Purvis Seeds	Seed dealer	Independent	1	Less than 5
Richardson Supplies	Oilfield supplies	Independent	0	5 to 9
Riverside Supplies	General farm supplies	Independent	1	5 to 9
Sagamore Livestock Supplies	Feed dealer	Independent	0	5 to 9
Smith Feeds	Feed dealer	Independent	0	5 to 9
Smithville Co-op	General farm supplies	Co-op	2	5 to 9
Sunshine Seeds	Seed dealer	Independent	2	5 to 9
Valley UFA	General farm supplies	Branch	2	Less than 5
Western Farm Supplies	General farm supplies	Co-op	1	Less than 5
Western Forest Supplies	Reclamation supplies	Independent	0	5 to 9
William Torsten	Farmer	Independent	0	5 to 9

EXHIBIT 4	Hannas Seeds Dealer Sales			

Name	Pounds Sold 1996-1997	Pounds Sold 1997-1998	Pounds Sold 1998-1999	Pounds Sold 1999-2000	Total
Agri Farm Supplies	4 460	3 430	4 230	7 735	19 855
Alberta Agro Services	0	950	750	9 060	10 760
Alberta Ranch & Farm	0	0	265	0	265
Alberta Seed Cleaning	9 655	165	1 895	165	11 880
Aylmer UFA	0	0	280	1 795	2 075
Bruce Seeds	5 150	14 467	9 290	22 055	50 962
Cedarview Co-op	8 712	9 870	18 604	165	37 351
Clarence Seed Cleaning	1 495	16 150	19 625	10 965	48 235
Dartmouth Supplies	47 370	36 525	42 663	34 305	160 863
Drumbo Co-op	0	3 525	15 497	11 256	30 278
Eccles Co-op	31 969	33 985	45 192	23 050	134 196
Eyckville Fertilizer	8 430	11 905	13 710	1 660	35 705
Fowler Farm & Ranch	12 930	29 335	12 139	18 515	72 919
Francesville Agri Supplies	3 765	0	0	535	4 300
Grimsby UFA	0	200	1 924	2 635	4 759
Harry Krabbe	0	875	1 750	55	2 680
Harvard Fertilizer	15 684	11 265	13 657	1 485	42 091
Hi Tech Agro	8 870	0	11 350	14 640	34 860
John Krug	29 060	36 265	25 370	33 545	124 240
Laroche County Supply	975	2 900	2 860	2 575	9 310
Lawrence Seed Cleaning	18 787	17 295	13 615	1 000	50 697
Len's Feed Store	2 098	1 510	2 885	1 500	7 993
Lloyd's Seed Cleaning	705	2 360	4 960	4 870	12 895
Muller Feed Mill	0	100	50	0	150
Parkview Fertilizer	12 898	17 475	46 261	50 674	127 308
Philip Reynolds	3 190	2 275	6 517	14 085	26 067
Purvis Seeds	51 533	81 010	61 808	49 465	243 816
Richardson Supplies	13 701	22 335	7 455	47 515	91 006
Riverside Supplies	2 745	2 695	630	2 355	8 425
Sagamore Livestock Supplies	15 385	10 770	15 288	9 341	50 784
Smith Feeds	350	1 760	5 655	3 715	11 480
Smithville Co-op	4 165	0	100	0	4 265
Sunshine Seeds	2 550	10 135	25 691	14 978	53 354

EXHIBIT 4	Hannas Seeds Dealer Sales (continued)				
Valley UFA	0	1 200	6 710	5 250	13 160
Western Farm Supplies	0	700	6 111	11 745	18 556
Western Forest Supplies	26 850	19 085	15 218	37 395	98 548
William Torsten	110 640	16 045	12 868	19 245	28 798
	354 122	408 562	462 873	459 329	

Contact with dealers was minimal and irregular. Warren made it a point to personally visit each dealer at least once a year, and supplemented this with phone calls, letters, faxes, and emails. Most competing companies had sales reps that would call on dealers on a much more frequent basis.

Hannas dealers were allowed the industry standard 15% margin on all seed products they sold. So, for example, if a dealer purchased 1000 pounds of Climax Timothy, which had a retail price of $1.75 per pound, they would be invoiced for $1487.50.[3] Hannas Seeds paid all freight on dealer sales except in cases where dealers would place an order for a couple of bags they needed in a hurry. This was usually shipped via courier and paid for by the dealer. If a dealer wanted to pick up an order from the Hannas warehouse, the invoice would deduct the cost of shipping. Because of larger volumes, shipping costs to dealers averaged only $0.02 per pound. All accounts were expected to be settled in 30 days. In the case of a few very large dealers, Hannas would rent a large truck trailer, load it with seed, and drop the truck off at their yard. At the end of the season, Hannas would pick up the truck trailer and invoice them for what was sold.

Other than margin, payment terms, and shipping, Hannas had not developed any dealer policies in areas such as sales incentives, training, exclusivity, or territory protection. Although Patricia was pleased with the growth of dealer sales over the last ten years, she was sure this aspect of the business could be improved by expanding the number of dealers and by getting existing dealers to increase sales.

Many of the current Hannas dealers had been recruited in the early 1990s when this was a priority task for Patricia. Lately, growth in dealer numbers had declined because Patricia was not able to devote as much time to this activity. In fact, recruiting dealers was a very time-consuming process. The first step was to identify prospects, and then it was necessary to contact these businesses and sell them on the benefits of carrying Hannas products. If a prospect did not carry forage seeds, it was much easier for Patricia to sell them on the idea of adding this product line than it was to sell a dealer currently carrying forage seeds on changing brands or adding a second brand. Patricia had no idea how many potential Alberta farm supply dealers currently did not carry any forage seed products, but estimated it might be 20%. The data in Exhibit 3 shows Patricia's estimate of the number of competing brands of forage seed carried by existing Hannas dealers.

In addition to recruiting new dealers, Patricia felt there was a lot of opportunity in working with existing dealers to help them increase sales of Hannas products. In reviewing sales by dealer (Exhibit 4) she noted that there was a lot of variability from dealer to dealer and, for any dealer, from year to year. Only a few dealers had shown a steady increase in sales over the past five years. She was not sure why this was the case, but speculated that it might be due to dealers starting to carry more than one line of forage seeds or dealer dissatisfaction or apathy. In an effort to understand the perspectives of dealers more fully, Patricia interviewed a number of dealers on a fairly wide range of topics. These interviews revealed a number of issues:

- Some dealers were unhappy with the fact that Hannas sold seed direct as well as through a dealer system. They felt that some customers would come to their dealership to obtain information on forage seeds and then go to the Hannas Customer Appreciation Day to purchase their needs at a 10% discount.
- Other dealers expressed some concern over the fact that Hannas had established two or more dealers in proximity to each other leading to some local competition for sales. In a few cases, these dealers said there was occasional price cutting at the local level to secure sales.
- There was fairly general concern over the fact that Hannas did not provide sales support for its dealers. Although Hannas did provide brochures listing its products and some technical information on each product, this was the only thing Hannas did.
- A number of dealers mentioned that the financial rewards for carrying Hannas products were not adequate.
- Some dealers mentioned that they could not afford the time and expense to aggressively sell forage seeds. This line represented such a small portion of their business that it not worth it to devote much effort to selling it. If farmers asked for a forage seed, they would take the order and fill it, but that was the extent of their involvement.
- A few dealers expressed concern over occasional delays in receiving orders.

FUTURE DIRECTION

Patricia and Warren were at odds in terms of how to expand sales of forage seeds in the Alberta market. Warren was strongly in favour of gradually phasing out dealer sales and putting major effort into direct sales. He felt it would not be possible to get a consistently strong effort from dealers to provide the sales growth Hannas Seeds required to meet company objectives. In his mind, using the margin currently allowed dealers to fund other marketing efforts would have greater payoff. Some of the activities he had in mind included the use of company salespeople to call on large accounts, greater use of advertising and direct mail, the possibility of having Customer Appreciation Days at other locations in Alberta, and the use of the Internet. He also noted that a substantial increase in direct sales would require hiring at least one more person in the office, since the three current employees were operating at maximum capacity at the present time.

Patricia, on the other hand, had serious concerns about direct distribution. She felt that some face-to-face contact with customers was required to sell forage seeds and that it would simply be too costly for Hannas to do this itself. Having dealers allowed for this face-to-face contact at a reasonable cost. She was, however, concerned about the ability of the company to attract good new dealers and motivate existing dealers to sell larger volumes of seed. She realized the company needed to review its distribution policies, particularly those policies related to compensating and motivating dealers. She also wondered whether it was possible to operate a system of direct distribution along with dealer sales.

Notes

1. The average retail price of a pound of forage seed was approximately $2. Direct costs of producing and processing the seed were about $1.25 per pound.

2. Each of the office staff was paid $30 000 in salary and benefits. Warren's salary and benefits totalled $75 000 in 2000.

3. The difference between the retail value of $1750 and the purchase price of $1487.50 is the margin the retailer earns.

MediaSpark

Doug Lionais, Sherry Finney, and Melissa Cameron

In September of 2001, Mathew Georghiou, the president and CEO of MediaSpark (www.mediaspark.com) in Sydney, Nova Scotia, finished a phone conversation with IBM Canada. IBM had just informed Georghiou that they were interested in exclusively carrying MediaSpark's new product, GoVenture Entrepreneur (www.goventure.net) in the Canadian market. Georghiou had been researching possible distribution channels for GoVenture in North America. The phone call with IBM completed Georghiou's research and he now needed to sift through the information and decide how he was going to get his product to market.

BACKGROUND

Georghiou completed a two-year engineering diploma at Cape Breton University (then University College of Cape Breton), before transferring to Dalhousie University in Halifax, Nova Scotia, to complete his Electrical Engineering degree. After Georghiou's second year at Dalhousie, IBM awarded him a sixteen-month internship in Toronto, an offer which he took. In 1991, Georghiou received a national award for innovation during his internship, which led IBM to guarantee him a position upon graduation. After graduating in 1993, Georghiou immediately moved back to Toronto to work for IBM. While employed at IBM, Georghiou gained much experience in the engineering field, which included programming and computer product manufacturing.

Georghiou had a vision to establish his own business and left IBM in 1994. He moved back to Sydney, Nova Scotia, and with personal savings and financing from Enterprise Cape Breton Corporation (ECBC), he established MediaSpark. The business began in the basement of his home; after only two years, he needed to expand and he relocated his offices downtown. MediaSpark focused on technology and design; the business offered a wide range of services such as multimedia production, Internet development, elearning, technology consulting, and image and print design.

GOVENTURE ENTREPRENEUR

In 2000, MediaSpark launched GoVenture Entrepreneur, an educational software program that simulated establishing and running a small business (Exhibit 1). This software created a practical replication of an entrepreneur's business start-up, daily management, and personal activities. Georghiou felt GoVenture Entrepreneur would be a perfect learning tool for any business education class because it provided students the opportunity to gain experience and knowledge without risk. Georghiou described GoVenture Entrepreneur as a "flight simulator for business."

In the GoVenture Entrepreneur simulation, participants establish and manage a small business start-up. The program simulates all aspects of entrepreneurial decision making, including business and personal outcomes. Performance evaluation tools included in the simulation allow the user and/or the instructor to set goals, adjust performance evaluation weightings, and measure outcomes in terms of business success and personal work–life balance. MediaSpark designed the product to be as flexible as possible for teachers.

MediaSpark identified the broader market for GoVenture Entrepreneur as middle school to adult; however, the primary target was high school classes. Georghiou saw GoVenture Entrepreneur as enhancing the existing curriculum. MediaSpark positioned it for use in business, marketing, and entrepreneurship courses. Georghiou identified three general ways of using GoVenture Entrepreneur in the classroom. First, educators could use GoVenture Entrepreneur as an introduction to demonstrate the purpose of learning the concepts in the course. Second, they could use it to end a course as a capstone module to apply the lessons of the course. Third, educators could use it throughout a course to complement ongoing lessons.

To serve the educational market, MediaSpark developed a number of support materials for GoVenture Entrepreneur. For example, institutions that purchased software licences received an "Experiencing Entrepreneurship" text. MediaSpark developed this book as an easy-to-use summary of the subject that educators could use either as a textbook or as a complement to existing textbooks. MediaSpark's educational bundle also included an instructor's manual, lesson plans focusing on different topics, and a test bank.

THE MARKET

Georghiou divided the educational publishing industry between the K-12 market and the university market. Georghiou's target market fell in the K-12 category. Georghiou felt the market in the United States was much larger than the Canadian market, with more growth in the

EXHIBIT 1	MediaSpark GoVenture Entrepreneur Website

The most realistic **entrepreneurship** simulation ever!

GoVenture Entrepreneur is a highly visual and realistic business simulation that recreates the day-to-day experiences involved in starting and running a small business.

Like a flight simulator for small business, Entrepreneur engages you in realistic situations and problems. Take your own test flights at your own speed. Within the world of Entrepreneur, the decisions and the consequences are highly realistic. So, virtual entrepreneurs rapidly gain the authentic wisdom that normally only comes from on-the-job experience.

The GoVenture Experience

- **Experience** what it is like to manage numerous business and personal tasks.
- **Make** necessary compromises to reach both business and personal success.
- **Learn** what you need to know to start a business in minutes, not months.

This simulation makes learning about being an entrepreneur fun. You can run the simulation for as long as you want. You can dive in using the Quick Start feature or take the time to go through the Personal and Business Profiles to select and start a business. You can conduct business, get advice, attend training seminars, and even close or sell your company. At any point, you may save your simulation and return to it later.

There is no penalty for failure, so if your first business doesn't succeed, try another. You can even control how fast the simulation time clock runs!

You can check your own personal financial status or your company's at any time. Review the business's financial statements and charts on recent operations. If you're doing well, you can pay yourself a bonus and buy one of those items on your wish list.

Watch out for random events—you could become injured and have to stay home for a while. Or if you forget your spouse's birthday your stress level may go up. If your stress level is too high, you may have to take some time off from the company. Can your employees run it without you?

The simulation immerses you in a life-like world of entrepreneurship and small business—a world where you still have to remember to pay your bills and get enough sleep.

EXHIBIT 1	MediaSpark GoVenture Entrepreneur Website (continued)

It is an engaging experience, which makes learning fun, as you build an understanding of what it is like to be an entrepreneur and to meet the challenges of starting and running a small business.

The Entrepreneur CD-ROM simulation can be used in schools, in self-paced home or work study, in life-long learning programs, and in corporate training initiatives for employees or customers. Never before has it been so easy to experience the life of an entrepreneur.

Source: www.goventure.net/home.cfm?ID8. Reprinted with permission of MediaSpark Inc.

educational software sector. There were 90 000 to 100 000 elementary and secondary schools in the United States while there were only 16 500 in Canada, and Canada's K-12 enrolment was 5.3 million students, approximately one-tenth the size of that in the United States. According to market studies that Georghiou had reviewed, U.S. schools spent $5.50 per student on software and the market for CD-ROMs in schools approximated US$300 million. Georghiou hoped to generate significant sales in both the Canadian and U.S. markets, but the focus was on the U.S. market due to its larger size and greater access to funding.

MARKETING AND PRICING STRATEGY

Georghiou was concerned about how to sell and distribute the product. The education market was accustomed to purchasing texts rather than multimedia products. Whereas a catalogue description can describe a text fairly well, Georghiou felt that educators would need to experience GoVenture Entrepreneur before considering it for use in the classroom. Georghiou felt that it would be difficult to convince educators of the value of his product as either a text complement or as a text replacement without a hands-on trial. Georghiou commented, "To sell the product, people need to see it; they need to try it out for themselves." Thus, he was only interested in marketing channels that placed the product in educators' hands for a decision or at least provided an opportunity to demonstrate the product in action.

The price of GoVenture Entrepreneur varied depending on the user and country. Georghiou identified six user groups: individuals, educational K-12, educational post-secondary, home school, non-profit or government, and all others. He wanted his initial target market to be the educational K-12 and offered this segment a 50% price reduction for a limited time in an effort to break into the market. The regular price varied per package depending on the quantity purchased (Exhibit 2). The cost of goods sold was generally 5% to 10% of the suggested retail price.

DISTRIBUTION CHANNELS

Georghiou identified two basic distribution alternatives for GoVenture Entrepreneur: direct or indirect. Indirect distribution channels would include catalogue companies, textbook publishers, or software publishers. If Georghiou was to sell directly, MediaSpark would have to handle the full advertising and distributing duties.

EXHIBIT 2	MediaSpark GoVenture Entrepreneur Pricing

GoVenture Entrepreneur Product Price

	1 SEAT*	5 SEAT*	30 Seat*	SITE**
GoVenture Entrepreneur Software Licence - Educational (USD)	$ 199	$ 349	$ 749	$ 1199
GoVenture Entrepreneur Software Licence - Educational (CAD)	$ 199	$ 499	NA	$ 1499

Software Licence Includes:
- Licence for a specified number of concurrent user(s). See Software Licence Descriptions below for important information.
- 1 CD-ROM for Windows (GoVenture Entrepreneur is also compatible with Macintosh). Program can be copied from CD to computer hard drives or network drive.
- User Guide.
- Performance Reports (built into the software).
- FREE Experiencing Book (text on entrepreneurship).
- FREE Education Bundle (including instructor guide, lesson plans, and test bank).
- FREE Value Option for One Year (includes additional customer service support).

*SEAT Licence: This licence allows for many people to use the software at the same organization (or school) at one physical address location. The number of seats purchased determines how many computers may run the software concurrently (at the same time). For example, a 5-Seat Licence allows for the software to be run on up to five computers at the same time. In this example, the software may be installed on a network, or installed on more than five computers, but the software may not be run on more than five computers concurrently. Individual Seats cannot be shared amongst different organizations (or schools).

*SITE Licence: This licence allows for use of the software on all your organization's (or school's) computers at one physical address location at any time. There are no limits on how many computers may run the software concurrently—as long as they are on the same site (one physical address location). A SITE Licence cannot be shared amongst different organizations.

Educational product catalogue companies sold thousands of products to educational institutions through published or online catalogues. The larger publishers would send out educational catalogues to most schools in North America, though Georghiou questioned how many actually got to teachers he wished to reach. Catalogue companies would typically only list a product in exchange for an exclusive deal. Thus, Georghiou would not be able to sell GoVenture Entrepreneur in the same region through any other channel. Georghiou had researched the reseller discount for all possible distribution channels. The reseller discount was the percentage of the final price that the reselling company retained. For catalogue companies, Georghiou reported the reseller discount to be between 20% and 35%.

Georghiou's second indirect option, textbook publishers, supplied most schools with their core textbooks. Textbook publishers differed from catalogue companies as they employed a sales force as well as a published catalogue of products. Sales representatives would travel to schools and trade shows to present the product catalogue, and potential purchasers would have a better chance of seeing a demonstration of the product. Textbook publishers, however, would also require an exclusive deal to carry a product and would demand a reseller discount of 40% to 60%.

Georghiou had identified two main textbook publishers: Glencoe McGraw-Hill and Southwestern. Georghiou knew that Glencoe was already carrying a competing product: Virtual Business (www.knowledgematters.com). Georghiou had heard that Southwestern had turned down his competitor's product, but thought it would likely want to pick up a competing product since Glencoe started carrying Virtual Business. Georghiou identified Southwestern as the leading business education provider to the K-12, higher education, and professional markets in the United States. It did not, however, distribute in Canada. Its main focus was textbooks; however, it had distributed some interactive software in key-boarding, marketing, management, and accounting. Glencoe also focused on textbooks with a small number of software titles (like Virtual Business).

Because of the technological nature of his product, Georghiou also considered soft-ware distribution companies as a third indirect distribution channel. A software distributor could give Georghiou's product more profile when compared to being "lost in the thousands of traditional text products in a publisher's catalogue." Again, software distributors would require an exclusive deal to carry a product. Georghiou found that the software distribution market was highly fragmented. There were no companies that operated in both the Canadian and U.S. markets. Furthermore, in the United States, there were very few national distributors; many were small companies that would carry other firms' products as well as their own. The reseller discount for software distributors was comparable to that of textbook publishers at 40% to 60%.

One option within the United States was to distribute through a non-profit company called MarkED, a consortium of 40 state education departments and other organizations. As an industry-run organization, MarkED would lend credibility to the products it supported. MarkED sold products through a catalogue it distributed to its constituent organizations. However, it did not have a sales force to complement the catalogue and Georghiou could not be sure that the catalogue would reach the right teachers.

In Canada, the software distribution choices were much different. The most prominent distributor was IBM, which operated a software distribution division in Canada.[1] Established in 1880, IBM was the world's largest and most recognizable information technology company. IBM Canada had its own sales force that was already distributing to schools. Since 1995, IBM invested $75 million in its Reinventing Education program, which it established to break down barriers to academic achievement. IBM estimated that this program would reach 100 000 teachers and 10 million students in 10 countries by the end of 2004. IBM provided research and technical expertise, as well as equipment and cash contributions, to improve teaching and learning. The educational software currently available to the K-12 market focused on reading, language arts, mathematics, and science. In

---

[1] IBM also sold software in the United States, but it was in the midst of changing its strategy and moving towards carring only a very small number of products. Because it was undergoing some changes, MediaSpark saw no real opportunity to work with them.

addition to this, IBM supplied many schools with the interface and Internet software for their computers, as well as interactive white boards.

Georghiou felt that IBM was a good candidate because it was technology based, had brand recognition, and was already distributing to schools. IBM had proposed a two-year exclusive deal with MediaSpark to distribute to the K-12 educational market. Georghiou's only reservation was that he felt IBM may focus its attention on its hardware sales rather than software.

Finally, Georghiou could also consider an in-house direct distribution channel. MediaSpark currently employed only one marketing/sales person. Georghiou estimated that to effectively market GoVenture, he would have to hire five to ten sales representatives and an additional two to three marketing people located in various areas throughout Canada and the United States. The majority of his sales would originate from trade shows, events, and inside sales calls. Georghiou expected that MediaSpark would have to appear at over ten trade shows in the United States and at least two in Canada. MediaSpark's sales team would have to be responsible for inside sales calls, email campaigns, direct mail, CD demos, seminars, public speaking, and catalogue sales. Georghiou estimated that if MediaSpark did market and sell GoVenture independently, he would not be able to hire all the sales representatives he required and would have to survive with only one or two marketing/sales people. In such a situation, Georghiou himself would likely attend a number of trade shows and make sales trips throughout the year. The advantage of selling in-house was that MediaSpark would make a much higher margin on each unit sold as there would be no reseller discount. However, trade shows were expensive and the need to sell GoVenture Entrepreneur may distract MediaSpark from new product development.

THE DECISION

Georghiou struggled with the distribution decision. He first had to decide whether or not to go with a third-party distributor and if he did, which one or ones to go with. Georghiou was most worried about the exclusivity required by distributors. In essence, if Georghiou went with a distributor, he was putting all his eggs in one basket; he had to have absolute confidence in the distributor he chose. If the distributor did not succeed in selling the product, Georghiou would have no other avenues to make a sale. Georghiou worried that his product would be one product among many in any distributor's product line and that they may put more focus on other products. The lack of technological knowledge of some of the potential distributors was another worry. As Georghiou explained, "Success depended on leveraging a distributor's brand awareness and market reach to sell more units than we can on our own."

TFI Food Equipment Solutions

H. F. (Herb) MacKenzie and James Doyle

It was early 2007, and Alex Pettes had just recently been appointed as president of TFI Food Equipment Solutions (TFI) (www.tficanada.com) of Brampton, Ontario. Sales for 2006 were approximately $20 million, just slightly below 2005 sales. In fact, sales had been reasonably stable for several years, but Alex was now considering how he could take TFI to the next stage in its growth. TFI was a well-established, privately owned industrial distributor that began in 1954. Its two major product lines were Henny Penny and Taylor. TFI held exclusive rights to sell both lines of products in Ontario, and in the four Atlantic provinces (New Brunswick, Nova Scotia, Prince Edward Island, and Newfoundland and Labrador). Alex recently secured for TFI the Canadian rights for One-Shot Corporation's "Revolver" and for R-O International's automatic French fry machine. Both products were manufactured outside Canada and had to be imported. The issue that Alex Pettes was considering was how and to what extent TFI should develop the national market for these two new product lines. In the back of Alex's mind was also a recent change that one of his current key suppliers was making in the U.S.

This case was written by H. F. (Herb) MacKenzie and James Doyle, both at Brock University, Faculty of Business, St. Catharines, ON L2S 3A1. It was prepared as a basis for class discussion and is not intended to illustrate effective or ineffective handling of a management situation. Copyright © 2007 by H. F. (Herb) MacKenzie. Reprinted with permission.

market, and Alex could not help wondering whether this might eventually have implications for his Canadian operations.

> I was able to convince Henny Penny to keep him [John Frishman] out of our territory, and all of Canada. We have built this territory without his involvement, and we will continue to have exclusive rights here, I understand. Still, I worry about the long-term implications of what is happening in the United States.

COMPANY BACKGROUND

TFI is a well-established industrial distributor headquartered in Brampton, Ontario, that in 2006 earned approximately 90% of its sales revenue (divided equally) from sales of its two major product lines: Taylor (a division of Carrier Commercial Refrigeration Inc. of Rockton, Illinois, www.taylor-company.com), and Henny Penny Corporation (headquartered in Eaton, Ohio, www.hennypenny.com). Both Taylor and Henny Penny produce equipment for use in restaurants, stores, and institutional food service operations. Taylor focuses on ice cream and beverage equipment (batch ice cream machines, shake and slush machines, etc.). Henny Penny manufactures equipment for food service applications (fryers, rotisseries, blast chillers/freezers, heated food display units, holding cabinets for storing cooked food while maintaining its quality, etc.). Essentially, there is no overlap or risk of cannibalization between the two product lines, and they do complement each other very well.

TFI has been recognized by both manufacturers for its sales performance. In 2003, TFI was named Henny Penny's "Distributor of the Year," and in 2004 and 2005, the company was named Taylor's "Distributor of the Year." Alex believes that the market potential for both product lines will continue to be strong, but he is concerned that growth might be difficult to achieve as long as he is restricted to his current sales territory. Sales for 2006 look like they will be down approximately 4% from 2005, but final sales figures will not be available for a few months yet. This small decline is certainly within normal sales variance, but Alex's greater concern is his desire to see TFI grow.

Alex Pettes is highly regarded by TFI employees, suppliers, and fellow distributors who sell the same and similar products in other regions of Canada and the United Sates. Deeply knowledgeable in sales and marketing, Alex came to the position of president of TFI after several years as vice-president of sales and marketing. During his period in the previous position, the company achieved considerable success. Alex developed many of the important relationships TFI has with its suppliers and customers, and he was instrumental in the establishment and growth of the firm's sales force. Now, as president, Alex reports directly to the two owners, Tom and Jerry Kappus, who are currently the majority shareholders of the company. The owners have removed themselves from the daily operations of the company and are gradually selling their shares to Alex and two other minority shareholders. Due to his experience and expertise in sales and marketing, Alex is still closely involved in many of the important sales and marketing decisions that are made by the organization.

TFI has good relations with the other two industrial distributors who represent Henny Penny and Taylor in other regions of Canada. D.S.L. Inc. (www.dslinc.com) distributes Henny Penny and Taylor products throughout western and much of northern Canada (as well as Alaska, Washington, and Oregon). It has been in business since 1916 and has Canadian sales branches in Winnipeg, Manitoba; Calgary, Alberta; and Port Coquitlam, British Columbia. Bazinet Taylor Ltee (www.bazinet-taylor.ca), established in 1954, is the exclusive Quebec industrial distributor. Though there are no contractual arrangements, the three "sister" distributors often help each other by trading or transferring inventory when one has a need and another has inventory. Taylor products, for example, may take as long as eight weeks to get after a distributor places an order on the factory. Being able to transfer, loan, or trade inventory, therefore, helps all of the distributors provide better customer service, and sometimes reduce inventory if there is an over-stock situation, or when older models of equipment must be sold. Arrangements are also made among distributors for installation, parts, or service when a product is sold by one distributor, but is being delivered and installed in the territory of another distributor.

THE TFI SALES FORCE

TFI currently employs two types of salespeople who sell to two distinct markets. There are four salespeople who serve national accounts. Judi Saliba, Joanne Shearer, and Vico Singh sell to such companies as 7-Eleven, Wendy's, Burger King, McDonald's, Harvey's, KFC, Milestone's Grill & Bar, Mac's Convenience Stores, Esso, and other large, multi-outlet businesses. Dean Robinson serves the supermarket chains, such as Loblaws, Sobeys, A&P, and Wal-Mart. Because of their size, these accounts generally receive discounts on the products they buy, and these discounts can be as high as 25% from TFI list prices depending on the particular products, the number of product-units purchased, and the overall size of the sale. (Exhibit 1 illustrates pricing and product information for three models of Taylor single flavour soft serve machines.) These accounts contribute approximately 43% of total

EXHIBIT 1	An Example of Product and Pricing Information		
	Taylor Single Flavour Soft Serve Machines		
	Model 142	Model C707	Model C706
Capacity	93 cones / hr	284 cones / hr	426 cones / hr
Impact	3 cones	25+ cones	40+ cones
Production	3.3 gal / hr	10 gal / hr	15 gal / hr
	12.4 l /hr	37.9 l / hr	56.8 l / hr
Weight	180 lb	335 lb	385 lb
	81.8 kg	152 kg	174.6 kg
Width	16.0"	18.25"	18.25"
	406 mm	464 mm	464 mm
Depth	24.5"	32.5"	34.0"
	622 mm	864 mm	864 mm
Counter clearance	4"	33.88"	33.88"
	101 mm	860 mm	860 mm
Price - Single Unit	$7 899 each	$13 890 each	$17 943 each
Price - Multiple Unit	$7 346 each	$12 918 each	$16 687 each

Source: Information taken from TFI 2006 price list.

company sales revenue (national accounts—15%, supermarket chains—24%, and McDonald's—4%). Each of these salespeople receive annual base salaries ranging between $50 000 and $70 000, and commissions on sales of between 1% and 4%. Commissions earned by these salespeople typically add 40% or more to their base salary. The national accounts market is relatively stable and predictable, although Alex can recall a circumstance where one grocery chain required a large amount of equipment with very short notice as it was preparing for a store "grand opening" and had forgotten to order its equipment with sufficient lead-time. With considerable effort, TFI delivered all of the equipment to the customer's satisfaction. Most equipment, however, was planned and ordered long in advance of need, so that salespeople generally filled a high-service, customer relationship role.

Ten salespeople service the "independent" market. It is very different from the multi-outlet market, and contributes approximately 31% of the company's total sales revenue. Comprising primarily small, locally owned operations, including convenience stores and independent restaurants, this market is divided into numerous exclusive territories. In each territory, a TFI salesperson has been granted permission to sell the complete TFI product line, including Henny Penny and Taylor. The busiest sales period for this market is the few months leading to the summer season when consumer demand is high for ice cream and cool beverages. On average, salespeople are expected to sell $400 000 of equipment annually (which usually works out to about 35–50 sales), and, apart from the provision of company vehicles and reimbursement of out-of-pocket expenses, are compensated by commission which generally ranges between 12% and 18% of sales. These salespeople have considerable flexibility in negotiating selling prices with customers; however, when discounts are given, the salesperson's commission is reduced accordingly. Alex was recently forced to terminate agreements with two of TFI's salespeople for consistent underperformance in their sales territory. Fortunately, this is uncommon as losing salespeople creates a disruption to operations while new salespeople must be hired and trained.

Parts and service revenue contributed approximately 26% of total sales revenue.

A RECENT CHANNEL CHANGE IN THE UNITED STATES

Recent changes to Henny Penny's distribution strategy in the United States concerned Alex, at least for the longer term. He needed to consider what he should do in case similar changes were implemented in the Canadian market. Henny Penny was beginning to upset some of its U.S. distributors by forming a strategic alliance with J. Frishman Associates of Pompano Beach, Florida, to sell one of its products, the combi-oven, to the institutional market. Henny Penny's U.S. distributors claimed that this move was tantamount to the creation of a dual distribution system that was sure to harm sales in their respective territories. Though sales for the manufacturer would likely increase, distributors were starting to argue that what was good for Henny Penny may not be so good for them; Alex Pettes expected this issue would cause considerable tension at an upcoming meeting of North American distributors, which Henny Penny had scheduled to be held in Las Vegas, Nevada. Although Henny Penny had indicated to Alex that it did not have similar plans for Canada, he was somewhat concerned with the possibility of changes in its distribution strategy in his territory if this new channel structure proved successful in the United States. Alex was aware, however, that, sometimes, legitimate reasons existed for dual distribution systems, and he wondered what the impact would be for TFI if this happened.

NEW OPPORTUNITIES FOR TFI

Alex Pettes was characteristically enthusiastic about the market potential for the two new products that TFI recently added to its product mix. The Revolver system (www.one-shot.com) is a single portion blending machine that is described as "the 'blend in cup' beverage system." It can blend a host of favourite drinks, including iced cappuccino, malts, milkshakes, etc. The machine can sit on a countertop as it is only 9" (229 mm) by 9.25" (234 mm) in size, stands only 30.5" tall, and weighs only 35 lb (16 kg). The countertop unit provides users with unparalleled convenience; as an "all-in-one" system, the Revolver requires no clean-up. The machine uses a patented and unique design, and the cup lids come equipped with a built-in blade that mixes milkshakes and smoothies within the cup. A Revolver system would list for approximately $2200, approximately double the cost to TFI. Alex is confident that the user-friendliness and low cost of the Revolver will make it very attractive to every business from national accounts to independent convenience stores and small restaurants and cafés.

The second product is an automatic French fry vending machine manufactured by R-O International (www.rointernational.com). The machine produces hot French fries, "coin-to-cup" in just 45 seconds. It is 40" (1016 mm) by 40" (1016 mm) by 72" (1828.9 mm) high, and weighs 970 lb (439.9 kg). The machine is a revolutionary and innovative product that cooks French fries without oil, and it accepts multiple payment types: coins, tokens, cards, etc. The unit is also self-cleaning and claims to generate a gross margin for businesses of 70%. Alex is also convinced that this product has tremendous market potential. In particular, Alex feels that the automatic French fry unit should perform well in convenience store chains (which was a key motivating factor in taking on the product), and in institutional settings such as university and college campuses. A typical French fry vending machine would list for approximately $20 000, again, approximately double the cost to TFI. Alex does recognize, however, that this product is relatively new to the market and consumers are generally unfamiliar with it. Many consumers would most likely question the quality of French fries distributed through a vending machine.

THE DECISION

Having secured distribution rights for the Revolver system and the automatic French fry vending machine, Alex Pettes was now unsure how and to what extent he should penetrate the Canadian market. He really had two related decisions to make: (1) how should the new products be sold in territories where TFI did not currently operate, and (2) how should they be sold in existing TFI territories. Since TFI had exclusive rights to sell these products throughout Canada, both decisions were important as the two new suppliers expected national distribution in Canada. Alex was also concerned that the two new products would appeal to different types of customers, and a different sales strategy might be appropriate for each of them. Alex considered several alternatives:

- First, Alex wondered whether he should hire TFI company salespeople for the new territories, even though they would not be allowed to sell the other products that TFI salespeople currently sold. TFI had a strong market presence and was quite profitable in Ontario and the four Atlantic provinces selling mainly two product lines. Alex understood how to manage this type of sales force structure, and using company salespeople ensured that all important market information stayed inside TFI where competitors or potential competitors could not make use of it.

- Second, Alex wondered whether TFI's relations with Bazinet-Taylor Ltee and D.S.L. Inc., the other Taylor and Henny Penny distributors in Canada, could be leveraged. Alex believed that these two distributors would be willing to add the two new product lines to their product mix, assuming that they could earn a good margin by doing so. The question immediately became what Alex would be prepared to offer them as a discount from the list price if they would become sub-distributors for these products.

- Third, Alex considered the possibility of using manufacturers' agents to sell the new products in the new territories. There was considerable risk and uncertainty associated with the new products, and using manufacturers' agents would be a more conservative sales strategy. These salespeople would be paid strictly by commission, and would otherwise pay their own selling expenses. Of course, they would also represent other product lines as well as the two that they would sell for TFI.

- Finally, Alex wondered if he decided to hire TFI company salespeople for the new territories (the first alternative above), should he also consider an entirely new sales force for these products in Ontario and the Atlantic provinces as well? Alex was not so much concerned that the two new products would cannibalize sales from the existing product lines, but he was concerned that if current salespeople allocated too much of their time and effort to the new products, sales for Henny Penny and Taylor could be negatively affected. These two suppliers were too important to TFI to jeopardize losing either of them. Of course, if Alex did decide to hire new salespeople for these existing territories, having salespeople organized on the basis of product lines was only one alternative. Alex might also consider simply making each of the current sales territories smaller so that each salesperson could sell the complete product mix in their respective territories.

Alex was keen to ensure that any decisions he made would enable TFI to generate sufficient sales to satisfy the company's two new suppliers. At the same time, he wanted to ensure that the company's ability to maintain sales for his current products, particularly Henny Penny and Taylor, was not compromised.

Murray Industrial Limited

H. F. (Herb) MacKenzie

Murray Industrial Limited (MIL) was advertised as Newfoundland's most complete industrial supplier, and sold to industrial accounts throughout Newfoundland and Labrador from three locations across the province. Products sold included hydraulic hose and fittings, bearings, conveyor products, hand and power tools, and fasteners (nuts, bolts, etc.), as well as chain, packing, and general mill supply items.

According to Dave Rowe, "Our success has been largely due to our customer service strategy. We aim to provide superior service with a well-trained, motivated staff and a broad inventory of quality products. We have an ongoing commitment to in-house training and product seminars, and we have a 24-hour emergency service for all of our accounts."

Prior to 1991, MIL was a sub-distributor for Snowden Rubber, a Gates Rubber distributor located in Dartmouth, Nova Scotia. In 1991, an opportunity arose to become a distributor for one of North America's largest and best-known manufacturers of hydraulic hose and fittings when its Newfoundland distributor, Newfoundland Armature Works, went bankrupt.

Industrial distributors that sold hydraulic hose and fittings usually bought the more popular sizes and types of hose in full reel lengths and then cut them to fit particular customer applications. Frequently, distributors would attach hydraulic fittings or other special attachments to the shorter hose lengths as required by customers. When distributors bought full-length reels of hose (which varied in length with the size of the hose) or full-box quantities of fittings (which also varied with the size and style of fitting), they paid a standard distributor price for their inventory. If they desired to buy a cut-to-length piece of hose or a small quantity of fittings for special applications that might arise infrequently, they paid a 10% surcharge on the distributor price. For shipments that were needed urgently, manufacturers would often guarantee shipment within 24 hours, but charged a $10 special-order handling charge.

At the time negotiations between MIL and the manufacturer began, the manufacturer had a distribution centre in Dartmouth, Nova Scotia, and prepaid shipments from there to distributors throughout Atlantic Canada. It offered a prompt payment discount of 2%-25th following, and co-op allowances to share promotion costs with distributors. Within a month (and before an agreement was signed), the Dartmouth warehouse was closed and the salesperson was let go. Shipments were still prepaid but came from Toronto, and the salesperson that serviced the Atlantic provinces operated from Quebec. After about three months, the manufacturer's policy changed, and shipments became F.O.B. Toronto, and the prompt payment discount was eliminated.

MIL increased sales by establishing sub-distributors in remote regions, and hydraulic hose eventually accounted for about 8% of the company's total sales, and helped increase sales for complementary products. The largest customer MIL had was Royal Oak Mines, a gold mine located about 1½ hours from Port aux Basques, and accessible only by air or water. It accounted for 35% of MIL's hydraulic hose sales.

Within a year, MIL began to have problems getting inventory. Back-order rates increased. The manufacturer closed its Toronto and Edmonton distribution centres in 1993, and decided to supply the Canadian market from the United States. The manufacturer sales force was reduced from six to two representatives in Canada. Distributors were reduced from 140 to 40 (MIL was the 22nd-largest at the time). All co-op policies were eliminated, and the Canadian price sheets were removed so that Canadian distributors had to purchase from U.S. price sheets and add exchange, duty, brokerage, transportation, and whatever markup they needed. Dave Rowe said:

> Our biggest problem was that they didn't plan for the change to the distribution system. Service continued to worsen from Toronto as inventory that was sold from there was not replaced, and we were told we couldn't order from the U.S. until July 1, 1993, when it would be organized to serve us. We haven't seen a salesperson since early 1993, and any contact we have had with them since then has been initiated by us. Service started to affect our relationships with our customers. We eventually lost the Royal Oak Mines account, and they started buying Gates Rubber products. We were stuck with about $50 000 in inventory that we stocked specifically for them. When we approached the manufacturer, they refused to help us beyond their normal return goods policy. They were willing to take back up to 2% of our annual purchases as long as the material was still in new condition and was still a standard item listed in their catalogue. We had to pay return freight and a 15% restocking charge. It was also their policy not to accept return of any hose products after one year as hose quality deteriorated with time. While their pricing and inventory management practices were standard for the industry, we felt they had an obligation to help us as they were largely to blame for our lost customer.

What responsibility should the manufacturer have for the lost account (Royal Oak Mines)? What can Dave Rowe do? What must he consider before taking any action?

Wee Piggies & Paws

H. F. (Herb) MacKenzie and James Doyle

"Do what you love, never forget your priorities, and everything will fall into place."
—Debbie Cornelius

Equipped with an idea and an interest in enabling moms to generate incomes for their families from home, Debbie Cornelius wondered how best to expand her venture from a small, home-based business in St. Catharines, Ontario, to serve customers across the province, and even nationally. Mother to two young daughters, Katherine and Laura, Debbie founded Wee Piggies & Paws (www.weepiggies.com) in response to an opportunity she recognized for high-quality physical impressions of the hands and feet of babies and young children. Unimpressed by the "do-it-yourself" kits available on the market through retailers, Debbie searched for and developed relationships with suppliers of various higher-quality materials required for making these impressions. Reinforced by positive feedback from her husband, Blake, after she presented him with a Father's Day gift of their own children's handprints, Debbie began to make similar products for friends, who also encouraged her to think about starting her own business. It was not long before word spread, and customers from other areas of Ontario and abroad started contacting Debbie to

This case was written by H. F. (Herb) MacKenzie and James Doyle, both at Brock University, Faculty of Business, St. Catharines, ON L2S 3A1. It was prepared as a basis for class discussion and is not intended to illustrate effective or ineffective handling of a management situation. Copyright © 2007 by H. F. (Herb) MacKenzie. Reprinted with permission.

have her make plaques and other gift and display items for them. Debbie quickly recognized the potential of her business to provide her with a reasonable income and, at the same time, let her work from home where she could continue to spend quality time with her two young daughters. Being able to spend quality time with her children while they were so young was an important motivator that Debbie had for establishing this as a home-based business.

It did not take Debbie very long to recognize as well that she had a potential business model that could be franchised to other young mothers who also had entrepreneurial drive, and who might like the benefits of operating a successful home-based business. At first, she called a number of local lawyers, but had difficulty getting anyone to return her telephone calls. When she finally did make contact with one lawyer, he admitted that the reason he failed to respond to her numerous requests was that he was unconvinced she would proceed with franchising her business. A call to the Canadian Franchise Association (CFA) provided Debbie with the name of a lawyer who was a franchise specialist in London, Ontario. He assured Debbie that franchising, at least from the perspective of beginning operations, was certainly doable, and the legal issues could be managed quite easily.

FRANCHISE POSSIBILITIES

Debbie had to consider what she could offer to potential franchisees, what types of people would be acceptable as franchisees, how she would market Wee Piggies & Paws as a franchise opportunity to prospective franchisees, and how she would structure franchisee payments to ensure that both she and the franchisees were happy with the business relationship. To Debbie, the relationships she would develop with her franchisees were very important. She dreamed of building a network of moms dedicated both to their families and to their Wee Piggies & Paws franchise. She saw franchisees as both business partners and as friends, and this made the selection of franchisees a critical decision.

The first question—what she could offer to potential franchisees—was easy to answer. Franchisees would have access to training, sources of high-quality materials and supplies, marketing support, and the Wee Piggies & Paws brand name. Most important, franchisees would not need to make large investments in buildings, land, equipment, or inventory, but for a very modest investment could own a business that could easily generate from $2000 to $4000 sales revenue per month or more, depending on the size of the market they served and their ability to market themselves in their region. Sales, depending on the particular products sold, could generate contribution margins of 60 to 80 percent. Debbie also planned to provide protected territories for each franchisee. That is, Debbie would not saturate the market by establishing one franchisee in close proximity to another franchisee, where they would then be in direct competition with each other.

Concerning acceptable franchisees, Debbie was hoping to find young mothers much like herself; that is, those who were motivated to succeed in their own home-based businesses and who valued the opportunity to spend extra time with their young families. She was also interested primarily in those who were able to demonstrate good interpersonal skills and a selling aptitude. Debbie would also select only franchisees who would agree to buy supplies from the sources she provided because she was very concerned with quality assurance. Since franchisees would be selling products under the brand name Wee Piggies & Paws, it would not take long for poor-quality products to ruin the brand image in the marketplace, and this would devalue the brand name for all franchisees.

Finding franchisees did not appear to be difficult. Debbie had seven people who had identified themselves as interested, but the bigger question was how to grow the number of franchisees quickly. She needed to think about how to market the franchise opportunity beyond the initial interested group. Although membership in the Canadian Franchise Association was reasonable at first, it would quickly become expensive as locations increased. Even for a small operation, the expense would be several thousand dollars. Attending franchise trade shows was another option. There were several in Canada each year. However, cost, to Debbie, was also prohibitive. Simply attending one trade show could easily cost $5000 or more. While she would need to give this issue some additional thought, Debbie decided that her short-term solution was to work with the interested group and make them so happy they would spread the word to others, and potential franchisees would seek her. For more remote locations, Debbie would have to decide whether to continue with the same franchise strategy, or whether to seek a master franchisee who would then have the rights to seek and establish smaller franchisee locations. If she decided on this option, then she would need to give more thought to how she would structure franchisee payments from the master franchisee and the smaller franchisee locations to herself.

The difficult question was deciding how to structure payments from franchisees for the rights to own a franchise location. Her decision was complicated by her strong desire to rapidly grow a successful franchise operation, her own financial needs and the need to compensate herself for her own time and the risks she would be taking, and her strong desire to provide mothers of young families with effective means of generating incomes for their families from their own home-based businesses. Her discussions with the franchise lawyer did provide her with some guidelines, and she did some research into how other franchisors structured their franchisee payments. However, she quickly realized that she would have to make the final decision herself.

Through her research, Debbie understood that franchisor compensation usually involved some combination of an initial franchise fee and some form of ongoing royalty payments, usually based on the franchisee's performance. Debbie was aware that Wee Piggies & Paws, while very successful as her own home-based business, lacked any history of success as a franchise. That suggested to her that she might have to charge a lower initial fee to franchisees while she established the business, and that she might be able to increase it as brand equity in the Wee Piggies & Paws brand name increased. While Tim Hortons and McDonald's might charge many thousands of dollars to a franchisee for a single location, it would certainly be unreasonable for Debbie to attempt to do so. While she knew that she could not price her franchise opportunity too high, she also did not want to undercharge because she wanted to attract only people who were committed to making their location a success.

When considering ongoing royalty payments, Debbie discovered that there was also a considerable range that franchisees were charged for these. Some franchisors charged as little as 2 percent of sales revenue, while others charged as high as 8 percent or more. Most charged between 4 and 6 percent. Royalties were usually based on sales revenue and not on profit. Moreover, Debbie understood that her success as a franchisor would largely be dependent on the quality of her relationships with her franchisees as she expected them to play a critical role in marketing and growing the Wee Piggies & Paws brand. She wondered what effect her choice might have on this, and even whether royalties might be the best way to generate an ongoing revenue stream for herself. One alternate revenue stream, or even one that could be used in addition to royalties, was to require that franchisees buy all materials and supplies through her. Selling materials and supplies added a whole new dimension to the franchise business, but many franchisors were doing it.

THE DECISION

Debbie spent a lot of time wondering how to set her franchise fees, but she knew that her lawyer wanted her to make a decision so it could be included in the franchise agreements that she would then sign with her chosen franchisees. She could have high or low initial fees, and high or low royalty fees. Debbie was sure that her initial decision was critical to her future success. While she might have some flexibility to make changes in the future as new franchisees were selected, the choices made at the time a franchisee was granted rights to a franchise location would essentially "lock" her in to a particular compensation structure as even minor changes would be costly administratively, and might damage relationships with the franchisees involved. She wondered also whether one of the two forms of compensation was inherently more flexible than the other, and if this flexibility could be used in the future to her benefit. In the back of her mind, Debbie was also considering whether franchising opportunities could one day be offered outside of Canada, and if it would make more sense to standardize her compensation structure or whether some degree of localization was required. While she would have some degree of oversight of her Canadian franchisees, Debbie appreciated that it would be more difficult to monitor sales of international locations.

Literacy Partners of Manitoba

Natalie Turnley-Johnston,
Anne M. Lavack, and Gina Clark

Lorri Apps, executive director of Literacy Partners of Manitoba (LPM), was stuck in slow traffic on her way to the office on a crisp fall day in 2004. While she waited for traffic to move ahead, she mentally reviewed her successes from the previous fiscal year in the area of sponsorships and partnerships. She was pleased about the past year's achievements, but felt that there might be opportunities in the coming year that could bring even greater success to her organization. Were there new strategies that should be followed? Were there other opportunities to be sought out? As she neared the office, she decided that at some point today, she would sit down and give serious thought to a strategy for sponsorships and partnerships for the upcoming year.

ABOUT LITERACY PARTNERS

Literacy Partners of Manitoba (LPM) was established in 1987 as a charitable non-profit organization committed to encouraging adult and family literacy. Its primary goal is to promote increased literacy through the provision of literacy-related resources. LPM has

This case was prepared by Natalie T. Johnston with assistance from Gina Clark, under the supervision of Anne M. Lavack, Ph.D. in the Faculty of Business Administration at the University of Regina. The case is based on information publicly available on the Internet and elsewhere. The case is intended to provide a basis for classroom discussion and learning, and is not intended to portray methods or decisions that are right or wrong. Copyright © Anne M. Lavack Reprinted with permission.

a variety of ways of doing this, such as informing the public about existing literacy issues, providing literacy training to teachers and volunteers, or offering resources and information related to current and developing literacy-related programs in Manitoba. Activities carried out by LPM include building the literacy network, raising public awareness of literacy issues, training parents and teachers, and providing information and resources to existing and emerging literacy programs across the province. LPM also plays a role as part of the "Movement for Canadian Literacy," which seeks to inform the federal government and the public about adult literacy issues.

Literacy has an enormous impact on society, which is not only apparent in the labour force and the economy, but also in family life. The International Adult Literacy Survey revealed that 39 200 Manitoba adults between the ages of 20 and 64 have less than a grade nine education. Furthermore, 22% of people from Manitoba have problems meeting everyday reading demands, and 18% have serious difficulty with literacy in general. The economic costs of low literacy amount to $10.7 billion annually in Canada, with Manitoba's portion accounting for over $374 million each year. Because literacy is so important to society and the economy, Literacy Partners has an enormous role to play in acting as the voice for literacy in Manitoba.

LPM has a complement of three staff members, three part-time regional coordinators, and several consultants. (See the organizational chart in Exhibit 1.) The three paid staff members include the executive director, an office manager, and a part-time financial manager.

LPM has a volunteer board of directors, comprising four executive committee members and seven members-at-large. The board directors have different qualifications and a variety of occupations; they are learners, tutors, arts educators, and professors. These different backgrounds provide LPM with a variety of perspectives and ideas, and they help to reflect the diversity in their membership.

LPM is a member-based organization with approximately 300 members, including organizations such as universities, community colleges, schools, and libraries, as well as individuals employed as instructors, tutors, and learners in literacy programs. There are five membership categories: Regular, Volunteer, Learner, Non-Profit Organizations, and For-Profit Organizations. The corresponding fees for these categories are $36, $12, $5, $100, and $250. The membership for Non-Profit Organizations provides membership privileges for four people, and the For-Profit Organizations' membership, although only for two people, provides members with a charitable receipt of $150 for tax purposes. All of the membership fees, except for those for Volunteer Tutors and Learners, are pro-rated, and there are reduced rates available for those who choose to join during the year.

There are many advantages of being a member of LPM; LPM provides its members with access to a lending library, a literacy listserv, the website www.elit.ca, special events, and access to the LPM display. Members also receive free promotional materials, copies of LPM's quarterly newsletter, and invitations to the annual general meeting and open houses at LPM. These services enable LPM members to stay up-to-date with developments in the field of adult literacy, and to have access to resources that can help them provide better programs for adult learners.

SERVICES AND ACTIVITIES OF LPM

LPM conducts a wide range of activities aimed toward achieving their goal. The following is a sample of some of the key services that they offer:

EXHIBIT 1   LPM Board and Staff

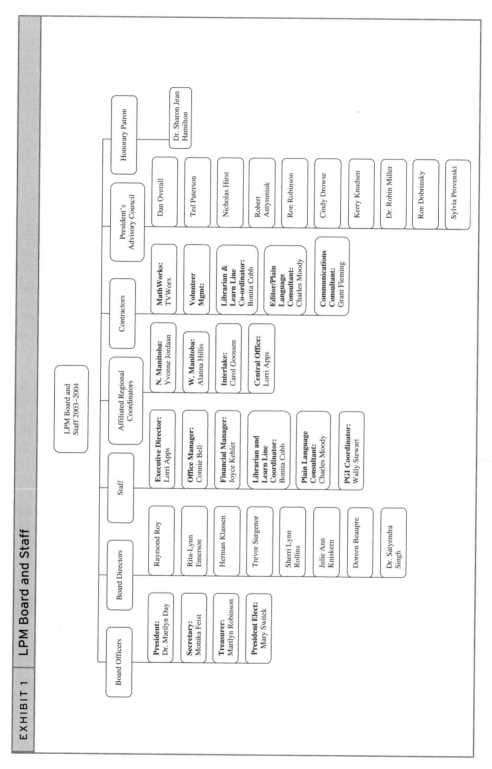

Learner Bursaries

LPM provides a number of learning bursaries for its members. These bursaries include the Katherine Aird Hamilton Bursary for Literacy Workers, PGI Learner Bursaries, and Raise-a-Reader Funding. The Katherine Aird Hamilton Bursary is for the amount of $500 and seeks to support adult literacy instructors in their professional development. The PGI Learner Bursaries, which are awarded to the recipient's literacy program, give short-term financial assistance in emergency situations for supplies, transportation, or child care to a maximum of $900 per person. The Raise-a-Reader Funding has a limit of $1500 and priority is given to literacy programs based on need, community-based connections, and the expected impact on families.

Resource Centre

LPM also has a resource centre that is the only province-wide lending library in Manitoba focusing on adult literacy. The library contains over 40 000 items, and contains a variety of software, books, literacy kits, and videos. The catalogue for the library is available online. LPM also provides a structured editing service for communicating with adult learners. LPM offers help with writing for low-literacy readers, including communication training sessions that can help organizations write documents in plain language accessible to low-literacy readers.

LEARN Line

The LEARN Line links people to programs, so that those who are interested in upgrading their literacy skills can phone in and be referred to the most appropriate literacy programs. The LEARN Line, which was advertised on Global TV, the Yellow Pages, newspaper and radio ads, and through posters and discreet referral cards, received over 500 calls during the past year alone. A follow-up study of callers found that among those who did not immediately enrol in a literacy program, the majority were planning to do so in the future. As well, over 100 people called the LEARN Line last year to inquire about volunteering in literacy programs.

Funding for the first three years of the LEARN Line was provided by the National Literacy Secretariat (NLS). In the following four years the province of Manitoba has supplied funding to cover the $40 000 cost of providing a counsellor for the LEARN Line, as well as funding for regular database updates and publicity.

ADVOCACY GOALS OF LPM

In the past year alone, there has been a 13% increase in the number of participants in adult literacy programs, thanks to the hard work of Literacy Partners of Manitoba. LPM continues to set high goals for further improving adult literacy; among these are the following:

- LPM wants Canada to adopt a national literacy strategy, due to the fact that it is one of the few industrialized nations without such a strategy in place.

- LPM hopes to see support for adult literacy in federal student scholarship strategies and student loans. This may include reimbursing adult learners for their child care, transportation, and material costs.

- LPM would like to see a portion of the National Child Tax Credit going toward supporting family literacy.

- LPM feels that Aboriginal Peoples' projects are an important area in which National Literacy Secretariat funds should be invested.

- LPM hopes that a minimum 25% of the Canadian Learning Institute's recent budget of $100 million dollars will be directed to adult and family literacy.

FINANCIAL STATUS

LPM has seen steady improvement in its financial position over the last several years. (See five-year financial statements in Exhibit 2 and Exhibit 3.) Revenues and net assets have both shown steady growth over this period. Each year, LPM strives to either maintain a balanced budget or produce a small surplus. Their physical facilities were substantially increased in 2004 because of generous donations from CanWest Global Communications and the Winnipeg Foundation that allowed LPM to move into a larger office space.

GOVERNMENT FUNDING

The largest source of funding support for LPM comes from the NLS of the federal Human Resource Development Centre (HRDC). Last year, NLS provided over $200 000 to LPM. (See Exhibit 4 for a partial list of LPM projects and funding agencies.)

NLS has demonstrated a willingness to fund new pilot projects, such as the LPM, to help them get started. Other sources of funding, such as the province of Manitoba, are more likely to provide support for literacy projects if the methods, materials, and models have been piloted and tested. NLS provides seed money for these projects, with the hope that the province or other funding agencies will later be willing to provide support to continue running successful programs.

Adult Learning and Literacy (ALL), a department of the government of Manitoba, also provides an operating grant of about $40 000 to LPM each year to share the costs of running the LEARN Line. ALL has also provided funding in the past for other LPM projects, such as extending their successful social marketing campaign with a contribution of $40 000 several years ago.

SPONSORSHIPS AND PARTNERSHIPS

While the majority of revenues come from government grants, the organization has become increasingly successful at creating alliances with businesses and non-government organizations.

Many of the companies that assist Literacy Partners of Manitoba do so out of the belief that by enhancing the skills of their workforce, they achieve a competitive advantage that may result in a financial return. Focusing on adult literacy means helping adults to be better prepared for the workplace and everyday life by enhancing essential literacy skills. A 1% increase in the average literacy skills of a worker can result in a permanent increase of 1.5% in gross domestic product (GDP) per capita. This increase means that improving adult literacy has a permanent and positive effect on the Canadian economy as a whole. Research has also shown that when literacy skills are increased, there is a

| EXHIBIT 2 | Literacy Partners of Manitoba, Inc. Statement of Revenue and Expenditures Year Ended August 31 |

	2000	2001	2002	2003	2004
Revenue:					
Grants	$256 030	$412 454	$332 873	$320 025	$323 469
Membership Fees	2 520	6 030	3 855	3 560	4 092
Conferences Fees	435	1 510	3 268	4 665	1 756
Investment Income	6 513	878	10 889	2 735	990
Partnership Income	-	-	-	6 400	1 298
Donations	3 371	1 668	7 870	13 819	98 047
Fundraising	15 666	26 683	14 148	28 381	12 759
Other	325	32	592	25 580	-
Total Revenue:	$284 860	$449 255	$373 495	$405 165	$442 411
Expenditures:					
Bank Charges	n/a	28	110	209	220
Bursaries	n/a	7 495	4 064	8 994	3 793
Donation	n/a	-	-	8 000	300
Facilities	n/a	28 358	26 778	28 681	88 097
GST	n/a	5 760	3 605	3 343	5 246
Honoraria	n/a	26 790	32 840	8 934	9 160
Insurance	n/a	1 838	1 944	2 332	2 805
K.A. Hamilton Scholarship	n/a	-	-	-	8 955
Materials	n/a	43 560	26 048	37 110	16 545
Membership Fees	n/a	1 366	1 433	992	1 433
Professional Development	n/a	1 710	1 607	844	350
Professional Fees	n/a	1 775	2 375	2 478	2 537
Program Subsidies	n/a	-	-	12 850	16 365
Publicity	n/a	44 949	13 165	18 909	19 738
Salaries and Benefits	n/a	163 993	187 032	167 089	163 898
Subcontracts	n/a	79 993	32 431	54 715	56 481
Travel	n/a	38 960	34 076	20 126	32 924
Total Expenditures:	$284 411	$446 575	$367 508	$375 606	$428 847
Surplus (loss)	$449	$2 680	$5 987	$29 559	$13 564

EXHIBIT 3	Literacy Partners of Manitoba, Inc. Statement of Financial Position Year Ended August 31				
	2000	**2001**	**2002**	**2003**	**2004**
ASSETS:					
Cash and Temporary Investments	$ 61 975	$ 3 512	$264 182	$142 190	$251 369
Accounts Receivable	190 000	9 672	3 114	7 553	11 819
GST Recoverable	1 988	-	-	-	-
Prepaid Expenses	844	844	-	-	-
Total Assets:	**$254 807**	**$284 028**	**$267 296**	**$149 743**	**$263 188**
LIABILITIES:					
Current Liabilities:					
Accounts Payable & Accrued Liabilities	$ 10 047	$ 15 955	$ 11 973	$ 9 558	$ 5 386
Deferred Contributions	184 052	190 685	185 948	41 251	145 304
Total Liabilities	**$194 099**	**$206 640**	**$197 921**	**$50 809**	**$150 690**
NET ASSETS:					
Internally Restricted Net Assets	$40 000	$40 000	$40 000	$40 000	$ 40 000
Externally Restricted Net Assets	20 708	-	-	-	-
Unrestricted Net Assets	-	37 388	29 375	58 394	72 498
Total Net Assets:	**$60 708**	**$77 388**	**$69 375**	**$98 934**	**$112 498**
Total Liabilities & Net Assets:	**$254 807**	**$284 028**	**$267 296**	**$149 743**	**$263 188**

corresponding decrease in health care costs, poverty, and crime. Investing in literacy makes good business sense.

CanWest Global Communications has been a major sponsor, assisting LPM in acquiring a larger office space to capitalize on their success. CanWest Global Communications is an international company that is responsible for a variety of newspapers, radio and television stations (including Global TV), and a film and TV distribution and production operation.

The Manitoba Lotteries Corporation, another major sponsor, recently donated $100 000 to allow for the development of the MathWorks tele-learning series. The series consisted of ten half-hour shows about math upgrading and was seen by thousands of adult learners. Numeracy is considered to be a very important part of literacy, and adult learners benefit substantially from improving their math skills.

FOUNDATION GRANTS

LPM actively applies for grants from foundations. Most foundations have relatively strict guidelines regarding the types of products that they are willing to fund. However, LPM has had substantial success in working with the Winnipeg Foundation. The Winnipeg Foundation is the second-largest community foundation in all of Canada, and has nearly

EXHIBIT 4	Examples of LPM Projects Undertaken and the Funding Agencies Responsible (2003–2004)

Project Title	Funder & Amount	Main Activities
Promoting Integration of Literacy	National Literary Secretariat, HRDC $130 000 x 2 years	• Publicized the need and benefits that increased public support and involvement would have on adult literacy programs and projects • Created "Unique benefits of adult and family literacy programs" campaign • Distributed 5000 newsletters and new numeracy and family literacy materials • Developed two partnership workshops
Literacy on the Move	NLS, HRDC project $49 893	• Pursued a new marketing and communications strategy • Executed seven special events • Updated materials for literacy practitioners and distributed them • Increased contact with rural/urban/Aboriginal Peoples media and corporate partners
LEARN Line and Speaker Bureau	Province of Manitoba $40 000	• Advertised and operated the LEARN Line • Trained ten learner-speakers • Created and maintained a database for volunteer opportunities
Moving the Markers	The Winnipeg Foundation $25 000	• Moved LPM office to create an Adult Learning Resource Centre with new equipment • Revised website to offer workshops online
PGI 2003	Business Sponsors $25 000	• Mounted the 14th annual PGI golf tournament for literacy to support learner bursaries and lending library
Population Health	Health Canada $48 000	• Delivered and evaluated the impact of training in plain language • Hosted Rural Development Institute training • Catalogued and distributed plain language materials about health

EXHIBIT 4	Examples of LPM Projects Undertaken and the Funding Agencies Responsible (2003-2004) (continued)	
Self-Generated Donations and Fees	$5000	• Board travel and membership meetings, distance subsidies, reimburse and recognize volunteers, solicit community partners
Building on Success	National Literary Secretariat $5614	• Prepared and presented photo-montage and briefs for input into municipal, provincial, and federal policy on public libraries and adult learning
Marketing our Message	National Literary Secretariat $5614	• Power Lunch and keynote speaker • Consulted with the field on new strategies for measuring the impact of community-based literacy programs
Resources on the Move	The Winnipeg Foundation $4715	• Took samples of the library collection out to various audiences
Welcome Kits	Thomas Sill Foundation $1746	• Ordered and circulated a new collection of top ten resources in adult literacy professional development in travelling trunks and 100 other items.

1500 endowment funds. Two of these are funds that directly support literacy: the LPM Endowment Fund and the Literacy for Life Fund. The Winnipeg Foundation has provided financial support to LPM to help with a variety of projects, including the very popular *Family Literacy in a Box* demonstration kits, which have been used throughout the province.

FUNDRAISING

Because LPM is a non-profit organization, it relies heavily on sponsorships, partnerships, and fundraising in order to raise the funds necessary to carry out its goals. Exhibit 5 details some of the recent fundraising activities that LPM has undertaken.

Raise-a-Reader

One of the most successful fundraisers is the Raise-a-Reader event. Raise-a-Reader is based on the idea that "the child who reads becomes the adult who succeeds," and has been a great success. During this fundraising campaign, members and volunteers for Literacy Partners of Manitoba gave out copies of the *Free Press* newspaper in exchange for donations to literacy. In 2003, their hard work raised over $50 000. The CanWest Global Foundation supported this campaign by securing the participation of all Safeway stores in Manitoba as outlets to drop off used books.

PGI Golf Tournament

The Peter Gzowski Invitational Golf Tournament is the largest fundraising event for literacy in Manitoba. It has become increasingly popular, with more people participating and more money being raised each year. So far, this fundraiser has generated over $7 million for adult learners in general, with over $240 000 of this amount going to support adult literacy in Manitoba. The $240 000 was used toward learner bursaries, the LEARN Line, and the LPM lending library. The money is used to assist adult learners with the costs of child care, materials, and transportation. The PGI Tournament was successful through the dedication of all

EXHIBIT 5	Recent Fundraising Activities & Proceeds	
Fundraising Event	**Year**	**Proceeds to Date**
Peter Gzowski Invitational Golf Tournament	Began in 1986; continues annually.	$240 000
Raise-a-Reader	Began in 2003; continues annually	$64 000
A Christmas Carol– Live reading with CBC celebrities	2003	$600
Family Literacy Day– Luncheon with Justice Murray Sinclair	2004	$300

the participants, literacy workers, second-chance learners, prize donors, committee members, and sponsors and supporters. These supporters included organizations such as Starbucks Coffee Co., the Kinsmen Club of Winnipeg, the *Winnipeg Sun,* and the Steering Committee of Workplace Education Manitoba.

CONCLUSION

It had been a long day, and Lorri Apps had finally found a few quiet moments to think about her sponsorship strategy for the coming year. Although there was widespread corporate support for the annual PGI Golf Tournament, only about $25 000 per year was raised as a result of the golf tournament. Large corporate donors were needed to support some of the new initiatives that LPM was planning. These initiatives included a follow-up to the highly successful MathWorks videos, which would focus on a somewhat more advanced level of mathematics. As well, sponsorship was needed to help create a series of videos that would focus on reading and writing.

Lorri was concerned about LPM's heavy reliance on government funding from the National Literacy Secretariat and the province of Manitoba. It would be desirable to diversify the revenues for the organization, so that more revenues were being obtained from non-government sources. However, this was easier said than done.

To date, there were only two major sponsors. CanWest Global Communications was a media conglomerate that owned major newspapers across Canada, so promoting literacy made good business sense for their business. It was a natural tie-in, and was something that the company and its employees could feel good about supporting.

The Manitoba Lotteries Corporation was the second major sponsor. As a Crown corporation, this organization was responsible for operating two major casinos in Winnipeg, managing a network of VLT machines across Manitoba, and selling lottery tickets across Manitoba (including Lotto 6/49, Sports Select, and break-open tickets). The clientele for many of its products tended to skew toward the lower socio-economic bracket. Since those of lower socio-economic status also tended to be lower in literacy, it made sense for Manitoba Lotteries Corporation to be involved in promoting literacy.

Lorri wondered whether there were other organizations that might be a natural fit for sponsorships. Such organizations needed to be fairly sizeable so that they could afford a substantial sponsorship commitment. At the same time, it was ideal if the organization could be sold on literacy as a business investment, since this would make the organization more supportive of the cause. It was also desirable for the selected organizations to provide a good "fit" with the goals of LPM, so that the relationship would be mutually beneficial.

Lorri started to page through the list of the Top 100 Businesses in Manitoba. (See Exhibit 6.) She was sure that there must be businesses out there that would be good sponsorship prospects. It was just a question of identifying them and developing a convincing approach.

| EXHIBIT 6 | *Manitoba Business Magazine: Top 100 Companies (2003)* |

Rank	Company	Gross Revenue 2003	Net Income or <Loss> 2003	Total Number of Employees	Manitoba Employees	Nature of Business
1	Great-West Lifeco Inc.	13 429 000 000	1 236 000 000	19 000	2500	Financial Services
2	Cargill Limited	3 654 293 000	N/A	6 105	441	Agri Business
3	Canadian Wheat Board	3 339 872 000	3 152 775 000	487	457	Grain Industry
4	Agricore United	2 726 631 000	<2 384 000>	2 743	2743	Agriculture
5	CanWest Global. Communications Corp	2 651 334 000	46 088 000	10 400	700	Media
6	IGM Financial Inc.	1 874 181 000	539 081 000	3 134	1114	Insurance
7	Manitoba Hydro	1 869 000 000	71 000 000	5 800	5800	Energy Utility
8	The Wawanesa Mutual Insurance Company	1 615 522 000	76 206 000	1 747	318	Insurance
9	Manitoba Telecom Services Inc.	844 700 000	85 800 000	3 400	3400	Telecommunications
10	The North West Company	783 000 000	35 700 000	5 288	1600	Retail
11	Standard Aero	759 969 000	21 553 000	2 645	1331	Aviation MRO
12	NFIL Holdings Corp.	691 000 000	N/A	1 800	1070	Bus Mfg.
13	Ridley Inc.	665 000 000	10 400 000	1 080	180	Mfg. Formulated Livestock Feeds
14	Manitoba Public Insurance	641 471 000	<22 794 000>	1 300	1300	Public Auto Insurer
15	Winpak Ltd.	513 286 000	34 811 000	1 802	544	Packaging
16	N.M. Paterson & Sons Limited	475 800 000	N/A	300	150	Agribusiness
17	Palliser Furniture Ltd.	471 009 000	N/A	4 329	2628	Furniture Mfg.
18	ProCurity Pharmacy Services Inc.	428 693 321	N/A	107	86	Pharmaceutical Distribution

EXHIBIT 6   *Manitoba Business Magazine: Top 100 Companies (2003)* (continued)

19	Manitoba Lotteries Corporation	410 838 000	265 484 000	2000	2000	Gaming
20	The Megill-Stephenson Company Limited	316 463 648	N/A	547	547	Automotive
21	Gendis Inc.	311 731 000	‹9 144 000›	3400	800	Retail Merchandiser
22	National Leasing Group Inc.	210 782 500	N/A	182	170	Asset-Based Financing
23	Boeing Canada Technology Winnipeg Division	198 263 787	14 964 370	875	875	Aircraft Parts Mfg.
24	TruServ Canada Cooperative Inc.	194 581 000	N/A	400	400	Retail and Distribution
25	Pollard Banknote Limited	188 034 000	N/A	1350	525	Security Printing
26	Cangene Corporation	186 213 000	40 090 000	600	383	Pharmaceutical Mfg.
27	Dairy Farmers of Manitoba	184 636 805	97 238 000	29	29	Raw Milk Marketing
28	Buhler Industries	181 162 000	11 630 000	800	600	Mfg.
29	Princess Group Inc.	180 420 000	N/A	1066	376	Retail
30	Ceridian Canada Ltd.	180 100 000	N/A	1365	312	Managed HR Solutions
31	Reimer Express Lines Ltd.	170 000 000	N/A	1500	500	Transportation
32	Old Dutch Foods Ltd.	149 816 000	N/A	500	180	Snack Food Mfg.
33	Maxim Transportation Services Inc.	135 000 000	N/A	300+	175	Truck Leasing and Rentals
34	Red River Cooperative Ltd.	135 000 000	14 800 000	15	15	Petroleum
35	Boyd Group Income Fund	129 600 000	1 480 000	1300	165	Collision Repair
36	WGI Westman Group Inc.	125 207 000	N/A	700	700	Steel Mfg.
37	Canad Inns	116 000 000	N/A	1500	1500	Hospitality
38	Portage la Prairie Mutual Insurance Company	111 373 012	5 908 835	178	78	Insurance

EXHIBIT 6	Manitoba Business Magazine: Top 100 Companies (2003) (continued)				
39	Vansco Electronics Ltd.	104 668 692	3 463 000	749	670	Electronics Mfg.
40	Hytek Ltd.	103 123 156	N/A	275	275	Livestock Producer
41	FP Canadian Newspapers Limited Partnership	100 000 000	7 300 000	590	589	Newspaper Publishing
42	Arctic Glacier Income Fund	97 170 000	10 764 000	650	68	Mfg. & Dist. of Packaged Ice
43	Granny's Poultry Cooperative (Manitoba) Ltd.	94 900 000	N/A	388	388	Poultry Processor
44	Manitoba Crop Insurance Corporation	92 600 000	4 400 000	101	100	Crop Insurance
45	McDiarmid Lumber Ltd.	91 000 000	N/A	500	400	Home Centre Building Supplies
46	The Puratone Corp.	89 000 000	N/A	260	250	Hog Production/Feed Mfg.
47	Friesens Corporation	84 000 000	N/A	500	490	Book Mfg.
48	Steinbach Credit Union Ltd.	74 000 000	8 055 581	279	279	Financial Services
49	B.A. Robinson Co. Ltd.	70 000 000	N/A	1704	80	Dist. Plumbing Heating and Lighting
50	E.H. Price Ltd.	70 000 000	N/A	554	462	Mfg.
51	Allmar International	68 526 000	N/A	315	150	Dist. of Construction Products
52	The R.G. Mazer Group	66 257 000	N/A	175	175	Farm Machinery Retail
53	Tundra Oil and Gas Ltd.	62 867 000	N/A	38	37	Oil & Gas Exploration and Production
54	Roy Legumex Inc.	61 400 000	N/A	35	35	Special Crop Processor
55	Cambrian Credit Union	51 615 000	6 673 000	210	210	Financial Services
56	Pembina Consumers Co-op (2000) Ltd.	48 600 000	3 129 000	110	110	Retail
57	Winnipeg Airports Authority Inc.	46 100 000	15 500 000	119	119	Airport

EXHIBIT 6 **Manitoba Business Magazine: Top 100 Companies (2003)** (continued)

58	Heritage Co-op	43 700 000	N/A	260	260	Retail
59	Ste. Anne Co-operative Oil Ltd.	39 227 910	4 999 396	49	49	Bulk Fuel and Gas Bars
60	Twin Valley Co-op Ltd.	38 769 747	1 936 386	85	81	Retail
61	Assiniboine Credit Union Ltd.	38 104 323	3 291 969	214	214	Financial Co-operative
62	Swan Valley Consumers Ltd.	37 885 000	1 762 000	130	130	Retail Co-operative
63	Wardrop Holdings Inc.	37 000 000	N/A	400	180	Engineering Consulting
64	Red River Valley Mutual Insurance Company	36 187 000	4 292 000	40	40	Property and Casual Insurance
65	Bee Maid Honey Ltd.	34 000 000	N/A	61	32	Honey Processing
66	Delmar Commodities Ltd.	33 302 676	N/A	19	19	Grain Elevator
67	IQON Financial	31 400 000	<400 000>	61	50	Financial Services
68	Concord Projects Ltd.	27 525 739	N/A	20	20	Construction
69	Lakeview Management Inc.	25 649 018	1 644 837	500	500	Hotel Mgmt./Dev.
70	North American Lumber Limited	24 000 000	N/A	150	50	Retail and Wholesale Lumber
71	Premier Printing Ltd.	23 948 000	793 000	115	87	Commercial Printing
72	Astra Credit Union Ltd.	22 538 574	2 576 519	120	120	Credit Union
73	Midwest Detroit Diesel-Allison Ltd.	21 730 859	N/A	90	60	Distributor
74	Emerging Information Systems Inc.	21 100 000	2 000 000	227	225	Software Developer
75	Sun Gro Horticulture	21 000 000	N/A	100	100	Peat Moss and Growing Mixes
76	Carman Co-op (1959) Ltd.	20 824 502	1 400 270	85	85	Retail
77	Valleyview Co-op Ltd.	20 078 821	1 089 305	74	74	Retail

EXHIBIT 6 | Manitoba Business Magazine: Top 100 Companies (2003) (continued)

78	Wellington West Capital Inc.	19 571 572	87 435	225	115	Investment
79	North of 53 Consumers Co-op Ltd.	17 688 285	294 811	52	46	Retail
80	Gilbert Plains Consumers Co-operative Limited	17 534 211	1 575 143	29	29	Agricultural Retailer
81	Prairie Flour Mills Ltd.	16 700 000	N/A	12	12	Flour Milling
82	Salisbury House of Canada Ltd.	15 904 615	N/A	550	550	Restaurant
83	Initial Security	15 000 000	N/A	9000	900	Security
84	Cloutier Agra Seeds Inc.	15 000 000	N/A	13	13	Grain Marketing
85	Crosstown Credit Union Limited	14 824 273	2 012 862	47	47	Financial Services
86	Hayhurst Elias Dudek Inc.	14 053 000	N/A	143	121	Insurance Brokerage
87	Flo Form Countertops	13 460 796	N/A	165	75	Countertop Mfg.
88	Florists Supply	11 403 000	N/A	70	40	Wholesale Florist
89	Intergraphics Decal Limited	11 276 307	878 684	100	98	Decal Mfg.
90	Boissevain Consumers Co-operative	10 570 483	546 076	58	58	Retail
91	Winnipeg Convention Centre	10 300 366	N/A	575	575	Convention Centre Facility
92	RW Packaging Ltd.	10 135 421	122 577	52	31	Consumer Goods
93	Carpathia Credit Union Limited	9 475 827	548 288	54	54	Financial Services
94	Perimeter Industries Ltd.	9 205 000	N/A	65	65	Carton Mfg.
95	Entegra Credit Union	8 131 400	900 651	38	38	Financial Services
96	Shelmerdine Nurseries and Garden Center Ltd.	6 599 000	N/A	170	170	Retail Garden Centre & Landscaping
97	McElhoes & Duffy	6 250 000	N/A	9	9	Insurance Broker

EXHIBIT 6

Manitoba Business Magazine: Top 100 Companies (2003) (continued)

98	Southport Aerospace Centre Inc.	5 799 358	100 298	25	25	Property Management
99	Encore Business Solutions Inc.	5 316 000	N/A	35	35	Business Solutions & Software Devt.
100	Springfield Industries Ltd.	5 200 000	N/A	60	60	Mfg.

"The Holey War": Robin's Donuts versus Tim Hortons

Ian Spencer

In July 2001, Wally Ballou, manager and part-owner of Robin's Donuts in Summerside, P.E.I., was wrestling with a tough problem: how to use media advertising, special promotions (incentives), public relations, and personal selling to increase Robin's sales and take market share away from Tim Hortons. As he pondered this challenge, Wally jotted down some relevant background information he planned to turn over to Tim Carroll, a retired marketing consultant and friend. Wally was enthused that Tim had agreed to help because he was just about out of ideas and needed a fresh approach. The following are Wally's jottings:

- Robin's opened in June 1999 and to date has gained only about 20% of the donut shop market in Summerside. The Tim Hortons franchise, which has operated for about ten years in Summerside, has the remaining 80%. Our shop is directly across the street from Tim Hortons on the way into town from the Trans-Canada Highway. My goal is to achieve a 30% market share, or about $500 000 in sales.

- Robin's Donuts has a small core of loyal customers. They like the coffee, the sweets, and the many deli items available at lunch. A few customers have patronized Robin's outlets in central or western Canada.

This case was written by Ian Spencer, Professor of Marketing, St. Francis Xavier University, Antigonish, Nova Scotia. Copyright © Ian Spencer, 2001. The assistance of all participants in the meeting is gratefully acknowledged. Reprinted with permission.

- Robin's sales are fairly consistent Monday to Friday, but fall off on the weekend. Sales are about 40% drive-thru, 40% eat-in, and 20% takeout.

- Most sales are to customers who live in or near Summerside. Other geographic market segments are people who live in western Prince Edward Island but at least five kilometres away from Summerside, and visitors to Prince Edward Island.

- About 20 000 people live in Summerside or within five kilometres of it.

- Last year a group of students at the University of Prince Edward Island conducted a survey for us. The survey revealed that almost everyone in the Summerside area had heard of Robin's and most had tried it. However, most had also returned to Tim Hortons. They had no real problems with Robin's. They just did not feel there was a good enough reason to switch.

- The thing is, we really are different from Tim Hortons. We have an extensive deli selection (salads, subs, and sandwiches) and several other items Tim Hortons does not carry (pizza pretzels, oatcakes, fruit sticks, and soon a line of deluxe pies).

- We have promoted Robin's quite aggressively:
  - Three commercials per week ($30 per spot) on Summerside radio station CJRW
  - A large sign in front of the building with messages changed each week or so
  - Discount coupons
  - Quarter-page ads ($200 per insertion) in the weekly newspaper, the *Journal Pioneer*

As well, I have personally dropped off coffee and donuts to various businesses in town to let them try our products.

- I think there are several opportunities to grow:
  - Pulling in more business from the highway
  - Getting current customers to drop in more frequently
  - Getting people who eat lunch out to try Robin's
  - Getting regular Tim Hortons customers to spend at least some of their donut shop dollars at Robin's; that is, to switch shops

5-to-10-a-day Program

Nicole Sali and Anne M. Lavack

It was a warm afternoon in the spring of 2004 when Ron Lemaire, marketing director of
the Canadian Produce Marketing Association, was sitting in his Ottawa office, munch-
ing on vegetables out of his lunch bag. As he crunched on a carrot stick, he pondered
some of the key issues surrounding the 5-to-10-a-day campaign to promote consumption of fruits and vegetables. While the campaign had been very successful during 2001
when he had a substantial media budget, now that he was limited to running public service announcements he was not sure if the campaign message was getting across. He
wondered if there was more that could be done to promote the program, given the limited budget that he had for the campaign.

5-TO-10-A-DAY PROGRAM

In the early 1990s, the Canadian Produce Marketing Association developed a campaign
to encourage Canadians to consume more fruits and vegetables. The slogan for the campaign, "Reach for 5-to-10 servings of fruit and vegetables daily . . . they're easy, tasty
and nutritious," communicated the key message. Although the Canadian Produce

Marketing Association ran the *Reach For It!* campaign for nearly seven years, an evaluation report commissioned in 1997 found that there was relatively little public recognition.

Around the same time, the World Cancer Research Fund issued its report entitled *Food, Nutrition and the Prevention of Cancer: A Global Perspective.* The report stated: "Diets containing substantial and varied amounts of vegetables and fruit will prevent 20 percent or more of all cases of cancer." This compelling statistic prompted the Canadian Produce Marketing Association to join forces with the Canadian Cancer Society and the Heart and Stroke Foundation in 1999 to create a more effective social marketing program to promote consumption of fruits and vegetables.

It was believed that the campaign should primarily target women aged 24 to 45, as research has shown that in 85 percent of households, it is the woman in the house who is most likely to do the major grocery shopping. The secondary target group consisted of children and others who influence the person making food-buying decisions.

To better understand the target, the trilateral partnership undertook a series of focus groups with women aged 25 to 45. The focus group results suggested that Canadians were unaware of the number of daily servings of fruits and vegetables needed for good nutrition, and were also unaware that fruits and vegetables play an active role in reducing the risk of cancer and cardiovascular disease.

DEVELOPING THE SOCIAL MARKETING CAMPAIGN

Until fairly recently, Canadians were typically unaware of the necessity of integrating sufficient fruits and vegetables into their diets. The social marketing campaign for the 5-to-10-a-day Program was developed to address these issues and boost fruit and vegetable consumption in order to improve the health of Canadians. Exhibit 1 outlines some of the key reasons why the 5-to-10-a-day Program was undertaken.

EXHIBIT 1	Why the 5-to-10-a-day Program Began

The 5-to-10-a-day Program was undertaken for a number of reasons:

- Cancer and cardiovascular diseases account for over 130 000 deaths in Canada annually.
- Over $155 billion per year is spent on Canadian health care, with almost $20 billion directed to cardiovascular diseases, and over $13 billion to cancer. Reducing the incidence of these diseases would result in significant cost savings for the health care system.
- Consumption of 5 to 10 servings of fruits and vegetables a day can decrease a person's risk of cancer by at least 20%.
- Only 30% of Canadians eat at least 5 to 10 servings of fruit and vegetables a day.
- Only 44% are aware that Canada's Food Guide calls for 5 to 10 servings a day.
- Only 7% are aware that fruit and vegetables can reduce the risk of cancer.
- Only 2% are aware of the protective effect of fruit and vegetables on heart disease, and 1% on stroke prevention capabilities.
- 85% of Canadians say that nutrition is important in choosing the food they eat.

Legitimacy in the 5-to-10-a-day campaign was achieved by placing the logos of the Canadian Cancer Society and Heart and Stroke Foundation, highly recognized and respected organizations within the community, on all campaign publications. To help guide the development of the 5-to-10-a-day campaign, an advisory committee was established. The committee was made up of representatives from the following organizations:

- The Canadian Cancer Society
- Heart and Stroke Foundation
- Canadian Produce Marketing Association
- Dieticians of Canada
- National Institute of Nutrition
- The City of Toronto Department of Public Health

Initially, the 5-to-10-a-day Program was promoted by using public service announcements in a variety of mass media outlets, including television, radio, and print ads. The public service advertisements provided examples of how to easily get five to ten servings a day of fruits and vegetables. (See Exhibit 2 for examples of print advertisements.) Ads included a 1-800 number that had been established through the Canadian Cancer Society, which featured trained operators who provided further information, referrals, and pertinent literature to consumers.

To ensure that the public was getting the message, from January to July 2001, an integrated media strategy was delivered on a national level. This campaign had a budget of $700 000, but it generated media value of over $13 million worth of airtime based on public service announcements. As a result, the campaign had relatively high levels of reach and frequency within the target group.

Since that time, the campaign has relied on public service announcements on television and radio. (See TV ad script example in Exhibit 3.) While radio and television stations are required to run a certain number of public service announcements (PSAs) for free, there are many non-profit organizations competing for this limited amount of free airtime. However, the 5-to-10-a-day Program has managed to obtain a significant amount of free PSA airtime.

Over the last few years, the TV and radio ads have continued to revolve around the concept that five to ten servings of vegetables and fruits a day helps to reduce the risk of cancer, heart disease, and strokes. Each ad gives examples of what classifies as a serving and which fruits and vegetables are better for people.

Mass media ads have been supplemented with in-store displays and grocery flyers to reach consumers where they shop for food. Programs have included an initiative by the Canadian Retail Trade Association, which incorporated the logo of the program onto produce bags and in millions of flyers each week. The Canadian Retail Trade Association also developed partnerships with local offices of the Canadian Cancer Society and the Heart and Stroke Foundation to create health promotion events, in-store sampling of fruit and vegetables, and other special events.

Community outreach through public health practitioners plays a major role in the campaign, and brochures are used to provide more information at public health clinics. Information is provided to schoolchildren through school boards, public health units, and other health centres. Some health units have expanded the 5-to-10-a-day Program using display systems, sampling booths, and training manuals in addition to the resource

EXHIBIT 2	5-to-10-a-day Program Posters

EXHIBIT 3	Example of a TV Ad Script

Video	Audio
A bowlful of salad being tossed by a guy holding tongs.	**Announcer:** "Hey, ever wonder what a serving of vegetables or fruits is?"
	Guy/Hand: "Hmm"
Tongs taken out of the bowl and banana caught by one of the hands that used to be holding the tongs. Banana taken away and only salad still appears.	**Announcer:** "Well if it fits in your hand, it's probably a serving. Here, like a banana."
	Guy/Hand: "Hmm"
Hand catches some broccoli. Broccoli is removed from screen and only salad still appears.	**Announcer:** "Or some broccoli."
	Guy/Hand: "Ahh"
Hand catches a pear. Pear is taken away by hand and only the salad still appears.	**Announcer:** "Here comes a pear."
	Guy/Hand: "Oh"
A hand catches a cluster of frozen peas.	**Announcer:** "And a half-cup of frozen peas"
The hand realizes the peas are cold and abruptly tosses them away, then shakes off and clenches it to try and get the chill out.	**Guy/Hand:** "Uh!"
Hand disappears off screen and only the salad appears.	**Announcer:** "I should have let them thaw first."
Image changes to another group of fruits and vegetables where a phone number and website appear for people to get more information about the program.	**Announcer:** "Eating 5 to 10 servings of vegetables and fruits each day is part of a healthy diet and helps to reduce the risk of cancer, heart disease and stroke. 5-to-10-a-day—it all adds up."

materials from the national program. Other health units have used the tips found on the website to include within nutritional flyers or other one-page information briefs on fruits and vegetables.

The 5-to-10-a-day website provides a variety of materials that can be used by people, either in the health profession or just for personal use:

• *Add it up!* posters provide easy-to-follow information along with photos that display what a serving of fruit and vegetables is and how to reach five to ten servings each day.

• *Freggie Tales Newsletter* is a four-page colour publication aimed towards children aged 6 to 12, providing them with facts about fruits and vegetables, games, produce trivia, and food safety tips.

- *Unlock Your Colours!* is a colourful booklet that provides the nutritional value of a list of fruits and vegetables based on their colour.

- *Grocery List with Magnet* is a colourful fridge pad along with a magnet that gives information as to what counts as a serving size.

- *Healthy Eating Brochure* gives a choice between four different 24-page brochures that provide serving size information, healthy eating tips, menu suggestions, health benefits of eating more fruits and vegetables, a weekly planning chart, and other information on healthy eating.

- *Serving Size Brochure* is a three-panel brochure that provides easy information and photos showing serving sizes for fruits and vegetables, in order to help people reach the goal of five to ten a day.

Exhibit 4 outlines each material available to purchase and provides the price of ordering each unit.

Effective public relations techniques are also used to gain more attention for the program; these public relations efforts are linked to campaign benchmarks such as the release of new research information about consuming fruit and vegetables.

EXHIBIT 4	Materials Available and Prices for Ordering Each Unit

Material Available	Prices per unit
Add it up! Posters	$0.50 per copy
Freggie Tales Newsletter	$0.24 per copy
Unlock Your Colours!	$0.18 per copy
Grocery List with Magnet	$1.00 per copy
Healthy Eating Brochure	$0.24 per copy
Serving Size Brochure	$0.06 per copy

CAMPAIGN EVALUATION

To ensure that the marketing strategies were correctly targeted, an evaluation survey was conducted after the 2001 campaign with a sample of over 2000 participants. Follow-up research was also conducted after the 2003 campaign. The research indicated that Canadians who were unaware of the 5-to-10-a-day Program consumed fewer servings of fruits and vegetables than those aware of the program. (See Exhibit 5.) The results from the survey also indicate that the program has been fairly successful in delivering the campaign message and brand, with approximately 25% of respondents aware of the campaign. Exhibit 6 outlines the vehicles through which the campaign message was seen or heard, by region and gender. Most respondents indicated they were made aware of the program through the TV advertisement. Exhibit 7 compares the 2003 survey results with the 2001 survey results.

Two key statistics are useful in assessing the overall success of the campaign. First, an impressive 41% of Canadians reported seeing ads or other materials for the 5-to-10-a-day campaign during the previous two-year period. Second, there has been a 9% increase in

EXHIBIT 5	Campaign Awareness - 2001

# of servings of fruit & vegetables per day	% aware of the campaign (n=506)	% not aware of the campaign (n=501)
None	1%	1%
1-4	51%	66%
5-9	43%	30%
10+	5%	3%
Total	100%	100%

Reading the above chart:
- Among those who were aware of the campaign, 43% ate 5-9 servings of fruit and vegetables per day.
- Among those who were unaware of the campaign, 30% ate 5-9 servings of fruit and vegetables per day.

EXHIBIT 6	Where did consumers see or hear about the 5-to-10-a-day Program? (2001)

Where did you see or hear the message?	National (n=506) %	By Region				By Gender	
		Atlantic (n=32) %	Quebec (n=101) %	Ontario (n=194) %	West (n=179) %	Male (n=101) %	Female (n=405) %
TV Advertising	66%	69%	72%	60%	69%	69%	68%
Health Professional	21%	28%	21%	19%	22%	13%	23%
Newspaper Editorials	20%	22%	32%	18%	15%	24%	19%
Radio	18%	22%	19%	17%	18%	20%	17%
News Stories	18%	19%	24%	16%	17%	16%	18%
In-Store Advertising	16%	16%	20%	14%	16%	12%	17%
Other	13%	9%	7%	14%	15%	7%	14%
Website/Internet	3%	-	4%	3%	4%	5%	3%

NOTE: The initial campaign ran from January to June 2001. Research conducted at the conclusion of the campaign was used to establish the levels of campaign awareness, as shown above.

EXHIBIT 7	Where did consumers see or hear about the 5-to-10-a-day Program? (2003 vs. 2001)	
Where did you see or hear the message?	National 2001	National 2003
TV Advertising	66%	77%
Health Professional	21%	25%
Newspaper Editorials	20%	19%
Radio	18%	17%
News Stories	18%	27%
In-Store Advertising	16%	36%
Other	13%	30%
Website/Internet	3%	6%

fresh produce sales during the same time period. These statistics were developed from the Ontario Farm Products Marketing Commission at their 13th annual Industry Seminar on the diet and health marketing trend.

CONCLUSION

Ron Lemaire had finished his lunch, and glanced at his watch to see if he still had time for a quick walk before getting back to work. As he walked, he thought back to last year's research on the 5-to-10-a-day campaign that was conducted by Ipsos Reid. The study had conducted focus group sessions in Calgary, Montreal, and Toronto, in order to examine women's views and challenges related to healthy eating. Results showed that the biggest obstacle to healthy eating was lack of time, including the time to plan, purchase, and prepare healthy foods for themselves and their families.

He wondered what the main message should be for the upcoming campaign for 2005. What themes should the campaign focus on? He knew that he would once again have to rely on public service announcements to deliver the main message to the public. He wondered what strategies he might use to ensure that he achieved good exposure for his PSAs.

Stavanger Safety Equipment

H. F. (Herb) MacKenzie

Hui Zhou, known to his English-speaking friends and business associates as Henry, was pleased with his recent appointment as Ontario sales manager for Stavanger Safety Equipment. Henry came to Canada from China in 1992 and completed his last year of secondary school in Toronto where he quickly became fluent in English. He then completed a four-year degree at an Ontario university and was fortunate to get a job with a consumer goods company. Within six months, Henry was promoted to a sales position, one he kept for almost four years before deciding to return to university for an MBA. He remained dedicated throughout his program to getting another sales job. This was one aspect of business he really enjoyed, and one where he had considerable aptitude.

Just before graduation, Henry met a fellow student who had worked for Stavanger Safety Equipment and who had left to pursue a career in finance. He mentioned to Henry that the company was looking for an Ontario sales manager, and that he would give Henry a great recommendation. Henry was not sure he was ready for a sales management position, but he was impressed with the company and the owners were impressed with Henry during his initial job interview. Henry was hired and he was told that his first task would be to "stir the pot" a bit. The owners had some concern that sales were not as good as they should be in Ontario, but they were unsure if or where there might be problems.

COMPANY BACKGROUND

Stavanger Safety Equipment Corp. (SSE) was a Canadian manufacturer of a broad range of safety clothing and equipment that it sold to general industrial accounts as well as to municipalities for use by police and fire departments. The company manufactured about 40% of the products that were in its product line, and supplemented these products with many that were manufactured overseas with the SSE brand name. The pricing policy of the company was to set the suggested list price of all products so that if any were sold at list price, the gross margin would be 35%; however, as will be explained shortly, the company gave discounts to all customers that it sold to, and only the company's distributors sold the products at full list price. In fact, in some regions, small distributors even charged a premium over the list price when they sold small quantities to individual consumers.

The company had regional sales offices across Canada and employed its own sales force, many of whom lived within their respective territories but who reported to a regional sales office. The largest regional office in Canada was located in Toronto. Nine salespeople reported directly to the Ontario region sales manager. Two salespeople served the Toronto area. One salesperson lived in each of London, Cambridge, Hamilton, Kingston, Ottawa, Windsor, and Thunder Bay.

Salespeople sold directly to municipalities and to selected large industrial accounts, referred to as "target user accounts." Otherwise, the company sold through a number of "distributors," which could range from small retail stores to wholesalers who sold to smaller industrial accounts. There was often some conflict between Stavanger Safety Equipment and its distributors as they were often competing for the same user accounts. Not all distributors were satisfied selling only to smaller accounts.

Management recognized the conflict and was prepared to let it continue as long as the company's overall goals were met. In particular, with the exception of the two Toronto area salespeople, management wanted each salesperson to sell 60% of his or her sales through distributors and 40% to user accounts. In the larger metropolitan area, the target split was established at 70% to 30% in favour of distributors because it was thought that since many of these distributors sold to customers throughout Ontario, they would have larger sales than might otherwise be expected. The company owners wanted to sell mainly through distributors because many sales would only be made if the products were immediately available for sale at the point where the customer wanted to make a purchase. On the other hand, the company wanted to maintain sales to important user accounts to reduce dependence on distributors. As well, the owners recognized that sales made to user accounts improved the company's gross margin.

Distributors received a 15% resale discount from list prices. They got an additional 2% discount when individual orders were between $5000 and $9999. For orders over $10 000, they received a 5% additional discount. Target user accounts got a 10% discount from the list price, but salespeople could negotiate discounts as high as 15% when necessary. However, they were discouraged as, when they gave larger discounts, they also received reduced commission on their sales. The discount structure was quite effective at keeping distributors from selling to target user accounts. Occasionally, however, a distributor would take a large order at a very low margin, and would then add additional items to the order to get a better price on those items for its own inventory.

THE STAVANGER SAFETY EQUIPMENT ONTARIO SALES FORCE

The first thing that Henry looked at was the total Ontario sales over the previous three years. There was nothing that immediately raised a concern. Sales increased each year; however, part of the increase could be attributed to annual price increases of 5% on January 1, 2005, and January 1, 2006. In all three years, the region achieved its target gross margins and sales quotas were surpassed by anywhere from 5% to 8%. In fact, during 2006, total sales reached $11.2 million, while the target sales quota was only $10.5 million (see Exhibit 1). It was apparent that if there were problems, they would be with individual salespersons.

When Henry looked at the sales data for individual salespersons, there were three salespeople with whom he had concerns: Antony Jones (Ottawa), Tom D'Video (London), and Bud Carson (Toronto). He wasn't sure there were problems, but he certainly had questions he wanted to ask. Henry decided to meet with each of them. The following summarizes what happened during each of the meetings.

Antony Jones

Henry took an immediate liking to Antony when the two first met. Similar to himself, Antony was not born in Canada but moved to Ottawa from Nigeria when he was very young. Antony got his entire education in Canada, however. He was tall and very thin with a friendly smile and an infectious laugh. Antony had been with the company for four years.

The questions Henry had concerning Antony's territory mainly concerned the increasing percentage of sales that were coming from distributors. Antony offered a defence: "I am very good at managing distributor accounts. You can ask any of them and they will tell you that they don't get better service from any other company that they represent. I like them, and I know how to manage them. I am not comfortable calling on user accounts. They just want to argue about price and they never appreciate what you do for them. Don't worry about me. Maybe my end-user sales are down, but I always deliver my total quota. If I wasn't making my quota, I could understand you wanting to get involved in my territory but since I am, I trust you will let me manage things myself."

Henry knew that there would be some concern if the owners of the company were aware of what was happening in this territory, but overall, the Ontario branch was nearly meeting its total target for user accounts. Henry decided to think about the situation before taking any further action.

Tom D'Video

Henry had a concern with Tom because he had been with the company for less than two years and his sales seemed to be steadily decreasing. He had not achieved his target sales during his first six months with the company in 2005, and he fell further behind in 2006. Early indications were that sales would continue to decline in 2007. Henry had just heard that one of Tom's most important user accounts had recently decided it did not want to see Tom again. When Henry contacted the company for a reason, the purchasing manager advised that he had told Tom on a previous occasion that he did not want Tom in the office smelling of tobacco. The purchasing manager stated that on Tom's next visit, the warning was repeated. Tom's clothing reeked of stale tobacco smoke and he had obviously just left his car. The purchasing manager commented, "There are far too many salespeople for me to buy from. I don't need to do business with someone who doesn't respect my office." Henry agreed that the purchasing agent was certainly within his rights, and he apologized for Tom's behaviour.

When Henry finally had a chance to speak with Tom, he decided to mention the decreasing sales performance first. Tom responded, "I know. I was waiting for Ken (the previous sales manager) to call me on this. I knew it would only be a matter of time before you did. I do take full responsibility for my behaviour. I have been making fewer calls than I should and, in fact, some days I simply stop selling early. I was committed to this job when I first took it. I was having some marital problems and I thought that if I took this job and moved back to London where my wife's family live, things would get better. Unfortunately, things got worse and we separated just over a year ago. I still haven't gotten over it. I have been drinking a bit too much and I spend a lot of time just too depressed to really do much. I am just starting to appreciate what this job means to me. I do like selling and I do like this company. If you will give me a chance to prove myself, I will certainly try. I want to succeed, and I know if I can simply get over my separation, I will."

At this point, Henry did not want to mention the lost account. He wanted some time to think what should be done. He made no promises to Tom other than to say that it was necessary to have some time to think about this and that the two of them would talk again in approximately two weeks.

Bud Carson

Henry was totally unprepared for what happened when he met with Bud Carson. Henry knew he would have to treat Bud with considerable respect as he was the oldest and most senior salesperson with the company. As well, he had the largest quota of all of the Ontario salespeople. Although he did not make his sales quota in 2006, he came very close and this was the only time during the previous three years when he did not. What concerned Henry most was that Bud's quota was growing at a slower rate than the annual price increases, so even if he met his sales quota, sales in his territory would not necessarily be improving. When he asked Bud why this might be happening, Bud became very loud and aggressive: "Until you can get someone who can handle the volume of sales that I can, you need to focus more on the other salespeople. However, since you raised the issue, I want to tell you that I am not happy with the way this company pays its commissions. We get 3% commission on all sales except when we give discounts to user accounts. Then, we are penalized as our commission percentage gets reduced as the discount we allow increases. If you look at my sales last year, you will see that I was just short of my total sales quota. Although I only got 24.8% gross margin on my sales to user accounts, I beat my total target gross margin by almost a whole percentage point. If you took the time to multiply my actual sales by my actual gross margin, you would see that I actually contributed more gross margin sales dollars than my quota. You should be thankful you have guys like me on the sales force, so leave me alone."

Henry wasn't sure what to do. There was certainly more he wanted to say, but he realized that now might not be the appropriate time. After several seconds of uncomfortable silence, he replied, "We will continue our discussion at a later time, after you have had some time to think about things."

EXHIBIT 1	Summary Information on Ontario Sales Performance 2004-2006					

	Actual 2006	Target 2006	Actual 2005	Target 2005	Actual 2004	Target 2004
Antony Jones (Ottawa)						
Sales (distributor)	842 428	600 000	727 765	540 000	701 901	510 000
Sales (end user)	269 557	400 000	255 609	360 000	256 675	340 000
Sales (total)	1 111 985	1 000 000	983 374	900 000	958 576	850 000
Gross margin (dist.)	21.6%	22.0%	22.0%	22.0%	22.2%	22.0%
Gross margin (user)	26.9%	26.0%	27.0%	26.0%	27.3%	26.0%
Gross margin (total)	22.9%	23.6%	23.3%	23.6%	23.6%	23.6%
Total accounts (dist.)	67		70		72	
Total accounts (user)	56		49		46	
Active accounts (dist.)	62		67		67	
Active accounts (user)	52		43		40	
Sales calls (dist.)	292		284		268	
Sales calls (user)	222		216		210	
Tony D'Video (London)*						
Sales (distributor)	513 244	600 000	241 540	270 000		
Sales (end user)	363 388	400 000	172 387	180 000		
Sales (total)	876 632	1 000 000	413 927	450 000		
Gross margin (dist.)	21.7%	22.0%	21.8%	22.0%		
Gross margin (user)	26.8%	27.0%	27.0%	27.0%		
Gross margin (total)	23.8%	24.0%	24.0%	24.0%		
Total accounts (dist.)	60		62			
Total accounts (user)	44		48			
Active accounts (dist.)	54		58			
Active accounts (user)	39		44			
Sales calls (dist.)	277		135			
Sales calls (user)	208		100			

* Tony joined SSE on July 1, 2005.

EXHIBIT 1	**Summary Information on Ontario Sales Performance 2004-2006** (continued)					
Bud Carson (Toronto)						
Sales (distributor)	933 222	980 000	905 900	945 000	962 853	910 000
Sales (end user)	422 905	420 000	451 564	405 000	435 098	390 000
Sales (total)	1 356 127	1 400 000	1 357 464	1 350 000	1 397 951	1 300 000
Gross margin (dist.)	21.6%	20.0%	21.2%	20.0%	21.0%	20.0%
Gross margin (user)	24.8%	26.0%	25.0%	26.0%	25.5%	26.0%
Gross margin (total)	22.6%	21.8%	22.5%	21.8%	22.4%	21.8%
Total accounts (dist.)	58		53		52	
Total accounts (user)	69		66		64	
Active accounts (dist.)	56		50		50	
Active accounts (user)	68		64		64	
Sales calls (dist.)	282		270		279	
Sales calls (user)	240		232		248	
Ontario (Sales)	11 233 334	10 500 000	10 402 111	10 000 000	9 906 867	9 500 000
Ontario (Gross Margin)	23.8%	23.8%	24.1%	24.0%	24.2%	24.0%

Industritech Inc.

H. F. (Herb) MacKenzie

Keith Thomas was excited as he walked into Industritech's head office in early 2002. It was Monday morning and he was about to begin his first two days with the company before flying to Calgary on Tuesday night. On Wednesday morning, Keith would begin work at the Calgary branch as sales manager for western Canada. For his first day, he was scheduled to meet with Tim Smith and Tony Appina, the company's two owners, and with Bill Stockley, the sales manager for eastern Canada. Keith would meet Adam Burden and Hank Matheson on Tuesday. Adam Burden was a senior salesperson who lived in Winnipeg and was responsible for Industritech sales in western Ontario and Manitoba. Adam was in Toronto to make a sales visit to the head office of a national account that was headquartered there, but that had several operating locations in his territory. Adam was scheduled to fly to Calgary with Keith and would introduce him to the rest of the staff there on Wednesday morning. Hank Matheson was a consultant who had just been hired to provide sales training to Industritech, but who had also been asked to provide advice or assistance to Keith while he established himself in his new position. While Keith was recognized as a very competent salesperson, he had no sales management experience prior to joining Industritech.

This case was prepared by H. F. (Herb) MacKenzie, Brock University, Faculty of Business, St. Catharines, ON L2S 3A1. It is intended as the basis for classroom discussion and is not meant to demonstrate either effective or ineffective management. Names and places in this case are disguised. Copyright © 2007 by H. F. (Herb) MacKenzie. Reprinted with permission.

KEITH THOMAS

Keith Thomas received his early education in Newfoundland, and moved to Cambridge, Ontario with his family in the mid-1980s when his father took a job in the automotive industry. Keith completed a sales program at a nearby community college in 1990 and was hired by a manufacturer of valves as an inside order desk salesperson. Within three years, Keith had demonstrated his ability to provide application assistance to customers and he was promoted to outside field salesperson, responsible for handling distributor accounts in Ontario and the Atlantic provinces. Keith worked closely with his distributors and was largely responsible for their sales growth over the next several years. In 2000, when the sales manager retired, the position was given to Jay Trerice, the salesperson who managed distributor accounts in western Canada. Keith was not surprised, although he was a little disappointed. Jay worked out of his home in Calgary, but he had a very good relationship with Industritech's senior management. Although Keith felt he was a better salesperson, he recognized that Jay was also very competent. Keith felt, unfortunately, that there were unlikely to be any opportunities for advancement in the near future as Jay was only a few years older than himself.

Keith began to think about looking elsewhere for a sales management job, but he did not actively pursue it until one of his distributors, Industritech, indicated that it was looking for a sales manager for western Canada. At first, Keith was unsure he wanted to apply as he was comfortable in his present position. He knew the products that he sold very well and one issue he had with working for a distributor was that he would have to learn about many different product lines. Industritech represented more than 300 manufacturers, and carried inventory for about one-third of them. The more he thought about it, however, the more he thought this might be just the challenge he needed. During the interview and hiring process, Keith was able to convince the owners of Industritech that he would be able to do the job. He knew a lot about valves and associated products, and he had enough technical aptitude that he could learn about the other products quickly. He had good planning skills, seemed to understand time and territory management issues, and he had a good understanding of the value of qualitative and quantitative sales performance analysis. He also recognized his weakness was likely to be his inexperience at handling "people issues," and knew that this would ultimately determine his success as a sales manager.

INDUSTRITECH

Industritech was a Canadian-owned industrial distributor with a head office and warehouse in Toronto, and offices and warehouses in Montreal and Calgary. The company had originally sold maintenance, repair, and operating (MRO) supply items such as hand tools, safety equipment, fasteners and fittings, and many items that were commonly bought by almost all types of businesses. It began operations in Toronto as Industrial Fasteners and Supplies Ltd. The company name was changed to Industritech in 1985 when more technical product lines, such as pneumatic and hydraulic valves and cylinders, electric motor control equipment, vibration dampening equipment, power cable reels, and solid and liquid level control equipment, were added. It bought the Montreal and Calgary locations of another industrial distributor that went bankrupt in 1988. Gradually, salespeople were hired who worked from these branches but who resided in the territories where they sold. In 2002, there were three of these salespeople: Adam Burden in Winnipeg, Bruce Stratton in Ottawa, and Rebecca MacIsaac in Halifax.

Tim Smith explained to Keith how the company's growth changed the way it managed sales. "At one time, things were very simple. We sold only MRO supplies. Everything came from our inventory and customers only bought from us when they needed supplies quickly for their operations. Now, however, things are more complicated. We assign all sales to one of three categories: warehouse (W), direct (D), or in-and-out (I&O). When we sell something that is normally an inventory item for us, the sale is coded as a warehouse sale. Those are usually the less technical, MRO supply items, or sometimes things that we inventory because we have promised to do so for specific customers. A direct sale is one where we place an order with a manufacturer, and the manufacturer then ships the order direct to our customer so that we don't have to physically handle it. We simply get an invoice from the manufacturer, and we in turn invoice our customer. These are usually more complex items or items that we could not afford to carry in inventory because the turnover rate or gross margin for them would be too low. In-and-out sales are orders that we have the manufacturer ship to one of our warehouses and that we then immediately reship to our customer. We may do that for any of several reasons. Maybe we don't want the manufacturer to know who our customer is. Sometimes we may wish to consolidate items to save freight or brokerage fees. Sometimes we may need to make some product modifications before items are shipped to our customer. Or, in some instances, we need to consolidate shipments in our warehouse because customers request it to save them freight expenses or order processing costs. As we have added more and more technical products, the percentages of direct and in-and-out sales have increased."

"It's created other problems for us too," added Tony Appina. "We have some salespeople who have adapted very well as the company has changed. One or two have resisted selling our newer product lines, maybe because they don't have the technical skills to be comfortable with them, or maybe because some people simply don't like change. We have one or two, like Adam Burden, who have focused almost exclusively on the newer product lines."

"Yes, that's true," Bill Stockley interjected. "But that's largely because salespeople such as Adam Burden who have territories more distant from our warehouses have to focus more on these types of products. Many customers buy MRO supply items from local sources where they are assured of faster deliveries. A customer in Winnipeg doesn't want to wait one or two days to get nuts and bolts or safety clothing from Calgary. On the other hand, vibration dampening shock mounts will take anywhere from four to twelve weeks regardless of where they are ordered from, and there may not even be a distributor located in Winnipeg that sells them."

Keith was following the conversation until there was a brief pause. He felt they were expecting him to ask a question or make a comment, so he said, "I guess you are telling me that when I look at the sales figures, I need to consider many factors when evaluating performance."

"Yes," said Bill, "and it gets even more complicated." He looked at Tony. "Should I tell him now?" Tony shrugged and Bill took that as a sign to continue. "I have a very unhappy salesperson here in Toronto," said Bill. "Annie Cormier worked for several years to sign a contract to become the sole supplier for all MRO supplies for National Cement, headquartered here in Toronto. She finally got the contract effective January 2000. The account means nearly $3 million annually for our company. National Cement has manufacturing plants from New Brunswick to Alberta. With our accounting system we split the credit for many of these sales based equally on three factors: where the order originates, where the shipment is delivered, and where the invoice is mailed."

"I can see how that could create problems," Keith interrupted, sorry he did as soon as he spoke. The conversation stopped, waiting for him to continue. "I mean, in some instances, the salesperson who is responsible for the sale might get credit for only one-third of the sale and in other instances they might get credit for two-thirds of the sale. When a salesperson in my territory has to service a sale and only gets credit for one-third of the sale because it was ordered from a centralized purchasing department in Toronto and invoiced to that office, he might feel he deserves more credit."

"But in this case," Bill continued, "National Cement places local orders that are then shipped to their local operating locations with the invoice following to its head office in Toronto. Annie was a bit upset that she only got one-third credit, but she was prepared to live with it. About a month ago, however, she came into my office in a rage. Arthur Melchuk, your most senior salesperson, has two of National Cement's operating plants in his territory. In January 2001, he convinced them to request that all invoices go to the local plants to be matched with receiving reports before being sent to head office, and the head office agreed even though that policy has not been implemented anywhere else. In effect, that gave Arthur 100% credit, and Annie got none. She just found out that she lost credit for $125 000 in sales last year that she feels should have been credited to her. If we can't come to some agreement on this, she's going to make my life miserable, and I agree with her."

Keith thought about it for a moment. "I can certainly sympathize with Annie and I'm sure we can solve the situation. But I must request that you give me a few months so I can get to discuss it with Arthur. Can we talk about this later, once I get settled?"

"I'll stall Annie. She's easy to manage as long as she knows I'm working for her, and she trusts me to do that."

"Well, I haven't even met any of my sales staff yet, and already I've got some people issues." At that point, Keith made a few notes in his folder and then the group decided it was time for lunch. They spent the rest of the day talking about where the company planned to go over the next few years and Keith quickly decided he was pleased to have taken his new position. He respected the two owners as he realized they knew their business well, and they were not simply putting in time until they decided to retire. They were committed to actively growing the company, but they seemed willing to delegate authority, at least where they felt it was warranted. Bill Stockley was an interesting person. In many ways, he seemed to be very much like Keith himself, and Keith thought they would get along very well.

When Keith arrived at the office on Tuesday morning, he was introduced to Adam Burden and Hank Matheson. Hank was preparing to make a sales call with one of the Toronto salespeople but had been scheduled to meet with Keith again later in the day. Adam was asked to spend the morning with Keith so they could talk about the Calgary operations. Keith had many questions he wanted very much to ask. He decided that he would ask some of them to Adam, but there were a few sensitive ones he thought best to save until he better understood his situation.

"Where do you want to start?" asked Adam.

"Well, I thought I'd like to know something about the man I'm replacing. What can you tell me about Tom Morgan? What was his management style? What would you consider to be his strengths and weaknesses?"

Adam looked directly at Keith. "Okay." There was a lengthy pause. "Tom was not a strong manager, but he did a reasonable job and I respected him a lot. Everyone liked him because Tom found it very easy to say yes, and very difficult to say no. He was smart enough to identify problems, but then never really wanted to solve them. He was a good man with numbers and he used them a lot for planning. He shared all his analysis with everyone on a regular basis, but he was never willing to push people when they needed it. He knew most of the older products very well, but as I'm sure you know, the company has changed considerably in the past few years. Tom never kept up with the newer products, so he was always uncomfortable visiting customers with me because that's where I focus most of my attention. Consequently, I think he made one trip to Winnipeg in the last three or four years. I didn't really need him, but sometimes I felt very isolated from everything. If you ask some of the others in Calgary, you might get a different perspective."

"One thing I do promise you, Adam, is that you will see me more regularly. You may not see me as often as the other salespeople do, but you will see me regularly and for longer periods of time than the others do. Once I get organized, you'll get my plans and you'll see that once I make them I treat them seriously." Adam nodded, and Keith continued, "Can you tell me if I'm going to run into problems coming to the organization from outside?"

"What you really mean is whether someone else is going to be upset because they didn't get a promotion. Right? Another good question, Keith. But you're lucky in that regard. Arthur Melchuk is the oldest member of the sales force. I'm glad he didn't get the promotion although, again, I like Arthur a lot. I don't think he would like the responsibility. He's been around a long time and he's very comfortable in his territory. Besides, he'll be retiring in four or five years so it might not make sense to promote him now. I'm the second most senior salesperson but I'm certainly not interested. I don't plan to leave Winnipeg. I don't know about Frank Kennedy. He certainly is an excellent salesperson, but he's a very independent guy. He gets along well with his customers, but he sometimes causes friction internally. He's not disliked, mind you. But I don't think he would get any support as sales manager either."

They continued to talk over lunch when Keith asked directly what Adam expected of him. Keith decided they were going to get along well and he was glad to have someone with Adam's maturity on his sales force. As the lunch proceeded, Adam seemed to grow more hesitant until Keith finally noticed. "I think there is something else you want to tell me, but you're not sure how to say it. I know we have only just met but I hope you feel comfortable enough to trust me with any problems you have. I am committed to working with you and for you wherever I can, and I hope we can be open with each other."

"Yes . . . no . . . I mean, I don't have any problems right now. I'm very happy and I'm sure we'll get along well. But, yes, I do have something I want to mention because I think it's important and you should know. I am hesitant though because I don't want anyone to know I was the source of the information, and I don't want to tell you where I got the information."

"You have my word. I won't ask where you got your information, and I won't tell anyone that I heard it from you. If it concerns the company, I would appreciate knowing, but if you're very uncomfortable and prefer to not tell me, I can respect that too."

"Well, it concerns another salesperson. Sheldon Armstrong covers northern Alberta and Saskatchewan. He basically goes to Saskatchewan every four weeks. I heard that he submitted an expense report for a trip to Saskatchewan last month but that he never left home. I won't tell you my source and you said you wouldn't ask, but I'm sure that everyone in the Calgary office knows about this."

"Thanks for your trust," said Keith. "That is information I should have, and I'll be sure to watch the situation." With that, they returned to the office where they separated so that Keith could spend some time with Hank Matheson. Hank had been scheduled to do some work at the Calgary branch, but that was now postponed until Keith had an opportunity to evaluate the branch situation. Hank would spend his immediate time in Toronto, but was "on call" to help Keith if needed. Keith thought it would be a good idea to make his own sales calls with his sales staff so that he could make his own assessments before having any outside involvement. Hank had agreed as that would give Keith an opportunity to get to know his staff better, and to do some of his own sales coaching.

"I really only have one question," Keith looked at Hank. "What exactly should I do tomorrow morning?"

"Let me ask a few questions first," replied Hank. "I heard you were a pretty strong 'numbers guy' so I expect you'll do a careful analysis of the numbers before you decide anything. I've given them a scan, but I have been asked not to discuss them with you for a few weeks unless you have some specific questions. Tim and Tony want you to make your own assessment first. I must ask though whether you plan to make sales calls with your salespeople?"

"Regularly. I have seen many sales managers who let this responsibility slip and I am committed to not do that. I plan to spend at least one day every month with each salesperson except Adam, the guy in Winnipeg. Because he is farther away, I plan to visit him quarterly, but I'll spend several days with him during each visit."

"Tom Morgan didn't do that, so I'm sure you'll get some resistance as soon as you announce your intentions."

"All the more reason to announce them immediately and to follow through quickly. They need to see my commitment to that and that my main purpose is to help them. I also want them to see that I do it regularly and I do it with everyone. Otherwise, it might be taken as a sign there are problems with specific people. I also think that once they see my intentions are good, it can be motivating for them."

"All right. That's certainly a reasoned approach," Hank responded, impressed with the answer. "Then, if that's your approach, I would recommend you call a group meeting tomorrow morning to introduce yourself. Give them some of your philosophy as a sales manager and as a manager in general. Let them know that you will be making sales calls with them every month and that you are looking forward to helping them grow personally and professionally. Promise to meet with them all individually in the next few days, but ask for some time to properly evaluate the region before you do that. Then, spend a few days doing your analysis. You won't have to ask all of your salespeople to meet individually with you. My hunch is that you will get a visit or two before you even finish your sales analysis. Anyway, that's my advice."

Keith looked puzzled. "Are you saying I should do things differently, Hank?"

"No. Not at all. You asked for my advice. I took what you gave me and added a few points to it for you to consider. I think your approach is the right one but unless I miss my guess, you will get some resistance early. The sooner you get a feel for the sales figures, the sooner you'll be able to predict from where."

"Any other advice?" Keith asked.

"Yes. Once you have looked at the sales figures by salesperson, you should look at how they are allocating their time across accounts."

"The old 20/80 rule," Keith commented.

"Yes, but in this company, you might want to group customers into the old A-B-C classification scheme. Maybe include each salesperson's 10 largest customers as "A" accounts, their 20 smallest customers as "C" accounts, and classify all the rest as "B" accounts.

"Have you already done this?" Keith asked.

"No. Just experience. I do have a sense of account distribution in this industry, by size of account. I may be wrong, but if there is anything of interest, this data should let you find it."

With that, the two men parted company, promising to be in contact within the next two weeks.

THE FIRST FEW DAYS AT THE CALGARY BRANCH

On Wednesday morning, Keith and Adam arrived early and went immediately to Keith's office. When the sales secretary arrived, Adam motioned her into the office and closed the door so they could all talk. Keith was also hoping to wait until everyone else arrived before meeting them as a group. Keith mentioned that as the branch sales secretary, she would be working for him as well as the sales staff, and he trusted she would handle any sensitive material she might see as confidential within the office. They continued to make casual conversation and Keith realized he liked her a lot. Gillian Strong was the type of person who would make an excellent administrative assistant. She was quite serious but friendly, and she had a lot of confidence and poise.

Shortly after 9:00, Gillian invited everyone to the boardroom. Once they were inside and seated, Keith and Adam entered, and Adam made the introductions. He pointed out each person in the room and told Keith who they were before Keith made his own introduction. "Let me tell you first how pleased I am to be here. I have been an employee of Industritech for only two days but I am excited about this company. I know Tom Morgan managed this branch for nearly 20 years, and I am sorry he didn't live to see his scheduled retirement next year. I do hope to gain the same support that you gave him as we continue to grow this branch in the years ahead. I promise to all of you my full support. I am dedicated to helping each and every one of you to develop personally and professionally, whether you are in sales or in sales support positions. I plan to spend the next few days assessing sales data for this branch and then I will meet with you individually to see how I can help you. You won't see much of me for the next few days. After my tour of the office and warehouse, I want to analyze our performance for the last few years. I will, however, have my door open and you will always find it open to you if you wish to discuss anything with me. Once I get a better understanding of our operations, I will begin making regular sales calls with each of the salespeople on a monthly basis." Before he could continue, Arthur Melchuk interrupted.

"Not with me, you won't. I've been with this company for 20 years. I have the highest sales in this branch. I know my customers and my territory," Arthur challenged.

"We can discuss this when me meet in the next week or so, Arthur." Keith tried to change the subject.

"You can make calls with the others if you wish, but you won't be making any with me. I don't need any help or interference." Arthur had become more aggressive.

"I'm sorry, Arthur. This is not open for discussion. Once I understand more about your accounts, I'll be in a better position to select which customers we will visit together." This time, Keith was successful at changing the topic as he asked Rick

Mansour, the office manager, to give him a tour of the office and warehouse. But, he noticed that Arthur had left the boardroom and didn't seem to be in the office while Rick showed him around.

For the rest of the week, Keith stayed mostly in his office reviewing sales figures. When he looked at recent expense reports from the sales force, he knew he had justification to speak to Sheldon Armstrong without having to acknowledge that he was suspicious because of a conversation with another employee. Keith asked Sheldon to come to his office for a minute and when he did, Keith closed the door behind him. After a few social comments, Keith looked directly at Sheldon and confronted him with the reason for wanting the meeting. "Sheldon, I don't know quite how to put this to you, so I'll be somewhat direct. I have reason to suspect that you submitted an expense report last month for a trip you did not take." Keith expected Sheldon to either show some embarrassment, or to become defensive and ask where the information originated, but he did not. "Yes. I did. In fact, I did it twice in the last year. Tom suggested that I do it because I get the lowest base salary on the sales force, and he had no way to get me up to what we both agreed would be appropriate. An alternative, he suggested, would be for me to submit a few expense reports and claim some expenses. It would be tax-free and would raise me to the same income level as some of my peers."

"Does anyone other than you or I know about this?" Keith asked.

"It was supposed to be a secret between Tom and me. But, if no one else knows, you now have me curious as to how you became suspicious."

"It was simple, really. All your expense reports for travel show hotel receipts, and credit card receipts for gas and meal expenses. This expense report shows handwritten receipts from a bed and breakfast, and cash receipts for meals and gasoline." Keith nodded toward an expense report on his desk.

"Yes, I know. But Tom knew too and he approved my expenses."

"Okay. I can accept that. Mind you, I'm not happy with it and I certainly won't be party to it in the future. I am pleased it was done with Tom's blessing. If there is a problem with your salary, I'll find some way to compensate you appropriately, but it won't be on your expense account. We can talk about this at a more appropriate time. I'd like to have breakfast with you on Monday morning if you can manage it. This is just a way to meet people outside the office so we can get to know each other better. I'm hoping to eventually have a breakfast meeting with everyone a few times each year." They agreed to meet first thing the next week, and Keith got back to analyzing his sales figures.

By the weekend, Keith had put together the information he thought he needed (see Exhibits 1, 2, and 3). His major problem was immediately apparent, but he wasn't sure what to do about it. He wished he had some advice, and he looked forward to discussing it with Hank Matheson. But he knew Hank's first response would be to ask what he found in the sales data, and what his own recommendations would be. Keith thought back to his job interview and his first few days at head office. He was certainly right that his biggest problems were likely to be people problems.

EXHIBIT 1	Salespeople			
	Active Accounts	Sales Calls	Direct Selling Expenses	Gross Margin
Terry O'Brien	87	843	$ 118 645	$ 201 613
Adam Burden	77	868	124 688	171 054
Sheldon Armstrong	103	930	108 227	236 873
Frank Kennedy	122	1240	94 566	311 052
Arthur Melchuk	130	1146	104 258	324 335
Total	**519**	**5027**	**$ 550 384**	**$ 1 244 927**

EXHIBIT 2	Sales by Salesperson, 1997–2001					
		Sales ($000)				
		2001	2000	1999	1998	1997
Terry O'Brien	W	464 661	454 214	433 824	424 071	388 699
	D	209 400	190 302	182 901	160 422	140 238
	I&O	191 230	186 745	173 209	151 265	145 256
	Total	**865 291**	**831 261**	**789 934**	**735 758**	**674 193**
Adam Burden	W	368 908	347 371	336 600	323 540	317 655
	D	187 607	173 206	151 390	140 243	125 751
	I&O	231 750	201 202	189 879	160 444	153 243
	Total	**788 265**	**721 779**	**677 869**	**624 227**	**596 649**
Sheldon Armstrong	W	608 377	567 463	525 429	527 539	466 848
	D	152 346	142 302	130 917	115 231	118 918
	I&O	222 153	208 962	190 902	170 345	163 183
	Total	**982 876**	**918 727**	**847 248**	**813 115**	**748 949**
Frank Kennedy	W	833 214	771 494	694 414	638 836	587 165
	D	185 901	184 129	170 774	145 148	157 236
	I&O	266 222	254 562	232 938	191 452	204 376
	Total	**1 285 337**	**1 210 185**	**1 098 126**	**975 436**	**948 777**
Arthur Melchuk	W	1 006 865	888 342	654 449	634 529	645 287
	D	129 567	108 241	106 789	94 536	109 258
	I&O	283 766	263 998	238 756	242 873	232 388
	Total	**1 420 198**	**1 260 581**	**999 994**	**971 938**	**986 933**

EXHIBIT 3	Sales Force Sales Calls and Sales Revenue ($000) by Account Importance		
	Top 10 Accounts	Middle Accounts	Smallest 20 Accounts
Terry O'Brien	108 – 302 599	552 – 512 816	41 – 49 876
Adam Burden	112 – 397 256	578 – 342 253	32 – 48 756
Sheldon Armstrong	128 – 414 215	545 – 488 907	47 – 79 754
Frank Kennedy	188 – 523 336	807 – 670 801	104 – 91 200
Arthur Melchuk	133 – 878 662	822 – 402 548	166 – 138 988
Total	**669 – 2 516 068**	**3304 – 2 417 325**	**390 – 408 574**

Health Care Corporation of St. John's: Meal Delivery System

H. F. (Herb) MacKenzie

This case is designed to provide some insight into the purchasing process for expensive items, and to provide students with an opportunity to actually be involved in the negotiating process through a practical simulation. There are few marketing cases that involve experiential learning within one or two classes.

BACKGROUND

On April 5, 1998, Health Care Corporation (HCC) of St. John's called for tenders for a meal delivery system to service six locations within the city: General Hospital, Grace General Hospital, Janeway Child Health Centre, Leonard A. Miller Centre, St. Clare's Mercy Hospital, and Waterford Hospital. HCC was building an off-site food production, assembly, and distribution centre that would be responsible for providing all the food meal requirements for the six hospitals. The meals would be delivered to the six locations by refrigerated truck three times every day, and would then be rethermalized (reheated) at each site.

Along with an advertisement in the local newspaper, the request for proposal (RFP) was sent to five companies. The bill of material included 48 retherm units and 144 transfer carts (99 carts holding 24 trays each, and 45 carts holding 30 trays each). The bill of material also included plastic trays with lids, 6 oz. china soup bowls with lids (1 ounce = 29.57 millilitres), and coffee mugs with lids, in sufficient quantities to fill all of the transfer carts.

When the RFP closed on April 24, 1998, three companies submitted bids; however, only two of them, Grande Cuisine Systems and Burlodge Canada, committed to making on-site presentations to demonstrate their systems. A copy of the Grande Cuisine Systems quotation is shown in Exhibit 1.

A formal procedure was developed so that the two systems could be fairly compared. Each system was tested with delivery and rethermalizing of 14 different test menus including, for example, a breakfast of cheese omelette and grilled ham with whole wheat toast; a lunch of macaroni and cheese with garlic bread and salad; a dinner of roast turkey, dressing, peas, mashed potato, and gravy. Other evaluation criteria that HCC used included a maintenance assessment, an ergonomic evaluation, an evaluation of warranty and service, and a formal company presentation by each of the companies. Burlodge Canada made the first presentation, followed by Grande Cuisine Systems.

Ted Mussett, the Atlantic provinces salesperson for Grande Cuisine Systems, arranged to have one system shipped to St. John's for testing. After the test period, Nigel Myles, vice-president of operations for Grande Cuisine Systems, travelled from Montreal to make the presentation with Ted. The two men met with Bruce Gorman, director of materials management for the Health Care Corporation, and Jean Day, director of food services for Nova Services, a division of Beaver Foods Limited. Bruce's role was to ensure that the RFP was written so that several companies could compete. He also was responsible for ensuring that the bidding and evaluation processes were fair to all companies that were hoping to be awarded the contract. Jean's role was to help evaluate the food delivery system as it would be employees of Nova Services that would have to use the system once it was purchased. Nova Services had the service contract from HCC to supply food services to all of its hospitals. Nova Services would manage the central food preparation facility, and be responsible for food delivery to and distribution of food within the off-site locations.

THE FOOD DELIVERY SYSTEM

The system Grande Cuisine decided to offer was a combination of the Ergoserv (see Exhibit 2) and the Double-Flow Terminal (see Exhibit 3). The Ergoserv is actually made up of two parts, the Ergosert, which is the outside shell, and a stainless steel insert that holds the trays. The Ergoserv is divided vertically in two sections and both sections are refrigerated when the unit is attached to the Double-Flow Terminal. Approximately 40 minutes before meals are to be served, one section of the Ergoserv is rethermalized. This heats the items on one side of the tray while keeping the items on the other side cold.

The Double-Flow Terminal is a stationary unit kept at the six off-site locations. One of the major advantages of the Grande Cuisine system is that the Ergosert can also be

EXHIBIT 1	Grande Cuisine Price Quotation

For: Health Care Corporation of St. John's

RFP #1998-0445

Meal Delivery System

Description	Unit Price	Quantity	Total Cost
Double-Flow Retherm Cart–24	14 982.00	33	494 406.00
Double-Flow Retherm Cart–30	15 118.00	15	226 770.00
Ergosert Transfer Cart–24	6 890.00	99	682 110.00
Ergosert Transfer Cart–30	7 073.00	45	318 285.00
Ergoserv Insert–24	2 830.00	99	280 170.00
Ergoserv Insert–30	2 924.00	45	131 580.00
Trays	35.00	3726	130 410.00
8" high-heat lids	11.10	3726	41 358.60
6 oz. soup bowl (china)	4.95	3726	18 443.70
Lid for bowl	1.60	3726	5 961.60
Coffee mug and lid	3.00	3726	11 178.00
Grand total			**$2 340 672.90**

Options

48 Timers		360.00 ea.	17 280.00
48 Polycarbonate doors for the double-flow terminal		956.00 ea.	45 888.00
144 Lockable doors for the Ergoserv		120.00 ea.	17 280.00

Special Terms and Conditions

Buy-back for current RXCF system	185 000.00
Estimated freight to St. John's	34 300.00

Standard Terms and Conditions

Delivery	26 weeks from order date
Penalty for late delivery	$5000 per month
Cancellation charges (if client cancels order)	5% of total contract price
Warranty	3 years, parts and labour; 5 years on Double-Flow units
Terms of payment	50% with order; 50% on delivery
Inflation escalator	3% per year
F.O.B. point	Montreal, QC

kept at the off-site locations, preventing damage that might occur if the unit had to travel to and from the central food preparation site. The only items that had to be transported were the stainless steel inserts and the trays of food. When these items arrive at the off-site locations, the insert is pushed into the Ergosert, and the Ergoserv is then connected to the Double-Flow Terminal (see Exhibit 4). When the food has been rethermalized, the Ergoserv is disconnected and taken to the location within the hospital where needed. The insert is removed from the Ergoserv and trays are taken from the insert and distributed to patients. At the same time, the Ergosert can be returned to the kitchen area. This prevents staff from reloading the insert back in the Ergosert with dirty food trays and utensils that could make the whole unit unsanitary, requiring additional cleaning effort. In this way, the inserts and food trays are returned directly to the loading dock area where they go back to the central food preparation area to be cleaned and reloaded with the next meals.

NEGOTIATION SIMULATION

Your instructor will normally divide you into groups of four and one person will play each of the roles identified in the case: Ted Mussett and Nigel Myles (Grande Cuisine Systems), Bruce Gorman (HCC), and Jean Day (Nova Services). Your instructor will also provide each person with additional details of each role, with instructions. Using this additional information, the two teams are to negotiate an agreement that both agree to accept. Exhibit 5 is a contract that is to be completed and signed

| EXHIBIT 2 | Ergoserv (made up of the Ergosert and stainless steel insert) |

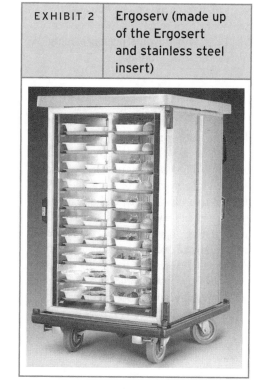

| EXHIBIT 3 | Double-Flow Terminal |

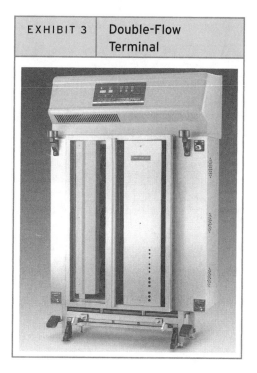

to finalize the negotiations between the two companies (a copy of the contract will be provided to the person playing the role of Bruce Gorman).

CASE PURPOSE

Negotiations play an important part in the selling of many products in business and organizational marketing (and in consumer marketing, too). One of the best ways to teach negotiating skills is through role-playing and similar experiential exercises. Hopefully, students will learn from the opportunity to participate in a realistic exercise such as this. Further, the exercise provides the basis to discuss various negotiation strategies and tactics appropriate for business and organizational buyers and sellers.

| EXHIBIT 4 | Ergoserv Being Connected to the Double-Flow Terminal |

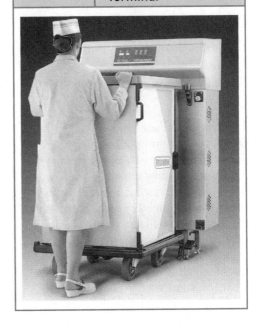

EXHIBIT 5	Final Contract

HCC Meal Delivery System

Description of final system if not completely as described in the Grande Cuisine Systems quotation:

_____

_____

_____

_____

System Price: _____

Options if taken:

   Timers: _____

   Polycarbonate doors for Double-Flow terminals   _____

   Locking doors for the Ergoserve   _____

   Buy back for the RXCF system   _____

   Freight   _____

TOTAL: _____

Standard Terms and Conditions

Delivery	_____	weeks from order date
Penalty for late delivery	_____	per month
Cancellation charges (if client cancels order)	_____	% of total contract price
Warranty	_____	years, parts and labour
	_____	years on Double-Flow units
Terms of payment	_____	
Inflation escalator	_____	% per year
F.O.B. Point	_____	

Signatures: _____   _____

           Health Care Corporation of St. John's   Grande Cuisine Systems

Some Ethical Dilemmas in Business-to-Business Sales

H. F. (Herb) MacKenzie

The following were actual situations experienced by the case writer during more than 15 years in business-to-business sales and sales management. The names of firms and individuals have been disguised due to the nature of the material in this case.

HALCO MANUFACTURING

Dave MacDonald was excited when he got the unexpected phone call from Nicki Steele, a senior buyer from Halco Manufacturing.

"I know it's a year since we bought that prototype reel from you, but we just got a contract from the government to build ten more 'bear traps' and we desperately need to hold our price on these units. Could you possibly sell us ten new reels at the same price you charged last year?" Nicki inquired.

"I'll see what I can do and call you back today," Dave replied.

Dave immediately retrieved the file from the previous year and saw that they had supplied the reel for $6990 F.O.B. the customer's warehouse. There was a breakdown of the pricing on the file:

Manufacturer's list price	$4000.00
Special engineering charge (25%)	1000.00
Total list price	5000.00
Distributor discount (20%)	1000.00
Distributor net cost	4000.00
Estimated currency exchange (8%)	320.00
Estimated duty (22½%)	972.00
Estimated freight	245.00
Estimated brokerage	55.00
Estimated distributor cost, F.O.B. destination	5592.00
Markup (25%)	1398.00
Selling price, F.O.B. destination	$6990.00

There were some notes on the file that Dave reviewed. The reel was designed as part of a "bear trap" on Canadian navy ships. These bear traps would hook onto helicopters in rough weather and haul them safely onto landing pads on the ship decks. The reel was really a model SM heavy-duty steel mill reel, except some of the exposed parts were to be made of stainless steel to provide longer life in the salt-water atmosphere. There was a special engineering charge on the reel as it was a non-standard item that had to be specially engineered. The manufacturer had suggested at the time they quoted that Dave could keep the full 20% discount as they thought there was only one other manufacturer capable of building this unit, and their price would likely be much higher.

When Dave got a price from the manufacturer on the ten new units, he was surprised they quoted a price of only $3200 each, less 40/10%. When he asked for the price to be verified, the order desk clarified the pricing. First, there had been a 20% reduction in all SM series reels. That made the manufacturer's list price only $3200. Then, because there was a large quantity, the distributor discount was increased to less 40/10% instead of the 20% that was given on the original reel.

As Dave estimated his cost, things got better. The original reel was imported from the United States at 22½% duty as "not otherwise provided for manufacturers of iron or steel, tariff item 44603-1." In the interim, the company Dave worked for got a duty remission on series SM steel mill reels as "machinery of a class or kind not manufactured in Canada, tariff item 42700-1" and the duty was remitted (and the savings supposedly passed on to the end customer). The currency exchange rate also improved in Dave's favour, and the estimated freight and brokerage charges per unit dropped considerably because of the increased shipment size. Dave estimated his new cost as shown in the chart on page 328.

Now that he had all the figures, Dave had to decide what the selling price should be to his customer.

CROWN PULP AND PAPER LTD.

Bill Siddall had been promoted to the position of salesperson, and he was pleased when he received an order for nearly $10 000 of stainless steel fittings from the new pulp mill being built in his territory. Unfortunately, he quoted a price that was 40% below his cost.

Manufacturer's list price	$ 3200.00
Distributor discount (40/10%)	1472.00
Distributor net cost	1728.00
Estimated currency exchange (2%)	35.00
Estimated duty (remitted)	0.00
Estimated freight	85.00
Estimated brokerage	14.50
Estimated distributor cost, F.O.B. destination	$ 1862.50

"We have to honour the price quoted," Bill insisted.

"I know if you let me talk to Rory, he'll let us raise the price," replied Dave MacDonald, the sales manager. "Rory used to be the purchasing agent at one of my best accounts before he came to the mill."

"No. You gave me responsibility for this account, and I want to build a good relationship with Rory myself. He gave us the order over two weeks ago. He can't change suppliers now because he needs the material next week, and I don't want to put him on the spot now because it would be unfair. Since this is our first order, I would like to supply it without any problems. We'll get back the money we lost on this order many times if we can get their future business. This material is needed for a small construction job, and they haven't even started to consider their stores inventory yet."

After much discussion, it was agreed that the order would stand, but Dave would call the fitting manufacturer's sales manager, Chuck Knowles, as the two men were good friends.

"We need some help on that last order we placed with you. Bill sold it at 40% below our cost," said Dave.

"How could that happen?" Chuck seemed amazed.

"Well," replied Dave, "you give us a 25% distributor discount and we gave 10% to the customer due to the size of the order. What we forgot was to double the list price because the customer wanted schedule-80 wall thickness on the fittings instead of standard schedule-40. This was Bill's first large inquiry and he made an honest mistake. He doesn't want me to get involved with the customer, and I don't want to force the issue with him, so I'm hoping you can help us on this one order. We expect to get a lot of business from this account over the next few years."

"I'll split the difference with you. What you're selling now for $0.90, you're paying $1.50 for, and if I give you an additional 20% discount, your cost will come down to $1.20. Can you live with that?" Chuck asked.

"It's a help. We appreciate it. We'll see you on your next trip to our territory, and I'll buy lunch."

"A deal. See you next month." The conversation ended.

When it was over, Dave was feeling reasonably satisfied with himself, but he still felt somewhat uneasy. He had promised not to call Rory, and he had promised not to interfere with the account, but he still thought something could be done.

On Saturday morning, Dave went to the Brae Shore Golf Club. He was confident Rory would be there. Sure enough, at 8 a.m., Rory was scheduled to tee off. Dave sat on the bench at the first tee and waited for Rory to appear. Promptly, Rory arrived with Bob Arnold, one of his senior buyers. The three men greeted each other pleasantly and Rory asked who Dave was waiting for.

"Just one of my neighbours. He was supposed to be here an hour ago but I guess he won't show."

"Join us. We don't mind. Besides we might need a donation this fall when we have our company golf tournament. We'll invite you of course, and we'll invite Bill if he plays golf."

"He doesn't play often, but he's pretty good. Beat me the last time we played. How is he doing at your mill? Is everything okay?" Dave asked.

"Checking up on him? Sure. He's fine. He made a mistake the other day when he went to see our millwright foreman without clearing it through my office first, but he'll learn. He'll do a lot of business with us because we want to buy locally where possible, and you have a lot of good product lines. I think he'll get along well with all of us as well. He seems a bit serious, but we'll break him in before long. We just gave him a big order for stainless fittings a few weeks ago, but we told him to visit at 10 o'clock next time and to bring the donuts."

"I know," replied Dave. "Unfortunately, we lost a lot of money on that order."

"Your price was very low. I couldn't understand it because I knew your material wasn't manufactured offshore. Did you quote the cheaper T304 grade of stainless instead of the T316 we use?"

"No. We quoted schedule-40 prices instead of schedule-80. The wall thickness for schedule-80 is twice as thick, and the price should have been double as well."

"Heck. Double the price. We'll pay it. I'll make a note on the file Monday. I know you're not trying to take us and I can appreciate an honest mistake. At double the price, you might be a bit high, but you know we want to place the order with you anyway because you're local. Eventually we'll want you to carry some inventory for us, so we might just as well make sure we're both happy with this business."

STRAIT STRUCTURAL STEEL LTD.

Dave MacDonald was sitting in the outer office waiting to see Stan Hope, the purchasing agent for Strait Structural Steel, a new account that had just begun operations in a remote, coastal location about 64 kilometres from the nearest city. Stan had telephoned Dave the previous week and had an urgent request for four large exhaust fans that were required to exhaust welding fumes from enclosed spaces where welders were at work. The union had threatened to stop the project unless working conditions were improved quickly, and although Dave didn't sell fans at the time, he found a line of fans and negotiated a discount from the manufacturer, along with an agreement to discuss the further possibility of representing the fan manufacturer on a national basis.

When Stan gave the order to Dave for the fans, the two men discussed other products that Dave sold. Dave sold products for a company that was both a general-line and specialty-line industrial distributor. Included in the general-line products were such items as hand and power tools, cutting tools (drills, taps, dies), safety equipment, wire rope and slings, fasteners (nuts, bolts), and fittings (stainless steel, bronze, and carbon steel flanges, elbows, tees). Included in the specialty-line products were such items as electric motors and generators, motor controls, hydraulic and pneumatic valves and cylinders, rubber dock fenders, and overhead cranes. When the men finally met, they were almost instantly friends, and it was obvious that the opportunities for them to do further business were great. "One item that really interests me," said Stan, "is PTFE tape. We need some and we will be using a lot of it."

"We have the largest stock of PTFE tape in the country," replied Dave. We import it directly from Italy, but it's high-quality and the same standard size as all others on the market; $\frac{1}{2}$" wide, .003" thick, and 480" long (1 inch = 2.54 centimetres). How much are you interested in?"

"Let's start with 400 rolls," Stan suggested.

PTFE tape was a white, non-adhesive tape used as a pipe thread sealant. It was wrapped around the threads of pipe or fittings before they were screwed together to make a leakproof seal. The tape first came on the market in the late 1960s at prices as high as $3.60 per roll, but since then prices had dropped considerably. North American manufacturers were still selling the tape for list prices near $1.80, and were offering dealer discounts between 25 and 50% depending on the quantities that dealers bought. Dave was importing the tape from Italy at a landed cost of $0.17 per roll.

"We have a standard price of $1 per roll as long as you buy 200 rolls," Dave offered.

"No question. You have an excellent price. How much would you charge M H Sales?"

"I don't know. Who is M H Sales?" asked Dave.

"A small industrial supply company located in my basement. The 'H' is for Hope. I share the company with Bruce Malcolm, the 'M,' and he's in purchasing at Central Power Corporation. M H Sales is a small company and we are looking for additional products to sell. Between Strait Structural and Central Power, we could sell several thousand rolls of PTFE tape each year."

MCCORMICK GLEASON LIMITED

Dave MacDonald telephoned Clarey Stanley, a senior buyer at McCormick Gleason Limited. "Clarey, I'm calling about that quote we made on Lufkin tapes. Can we have your order?"

"Sorry. Your price was high. I gave the order to Ken Stafford. You need a sharper pencil."

"How much sharper?" Dave asked.

"I can't tell you that. But you were close." Clarey replied. "By the way, Kenny called me from the stores department this morning and he has a large shipment of electric relays that was delivered yesterday. They weren't properly marked and he can't identify the ones with normally open contacts from the ones with normally closed contacts. Do you want them returned, or can someone see him and straighten it out here?"

"Tell him I'll see him immediately after lunch. I can tell them apart and I'll see they get properly identified."

When the conversation ended, Dave made a note to see Clarey about the tapes. There was a problem somewhere. Dave knew his cost on Lufkin tapes was the lowest available, and he quoted 12% on cost because he really wanted the order. The order was less than $1500, but it meant that Dave could place a multiple-case order on the manufacturer and get the lowest possible cost for all replacement inventory. That would increase the margin on sales to other customers who bought smaller quantities. There was no possibility that

Stafford Industrial, a local, one-person, "out-of-the-basement" operation that bought Lufkin tapes as a jobber, not as a distributor, could match his price.

That afternoon, while waiting to see Ken MacKay, the stores manager, Dave noticed a carton from Stafford Industrial Sales being unloaded from a local delivery van. Although he knew that Stafford supplied quite a few maintenance, repair, and operating (MRO) supplies to this customer, Dave decided to play ignorant.

"What do you buy from Stafford Industrial?" he asked the young stores clerk who was handling the package.

Opening the carton, the clerk read the packing slip. "It says here we ordered 144 measuring tapes, $\frac{3}{4}$" wide by 25' long" (25 feet = 7.6 metres).

"Are those things expensive?" Dave asked.

"Don't know. There's no price on the packing slip. Clarey Stanley in purchasing ordered them. You could talk to him." The clerk continued to unpack the shipment. As he did, Dave noticed the tapes were manufactured offshore and were poor-quality compared to the Lufkin tapes that he sold, and that he quoted to Clarey Stanley the previous day.

"Aren't those supposed to be Lufkin tapes?" Dave asked.

"Not that I know. The packing slip just says tapes. Wait and I'll haul our copy of the purchase order." The clerk went to a filing cabinet next to his desk and returned with a carbon copy of the purchase order. "No, it just says tapes. It doesn't specify any brand."

There was something wrong, and Dave was determined to get an answer.